SOCIAL JUSTICE, CRIMINAL JUSTICE

Social Justice, Criminal Justice is a thought-provoking examination of the US legal system, focusing on how criminal justice and social justice are related. The book provides a solid foundation of key philosophical and theoretical issues and goes on to examine the function of the law as it relates to social justice issues. The authors present and explain the foundational legal documents of the United States, and critically examine how those same documents, which espoused the rhetoric of equality for all, contribute toward the perpetuation and maintenance of a system of exclusion for groups with minority status, such as racial and ethnic minorities, the poor, women, and the LGBT (lesbian, gay, bisexual, transgender) community.

Succinct but comprehensive, this text offers a careful examination of possible relationships between social justice theory and criminal justice practice and illuminates the role that the legal system has played in both preventing and assisting social change and power dynamics. For each identified group, important landmark court decisions are used to demonstrate the plight of the powerless and the quest for equal rights. The book provides an important perspective and understanding of the relationships among criminal justice, social justice, and the law. Suitable for undergraduate and early graduate courses in Social Justice, Justice Studies, Critical Issues, Ethics, and American Government and Law, this text provides easily digestible content for those interested in thinking critically about the US legal system.

Cyndy Caravelis is an Assistant Professor at Western Carolina University. Her current research interests include the relationship between social threat and social control, the effect of inequality on crime, theoretical criminology, and the death penalty. Her research on sentencing inequality has been published in journals such as *Justice Quarterly* and the *Journal of Quantitative Criminology*. In addition to her academic endeavors, she has extensive field experience in the criminal justice system, including work as a legislative analyst, a crime intelligence analyst, and an academic instructor in both male and female correctional institutions.

Matthew Robinson is a Professor of Government and Justice Studies at Appalachian State University. Robinson is the author of more than a dozen books on varied topics, including criminological theory, crime prevention, corporate crime, criminal justice, capital punishment, and the drug war. He is Past President of the North Carolina Criminal Justice Association and Past President of the Southern Criminal Justice Association.

A range of further resources for this book are available on the Companion Website at www.routledge.com/cw/Caravelis

"This book makes a unique and impressive contribution to an emerging field of study. It uses a thorough array of philosophical, theoretical, empirical and practice-related insights to examine how law can promote or thwart the interface of social and criminal justice—especially for marginalized groups. It will be an important resource for courses in criminology, criminal justice, sociology and political science."

Ted Chiricos, Florida State University

SOCIAL JUSTICE, CRIMINAL JUSTICE

The Role of American Law in Effecting and Preventing Social Change

Cyndy Caravelis and
Matthew Robinson

Routledge
Taylor & Francis Group

NEW YORK AND LONDON

First published 2016
by Routledge
711 Third Avenue, New York, NY 10017

and by Routledge
2 Park Square, Milton Park, Abingdon, Oxon, OX14 4RN

Routledge is an imprint of the Taylor & Francis Group, an informa business

Library of Congress Cataloging in Publication Data
Caravelis, Cyndy, author.
Social justice, criminal justice : the role of American law in effecting and preventing social change / Cyndy Caravelis and Matthew Robinson.
pages cm
Includes bibliographical references and index.
1. Criminal justice, Administration of —United States. 2. Social justice—United States. 3. Criminal law—United States. 4. Sociological jurisprudence. I. Robinson, Matthew (Matthew B.), author. II. Title.
KF9223.H84 2016
364.973—dc23
2015028764

ISBN: 978-1-138-95505-9 (hbk)
ISBN: 978-0-323-26451-8 (pbk)
ISBN: 978-1-315-64743-2 (ebk)

Typeset in Bembo
by Swales & Willis Ltd, Exeter, Devon, UK

CONTENTS

ILLUSTRATIONS

Figures

Tables

Activity Boxes

1

WHAT ARE JUSTICE AND SOCIAL JUSTICE?

> The American people have this lesson to learn, that where justice is denied, where poverty is enforced, where ignorance prevails, and where any one class is made to feel that society is an organized conspiracy to oppress, rob, and degrade them, neither persons nor property would be safe.
>
> *Frederick Douglas, 1886*

Just about everyone believes in *justice*. Yet, people sometimes disagree about what justice means. The opposite of justice—*injustice*—may be easier to understand, because we know it when we see it. The quote above from Frederick Douglas, former slave and famous abolitionist, speaks to a form of injustice that Americans increasingly reject, as our society and its people progress across time. America has been, and is increasingly becoming, not only a tolerant nation, but one that embraces all people, regardless of class, race, ethnicity, gender, religion, sexual orientation, and so forth. Yet, clearly there is much work left to be done.

This book is about justice and its opposite—injustice. In it, we identify ways in which American society generally, and criminal justice agencies in particular, strive to be just and eradicate injustice. We also show ways in which both sometimes fall short of our ideals of justice, remaining unjust and even at times reinforcing injustice. So this book is about relationships between criminal justice and social justice.

In this chapter, we define some of the key terms used throughout the book, including *justice, criminal justice, social justice,* and *human rights*. Further, we outline major theories of justice that are applied to criminal justice practice later in the book. These theories include *utilitarianism, libertarianism, egalitarianism,* and *virtue-based theories*. Since we apply these theories to various topics throughout the book, it is important to understand their meaning. The main purpose of this chapter is to introduce you to the topics of social justice and criminal justice.

Activity 1.1 Justice and Injustice

What does the term *justice* mean to you?

What about *injustice*?

How would you define these terms?

What Is Justice?

The answer to the question of "what is justice" depends on who is being asked. For example, to a person who has been harmed by another (e.g., a crime victim), justice may be about holding the guilty accountable—making sure he or she is punished in order to achieve retribution. *Retribution* is often associated with punishment of criminals and generally means giving people what they deserve based on the harms they cause. For example, one form of retribution is capital punishment, reserved exclusively in practice for those convicted of murder. When a murderer is executed, it is a statement by society that taking a life demands the sacrifice of the killer's life as a form of retribution; think of it as a payment made by the offender to right the wrong he or she committed (Kant, 1887).

We can call the form of justice rooted in retribution *retributive justice*, which generally means punishing an individual who commits a crime. Retributive justice assures that victims of crime are served by their government.

Yet, to a person who has been arrested and who might be facing a criminal trial, justice may be more about being treated fairly by agencies of criminal justice and having his or her rights protected. As citizens of the United States, people are granted numerous rights, most notably from the Bill of Rights of the US Constitution. Examine the rights granted to us in Table 1.1.

Notice that, of these rights, Amendments IV, V, VI, and VIII have the most relevance for criminal justice. The Fourth Amendment grants you the right to be protected from unreasonable searches and seizures by the police and requires them to get a warrant based upon probable cause in order to search or seize you or your property. The Fifth Amendment guarantees you *due process of law*, meaning that, for you to be held and prosecuted for a crime, the government must follow the rules of procedure as established by the US Constitution and upheld by US courts. Specific rights granted by this Amendment include the right to a grand jury hearing, freedom from *double jeopardy* (meaning you cannot be tried twice for the same offense), freedom from *self-incrimination* (meaning the government cannot coerce you to testify against yourself so that you have the right to remain silent), and the right to just compensation for government seizure of your property.

The Sixth Amendment gives you the rights to notice of any criminal charges against you, speedy and public trials, and impartial juries. It also guarantees you the right to confront witnesses against you, to offer witnesses on your behalf, and to be granted an attorney to assist you with your defense. Finally, the Eighth Amendment bans excessive bails, excessive fines, and cruel and unusual punishments.

The form of justice rooted in due process of law is commonly referred to as *procedural justice*, which generally means assuring fairness in the criminal justice process by protecting people's rights as they are processed through the system of police, courts, and corrections. Procedural justice assures that people accused of crime are served by their government.

TABLE 1.1 The Bill of Rights

Amendment I

Congress shall make no law respecting an establishment of religion, or prohibiting the free exercise thereof; or abridging the freedom of speech, or of the press; or the right of the people peaceably to assemble, and to petition the Government for a redress of grievances.

Amendment II

A well regulated Militia, being necessary to the security of a free State, the right of the people to keep and bear Arms, shall not be infringed.

Amendment III

No Soldier shall, in time of peace be quartered in any house, without the consent of the Owner, nor in time of war, but in a manner to be prescribed by law.

Amendment IV

The right of the people to be secure in their persons, houses, papers, and effects, against unreasonable searches and seizures, shall not be violated, and no Warrants shall issue, but upon probable cause, supported by Oath or affirmation, and particularly describing the place to be searched, and the persons or things to be seized.

Amendment V

No person shall be held to answer for a capital, or otherwise infamous crime, unless on a presentment or indictment of a Grand Jury, except in cases arising in the land or naval forces, or in the Militia, when in actual service in time of War or public danger; nor shall any person be subject for the same offence to be twice put in jeopardy of life or limb; nor shall be compelled in any criminal case to be a witness against himself, nor be deprived of life, liberty, or property, without due process of law; nor shall private property be taken for public use, without just compensation.

Amendment VI

In all criminal prosecutions, the accused shall enjoy the right to a speedy and public trial, by an impartial jury of the State and district wherein the crime shall have been committed, which district shall have been previously ascertained by law, and to be informed of the nature and cause of the accusation; to be confronted with the witnesses against him; to have compulsory process for obtaining witnesses in his favor, and to have the Assistance of Counsel for his defence.

Amendment VII

In Suits at common law, where the value in controversy shall exceed twenty dollars, the right of trial by jury shall be preserved, and no fact tried by a jury, shall be otherwise re-examined in any Court of the United States, than according to the rules of the common law.

Amendment VIII

Excessive bail shall not be required, nor excessive fines imposed, nor cruel and unusual punishments inflicted.

Amendment IX

The enumeration in the Constitution, of certain rights, shall not be construed to deny or disparage others retained by the people.

Amendment X

The powers not delegated to the United States by the Constitution, nor prohibited by it to the States, are reserved to the States respectively, or to the people.

The *criminal justice system*, as you will see, tries to achieve both of these justice-related goals—holding the guilty accountable for the harms they inflict on others (i.e., retributive justice) while simultaneously treating people fairly by protecting the rights they enjoy as American citizens (i.e., procedural justice). The scales of justice, illustrated in Figure 1.1, are kept in balance when the rights of victims and the rights of defendants are both served by criminal justice agencies concerned with retributive justice and procedural justice. Yet, these goals often conflict, meaning that Americans ultimately have to choose which goal is more important to them and thus worthy of greater emphasis (Robinson, 2009).

In addition to these conceptions of justice, there are also broader definitions of justice which focus on issues other than crime and outside of the criminal justice system. As you'll see later in the chapter, there are theories of justice that highlight other issues, including happiness or utility, liberty or freedom, equality or egalitarianism, and virtue or morality. Given the focus of this book on links between social justice and criminal justice, first it is important to briefly discuss the concept of criminal justice.

What Is Criminal Justice?

Criminal justice is a term that describes the efforts of government agencies at the local, state, and federal levels to reduce crime and achieve justice for crime victims (retributive justice) while also protecting the due process rights of criminal defendants (procedural justice). These agencies include lawmakers, police, courts, and correctional facilities (Lab, Williams, Holcomb, Burek, King, & Buerger, 2010).

The *criminal justice system* is the term used to describe the work of these agencies, whereby the:

- *Law* defines harmful acts as crimes, specifies possible punishments, and sets forth rules of due process that must be followed by police, courts, and corrections;
- *Police* investigate alleged crimes and apprehend people suspected of breaking the law;

FIGURE 1.1 Scales of Justice.

- *Courts* determine the legal guilt of those accused of crimes and sentence those found guilty to some form and term of punishment;
- *Correctional agencies* carry out the punishment determined by the courts.

Although each of these agencies of criminal justice clearly has its own goals, they are also expected to work together to achieve common goals of larger society. These include crime control and due process. *Crime reduction* refers to all the efforts of criminal justice agencies to reduce crime, including arresting and prosecuting alleged offenders, convicting and punishment the guilty, and preventing crime in the first place (e.g., directed police patrols in areas where crime is likely to occur). Crime control is generally aimed at achieving the goal of retributive justice.

Due process refers to all the efforts of criminal justice agencies to make sure that an individual's Constitutional rights are protected as a person is processed through the system, or to make sure that we achieve procedural justice (David & Bruce, 2012). These rights were illustrated in Table 1.1. Because of due process, police, courts, and correctional agencies are not only charged with trying to reduce crime in society, but they must do so in ways that protect our rights. That is, they cannot violate your rights established by the US Constitution when trying to gather and present convincing evidence of your guilt for crimes with which you are charged.

Yet, exceptions are often granted to criminal justice agencies when dealing with criminal suspects as well as those convicted of crimes, in the name of public safety. For example, police can search a person or his or her property without a warrant in numerous circumstances including when there are *exigent circumstances*; courts can convict someone without a trial if a defendant waives his or her right to one; correctional agencies can restrict the speech, movement, and possessions of offenders in the name of the safety of officers working in jails and prisons (Chemerinsky, 2009). So, while these rights are not absolutes, the point is that citizens of the United States are entitled to due process, which assures them some measure of protection against their own government.

Both crime control and due process are valued by Americans. This reality is captured nicely in the very symbol we commonly use to depict American criminal justice—Justitia, or the lady justice—shown in Figure 1.2. Although the meaning of the symbols in the figure is debatable, people generally equate the sword held by Justitia with crime control (i.e., punishment or retributive justice) and the blindfold with due process (i.e., fairness or procedural justice). Further, the scales are most often thought to represent balance; in the American justice system, this could be seen as an indication that society has a vested interest in both retributive justice and procedural justice and that it is in the interest of justice not to emphasize one form of justice at the expense of the other.

Here, considering two fictional models of justice can help us understand this issue better. In 1968, Herbert Packer published his book, *The Limits of the Criminal Sanction*. In it, he presented two models of criminal justice as ideals of two different conceptions of justice, one focused on retributive justice and the other on procedural justice. Packer attempted to describe two polar extremes—one model most concerned with maintaining order in the community by reducing crime in order to provide justice for victims and the other with preserving individual rights in order to provide justice for defendants. Packer's purpose in creating these models seems to have been to pose a challenge for citizens to decide which model they liked best and wanted their real criminal justice system to be most like (Packer, 1968).

FIGURE 1.2 Justitia, the Lady Justice.

Table 1.2 depicts these models at opposite ends of a continuum. On one extreme, the *crime control model* aims to protect the community by lowering crime rates, even if it means that innocent people are sometimes wrongly convicted of crimes. The crime control model tries to protect people from criminals by assuring high conviction rates. It does this by relying on informal processes such as *plea bargaining* (when a prosecutor and defense attorney agree out of court to an appropriate sentence for an accused criminal) to expedite criminal justice operations rather than slower and more costly criminal trials. So, very few criminal trials are held, because they are expensive and unnecessary for establishing legal guilt.

Efficiency is the most important value of the crime control model, for it is imperative that the criminal justice system operates as quickly as possible in order to keep up with the large numbers of criminal cases that enter it each day. Packer's metaphor for this model was an "assembly line" because individual defendants would be quickly processed through the criminal justice system outside of the courtroom through plea bargaining rather than criminal trials.

On the other extreme, the *due process model* aims to protect individual liberties at all costs even if it means that sometimes guilty people go free. The due process model tries to uphold Constitutional protections by placing a high value on the adversarial nature of justice. Here, a prosecutor and defense

TABLE 1.2 Crime Control and Due Process Models

	Crime Control Model	*Due Process Model*
Most important goal	Reduce crime	Protect rights
Cherished value	Efficiency	Reliability
Metaphor	Assembly line	Obstacle course
In practice	Increase powers of police, prosecutor	Decrease powers of police, prosecutor

attorney battle it out in court, utilizing criminal trials (where alleged victims are served by the prosecution and alleged offenders are represented by defense attorneys in an adversarial process in a battle in open court to find the truth).

Reliability is the most important value of the due process model, for it is imperative that the right person be convicted of the crime of which he or she is accused. Packer's metaphor for this model was an "obstacle course" because, in order to ensure that no innocent persons were wrongfully convicted, the prosecution would have to overcome numerous obstacles in order to convict anyone.

Justice is an important value in both models, but proponents of each model view justice quite differently. Supporters of the crime control model value retributive justice more and thus favor devoting resources to the agents of criminal justice who carry out crime control efforts (e.g., police who investigate alleged crimes and prosecutors who charge and try to convict alleged offenders). Supporters of the due process model value procedural justice more and thus favor devoting resources to the agents of criminal justice who protect due process efforts (e.g., defense attorneys who make sure the rights of the accused are considered and judges who make sure they are ultimately upheld).

Activity 1.2 Models of Criminal Justice

Which fictional model of criminal justice do you like better, the crime control model or the due process model?

If the criminal justice system in the real world had to more closely resemble the crime control model or the due process model, which would you choose? Why?

As for Americans, there is evidence that both retributive justice and procedural justice are important to us. That is, depending on how questions are asked, Americans say they want the guilty to be held accountable for their criminal behaviors and that they still value their rights as citizens (Roberts & Stalans, 1999; Wood & Gannon, 2008). In Chapter 2, we examine public opinion and discuss evidence that this is true.

What Is Social Justice?

Note that *social justice* is not an explicit goal of criminal justice in either the crime control or the due process models of criminal justice, although some have argued that criminal justice can help bring about social justice (Robinson, 2010). This is due to the fact that social justice is a type of justice that exists in larger society, beyond the realm of criminal justice.

Social justice can be defined in many ways. One definition is "promoting a just society by challenging injustice and valuing diversity." It exists when "all people share a common humanity and therefore have a right to equitable treatment, support for their human rights, and a fair allocation of community resources." In conditions of social justice, people are "not to be discriminated against, nor their welfare and well-being constrained or prejudiced on the basis of gender, sexuality, religion, political affiliations, age, race, belief, disability, location, social class, socioeconomic circumstances, or other characteristic of background or group membership" (Toowoomba Catholic Education, 2006). Later in this book, we will examine the social construction of differences for the aforementioned groups before evaluating how laws have been used both to oppress and to restore each minority group towards the end of achieving social justice.

As a rule, social justice is generally equated with the notion of equality or equal opportunity in society. Although equality is undeniably part of social justice, the meaning of social justice is actually much broader (Scherlen & Robinson, 2008). Further, "equal opportunity" and other phrases such as "personal responsibility" have been used to diminish the prospect of realizing social justice by justifying enormous inequalities in modern society (Berry, 2005). This is because, as long as society supposedly values and takes steps to assure equal opportunity in society, failure to achieve success can be blamed on laziness or a lack of effort on the part of those who fail.

For example, as Americans believe that the *American Dream* is possible for all, they will be less likely to acknowledge structural barriers such as discrimination that make it more difficult to achieve (Robinson & Murphy, 2009). Evidence also exists that how we view the causes of crime and how we prefer to address it (e.g., punishment or rehabilitation) is impacted by whether we attribute outcomes to *situational factors* (i.e., things within our social environments such as opportunity and discrimination) or *dispositional factors* (i.e., things unique to individuals such as effort and hard work) (Thompson & Bobo, 2011).

The most recent theories of and scholarly statements about social justice illustrate the complex nature of the concept. Each of the following theories of justice is about social justice—justice in society—but each emphasizes a different concept or value.

Major Theories of Justice

There are several theoretical approaches to justice. Each major approach to justice is organized around a different principle. According to a leading justice scholar Michael Sandel (2009), there are three broad issues discussed and debated by scholars of justice theory—welfare, freedom, and virtue. Stated simply, *welfare* refers to providing a good life for people, *freedom* refers to protecting people's liberty, and *virtue* refers to morality. Table 1.3 illustrates some things that would likely be seen as important by people who value welfare, freedom, and virtue.

As you can see, those who value welfare are most concerned with helping other people, especially the most needy or least advantaged, as well as assuring happiness for as many people as possible. Those who value freedom are most concerned with rights and liberties, such as property rights; the right not to be discriminated against based on factors such as social class, gender, race, and so forth; and civil liberties such as those established by the Bill of Rights to the US Constitution. Finally, those concerned with virtue are most concerned with things like values and morality or ensuring clear boundaries between right and wrong.

TABLE 1.3 Welfare, Freedom, and Virtue

For those concerned about	. . . things such as these would matter most
Welfare	The needy, helping others, happiness
Freedom	Property rights, civil rights, civil liberties
Virtue	Values, morals, right and wrong

Different schools of thought about justice are associated with each of these three principles. In fact, at least four different approaches stem from these three principles: two stress the importance of freedom, one welfare, and one virtue. We begin with the school of thought most concerned with welfare.

Utilitarianism

The major school of thought that focuses on welfare, or general well-being and happiness of people in society, argues that what matters most for justice is the welfare of society, or its overall happiness. For example, Jeremy Bentham's (1789) *utilitarianism* says that whether something is just depends on whether it maximizes utility or the greatest happiness for the greatest number of people. To Bentham, it does not matter what the intent of an act is, only whether it benefits people, and especially a lot of people.

Happiness or welfare is obviously important to people, but it is not the only thing that matters for justice. In fact, a major criticism of this approach is that it does not respect the rights of people in society. So for example, let's say some policy stripped one small group of its rights and yet was found to contribute to the overall happiness of the rest of the people in society who comprise the majority. Would such a policy be seen as just? It is unlikely because, in America, the rights of minority groups are protected even when they are viewed as nontraditional or atypical. One example is religion; in the United States, people have the Constitutional right to practice whatever religion they see fit, and Congress has no authority to establish any religion (Eisgruber & Sager, 2010). So, if banning the right of one group to practice its obscure or strange religion made the majority of people in the country happier, it would still likely be viewed as unjust by citizens because they also have a strong preference for freedom or liberty.

Libertarianism

Some justice theorists argue that what matters most for deciding what is right or just is freedom— whether individual rights are respected and protected. This school of thought is called *libertarianism* because it holds that what matters most for justice is liberty. For some, this means protecting civil rights such as the right to vote and civil liberties granted to citizens through the US Constitution (e.g., Rawls, 1971).

Of course, liberties are not in fact absolute because restrictions on civil liberties are frequently made by courts when they serve other socially desirable outcomes. An example is gun control. While the US Supreme Court has held that the right to keep and bear arms applies to individuals, not many Americans believe that citizens should be able to possess tanks, grenade launchers, and such! Thus, a criticism of this approach is that it is too absolute, meaning that freedom ought to be restricted when it assists the government with its other duties such as its responsibility to prevent crime, illegal drug use, and terrorism (Fisher & Harriger, 2013).

For others a devotion to freedom means assuring the right of people to pursue, own, and control property with minimal governmental interference (e.g., Friedrich Hayek, 1960; Milton Friedman, 1962; Robert Nozick, 1974). The latter camp is often referred to as *free market libertarians* because most of their arguments revolve around the idea that freedom amounts to an unregulated economic market-place where the government allows people to freely engage in the exchange of property without undue interference.

While free market libertarianism seems to protect people's property rights such as the right to enter into work agreements and to sell property, a major criticism of the school of thought is that, without efforts to curb inequality, it inevitably leads to large inequalities in society. For example, free market economies tend to create huge gaps between the wealthy and the poor. In the United States in 2012, the top 10 percent of households controlled 50.4 percent of income and the top 1 percent had 19.3 percent of the income (Greenwood, 2013). Further, the average CEO of a corporation made 273 times more money than the average employee (DePillis, 2013). It turns out that many Americans have a problem with these realities, viewing them as unjust (Miller, 2003).

Egalitarianism

Given the fact that justice is often concerned with equality, many people challenge the tenets of libertarianism. Another school of thought is known as *egalitarianism*, which argues that what matters most for justice is equality of opportunity in society and taking care of the least advantaged citizens (e.g., Miller, 2003). Given that egalitarians value equality in society—including equality of all rights and liberties—their view of justice tends to be much broader than free market libertarians who focus squarely on economic issues.

There is also a basic disagreement between free market libertarians and egalitarians with regard to economic issues. The former end up arguing against government interference in property exchanges, even in cases where capitalism produces massive inequities between the wealthy and the poor, whereas the latter often argue for government intervention to make arrangements in society fairer for all and especially for the poor and needy. This is because the main concern of egalitarians is equality in society, and although egalitarians recognize that superior talent and effort ought to result in superior reward, they also argue that inequalities in today's society are not justifiable.

A criticism of egalitarianism is that the government has no right to tell people what they can do with their money or property. For example, is it right to coerce rich people to pay higher taxes in order to benefit the poor? What about mandating a minimum wage or even a living wage in order to assure that people who work will be able to afford basic necessities and pay their bills? Some would argue that justice demands companies do this, whereas others would obviously disagree on libertarian grounds (Pollin, Brenner, Luce, & Wicks-Lim, 2008).

Virtue-Based Theories

Finally, what is the role of virtue or morality for justice? Other justice theorists argue that what matters most for justice is virtue, or moral goodness and righteousness. Such approaches are often referred to as *virtue-based theories.* For example, Aristotle's (1280) theory suggests that justice demands giving people what they deserve or what they are due. This means honoring and rewarding those values or virtues that are worthy of honor and reward. In order to make such determinations, we must make decisions about what is good or righteous in the first place. There is a controversy between those, such as Michael Sandel (2009), who believe that justice theory cannot be silent on matters of virtue or the "good life" and those, such as John Rawls (1971), who always argued that it must be.

Immanuel Kant's (1785) view is also relevant here. According to Kant, whether something is just or not depends only on whether it is the right thing to do, regardless of the consequences. That is, whether something is just is determined by motive, or whether it is morally right. Something is morally right, according to Kant, if it respects the moral law, which requires us to treat each other as autonomous beings worthy of respect.

A major criticism of virtue-based approaches is, who decides what is moral or virtuous, especially when public opinion is often so divided on such matters? Evidence suggests that opinion on matters such as abortion, drugs, taxes, capital punishment, and many other issues is divergent and varied (Amaya & Lai, 2013; MacIntyre, 2007).

Table 1.4 summarizes these major theories of justice. The table demonstrates the major value of justice of each theory.

An example here will help you understand the major theories of justice presented in Table 1.4. Is the drug war consistent with social justice? The answer depends on the major school of thought one uses to address the question.

To a utilitarian, the most important issue would be whether the drug war contributes to overall happiness in society. If it could be shown that the drug war achieves undeniable benefits that contribute to the overall happiness in society (such as reducing drug abuse and addiction as well as drug-related crimes), then utilitarians would likely see the drug war as just; if not, they would see it as unjust (Inciardi, 2007; Kleiman, Caulkins, & Hawken, 2011).

To a libertarian, the major issue would be whether the drug war respects liberty or freedom? In a free society, shouldn't a person be able to experiment with and responsibly use drugs, as long as he or she does not hurt another innocent person? If so, libertarians would likely see the drug war as unjust (Boyum & Reuter, 2005).

But, isn't drug use—especially illegal drug use—immoral or wrong? A person concerned with virtue might say so, and in this case, the drug war would be seen as socially just. But of course, the issue of whether the drug war itself is virtuous or moral would also be important to know (Inciardi, 2007;

TABLE 1.4 Utilitarianism, Libertarianism, Egalitarianism, and Virtue-Based Theories

Utilitarianism	What matters most for justice is utility or happiness; something is unjust if it does not respect or violates happiness.
Libertarianism	What matters most for justice is liberty or freedom; something is unjust if it does not respect or violates freedom.
Egalitarianism	What matters most for justice is equality; something is unjust if it does not respect or violates equality.
Virtue-Based	What matters most for justice is virtue or morality; something is unjust if it does not respect or violates morality.

Yardley, 2012). For example, if the government lied in order to continue the drug war, you might call that immoral and thus unjust (Robinson & Scherlen, 2013).

Finally, to an egalitarian the most important question would be whether the drug war is applied equally or unequally in society. If the drug war is fought largely in inner-city areas inhabited by the poor and people of color, egalitarians would characterize the drug war as unjust; if not, they may see it as just (Inciardi, 2007; Provine, 2007).

This example ought to help clarify how these theories of justice can be used to assess any particular issue or policy in society. Whether that issue or policy is seen as just or not will depend on what school of thought one embraces in order to assess it—which theory of justice one finds most convincing and which major principle of justice one most embraces—welfare, freedom, or virtue.

Activity 1.3 Theories of Justice

Which theory of justice is most appealing to you?

Which theory of justice is least appealing to you? Why?

Which Theories of Justice Are Appealing to Americans?

In Chapter 2, we examine public opinion to show which of the preceding theories of justice are appealing to Americans, and explain why. Yet, we can go ahead and state unequivocally here that to some degree or another, *all* of these approaches to justice are supported by citizens. At the same time, Americans do not completely embrace any one theory of justice, likely because of serious problems with each.

For example, Americans value liberty or freedom. Thus, they like libertarianism and often see a social policy or issue as just or unjust based on whether it respects liberty. Yet allowing people to pursue their own economic interests through a free market system with no meaningful regulation inevitably produces inequality in society (not to mention dangerous products and hazardous workplaces). This is problematic to Americans because they also value equality. Thus, they like egalitarianism and consider whether a social policy or issue is just or unjust based on whether it promotes or inhibits equality in society. As it turns out, we do not support huge inequality in outcomes such as income and wealth. Figure 1.3 demonstrates the degree of inequality in contemporary American society. This level of inequality in society is *not* supported by most Americans.

Americans value the free market economic system (i.e., capitalism), but they recognize that not all Americans actually start off at equal starting places and that equal opportunity really does not exist in the United States. That is, some people have opportunities for success that others do not have, and many of these opportunities are structured by *social class*. Americans also know that very wealthy individuals and corporations enjoy benefits (e.g., tax breaks and loopholes, government subsidies and bailouts) to which they do not have access. So, most Americans favor some kind of government intervention in the capitalist economy, even if only to assure clean air and water, safe workplaces and consumer products, equal opportunity and pay in the workplace, and a level playing field for all (these are generally *not* concerns of corporations pursuing unlimited wealth).

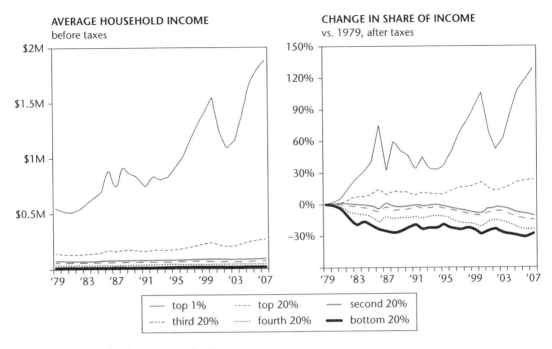

FIGURE 1.3 Inequality in American Society.

Source: Congressional Budget Office.

Although Americans value equality, this does not mean they believe every person should have identical levels of income and wealth, as in some kind of utopian socialist regime. Instead, due to their strong, Protestant work ethic, Americans believe that people who work harder and who develop valuable, specialized skills deserve to earn more and enjoy better standards of living than those who are lazy, do not work hard, or do not become educated and develop useful employment skills. So, there is an inherent conflict between our preferences for liberty and equality.

Americans also believe in happiness or utility, including doing the greatest good for the greatest number of people. Thus, we believe in utilitarianism and consider this issue when deciding when a social policy or issue is just or unjust. Yet, what if helping the majority seriously harms a sizeable minority, or violates the rights of another person? Respecting minority interests and individual rights makes fully accepting utilitarianism impossible. Because of our strong respect for liberty, we do not fully embrace utilitarianism.

Finally, it is fair to say that Americans are a moral people, and that we thus value virtue. We'll have more on this in Chapter 2, but, as noted earlier, there is a wide divergence of opinion on matters of virtue and morality. Further, it is also clear that US opinion on these issues changes over time. In Chapter 2, you'll see, for example, that US opinion on matters such as support for gay marriage and legalization of marijuana has rapidly changed in our recent history. The relevance here though is that, at times, our sense of justice (and injustice) is definitely impacted by what we think is moral (and immoral), virtuous (and evil or sinful).

Overlap Between Approaches

So you see, in spite of the divergent views and numerous subcultures that exist in our society, Americans generally believe in libertarianism, egalitarianism, utilitarianism, and virtue-based theories of justice to some degree or another. Thus perhaps it makes sense that leading thinkers from each school of thought have developed ideas that embrace more than one school of thought.

Although each approach is organized primarily around one major concept (i.e., welfare, freedom, or virtue), specific theorists have over time "borrowed" from the other schools of thought to build their own theories of justice. As such, there is significant overlap between these different theories of justice. For example, John Stuart Mill (a utilitarian) claimed that the best way to achieve maximum happiness in society is ultimately to protect people's liberties (like a libertarian) (Mill, 1869). Mill argued that individuals should be allowed to do whatever they want as long as they produce no harm to others. Mill is not considered a libertarian because his argument for liberty is not based on the argument that what matters for justice is freedom but instead that freedom is what has the most utility, or what makes people happy.

Another example is Friedman Hayek (a free market libertarian), who also wrote about the importance of enforcing equality in the law (like an egalitarian) (Hayek, 1960). Hayek noted that, although unequal outcomes in society are an inevitable result of competition in a free market system, everyone should still enjoy equal protection of the law so that they have equal opportunity to succeed. Since Hayek was not concerned with equality in society but instead just equal opportunity to participate in the free market, he is not considered an egalitarian.

Another example is John Rawls (an egalitarian), who stressed the importance of "equal liberty" (like a libertarian). Rawls's first principle of justice is that every citizen has the same basic rights, protected by the US Constitution (Rawls, 2003). Yet, Rawls is not seen as a libertarian because his theory is all about equality in society.

Finally, David Miller (also an egalitarian) presents a theory of justice containing three principles, one of which is desert (Miller, 2003). To Miller, in matters of "instrumental associations" such as work, justice requires that people get what they deserve (similar to the virtue-based theory of Aristotle and the argument of free market libertarians). Yet, Miller does not develop a virtue-based theory or a libertarian theory but instead presents a theory organized around the idea of equality in society, like an egalitarian.

Because the theories of John Rawls and David Miller are likely most consistent with the principles on which America was founded (more on this in Chapter 2), they are summarized below.

Two Examples of Contemporary Justice Theories

Two of the most prominent statements about justice, each of which posits its own theory of social justice, are John Rawls's (2003) *Justice as Fairness* and David Miller's (2003) *Principles of Social Justice*. While neither of these theories can be considered an exhaustive treatment of the subject matter, each offers a complex theory of social justice that illustrates its broad meaning.

Both conceptions of social justice are similar, so there is significant overlap between the main ideas of the theorists; this is likely due to the fact that they are founded on like principles and based on previously posited theories from significant historical political philosophers (Brighouse, 2005). Below, we thoroughly summarize the social justice theories of John Rawls and David Miller. Keep in mind as you are reading that both theories of justice are considered examples of egalitarianism that also have strong libertarian tenets, an approach that we will later show to be quite appealing to most Americans.

John Rawls

John Rawls posits a theory of social justice commonly referred to as *justice as fairness*. Rawls (2003: 5–6) set out to sketch a theory of social justice that would answer the questions: "once we view a democratic society as a fair system of social cooperation between citizens regarded as free and equal, what principles are most appropriate to it?" and "which principles are most appropriate for a democratic society that not only professes but wants to take seriously . . . that citizens are free and equal, and tries to realize that idea in its main institutions?"

Do Americans view themselves as a people who value freedom and equality? Do we like to think of ourselves as a democracy? If so, then Rawls's theory of justice as fairness is relevant for the United States.

Rawls develops his theory for a democratic system of government, and he assumes that society comprises a fair system of social cooperation between free and equal citizens. He also assumes that society is well organized and regulated by a public perception of justice. Further, he assumes that society is guided by rules and procedures that are publicly recognized and agreed to, that the rules specify fair terms of cooperation and are rooted in the notion of reciprocity or mutuality so that each person has a chance to promote his or her own advantage or good. Thus, his theory is aimed at determining the "political conception of justice for specifying the fair terms of cooperation between citizens regarded as fair and equal and as both reasonable and rational" (Rawls, 2003: 7–8).

To Rawls, social justice is about assuring the protection of equal access to liberties, rights, and opportunities, as well as taking care of the least advantaged members of society. Thus, whether something is consistent with social justice depends on whether it promotes or hinders equality of access to civil liberties, human rights, and opportunities for healthy and fulfilling lives, as well as whether it allocates a fair share of benefits to the least advantaged members of society.

Rawls's conception of social justice is developed around the idea of a *social contract*, whereby people freely enter into an agreement to follow certain rules for the betterment of everyone, without considering the implications of these rules for their own selfish gain. Rawls posits that rational, free people will agree to play by the rules under fair conditions and that this agreement is necessary to assure social justice because public support is critical to the acceptance of the rules of the game. These rules or principles "specify the basic rights and duties to be assigned by the main political and social institutions, and they regulate the division of benefits arising from social cooperation and allot the burdens necessary to sustain it" (Rawls, 2003: 7).

Rawls does not suggest that everyone will agree with what justice specifically requires in given situations, but rather that his conception of justice as fairness can fit into "conflicting doctrines" because of what he calls "overlapping consensus." That is, people agree enough about the basic principles of justice he offers that, even when they disagree about larger moral, religious or philosophical issues, they can still agree about issues of social justice (Rawls, 2003: 32–37).

Finally, Rawls does not posit an unrealistically utopian vision of what is justice but instead offers a theory of social justice that is "realistically utopian" (Rawls, 2003: 4). Rawls attempts to answer "[w]hat would a just democratic society be like under reasonably favorable but still possible historical conditions, conditions allowed by the laws and tendencies of the social world?"

Rawls's Major Principles of Justice

Rawls's theory of "justice as fairness" can be summarized with three primary principles. They are:

1. Each person has the same indefensible claim to a fully adequate scheme of equal basic liberties, which scheme is compatible with the same scheme of liberties for all;[1]
2. Social and economic inequalities are to satisfy two conditions: first, they are to be attached to offices and positions open to all under conditions of fair equality of opportunity;[2] and
3. second, they are to be to the greatest benefit of the least-advantaged members of society[3] (Rawls, 2003: 42–43).

According to Rawls, these principles are ordered, meaning the first principle (the *equal liberties principle*) should be achieved before efforts to achieve the second and third principles are attempted.

The ordering of the principles suggests that, to Rawls, equality is the most important element of social justice, as you would expect from an egalitarian. Equality means a fair distribution of each of the capacities needed "to be normal and fully cooperating members of society over a complete life" (Rawls, 2003: 18). Rawls explains that the priority of equality means that the second and third principles should "always be applied within a setting of background institutions that satisfy the requirements of the first principle (including the requirement of securing the fair value of the political liberties)" (Rawls, 2003: 46). Background institutions refer to basic structures of society (e.g., family, school, religion, economy, polity), which, when just, can be referred to as "background justice" (Rawls, 2003: 10).

The Scope of the Principles

Not only can Rawls's first principle be differentiated from the second in terms of priority or importance, each also has its own scope. That is, each is meant to have its own unique applications. According to Rawls, the first principle applies to the "constitutional essentials" whereas the second and third apply to "the background institutions of social and economic justice in the form most appropriate to citizens seen as free and equal" (Rawls, 2003: 47–48). That is, equal liberty is assured through the Constitution and equal opportunity and the difference principle are assured through other societal institutions (including criminal justice agencies).

Rawls explains that the principles of justice as fairness are adopted and applied in a four-stage sequence. The first is the adoption of the principles of justice to regulate a society. Rawls (2003: 15) asserts that these must be adopted behind a "veil of ignorance," which exists when there is a limit on information because:

> parties are not allowed to know the social positions or the particular comprehensive doctrines of the people they represent. They also do not know persons' race and ethnic group, sex, or various native endowments such as strength and intelligence, all within the normal range.[4]

The second phase is the constitutional convention, which sets forth the institutions and basic processes of governance. The third stage is the legislative stage, where just laws are enacted. Finally, the fourth stage is the application of the rules by administrators, the interpretation of the constitution and laws by the judiciary, and the following of the rules by members of society in the conditions required by justice as fairness.

When Are Inequalities Unjust?

Just because Rawls's conception of social justice values equality, this does not mean that equal outcomes will be achieved in society, or even that they can be. In fact, Rawls's second principle asserts that inequalities in society are acceptable as long as they meet two conditions. First, as per the *equal opportunity principle*, inequalities are acceptable if every person in society has a reasonable chance of obtaining the positions that lead to the inequalities. An example would be equal opportunity to achieve any job. Rawls (2003: 43) specifies that "fair equality of opportunity" requires "not merely that public offices and social positions open in the formal sense, but that all should have a fair chance to attain them."

Further, Rawls (2003: 44) is very explicit that beyond this:

> certain requirements must be imposed on the basic structure beyond those of the system of natural liberty. A free market system must be set within a framework of political and legal institutions that adjust the long-run trend of economic forces so as to prevent excessive concentrations of property and wealth, especially those likely to lead to political domination.
>
> *(Rawls, 2003: 53)*

Beyond political domination, extreme concentrations of wealth "are likely to undermine fair equality of opportunity [and] the fair value of the political liberties" (Rawls, 2003: 53). Rawls concludes the degree of inequality in American society is not justifiable.

Second, as per the *difference principle*, inequalities in society must be organized so that they are to the greatest benefit of the least advantaged members of society. After explaining that today's economic inequalities are simply not acceptable, Rawls explains the difference principle this way:

> To say that inequalities in income and wealth are to be arranged for the greatest benefit of the least advantaged simply means that we are to compare schemes of cooperation by seeing how well off the least advantaged are under each scheme, and then to select the scheme under which the least advantaged are better off than they are under any other scheme.
>
> *(Rawls, 2003: 59–60)*

With two competing arrangements of incomes in a society, the fairer of the two—and therefore the more just of the two—is the one that is to the greatest benefit of the least advantaged.

By the least advantaged, Rawls is referring to those who lack what he calls *primary goods* (Rawls, 2003: 53). Primary goods, according to Rawls, include:

> things needed and required by persons seen in the light of the political conception of persons, as citizens who are fully cooperating members of society, and not merely as human beings apart from any normative conception. These goods are things citizens need as free and equal persons living a complete life; they are not things it is simply rational to want or desire, or to prefer or even to crave.
>
> *(Rawls, 2003: 58)*

Such goods include:

- the basic rights and liberties: freedom of thought and liberty of conscience, and the rest;
- freedom of movement and free choice of occupation against a background of diverse opportunities, which opportunities allow the pursuit of a variety of ends and give effect to decisions to revise and alter them;
- powers and prerogatives of office and positions of authority and responsibility;
- income and wealth, understood as all-purpose means (having an exchange value) generally needed to achieve a wide range of ends whatever they may be; and
- the social bases of self-respect, understood as those aspects of basic institutions normally essential if citizens are to have a lively sense of their worth as persons and to be able to advance their ends with self-confidence (Rawls, 2003: 58–59).

The Relevance of Human Rights

It should also be noted that Rawls (2003: 13) acknowledges the importance of *human rights* as well. He writes: "A just world order is perhaps best seen as a society of peoples, each people maintaining a well-ordered and decent political (domestic) regime, not necessarily democratic but fully respecting basic human rights." *Human rights* are expansive and include rights in the following areas: general freedom; dignity; life; liberty; security; equality before the law; fair and public hearings by independent and impartial tribunals; presumption of innocence until proven guilty; freedom of movement and residence; right to seek and gain asylum from persecution; right to a nationality; the right to marry and have a family; right to own property; freedom of thought, conscience and religion; freedom of opinion and expression; freedom of peaceful assembly and association; the right to participate in government; the right to social security; the right to work by free choice and to have protection against unemployment; the right to equal pay for equal work; the right to rest and leisure; the right to an adequate standard of living, including "food, clothing, housing and medical care and necessary social services, and the right to security in the event of unemployment, sickness, disability, widowhood, old age"; the right to education; the right to participate in the community and "to enjoy the arts and to share in scientific advancement and its benefits"; and the right to the "protection of the moral and material interests resulting from any scientific, literary or artistic production of which [one] is the author." Additionally, people enjoy freedom from slavery or servitude, torture or cruel, inhuman or degrading treatment or punishment, discrimination, arbitrary arrest, detention, or exile, and arbitrary interference with privacy, among many others.[5]

In summary, Rawls concludes that, for something to be just, it must assure or protect equal liberties, provide for equal opportunity, and take care of the least advantaged members of society. It must also protect or assure human rights. Any institution or practice in society that fails to do this can be considered unjust.

Think of American criminal justice, including the law, police, courts, and corrections. Do these institutions help achieve these social justice outcomes or interfere with them? In this book, we'll provide some answers.

David Miller

David Miller posits a *pluralistic theory of social justice* that is built around those principles of justice that people actually hold. Miller (2003) develops his theory for a democratic system of government, and he assumes that society is a living organism comprising individuals, groups, and so forth who believe in social justice because it specifies the institutional arrangements that allow for full contributions by and well-being of members of the society. Further, his theory assumes a bounded society with members; that there are specific institutions to which the principles of social justice apply; and that the state is the agency capable of changing structures when necessary. The theory can be considered *pluralistic* or *circumstantial*, because different parts of his conception of social justice are more or less relevant depending on the circumstances. That is, social justice depends on the context of given situations.

Miller's goal was to discover those principles people actually use when judging whether parts of society are just or unjust. Miller created his theory from public opinion polls and studies of public opinion with regard to different elements of justice. He does this in part because, while social justice must be "critical" in nature so that changes toward more fairness in society can be achieved, it must not be utopian. That is, it must be supported by citizens and be realistically able to be achieved.

It is important to note that Miller finds that people's views of justice are actually pluralistic, in that they are determined by the context of a situation. This suggests that whether something is judged as just or unjust depends not only on the principles of justice that people hold but also in part on the nature of the situation.

To Miller, social justice deals with the distribution of good (*advantages*) and bad (*disadvantages*) in society, and more specifically with how these things should be distributed within society. Further, social justice is concerned with the ways that resources are allocated to people by social institutions. Some of the advantages relevant for social justice include money, property, jobs, education, medical care, child care, care for the elderly, honors and prizes, personal security, housing, transportation, and opportunities for leisure. Some of the disadvantages include military service, dangerous work, and other hardships. Keep in mind that Miller's theory applies to both *public goods* as well as *private commodities*.

Whether something is just or unjust thus depends on whether advantages and disadvantages are distributed appropriately in society. Miller explains that when:

> we attack some policy or some state of affairs as socially unjust, we are claiming that a person, or more usually a category of persons, enjoys fewer advantages than that person or group of persons ought to enjoy (or bears more of the burdens than they ought to bear), given how other members of the society in question are fairing.
>
> *(Miller, 2003: 1)*

Miller clearly points out that, when considering policies to allocate advantages and disadvantages, we must not judge them based on how they benefit us personally: "Justice is about assigning benefits whose values are established by their worth to the relevant population taken as a whole, and it must be *blind to personal preferences*" (Miller, 2003: 8, emphasis added). Further, Miller (2003: 22) says that "justice fundamentally requires us to treat people as equals; or we should understand justice as what people would agree to in advance of knowing their own stake in the decision to be reached."[6] Social justice efforts can not merely be rationalizations of self-interest.

To Miller, social justice is a social virtue that pertains to what you are due or owed, as well as what you owe others. It requires that everyone agrees to treat others as equals in a manner that is not egocentric or selfish. This does not mean that everyone has to agree on all procedures to bring about justice, for people generally agree on what justice demands (this is called the *stability of justice*).

Miller's Major Principles of Justice

To make his argument about whether something is just or unjust, Miller offers three major concepts—need, desert, and equality.

1. *Need* is a claim that one is lacking in basic necessities and is being harmed or is in danger of being harmed and/or that one's capacity to function is being impeded (Miller, 2003: 207, 210).
2. *Desert* is a claim that one has earned reward based on performance, that superior performance should attract superior recognition (Miller, 2003: 134, 141).
3. *Equality* refers to the social ideal that society regards and treats its citizens as equals, and that benefits such as certain rights should be distributed equally (Miller, 2003: 232).

Justice requires we take care of people's basic needs, achieve appropriate desert in society, and assure equality. Miller's (2003: 25) theory asserts that whether need, desert, or equality takes precedence depends on which "mode of human relationship" is being considered. This is because "we can best understand which demands of justice someone can make of us by looking first at the particular nature of relationship." A *mode of human relationship* refers to the different kinds of relationships that people have with one another.

Modes of Human Relationships

Miller specifies three basic modes of human relationships, including the solidaristic community, instrumental associations, and citizenship. A *solidaristic community* "exists when people share a common identity as members of a relatively stable group with a common ethos" (e.g., family relations). In this mode of human relationships, the principle of distribution according to need is most relevant:

> Each member is expected to contribute to relieving the needs of others in proportion to ability, the extent of liability depending upon how close the ties of community are in each case . . . Needs will be understood in terms of the general ethos of the community. Each community embodies, implicitly or explicitly, a sense of the standards that an adequate human life must meet, and it is in terms of this benchmark that the much-contested distinction between needs, which are matters of justice, and mere wants is drawn.
>
> *(Miller, 2003: 27)*

Miller is clear to differentiate *needs* (meeting what is minimally necessary to avoid harm) versus *wants* or *preferences*. Needs are also held to be community-specific rather than individual-specific and thus can vary across places.

Instrumental associations exist when "people relate to one another in a utilitarian manner; each has aims and purposes that can best be realized by collaboration with others" (e.g., economic relations). In this mode of human relationships, the principle of distribution according to desert is most relevant:

> Each person comes to the association as a free agent with a set of skills and talents that he deploys to advance its goals. Justice is done when he receives back by way of reward an equivalent to the

contribution he makes. A person's deserts, in other words, are fixed by the aims and purposes of the association to which she belongs; these provide the measuring rod in terms of which relative contributions can be judged.

(Miller, 2003: 28)

Desert is measured based on actual performance rather than efforts or attributes. It assumes that superior performance (not superior talents) should attract superior reward. Desert lies at the heart of a meritocratic system.

Finally, *citizenship* refers to "members of a political society" in "modern liberal democracies" who:

are related not just through their communities and their instrumental associations but also as fellow citizens. Anyone who is a full member of such a society is understood to be the bearer of a set of rights and obligations that together define the status of citizen.

(Miller, 2003: 30)

In this mode of human relationship, the principle of distribution according to equality is most relevant because everyone in the society is deemed equal in terms of certain rights. Here, every citizen deserves equal rights.

The Relevance of Human Rights

Because of the citizenship mode, human rights also play a significant role in Miller's theory of social justice. Miller explains that:

a central element in any theory of justice will be an account of the basic rights of citizens, which will include rights to various concrete liberties, such as freedom of movement and freedom of speech . . . an extensive sphere of basic liberty is built into the requirements of social justice itself.

(Miller, 2003: 13)

As introduced earlier, human rights are expansive and include rights in many areas.

When Are Inequalities Unjust?

Like Rawls, Miller holds that inequalities in society are at times just. There are at least two reasons for this. First, economic inequalities that motivate people to strive for more can sometimes be justified. Second, inequalities may result from differential claims on merit. That is, those individuals who are more meritorious because of their performances deserve more than those who are less meritorious because of their education, skills, and performances. Yet, Miller notes that today's economic disparities are not acceptable; thus he is in agreement with Rawls. Further, he asserts that citizens believe: (1) the gap between the rich and the poor today is too large; (2) the bottom wage is not a *living wage* (so that the poor cannot pay their bills even when they work); and (3) the amount of money being paid to those at the top has not been earned (Miller, 2003: 71).

In summary, Miller concludes that, for something to be just, it must assure or protect basic needs, provide for proper desert, and respect equality in society. It must also protect or assure human rights. Any institution or practice in society that fails to do this can be considered unjust. This is a good reminder of the limits of free market libertarianism as a school of justice. Think of American criminal justice once again, including the law, police, courts, and corrections. Do these institutions help achieve these social justice outcomes or interfere with them? In this book, we'll provide some answers.

Overlap in Rawls's and Miller's Theories of Social Justice

There is significant overlap in the theories of John Rawls and David Miller. For example, Rawls's equal liberties principle is most similar to Miller's principle of equality (every citizen deserves the same basic civil liberties and no societal practices should interfere with these rights). Rawls's difference principle is most similar to Miller's principle of need (arrangements in society should take care of the basic needs of all people in society and no societal practices should interfere with these needs). And Rawls's equal opportunity principle is most similar to Miller's principle of desert (every citizen should have the same opportunity to compete for reward based on performance and societal practices should be set up to assure this outcome). As noted earlier, the overlap in the theories is likely due to the fact that both theories are founded on like principles and based on previously posited theories from significant historical political philosophers.

Finally, recall that each principle has its own scope. For example, according to Rawls, the equal liberties principle applies to the establishment of "constitutional essentials." Thus, the equal liberties principle can be used to assess whether citizens enjoy equal liberties according to the law. Rawls's other principles apply to the main institutions of society, which would include the law, policing, courts, and corrections. As such, the equal opportunity and difference principles apply to the interpretation and application of the law by important societal institutions.

Similarly, according to Miller, each principle is more or less relevant depending on the mode of human relationship being considered. In matters of citizenship, the principle of equality is most important. Following this logic, as citizens in the United States, all of us should be treated equally in the eyes of the law (and in its application by agencies of criminal justice). This makes the principle of equality the most important when it comes to assessing matters of criminal justice because criminal justice is a series of government activities that are carried out in the name of citizens for purposes of assuring public safety and due process.

As for the principle of need, this is most relevant for solidaristic communities such as families. However, it is not irrelevant for criminal justice for at least three reasons. First, to the degree that all citizens of a society see themselves as members of an extended family—e.g., an "American family"—where all members are "in this together," the principle of need becomes even more important. Second, to the degree that criminality is driven by efforts to satisfy basic needs (e.g., stealing food to eat), need becomes relevant since punishing people for trying to satisfy basic needs will logically interfere with the ability of people to satisfy their basic needs (Little & Steinberg, 2006). Third, criminal justice processing can interfere with the basic needs of citizens as well, especially minorities and the poor (Lurigio & Loose, 2008), making it a significant source of inequality in society.

As for the principle of desert, this is most relevant for instrumental associations such as work. However, it is also not irrelevant for criminal justice for at least three reasons. First, many criminological theories assert that criminality is driven by a desire to seek monetary gain; these crimes are even referred to as *instrumental crimes* (Baumer & Gustafson, 2007). Second, if people cannot obtain wealth and their other goals through legal means, some will turn to criminality through *innovation*, or creating new (illegal) opportunities for success (Merton, 1938). To whatever degree people innovate because of diminished opportunities for legitimate success, criminal justice processing may be less deserved because of "mitigating" factors (Ashworth, 1994). Third, it is well accepted among legal scholars that punishment is aimed at satisfying desert; that is, giving offenders what they deserve, consistent with the notion of retributive justice (Ristroph, 2006).

How to Use the Theories

For the above reasons, it is entirely appropriate to use the theories of John Rawls and David Miller to assess the performance of government institutions, including the law, policing, courts, and corrections. We can use Rawls's theory of "justice as fairness" to determine if any institution, process or outcome in society is consistent with social justice. When an institution, process or outcome does not comport with any of Rawls's principles, we can conclude that it is not consistent with social justice. That is, something is not consistent with Rawls's conception of social justice if it interferes with any person's indefensible claims to equal basic liberties (the equal liberties principle); or if inequalities in society are not attached to offices and positions open to all under conditions of fair equality of opportunity (the equal opportunity principle); or if inequalities in society are not arranged to the greatest benefit of the least-advantaged members of society (the *difference principle*).

Similarly, we can use Miller's pluralistic theory of social justice to determine if any institution, process or outcome in society is consistent with social justice. When an institution, process or outcome is not in alignment with any of Miller's principles, we can conclude that it is not consistent with social justice. That is, something is not consistent with Miller's conception of social justice if it interferes with one's necessities or hurts one's capacity to function (i.e., need), if it interferes with claims based on desert, or if it impedes *equal opportunity* or treatment (i.e., inequality).

These theories can be used to assess any government policy to determine if it is consistent or inconsistent with this theory of social justice. Thus, any criminal justice policy—from policing, judicial processes, correctional punishments, and so forth—can be judged as consistent or inconsistent with social justice based on whether it is consistent or inconsistent with Miller's three principles of social justice. In this book, we will assess criminal justice practice using these theories, but also the other theories of justice identified in this chapter.

The reason we use the other theories as well is because Americans value principles from the theories of utilitarianism, libertarianism, and egalitarianism, as well as virtue-based theories. We turn to this issue in Chapter 2.

Summary

The term *justice* has different meanings to different people. For those victims of crime and their families, justice is usually equated with holding the guilty accountable. To those being processed through the criminal justice system, justice is often more about having their due process rights protected. But these definitions of justice pertain to the context of *criminal justice*, which refers only to the actions of criminal justice agencies including police, courts, and corrections.

Outside of the context of criminal justice, justice has additional meanings, as well. To some, justice is about liberty or freedom. To others, justice is about equality. To yet others, justice is about happiness or utility. Finally, justice to still others is about virtue or morality. These conceptions of justice are held by libertarians, egalitarians, utilitarians, and virtue-based theorists, respectively.

Social justice, one of the main topics of this book, is usually equated with justice in society, and specifically to equality of opportunity in society. Yet, social justice actually means much more than equality, as shown in this chapter. Social justice, according to scholars such as John Rawls and David Miller, is about liberty, equality, giving people what they deserve based on their actions, and taking care of the least-advantaged people in society. Our ultimate goal in this book is to show potential relationships between justice in broader society (i.e., social justice) and criminal justice practice in the real world.

Discussion Questions

1. What is retribution?
2. What is retributive justice?
3. Define due process of law.
4. What is procedural justice?
5. Define criminal justice and the criminal justice system.
6. What is crime control?
7. What is due process?
8. Compare and contrast the fictional crime control model of criminal justice with the due process model of criminal justice.
9. What is social justice?
10. Identify and define three broad issues discussed and debated by scholars of justice theory.
11. Compare and contrast utilitarianism, libertarianism, egalitarianism, and virtue-based theories.
12. What are the major limitations of utilitarianism, libertarianism, egalitarianism, and virtue-based theories?
13. Describe the overlap between the different theories of justice.
14. Summarize John Rawls's theory of justice—justice as fairness. Be sure to summarize his three principles of justice.
15. Summarize David Miller's theory of justice—the pluralistic theory of social justice. Be sure to summarize his three principles of justice.
16. Describe the overlap between the theories of Rawls and Miller.

Notes

1   This can be called the *equal liberties principle*.
2   This can be called the *equal opportunity principle*.
3   Rawls calls this the *difference principle*.
4   Criminal justice scholars often refer to *blind justice* when discussing how factors such as race, ethnicity, gender, social class, and other extra-legal factors should not impact outcomes of justice (Robinson, 2009).

5 For other examples, see the *Universal Declaration of Human Rights*, *Covenant on Civil and Political Rights*, *Covenant on Economic, Social, and Cultural Rights*, and other similar documents. "A Summary of Agreements on Human Rights" retrieved from http://www.hrweb.org/legal/undocs.html.

6 This is similar to Rawls's claim about the "veil of ignorance" and reminds us of the need in criminal justice practice for "blind justice."

References

Amaya, A., & Lai, H. (2013). *Law, Virtue, and Justice*. Oxford, UK: Hart Publishing.

Aristotle (1280 ed./1946). *The Politics*. Edited and translated by E. Baker. New York: Oxford University Press.

Ashworth, A. (1994). *Sentencing and Criminal Justice*. New York: Cambridge University Press.

Baumer, E., & Gustafson, R. (2007). Social Organization and Instrumental Crime: Assessing the Empirical Validity of Classic and Contemporary Anomie Theories. *Criminology, 45*(3), 617.

Bentham, J. (1789). *An Introduction to the Principles of Morals and Legislation*. Oxford, UK: Clarendon Press.

Berry, B. (2005). *Why Social Justice Matters*. Cambridge, UK: Polity Press.

Boyum, D., & Reuter, P. (2005). *An Analytic Assessment of US Drug Policy*. Washington, DC: American Enterprise Institute.

Brighouse, H. (2005). *Justice*. Cambridge, UK: Polity Press.

Chemerinsky, E. (2009). *Constitutional Law*. New York: Aspen.

David, G., & Bruce, F. (2012). *Criminal Justice in America: Crime Control and Due Process*. Dubuque, IA: Kendall Hunt.

DePillis, L. (2013). Congrats, CEOs! You're Making 273 Times the Pay of the Average Worker. *Washington Post*, January 26. Downloaded from: http://www.washingtonpost.com/blogs/wonkblog/wp/2013/06/26/congrats-ceos-youre-making-273-times-the-pay-of-the-average-worker/.

Eisgruber, C., & Sager, L. (2010). *Religious Freedom and the Constitution*. Cambridge, MA: Harvard University Press.

Fisher, L., & Harriger, K. (2013). *American Constitutional law, Volume Two: Constitutional Rights: Civil Rights and Civil Liberties*. Durham, NC: Carolina Academic Press.

Friedman, M. (1962). *Capitalism and Freedom*. Chicago, IL: University of Chicago Press.

Greenwood, F. (2013). Gap between US Rich and Poor Reaches Record Width. *Global Post*, September 20, 2013. Downloaded from: http://www.globalpost.com/dispatch/news/regions/americas/united-states/130910/gap-between-us-rich-and-poor-reaches-record-width.

Hayek, F. (1960). *The Constitution of Liberty*. Chicago, IL: University of Chicago Press.

Inciardi, J. (2007). *War on Drugs IV: The Continuing Saga of the Mysteries and Miseries of Intoxication, Addiction, Crime and Public Policy*. Upper Saddle River, NJ: Prentice Hall.

Kant, I. (1785/1887). *Groundwork for the Metaphysical of Morals*. New York: Broadview Press.

Kleiman, M., Caulkins, J., & Hawken, A. (2011). *Drugs and Drug Policy: What Everyone Needs to Know*. New York: Oxford University Press.

Lab, S., Williams, M., Holcomb, J., Burek, M., King, W., & Buerger, M. (2010). *Criminal Justice: The Essentials*. New York: Oxford University Press.

Little, M., & Steinberg, L. (2006). Psychosocial Correlates of Adolescent Drug Dealing in the Inner City. *Journal of Research in Crime and Delinquency, 43*(4), 357–386.

Lurigio, A., & Loose, P. (2008). The Disproportionate Incarceration of African Americans for Drug Offenses: The National and Illinois Perspective. *Criminal Justice Policy Review, 21*(2), 185–201.

MacIntyre, A. (2007). *After Virtue: A Study in Moral Theory*. Notre Dame, IN: University of Notre Dame Press.

Merton, R. (1938). Social Structure and Anomie. *American Sociological Review, 3*(5), 672–682.

Mill, J. (1869). *On Liberty*. London: Longman, Roberts & Green.

Miller, D. (2003). *Principles of Social Justice*. Cambridge, MA: Harvard University Press.

Nozick, R. (1974). *Anarchy, State, and Utopia*. New York: Basic Books.

Packer, H. (1968). *The Limits of the Criminal Sanction*. Stanford, CA: Stanford University Press.

Pollin, R., Brenner, M., Luce, S., & Wicks-Lim, J. (2008). *A Measure of Fairness: The Economics of Living Wages and Minimum Wages in the United States*. Ithaca, NY: ILR Press.

Provine, D. (2007). *Unequal Under Law: Race in the War on Drugs*. Chicago, IL: University of Chicago Press.

Rawls, J. (1971/2003). *A Theory of Justice*. New York: Belknap.

Ristroph, A. (2006). Desert, Democracy, and Sentencing Reform. *Journal of Criminal Law & Criminology*, *96*(4), 1293–1352.

Roberts, J., & Stalans, L. (1999). *Public Opinion, Crime, and Criminal Justice*. Boulder, CO: Westview.

Robinson, M. (2009). *Justice Blind? Ideals and Realities of American Criminal Justice*. Upper Saddle River, NJ: Prentice Hall.

Robinson, M. (2010). Assessing Criminal Justice Practice using Social Justice Theory. *Social Justice Research*, *23*, 77–97.

Robinson, M., & Murphy, D. (2009). *Greed is Good: Maximization and Elite Deviance in America*. Lanham, MD: Rowman & Littlefield.

Robinson, M., & Scherlen, R. (2013). *Lies, Damned Lies, and Drug War Statistics*. Albany, NY: State University of New York Press.

Sandel, M. (2009). *Justice: What is the Right Thing to do?* New York: Farrar, Straus and Giroux.

Scherlen, A., & Robinson, M. (2008). Open Access to Criminal Justice Scholarship: A Matter of Social Justice. *Journal of Criminal Justice Education*, *19*(1), 54–74.

Thompson, V., & Bobo, L. (2011). Thinking about Crime: Race and Lay Accounts of Lawbreaking Behavior. *The ANNALS of the American Academy of Political and Social Science*, *634*(1), 16–38.

Toowoomba Catholic Education (2006). Social Justice. Downloaded from: http://www.twb.catholic.edu.au/Pages/default.aspx.

Wood, J., & Gannon, T. (2008). *Public Opinion and Criminal Justice: Context, Practice and Values*. New York: Willan.

Yardley, T. (2012). *Why we Take Drugs: Seeking Excess and Communion in the Modern World*. New York: Routledge.

2

WHAT DO AMERICANS VALUE?

> Our American values are not luxuries, but necessities—not the salt in our bread but the bread itself. Our common vision of a free and just society is our greatest source of cohesion at home and strength abroad, greater even than the bounty of our material blessings.
>
> *Jimmy Carter, 1981*

Americans believe in themselves as a free and just people, *free* because we declared our independence from Great Britain and were willing to fight a war of independence to assure our liberties, and *just* because we established equal rights for all people in our founding documents. Of course, our national history has been plagued by serious inconsistencies between our ideals and actual practices. For example, contrast our statements of equal rights for all people in the US Constitution and the slaughtering of Native Americans, enslavement of Africans, and subjugation of women in the first three centuries of our nation (Zinn, 2005).

In spite of this history, Americans today believe we are a special people. The quote above from Jimmy Carter—made as he left office as President of the United States—speaks to the notion of *American exceptionalism*, the belief that our country is unique in the world because of our strong beliefs in freedom and justice. While this belief is largely not justified, America has been and remains in many places an example to people in many other countries, a place that President Ronald Reagan called in 1989, "still a beacon, still a magnet for all who must have freedom, for all the pilgrims from all the lost places who are hurtling through the darkness, toward home."

In the last chapter, we defined some of the key terms used throughout the book and outlined some major theories of justice that we will apply to criminal justice practice later in the book. In this chapter, we examine our founding documents—the Declaration of Independence and US Constitution—and show how these theories relate to the theories of utilitarianism, libertarianism, egalitarianism, and virtue-based theories that were introduced and examined in the last chapter. We also examine public opinion polls asking Americans about their values and priorities as a people. The point of this chapter is to demonstrate the values that Americans held at the time of our country's founding, as well as the values we currently hold.

The Declaration of Independence

The *Declaration of Independence* is the document the original 13 states of America used to state their independence from Great Britain in 1776. The document, depicted in Figure 2.1, states:

> When in the Course of human events, it becomes necessary for one people to dissolve the political bands which have connected them with another, and to assume among the powers of the earth, the separate and equal station to which the Laws of Nature and of Nature's God entitle them, a decent respect to the opinions of mankind requires that they should declare the causes which impel them to the separation.

Within the document, its authors go on to state the causes of concern of citizens of the "New World" against King George III of Great Britain. These grievances are depicted in Table 2.1. This list of grievances shows that the colonists' problems with the King were far greater than mere "taxation without representation," commonly believed to be *the issue* that led us to fight for our independence.

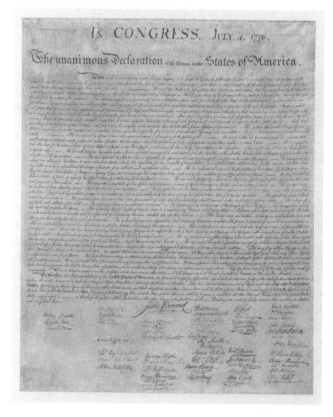

FIGURE 2.1 The Declaration of Independence.

TABLE 2.1 Grievances of Early Americans Against King George III of Great Britain

From the Declaration of Independence

- He has refused his Assent to Laws, the most wholesome and necessary for the public good.
- He has forbidden his Governors to pass Laws of immediate and pressing importance, unless suspended in their operation till his Assent should be obtained; and when so suspended, he has utterly neglected to attend to them.
- He has refused to pass other Laws for the accommodation of large districts of people, unless those people would relinquish the right of Representation in the Legislature, a right inestimable to them and formidable to tyrants only.
- He has called together legislative bodies at places unusual, uncomfortable, and distant from the depository of their public Records, for the sole purpose of fatiguing them into compliance with his measures.
- He has dissolved Representative Houses repeatedly, for opposing with manly firmness his invasions on the rights of the people.
- He has refused for a long time, after such dissolutions, to cause others to be elected; whereby the Legislative powers, incapable of Annihilation, have returned to the People at large for their exercise; the State remaining in the mean time exposed to all the dangers of invasion from without, and convulsions within.
- He has endeavoured to prevent the population of these States; for that purpose obstructing the Laws for Naturalization of Foreigners; refusing to pass others to encourage their migrations hither, and raising the conditions of new Appropriations of Lands.
- He has obstructed the Administration of Justice, by refusing his Assent to Laws for establishing Judiciary powers.
- He has made Judges dependent on his Will alone, for the tenure of their offices, and the amount and payment of their salaries.
- He has erected a multitude of New Offices, and sent hither swarms of Officers to harass our people, and eat out their substance.
- He has kept among us, in times of peace, Standing Armies without the Consent of our legislatures.
- He has affected to render the Military independent of and superior to the Civil power.
- He has combined with others to subject us to a jurisdiction foreign to our constitution, and unacknowledged by our laws; giving his Assent to their Acts of pretended Legislation.
- For Quartering large bodies of armed troops among us.
- For protecting them, by a mock Trial, from punishment for any Murders which they should commit on the Inhabitants of these States.
- For cutting off our Trade with all parts of the world.
- For imposing Taxes on us without our Consent.
- For depriving us in many cases, of the benefits of Trial by Jury.
- For transporting us beyond Seas to be tried for pretended offences.
- For abolishing the free System of English Laws in a neighbouring Province, establishing therein an Arbitrary government, and enlarging its Boundaries so as to render it at once an example and fit instrument for introducing the same absolute rule into these Colonies.
- For taking away our Charters, abolishing our most valuable Laws, and altering fundamentally the Forms of our Governments.
- For suspending our own Legislatures, and declaring themselves invested with power to legislate for us in all cases whatsoever.
- He has abdicated Government here, by declaring us out of his Protection and waging War against us.
- He has plundered our seas, ravaged our Coasts, burnt our towns, and destroyed the lives of our people.

(continued)

TABLE 2.1 *(continued)*

- He is at this time transporting large Armies of foreign Mercenaries to compleat the works of death, desolation and tyranny, already begun with circumstances of Cruelty & perfidy scarcely paralleled in the most barbarous ages, and totally unworthy the Head of a civilized nation.
- He has constrained our fellow Citizens taken Captive on the high Seas to bear Arms against their Country, to become the executioners of their friends and Brethren, or to fall themselves by their Hands.
- He has excited domestic insurrections amongst us, and has endeavoured to bring on the inhabitants of our frontiers, the merciless Indian Savages, whose known rule of warfare, is an undistinguished destruction of all ages, sexes and conditions.

According to the drafters of this document, they repeatedly "Petitioned for Redress in the most humble terms"; yet, they were "answered only by repeated injury" both by the King and the people of England. It is stated in the Declaration, therefore, that:

> We . . . the Representatives of the united States of America, in General Congress, Assembled, appealing to the Supreme Judge of the world for the rectitude of our intentions, do, in the Name, and by Authority of the good People of these Colonies, solemnly publish and declare, That these United Colonies are, and of Right ought to be Free and Independent States; that they are Absolved from all Allegiance to the British Crown, and that all political connection between them and the State of Great Britain, is and ought to be totally dissolved; and that as Free and Independent States, they have full Power to levy War, conclude Peace, contract Alliances, establish Commerce, and to do all other Acts and Things which Independent States may of right do. And for the support of this Declaration, with a firm reliance on the protection of divine Providence, we mutually pledge to each other our Lives, our Fortunes and our sacred Honor.

The most widely known part of the Declaration of Independence is the part that states the values that Americans supposedly held at the time—equality, liberty, and happiness. Its famous words are these:

> We hold these truths to be self-evident, that all men are created equal, that they are endowed by their Creator with certain unalienable Rights, that among these are Life, Liberty and the pursuit of Happiness.

> *(National Archives, 2012)*

Some of the key words from this statement include *equal, Rights, Life, Liberty,* and the *pursuit of Happiness.* Each of these terms clearly relates to equality, liberty, and happiness, suggesting that these are the values on which our country was founded. They also relate to many of the theories of justice introduced in Chapter 1, as will be examined later.

The US Constitution

The *US Constitution*, drafted after a revision of the Articles of Confederation proved impossible as well as insufficient for organizing a new government, occurred in 1787 and was ratified by all necessary states in 1788. The document, long and divided into seven articles, lays out the functions of the federal government as well as the appropriate roles of all parties involved. It is shown in Figure 2.2.

The first three Articles are probably the most important, as they address issues of the legislative, executive, and judicial branches of government, respectively. Specifically, Article I specifies the roles and responsibilities of the legislative branch of government, including the Senate and House of Representatives. Article II deals with the executive branch—specifically the powers of the President of the United States. Article III addresses the judicial branch of government, including the US Supreme Court and "such inferior Courts as the Congress may from time to time ordain and establish."

Yet, perhaps it is the words of the Preamble to the Constitution that are best known to Americans:

> We the People of the United States, in Order to form a more perfect Union, establish Justice, insure domestic Tranquility, provide for the common defence, promote the general Welfare, and secure the Blessings of Liberty to ourselves and our Posterity, do ordain and establish this Constitution for the United States of America.
>
> *(National Archives, 2012).*

FIGURE 2.2   The US Constitution.

Some of the key words from this document include Justice, domestic Tranquility, common defence, general Welfare, and Liberty. Although liberty is clearly a value stated in the Constitution—referring to freedom—other key values expressed by our "Founding Fathers" relate to public safety or our "common defence" and perhaps even social justice. For example, *domestic Tranquility* refers to peace in the land and Welfare refers to "being well," and both of these are obviously threatened not only by war but also by crime.

Many contemporary justice scholars have pointed out that America's efforts to reduce crime must respect justice by protecting our liberty. In fact, a review of the Bill of Rights, introduced in Chapter 1, illustrates that half of them deal with how government is to deal with people accused of crimes (Robinson, 2009). This clearly shows that, even at the founding of our country, due process rights were important to the founders (at least when it came to tactics of the federal government against some individuals). Recall that the Fourth Amendment grants you the right to be protected from unreasonable searches and seizures by the police and requires them to get a warrant based upon probable cause in order to search or seize you or your property; the Fifth Amendment guarantees you due process of law, the right to a grand jury hearing, freedom from double jeopardy, freedom from self-incrimination, and the right to just compensation for government seizure of your property; the Sixth Amendment gives you the rights to notice of any criminal charges against you, speedy and public trials, and impartial juries, as well as guaranteeing you the right to confront witnesses against you, to offer witnesses on your behalf, and to be granted an attorney to assist you in your defense; the Eighth Amendment bans excessive bails, excessive fines, and cruel and unusual punishments.

It was not until 1791 that three-quarters of the states finally approved the Bill of Rights. And it was not until the twentieth century that many of the rights contained within were finally applied by the US Supreme Court to state governments (as opposed to just the federal government). An example comes from the US Supreme Court case, *Mapp v. Ohio*, 367 U.S. 643 (1961) where the Court ruled that the Fourth Amendment protected an individual's Fourth Amendment rights from state government actions; prior to this ruling, the Fourth Amendment only precluded the federal government from using illegally obtained evidence against criminal defendants. The case dealt with an individual who had in her possession lewd and lascivious materials (in violation of state law) that were seized by the police when they were searching a home for a person wanted by the law. Since the police did not have a search warrant, the Court held 6–3 that the search violated the person's Fourth Amendment rights, and this was the first time the Court ruled in a way that applied these rights to state rather than federal matters.

Americans today view the Bill of Rights as part of the original document, one that gave them rights as citizens that cannot be eroded by the government. In fact, the US Constitution itself was actually a very radical idea and the Bill of Rights was even more so. As noted by Willis (1982: viii): "The framers were gambling on a new mood out in the country, created by new emergencies." It was "a fresh start entirely . . . an address to the people at large." In order to rally support for the new Constitution, the founders would have to engage in a propaganda campaign, arguing under pseudonyms in newspapers, pamphlets, and published speeches across the country, especially in the states of New York (where opposition to the idea of a Constitution was high), Pennsylvania, Massachusetts, and Virginia. The result was the book, *The Federalist Papers*, which contains the arguments of those who wanted to form a new government.

To understand this, you must remember that the new nation was being led by a loose set of agreements that bound the states—the *Articles of the Confederation*. People like Alexander Hamilton, James Madison, and John Jay—who would later author *The Federalist Papers*—argued that the Articles were insufficient to govern the new nation. As noted by Willis (1982: x), "a loose confederation could not possibly address itself to challenging times with any efficiency." Specifically, the Articles did not provide for a strong central government, meaning that the federal government could not regulate trade between states and foreign nations or force states to pay taxes, did not establish a uniform monetary system, was characterized by a weak judiciary, did not protect the nation from national or domestic threats, and made passing legislation very difficult.

Further, the national government had no mechanism in the executive branch to enforce its laws. Instead, each state printed its own money, entered into its own agreements, ran its own economy, and was essentially a nation unto itself. As noted by Bruns (1986): "Saddled with this weak government, the states were on the brink of economic disaster. The evidence was overwhelming."

Keep in mind that, not only did the new Constitution violate some sections of the Articles—many prominent individuals and groups also opposed the proposed new government. For example, Bruns (1986) writes that Rhode Island's leaders, made up of "men wedded to paper currency, low taxes, and popular government . . . refused to participate in what they saw as a conspiracy to overthrow the established government." Further, others like Patrick Henry (known for his famous quote, "Give me liberty or give me death") "refused to attend, declaring he 'smelt a rat.' He suspected, correctly, that Madison had in mind the creation of a powerful central government and the subversion of the authority of the state legislatures." And he along with others "believed that the state governments offered the chief protection for personal liberties. He was determined not to lend a hand to any proceeding that seemed to pose a threat to that protection."

The key battle in the fight for the Constitution was between the *Federalists*, who supported a Constitution, and the *Antifederalists*, who did not. The latter were concerned about the immense power the central government would have under such a system, the usurpation of state sovereignty, and the lack of a Bill of Rights that would guarantee individual liberties. According to Bruns (1986), in Pennsylvania "anti-Federalist rioters broke up a Federalist celebration and hung [James] Wilson and the Federalist chief justice of Pennsylvania, Thomas McKean, in effigy; put the torch to a copy of the Constitution; and busted a few Federalist heads." Further: "In New York the Constitution was under siege in the press by a series of essays signed 'Cato.' This motivated the counterattack by Alexander Hamilton, John Jay, and James in the form of *The Federalist Papers*. One critic, Patrick Henry said: 'What can avail your specious, imaginary balances, your rope-dancing, chain-rattling, ridiculous ideal checks and contrivances.'"

Fervent disagreement was also witnessed within the convention, causing great debate and arguing, as well as drafting and redrafting for months. The men who would become the founders considered various plans from different state representatives, ultimately rejecting some and compromising on others. This suggests that the US Constitution was not some divinely inspired form of perfect government that must be worshipped and never changed (as does the fact that it has been amended 27 times since), but also that the "original intent" of the founders really refers to a compromised product rather than some pure form of ideal virtues or values.

Activity 2.1 Original Intent

Go online and research the idea of the "original intent" of the US Constitution.

Be sure to read the brief article, "What 'original intent' would look like" by David Schultz: http://www.salon.com/2011/02/13/tea_party_schultz_constitution.

Do you think it would be possible to govern the US today using the philosophy of original intent? Would it be wise?

Do you agree with Schultz's argument that using original intent would mean Americans would be less free? Why?

How Social Justice is Emphasized in our Founding Documents

With those important points about the US Constitution in mind, it is possible to derive from America's founding documents a sense of what elements of social justice the founders valued. Recall from Chapter 1 that social justice has many meanings, depending on the context and on one's priorities and point of view. Generally speaking, social justice pertains to freedom, welfare, and virtue—where freedom refers to protecting people's liberty, welfare refers to providing a good life for people, and virtue refers to morality.

As noted in Chapter 1, libertarians assert that what matters most for deciding what is right or just is freedom—whether individual rights are respected and protected. For egalitarians, what matters most for justice is equality of opportunity in society and taking care of the least-advantaged citizens. Utilitarians focus on welfare and assert that what matters most for justice is the welfare of society, or its overall happiness. Finally, virtue-based theorists suggest that what matters most for justice is virtue, or moral goodness and righteousness.

Which of these approaches to justice is found or alluded to in the Declaration of Independence and US Constitution? This matters because it can give us a sense of what America's founders thought of justice when they declared our independence from Great Britain and formed our own country. Depending on one's perspective, you could argue that all of the major theories of justice are reflected in the words of the Declaration of Independence and the US Constitution. That is, the values of freedom (libertarianism and egalitarianism), welfare (utilitarianism), and virtue are all found in these documents.

Starting with the Declaration of Independence, let's go back to some of the key words from that document:

> We hold these truths to be self-evident, that all men are created equal, that they are endowed by their Creator with certain unalienable Rights, that among these are Life, Liberty and the pursuit of Happiness.

Remember that some of the key words from this statement include equal, Rights, Life, Liberty, and the pursuit of Happiness. In these words we see a reverence for libertarianism (Life, Liberty), egalitarianism (Rights, Liberty), as well as utilitarianism (Happiness). These were concepts at the time that were highly valued, suggesting a deep sense of morality or virtue inherent to the principles laid out in the document.

Of course, in the real world, the founders did not themselves live up to these principles (at least not by today's standards), but on paper they pronounced to the world the values for which the new America would eventually stand.

Returning to some of the most important words from the US Constitution—the Preamble—we see another strong statement of justice:

> We the People of the United States, in Order to form a more perfect Union, establish Justice, insure domestic Tranquility, provide for the common defence, promote the general Welfare, and secure the Blessings of Liberty to ourselves and our Posterity, do ordain and establish this Constitution for the United States of America.
>
> *(National Archives, 2012).*

Remember that some of the key words from this document include Justice, domestic Tranquility, common defence, general Welfare, and Liberty. In these words we see that the founders valued utilitarianism (general Welfare, domestic Tranquility, common defence), but also libertarianism (Liberty). The term Justice here is perhaps used as an egalitarian term or as a sign of one of our nation's virtues. As with the Declaration of Independence, the values found in the US Constitution were highly valued, hinting that these were the predominant virtues of the time, at least on paper.

Many people, including serious Constitutional scholars, disagree about what values the founders actually held when they wrote these documents. On the one hand, the founders used words like justice, liberty, and equality, but on the other, they clearly were not referencing all the values that those terms signify today. As one example, many of the founders owned slaves and treated them as property, a practice widely rejected today. Another example is that women were not seen or treated as equals to men; women did not even gain the right to vote until 1920 with the passage of the Nineteenth Amendment to the US Constitution.

Beyond the obvious contradiction of slave owners and oppression of women promoting ideals of liberty and equality, there is serious debate about what the founders intended in the first place. Given that no records were kept of the Constitutional convention, no reporters were allowed in, and so on, we must rely on the writings and speeches of the founders to infer their intent.

Critical Interpretations of the Constitution

Serious scholars have examined these documents and concluded that our founding documents were intended not to liberate but instead to constrict—to maintain the status quo inequality in society rather than to eradicate it. For example, Charles Beard, in *An Economic Interpretation of the Constitution of the United States* (1913), suggests the Constitution was intentionally biased against the poor. He points out that, of the five economic groups that existed in 1787, "the four poorest groups had no representatives at the convention: women, slaves, indentured servants, and propertyless white men" (Harrigan, 2000: 45). Every delegate involved in drafting the Constitution was a white male who owned enough property to be allowed to vote. According to Beard, 38 of the 55 delegates owned government bonds, 24 earned their living through banking or some other financial investment, 15 owned slaves, and 14 had investments in western lands. Feagin adds that, of the 55 delegates:

at least 40 percent have been or are slave owners, and a significant proportion of the others profit to some degree as merchants, shippers, lawyers, and bankers from the trade in slaves, commerce in slave-produced agricultural products, or supplying provisions to slaveholders and slave-traders.

(Feagin, 2000: 9)

Given the makeup of the delegates, was the Constitution drafted at least partly to protect their limited interests?

John Harrigan (2000: 47) suggests that three different types of provisions were written into the Constitution to protect the limited financial interests of wealthy, white male delegates:

- those that protected their private property rights;
- those that insulated the national government from popular rule; and
- those that minimized the influence of the lower-status population in the ratification process.

The protections of private property rights included provisions that benefited businesses engaged in trade and economy, bankers and creditors, slave holders, and holders of securities under the Articles of Confederation.

Joe Feagin explains that:

At the heart of the Constitution was protection of the property and wealth of the affluent bourgeoisie in the new nation, including property of those enslaved . . . For the founders, freedom meant the protection of unequal accumulation of property, particularly property that could produce a profit in the emerging capitalistic system. Certain political, economic, and racial interests were conjoined. This was not just a political gathering with the purpose of creating a new major bourgeois-democratic government; it was also a meeting to protect the racial and economic interests of men with substantial property and wealth in the colonies.

(Feagin, 2000: 10)

Popular rule was not set up in the Constitution because people did not directly vote for the president, the Court, or the Senate. Only House members were originally elected by the people, and people could vote only if their congressional districts had at least 30,000 people. This benefited the wealthy. Barriers to voting (such as property ownership requirements) were constructed to discourage a large percentage of people from voting.

Because of this, Harrigan concludes:

The lower-status population did indeed have nothing to say about the drafting of the Constitution and (whether by choice or coercion) had little to say about ratifying it. Important provisions in the Constitution protected economic interests that were more valuable to the upper-status population than to the lower-status population.

(Harrigan, 2000: 53)

Similarly, Joe Feagin (2000), in his book, *Racist America: Roots, Current Realities and Future Reparations*, traces the roots of American racism to the US Constitution and early Colonial America. He suggests that many of our country's founders, including Thomas Jefferson, Benjamin Franklin, and James Madison, were greatly influenced by assumptions in Europe about the inherent inferiority of African Americans to Caucasians. Thus, African Americans would specifically be counted only as three-fifths of a man according to Article I, Section 2 of the US Constitution.

Feagin (2000: 14) asserts that the US Constitutional Convention was something other than what we have learned about in school. He suggests the structure of the nation, as laid out in the Constitution:

> was created to maintain separation and oppression at the time and for the foreseeable future. The framers reinforced and legitimated a system of racist oppression that they thought would ensure that Whites, especially White men of means, would rule for centuries to come.
>
> *(Feagin, 2000: 14)*

According to Feagin, the country's founders owned slaves and benefited from the unequal treatment of African Americans with Caucasians:

> Men of politics like Thomas Jefferson, George Washington, Alexander Hamilton, Patrick Henry, Benjamin Franklin, John Hancock, and Sam Houston enslaved black Americans. Ten US presidents (Washington, Jefferson, James Madison, James Monroe, Andrew Jackson, John Tyler, James Polk, Zachary Taylor, and Ulysses S. Grant) at some point in their lives enslaved African Americans.
>
> *(Feagin, 2000: 15)*

Many lawmakers (members of both houses of Congress) were also slave owners, as were those who would interpret the law (members of the US Supreme Court). Not surprisingly, "few major decisions made by the federal legislative and judicial branches went against the interests of the nation's slaveholding oligarchy, and foreign and domestic policies generally did not conflict with the interests of those centrally involved with the slavery system" (p. 56).

Activity 2.2 US Constitution

Do you think the US Constitution was set up to grant rights to all people and to serve us all, or that it was established to serve the rights and interests of wealthy, white, landowners?

Explain.

In spite of these shortcomings, the founders established a country that would, over the passage of time, come to expand rights to more and more people. So, even whereas the ideals of America would not be realized in the short term, with strides by millions of people over decades, US practice would come to match the ideal more and more. That is, liberty, equality, and justice would become a reality for more people as they would stand up and challenge authority to assure victory. Later in the book, we'll provide numerous examples showing how Americans have achieved this.

Public Opinion Polls

What do Americans value today? As noted in Chapter 1, to some degree, *all* approaches to justice (i.e., libertarianism, egalitarianism, utilitarianism, virtue-based theories) are supported by citizens, just not fully embraced by them. Research based on public opinion polls suggests that our views of justice are contextual or circumstantial—i.e., they depend on the context or circumstances.

As noted in Chapter 1, Western citizens including Americans tend to prioritize equality in matters of citizenship. This means they value equal rights or liberty. When it comes to matters of instrumental associations such as work, they tend to prioritize desert. This means they also value liberty in the sense of property rights and earning money. And when it comes to solidaristic communities such as in families, they tend to prioritize need. This means they also value helping the least fortunate and assuring happiness for all (Miller, 2003). Thus, there is room for liberty, equality, and utility or happiness.

These values of justice sometimes conflict, so Americans are often conflicted about the implications for justice of some issues. Here is an example: in Chapter 1, we showed that Americans value liberty or freedom, making libertarianism popular. Yet, since Americans also value equality, egalitarian ideals are prominent. Since there can be an inherent conflict between our preferences for liberty and equality, whether we emphasize one or the other often depends on the context or circumstances. So, on the one hand, Americans respect liberty and believe murderers are responsible for their choices to permanently deprive their victims of their liberty; given this, they have historically supported execution of murderers as a legitimate form of retribution. That is, when murderers deprive their victims of their liberty by taking their lives, they deserve to lose their liberty by sacrificing their own lives (Pojman & Reiman, 1998).

On the other hand, since Americans have a strong affinity for equality, evidence of inequality in capital punishment practice has resulted in lowered support for the death penalty. Data from 2012 show that almost two-thirds of Americans (62 percent) say they support the death penalty, while 32 percent say they oppose the death penalty, and 6 percent are unsure (Sourcebook, Table 2.51.2012). As evidence of racial disparities in the application of the death penalty have surfaced in numerous states, support for capital punishment is found to be reduced (Robinson, 2009). A poll from 2011 found that only 52 percent of Americans believed the death penalty was fairly applied, versus 41 percent who said it was unfairly applied, and 6 percent who said they did not know (Sourcebook, Table 2.0005.2011).

It is possible that increased awareness of racial biases in capital punishment practice (a threat to equality) helps us understand the reductions in death sentences and executions in the US within the past decade. Further, it might help us understand why Americans increasingly say they support alternatives to the death penalty. Polls show that, when given alternative sentences such as life imprisonment without the possibility of parole (LWOP), support for the death penalty drops to about 50 percent (Death Penalty Information Center, 2013a). A 2010 poll, for example, found that 49 percent of respondents chose the death penalty as the most appropriate penalty for murder, versus 46 percent who chose LWOP, and 6 percent who did not know (Sourcebook, Table 2.49.2010). And, when given the alternative of LWOP plus restitution to the victim's family (LWOP + restitution, where the offender works in prison and his or her pay is sent either to the victim's family or a charity of their choosing), support falls even further. For example, a recent study in North Carolina found support for LWOP plus restitution at 78 percent (Death Penalty Information Center, 2013b).

Liberty

We do have some sense of whether Americans still value *liberty*—including both the right to own and control their own property (free market libertarianism) as well as more generally appreciation for freedom. For example, research from the Pew Research Center shows that 67 percent of Americans agreed that "most people are better off in a free-market economy, even though some people are rich and some poor." This is strong evidence that Americans support free markets and thus free market libertarianism. Yet, 70 percent of Americans also agree that the government has some responsibility to take care of the very poor and 51 percent say they think "the government should do more to help needy Americans, even if it means going deeper into debt." This is evidence of American concern for the needy, a sign of support for egalitarian ideals. Still, 69 percent say they worry that "poor people have become too dependent on government assistance programs."

Even though 80 percent of Americans thought at least some of the blame for the 2008 financial crisis was due to weak government regulation, support for regulation did not shift upward as a result. Still, about 54 percent of Americans agree that the government should exert more control over the economy than it has in the past (Allen & Auzier, 2009).

Given that a large majority of Americans generally do not trust the government—only 26 percent of Americans in 2013 said they can trust the government all or some of the time (Pew, 2013a)—it is safe to say that Americans are currently skeptical about government. Yet, this figure has varied widely across our history, and only plummeted below 50 percent during the George W. Bush Administration after climbing steadily in the 1990s under the presidency of Bill Clinton (the figure also fell during the presidency of Lyndon Johnson).

Trust in government is higher among Hispanics and African Americans than whites, as well as among younger people than older people, and is lower for Republicans and Independents than Democrats. Perhaps not surprisingly given the differences in their political ideologies:

> 76% of conservative Republicans regard the government as a threat to their personal rights and freedoms and 54% consider the government to be a "major" threat, an increase [from 2010] when 62% of them described it as a threat to their freedom and 47% said it was a 'major' threat.

Among Democrats, only 38 percent say the government poses a threat to their personal freedoms and 16 percent call it "major." So it is likely fair to conclude that free market libertarianism is most common among Republicans and is thus likely a function of or even a determinant of one's political ideology.

Given that the poll was taken during the Obama presidency, perhaps the results of the poll are the result of *ideology*—Republicans are more concerned with government when a Democrat is leading it. Another possibility is that Republicans tend to be more conservative, and part of the conservative ideology is skepticism of government; to conservatives, big government is the problem (Ginsberg, Lowi, Weir, & Tolbert, 2013).

Interestingly, however, conservatives are not afraid of or disapproving of big government when it comes to functions of crime control or preventing terrorism. Data consistently show that conservatives are more supportive of strong central government responses such as the wars on crime, drugs, and terrorism (Robinson, 2009).

Yet, in response to the question:

> Which comes closer to your view—the government should take all steps necessary to prevent additional acts of terrorism in the U.S. even if it means your basic civil liberties would be violated, (or) the government should take steps to prevent additional acts of terrorism but not if those steps would violate your basic civil liberties?

Seventy-one percent of Americans chose respecting civil liberties and only 25 percent said to prevent terrorism even if civil liberties were violated (Gallup, 2013). This is strong support for the libertarian school of thought.

Earlier in 2006 when evidence surfaced that President Bush had authorized a secret domestic spying program (Cole & Lobel, 2009; US Commission on Civil Rights, 2013), a majority of Americans also said they were concerned about collecting data on Americans by tapping phones without warrants, and that they disapproved of this practice. This was true even though 30 percent of Americans said they frequently or occasionally worried about being victimized by terrorism, further evidence of Americans' devotion to liberty.

Additional information on American opinion of privacy comes from the Pew Research Center:

> Most Americans are concerned that business and government are accessing too much of their personal information. Nearly three-quarters (74%) say they are concerned that business is collecting too much information about people like them. More than six-in-ten (64%) have the same concern about the government.

The right to privacy is not explicitly stated in the US Constitution or the Bill of Rights. Yet, it is implied in several Amendments including the First Amendment (which allows you to hold your own beliefs and state them or keep them privately), the Third Amendment (which allows you to keep soldiers out of your home during times of war thereby assuring your privacy), the Fourth Amendment (which allows you to keep your property and person private from the government unless they have a warrant based on probable cause to search it), and the Fifth Amendment (which allows you to not incriminate yourself by keeping certain information private).

Equality

As for measures that relate to egalitarianism—such as helping the least advantaged—more than half (56 percent) of Americans would like a smaller government that offers a smaller range of services, compared to 35 percent who would like a larger government offering a wider range of services. This suggests that, when asked general questions about the size of government, Americans tend to favor smaller government. At the same time, when asked about specific government programs, Americans do not want large cuts to them; instead they generally would like to keep spending allocations the same or actually prefer increases in spending to specific programs instead of cuts. This is found to be true for every program with the exceptions of spending on the State Department (which at the time of the poll was under scrutiny for the mishandling of a case involving an attack against a US Embassy in Libya) and providing aid to the world's needy:

> For 18 of 19 programs tested, majorities want either to increase spending or maintain it at current levels. The only exception is assistance for needy people around the world. Nonetheless, as many

say that funding for aid to the needy overseas should either be increased (21%), or kept the same (28%), as decreased (48%).

(Pew, 2013a)

According to data from Pew, the largest partisan divides between Republicans and Democrats are on the issues of the social safety net (i.e., social security and Medicare), protecting the environment through regulations, the power of labor unions, "equal opportunity," and the size and scope of government. Pew notes:

> There are partisan differences of 35 points or more in opinions about the government's responsibility to care for the poor, whether the government should help more needy people if it means adding to the debt and whether the government should guarantee all citizens enough to eat and a place to sleep.

As noted earlier, conservatives do not favor these kinds of programs whereas liberals are far more likely to favor them.

With regard to equal opportunity, Democrats tend to be more favorable than Republicans. Pew reports:

> Democratic support for doing whatever is necessary to improve the position of minorities, including the possible use of preferences, has increased in recent years. About half (52%) of Democrats agree that "We should make every effort to improve the position of blacks and other minorities, even if it means giving them preferential treatment." This has increased 11 points since 2007. Yet, Republicans' views have changed little over this period. Just 12% currently agree that all efforts should be taken, including the use of preferential treatment, to improve the position of minorities.

In spite of these differences, "an 86% majority says that society should do what is necessary to ensure everyone has an equal opportunity to succeed." So, in theory, Americans support equal opportunity; in practice, there are limits, especially for conservatives. This still serves as evidence of a strong preference for egalitarianism among Americans.

Interestingly, in spite of being aware of notable gaps between the rich and poor, a large portion of Americans (63 percent) disagree with the sentiment that "hard work offers little guarantee of success." That is, Americans tend to still believe that hard work can pay off. Yet, 76 percent of Americans agree that "today it's really true that the rich just get richer while the poor get poorer." Consistent with this is the finding that "46% say that circumstances beyond one's control are more often to blame if a person is poor, while 38% say that an individual's lack of effort is more often to blame; 11% blame both." Interestingly, people actually experiencing poverty are far more likely than are people not experiencing poverty to believe that circumstances beyond their control explain their situation. Taken together, these findings suggest that, even though Americans still believe in hard work and personal responsibility for economic success, they recognize that the wealthy do have advantages. This justifies government intervention in order to "level the playing field" to achieve egalitarian outcomes.

One advantage is the amount people earn for their work—rich people (if they work) have better jobs and thus earn more than poor people. According to Pew: "Nearly two-thirds of Americans (65%) say that most poor people in the US work but are unable to earn enough money; just 23% say the poor do not work." There is certainly ample evidence that a sizable portion of poor people are employed and simply do not earn enough money to get out of poverty. For example, the Bureau of Labor Statistics (2012) reports that, in 2010, there were 46.2 million people in the US who were living below the poverty threshold. Of these, 10.5 million were among the "working poor," meaning they spent at least 27 weeks working or looking for work but still did not earn enough to get themselves out of poverty. Thus, about 23 percent of poor people in the US are employed or looking for employment (and this number is an underestimate since it also includes young children, who obviously are not working or looking for work).

Even though more than 70 percent of Americans believe that the success of the country depends on the success of businesses, 61 percent of Americans believe the gap between the rich and the poor has grown in the past decade, a gap they believe is too large. A review of the research by Miller (2003) supports this conclusion. These findings are indicative of the conflict between our preferences as free market libertarians and egalitarians.

Additionally, "large majorities continue to say that business corporations make too much profit and fail to strike a fair balance between making profits and serving the public interest." And most agree that the free market system needs "government regulation to protect the public interest" even though "nearly as many say that government regulation of business usually causes more harm than good."

If it seems like there are contradictions in America's values, we believe it is safe to conclude there are. Plenty of data reflect this reality. For example, Pew reports that:

> Today, 59% agree that they are concerned about the government becoming too involved in health care. In 2009, during the early stages of debate about what would become the Affordable Care Act a year later [i.e., "Obamacare"], 46% expressed concern about growing government involvement in health care. Yet, even as concern about government involvement has grown, an overwhelming majority (82%) continues to agree that the government needs to do more to make health care affordable and accessible.

An obvious question is, how can government do more to make health care affordable and accessible without getting involved in health care in some way? American opinion on this issue is thus a good example of the oftentimes confused or conflicted nature of US public opinion.

Happiness

In addition to the popularity of libertarianism and egalitarianism, Americans also believe in and strive for happiness. Thus, as noted in Chapter 1, we believe in utilitarianism. Yet, here our respect for the rights of the minority can at times interfere with our desire to do the greatest good for the greatest numbers of people. In these cases, we do our best to protect the rights of those minorities, as we will show later in the book.

In 2006, in the latest *World Values Survey*, the United States ranked sixteenth in the world in terms of happiness, ahead of more than 80 other countries. Given that Americans are goal-driven, we might assume that Americans strive to be happy. The countries at the bottom of the list have a long history of authoritarian rule as well as poverty, two realities that run counter to happiness. The US ranks high on wealth and *social solidarity* (a sense that we're connected and all in this together), measures important for overall happiness.

According to Inglehart and Welzel:

> The unprecedented wealth that has accumulated in advanced societies during the past generation means that an increasing share of the population has grown up taking survival for granted. Thus, priorities have shifted from an overwhelming emphasis on economic and physical security toward an increasing emphasis on subjective well-being, self-expression and quality of life.
>
> *(Inglehart & Welzel, 2007)*

This is an important reminder of the link between economic success and happiness and may provide some support for the argument that free market libertarianism is still an important part of what it means to be American. Yet, it is important to note that data from the *World Values Survey* show that, from 1946 to 2006, levels of happiness in the US have been flat (Inglehart, Welzel, & Foa, 2007).

In support of the finding that Americans are generally happy, a recent Gallup poll found that 52 percent described themselves as happy and 54 percent as thriving. Yet, 42 percent said they were struggling, 3 percent suffering, and 10 percent stressed (Gallup, 2013a). Part of this is owing to the state of the US economy, as 7 percent describe themselves as unemployed and another 18 percent say they are underemployed. Another Gallup (2013f) poll found that 78 percent of Americans said they felt satisfied with their lives while 21 percent said they felt dissatisfied. Gallup also has a daily tracking poll that asks people whether they experienced "a lot of happiness and enjoyment without a lot of stress and worry" or "daily worry and stress without a lot of happiness and enjoyment." Roughly 50 percent on any given day indicate happiness and enjoyment whereas about 15 percent say worry and stress (Gallup, 2013h).

Meanwhile, only 24 percent said they were satisfied with the way things are going in the United States, while 74 percent were dissatisfied (Gallup, 2013g). This has trended sharply downward since about 2003, along with the performance of the economy and specifically with the decline in median family income during this time. Thus, it is reasonable to conclude that, in the short-term, levels of happiness trend along with economic performance.

Research from the Pew Research Center (2012) shows that 68 percent of Americans rate their personal economic situation as good, while only 31 percent say the national economic situation is good. These figures trend with the performance of the economy. For example, in 2011, only 18 percent rated the country's economic situation as good, and in 2007 (the year before the economic collapse), the number was 50 percent. Finally, research from the Harris Poll finds that, generally speaking, people who are older and who make more money, are generally the most happy, according to their happiness index that measures agreement with a large number of items related to happiness; their poll shows that only about one-third (33 percent) of Americans describe themselves as very happy.

Virtue

Recall that virtue refers to that which is moral or right. Based on the information above, Americans clearly value liberty, equality, and happiness. What else do Americans value? There are a few worldwide and national surveys we can use to assess this question. But the results often depend on who is asked. For example, According to Pew (2013b), there are large differences between Republicans and Democrats on the issue of "old-fashioned values" related to family and marriage. Pew notes:

> Just 60% of Democrats currently agree, down from 70% in 2007 and 86% in the first political values survey" that they have old-fashioned values about marriage and family. Republicans' views have shown far less change: currently, 88% say they have old-fashioned values about marriage and family.

Many would see this as a virtue issue, or one that deals with right and wrong. For example, is it right or wrong to allow gay people to get married? Should people have children out of wedlock? These kinds of questions pertain to "old-fashioned values" related to family and marriage. Yet, some would also see these issues as issues of equality because they pertain to issues such as marriage equality and parental rights.

Gallup results show that 59 percent of Americans in 2013 believe gay or lesbian relations are morally acceptable, a large increase from 2001 when only 40 percent did (Gallup, 2013b, 2013c, 2013d). Further, 65 percent of Americans believe gay relationships between consenting adults should be legal (versus 31 percent who believe they should be illegal), and 53 percent believe gay marriage should be recognized in the same way, with the same rights, as traditional marriage (versus 45 percent who disagree). This is clear evidence of how Americans have increasingly embraced equality, even for issues like gay marriage. But to others, this change is seen as an erosion of morals or virtue, at least in the "old fashioned" or traditional sense.

Interestingly, the same survey found 91 percent find birth control morally acceptable, 68 percent approve of divorce, 67 percent approve of an unmarried woman having a baby, 64 percent approve of gambling, 63 percent approve of sex between an unmarried man and woman, 62 percent approve of the death penalty, 60 percent approve of having a baby outside of marriage, 42 percent approve abortion, and 31 percent approve of pornography (Gallup, 2013), as shown in Table 2.2. Each of these could be related to issues of virtue or morality, at least for some; for others, these are issues of liberty or freedom.

The same Gallup survey found that 72 percent of Americans feel "the state of moral values in the country" is getting worse, while 20 percent think it is getting better, and 6 percent think it is staying the same. According to Gallup (2013e), only 19 percent of Americans rated the "overall state of moral values in this country" as excellent or good, while 36 percent rate them as fair and 44 percent rate them as poor. Clearly then, many Americans have concerns about morality or virtue.

Some findings from the *World Values Survey* also pertain to values or virtues, including the US measure for *secular-rational values*. This measure indicates the degree a nation is more secular or sacred (Welzel, 2007). The US ranks a bit closer to the "traditional pole" (meaning sacred or religious) than to the secular/rational pole, suggesting the importance of parent–child ties and deference to authority, as well as traditional family values. Thus many Americans reject practices they perceive as threats to tradition, including divorce, abortion, and euthanasia. Such nations also tend to have high levels of national pride as well as a nationalistic outlook (Inglehart & Welzel, 2010). However, the US also embraces secularity in practice, meaning Americans generally want to keep religion out of public life and are willing

TABLE 2.2 American Virtues

Percentage reporting that they find something morally acceptable or that they approve of it

Birth control	91%
Divorce	68%
Unmarried woman having a baby	67%
Gambling	64%
Sex between an unmarried man and woman	63%
Death penalty	62%
Having a baby outside of marriage	60%
Abortion	42%
Pornography	31%

Source: Gallup Poll, Moral Issues, http://www.gallup.com/poll/1681/Moral-Issues.aspx.

to allow people to pursue any religion they choose, a sign of tolerance that is more consistent with a secular–rational nation, as well as with libertarianism.

The figure for another measure from the *World Values Survey, self-expression values*, was quite strong and growing over time, suggesting Americans highly value individuality over conformity. That is, Americans embrace individuality more than people in other more traditional or reserved cultures. According to Inglehart and Welzel:

> Self-expression values give high priority to environmental protection, tolerance of diversity and rising demands for participation in decision making in economic and political life. These values also reflect mass polarization over tolerance of outgroups, including foreigners, gays and lesbians and gender equality. The shift from survival values to self-expression values also includes a shift in child-rearing values, from emphasis on hard work toward emphasis on imagination and tolerance as important values to teach a child. And it goes with a rising sense of subjective well-being that is conducive to an atmosphere of tolerance, trust and political moderation. Finally, societies that rank high on self-expression values also tend to rank high on interpersonal trust.
>
> *(Inglehart & Welzel, 2007)*

There is a link between these outcomes and democracy: specifically, in "a culture of trust and tolerance, in which people place a relatively high value on individual freedom and self-expression" and where people "have activist political orientations," democracy is likely to flourish. Perhaps one reason American democracy has been so successful is because we have created a culture that sustains it, one that embraces tolerance, self-expression, trust, and so forth. Our strong beliefs in liberty and equality—signs of our preferences for libertarianism and egalitarianism—may be seen as virtuous in themselves.

Criminal Justice Polls

Polls related to crime and criminal justice issues are also useful in helping us see what Americans value. For example, in response to the question:

Which of the following approaches to lowering the crime rate in the United States comes closer to your own view . . . do you think more money and effort should go to attacking the social and economic problems that lead to crime through better education and job training or more money and effort should go to deterring crime by improving law enforcement with more prisons, police, and judges?

a sizable majority of Americans (64 percent) say attacking social problems, versus 32 percent who say more law enforcement, and 4 percent who say they don't know (Sourcebook, Table 2.28.2010). This finding is consistent with utilitarianism, for it reflects the desire to better people's lives—the greatest happiness for the most people.

Another poll asked:

We are faced with many problems in this country, none of which can be solved easily or inexpensively. I'm going to name some of the problems, and for each one I'd like you to tell me whether you think we're spending too much money on it, too little money, or about the right amount.

Data for 2002, the latest year for which data are available, are shown in Table 2.3. As you can see, a majority of Americans believe we do not spend enough money on halting the crime rate, dealing with drug addiction, and improving the American educational system. Much smaller portions of Americans believe we spend too little on improving the condition of blacks or on welfare. These data also suggest an affinity of Americans for utilitarianism (because we want to increase overall happiness by bettering people's lives) as well as egalitarianism (because we want to improve the conditions of blacks who have historically been subjected to discrimination and differential treatment).

Another interesting finding is a poll from 2011 that found that 50 percent of Americans said they favored legalizing marijuana, versus 46 percent who said they did not favor this, and 3 percent who were unsure. These numbers changed slightly in 2012 to 48 percent who favored it, 50 percent who opposed it, and 1 percent who were not sure (Sourcebook, Table 2.67.2012). 2012 was the year that two states—Washington and Colorado—legalized marijuana and another state—Oregon—narrowly failed to, even though it was on the ballot (Oregon and Alaska legalized marijuana use in 2014). In 2010, an incredible 70 percent of Americans said they favored "making marijuana legally available for doctors to prescribe in order to reduce pain and suffering" (Sourcebook, Table 2.0038.2010).

TABLE 2.3 Public Opinion on Spending on Various Problems

Percentage reporting that we spend too little on various problems	
Halting the crime rate	56%
Dealing with drug addiction	57%
Improving the American educational system	73%
Improving the condition of blacks	31%
Welfare	21%

Source: Data is from Source: National Opinion Research Center, *General Social Surveys, 1972–2002*, Storrs, CT: The Roper Center for Public Opinion Research, University of Connecticut. (Machine-readable data files.) Table constructed by SOURCEBOOK staff.

Perhaps for some this issue is one that relates most to virtue or morality, although for others it is likely about the overwhelming social science evidence showing the ineffectiveness of US drug control policy (Robinson & Scherlen, 2013).

Public opinion on each of these issues varies widely depending on one's political ideology as captured by party affiliation. For example, support for the death penalty varies significantly by political party. In 2011, only 41 percent of Democrats supported the death penalty, versus 49 percent of Independents, but 72 percent of Republicans (Sourcebook, Table 2.54.2011). Also, when it comes to legalizing marijuana, 61 percent of Democrats favor this, versus 50 percent of Independents, but only 33 percent of Republicans (Sourcebook, 2.0021.2012).

The pluralistic nature of American opinion of criminal justice practice can be seen clearly when examining responses to the question:

> In your view, how should juveniles between the ages of 14 and 17 who commit violent crimes be treated in the criminal justice system—should they be treated the same as adults, or should they be given more lenient treatment in a juvenile court?

In response to this question, 59 percent say juveniles should be treated the same as adults, but 32 percent say they should be treated more leniently, and less than 1 percent say they should be treated harsher. Another 8 percent said it depends and 1 percent said they did not know. Table 2.4 illustrates how the answers depend on the different demographic characteristics of respondents.

As you can see, males, the less educated, and Republicans are more likely to indicate that they support treating kids like adults, whereas females, the more educated, and Democrats and Independents are more likely to suggest more lenient treatment for juvenile offenders. Similar patterns are seen for other issues, including gun control and immigration reform. Specifically, females, African Americans, older people, the most educated, and Democrats favor more strict laws regulating the sale of guns, while males, whites, the younger, the least educated, and Republicans favor keeping the laws the way they are now or make them less strict (Sourcebook, Table 2.64.2011). Similarly, when given the choice

TABLE 2.4 Public Opinion on the Treatment of Juveniles

How should juveniles between the ages of 14 and 17 who commit violent crimes be treated in the criminal justice system?

	Same as adults	More lenient	Tougher	Depends
Male	64%	29%	1%	5%
Females	55%	34%	less than 1%	10%
High school (or less)	68%	25%	less than 1%	6%
Some college	61%	27%	1%	9%
College grad	51%	41%	less than 1%	7%
College (post grad)	42%	49%	0%	9%
Independent	59%	35%	0%	5%
Democrat	55%	35%	less than 1%	9%
Republican	64%	24%	1%	10%

Source: Data compiled by SOURCEBOOK staff from The Gallup Organization, Inc.

between better border security or creating a path to citizenship to deal with illegal immigration, males and Republicans tend to favor the former while African Americans and Hispanics as well as Democrats and Independents tend to favor the latter (Sourcebook, Table 2.0035.2013).

Each of these findings is an important reminder of facts already established in this book. First, how Americans view justice largely depends on the context or circumstances. Second, whether Americans view something as just or not depends on which Americans you are talking about.

Activity 2.3 Democrats and Republicans

Why do you think Democrats and Republicans see things so differently?

And what do you think are the implications for justice?

Do Democrats and Republicans favor different theories of justice? Explain.

Summary

Americans believe in justice and see themselves as a free and just people. A review of the Declaration of Independence and the US Constitution illustrates that, from the very outset of our country, the founders believed in liberty, equality, happiness or utility, and virtue or morality. As such, several theories of justice—including libertarianism, egalitarianism, utilitarianism, and virtue-based theories—are all relevant and important to America.

Yet, there are clear differences between the ideals expressed in our founding documents and actual practice in the real world. For example, liberty, equality, and happiness were not applied to people of color and women from the foundation of our country; instead, Native Americans were slaughtered, Africans were enslaved, and women were oppressed in the earliest days of our country. Civil and human rights were earned by citizens as they forced their own government to grant them these rights over time—typically in the courts but also on the streets of America.

Polls today show that the principles of liberty, equality, happiness or utility, and morality are all still important to Americans. They also demonstrate clearly that we have progressed to a more progressive and tolerant people—characteristics vital not only to equality and our happiness, but also to our economic success as a nation. Yet, we remain a conflicted people; whether we prioritize liberty, equality, utility, or virtue often depends on the context or circumstances. Thus, no one theory can completely capture our views of justice.

Discussion Questions

1. Define American exceptionalism.
2. What is the US Declaration of Independence? What were some of the most important grievances filed against King George III of Great Britain?
3. Which major principles of justice are found in the US Declaration of Independence? Provide evidence.
4. What is the US Constitution? Contrast this document with the Articles of Confederation.

5. Which major principles of justice are found in the US Declaration of Independence? Provide evidence.
6. In what ways can the US Constitution be interpreted as serving limited interests? Discuss how the document allegedly was written to benefit the wealthy and the white.
7. What are the major values of Americans today according to public opinion polls?
8. Do Americans value liberty? Provide evidence.
9. Do Americans value equality? Provide evidence.
10. Do Americans value happiness? Provide evidence.
11. Do Americans value virtue? Provide evidence.
12. What do findings from criminal justice polls say about Americans' virtues?

References

Allen, J., & Auzier, R. (2009). Socialism, American Style. Downloaded from: http://www.pewresearch.org/2009/03/12/socialism-americanstyle/.

Beard D. (1913). *An Economic Interpretation of the Constitution of the United States.* New York: MacMillan.

Bruns, R. (1986). Web version based on the Introduction to *A More Perfect Union: The Creation of the United States Constitution.* Washington, DC: Published for the National Archives and Records Administration by the National Archives Trust Fund Board. Downloaded from: http://www.archives.gov/exhibits/charters/constitution_history.html.

Bureau of Labor Statistics (2012). Income, Poverty and Health Insurance Coverage in the United States. Downloaded from: https://www.census.gov/newsroom/releases/archives/income_wealth/cb12-172.html.

Cole, D., & Lobel, J. (2009). *Less Safe, Less Free: Why America is Losing the War on Terror.* New York: New Press.

Death Penalty Information Center (2013a). Public Opinion: 2012 Gallup Poll shows Support for Death Penalty Remains near 40-year Low. Downloaded from: http://deathpenaltyinfo.org/public-opinion-2012-gallup-poll-shows-support-death-penalty-remains-near-40-year-low.

Death Penalty Information Center (2013b). Public Opinion: Strong Majority of North Carolinians prefer Life without Parole over the Death Penalty. Downloaded from: http://deathpenaltyinfo.org/public-opinion-strong-majority-north-carolinians-prefer-life-without-parole-over-death-penalty.

Feagin, J. (2000). *Racist America.* New York: Routledge.

Gallup (2013a). Americans' Outlook for US Moral Values still Pessimistic. Downloaded from: from: http://www.gallup.com/poll/162740/americans-outlook-moral-values-pessimistic.aspx.

Gallup (2013b). Civil Liberties. Downloaded from: http://www.gallup.com/poll/5263/Civil-Liberties.aspx.

Gallup (2013c). Gay and lesbian rights. Downloaded from: http://www.gallup.com/poll/1651/Gay-Lesbian-Rights.aspx.

Gallup (2013d). In US, Record-High say Gay, Lesbian Relations Morally OK. Downloaded from: http://www.gallup.com/poll/162689/record-high-say-gay-lesbian-relations-morally.aspx.

Gallup (2013e). Moral Issues. Downloaded from: http://www.gallup.com/poll/1681/Moral-Issues.aspx.

Gallup (2013f). Satisfaction with Personal Life. Downloaded from: http://www.gallup.com/poll/1672/Satisfaction-Personal-Life.aspx.

Gallup (2013g). Satisfaction with the United States. Downloaded from: http://www.gallup.com/poll/1669/General-Mood-Country.aspx.

Gallup (2013h). Well-being. Downloaded from: http://www.gallup.com/poll/wellbeing.aspx?ref=f.

Ginsberg, B., Lowi, T., Weir, M., & Tolbert, C. (2013). *We the People: An Introduction to American Politics.* New York: WW Norton.

Harrigan, J. (2000). *Empty Dreams, Empty Pockets: Class and Bias in American Politics.* New York: Addison-Wesley Longman.

Inglehart, R., & Welzel, C. (2010). Changing Mass Priorities: The Link between Modernization and Democracy. *Perspectives on Politics, 8*(2), 554.

Inglehart, R., & Welzel, C. (2007). The WVS Cultural Map of the World. Downloaded from: http://www.world valuessurvey.org/wvs/articles/folder_published/article_base_54.

Inglehart, R., Welzel, R., & Foa, C. (2007). Happiness Trends in 24 Countries, 1946–2006. Downloaded from: http://www.worldvaluessurvey.org/wvs/articles/folder_published/article_base_106.

Miller, D. (2003). *Principles of Social Justice*. Cambridge, MA: Harvard University Press.

National Archives (2014). Declaration of Independence. Downloaded from: http://www.archives.gov/exhibits/charters/declaration.html.

National Archives (2014). Constitution of the United States. Downloaded from: http://www.archives.gov/exhibits/charters/constitution.html.

Pew Research Center (2012). Pervasive Gloom about the World Economy. Downloaded from: http://www.pewglobal.org/2012/07/12/pervasive-gloom-about-the-world-economy/.

Pew Research Center (2013a). As Sequester Deadline Looms, Little Support for Cutting most Programs. Downloaded from: http://www.people-press.org/2013/02/22/as-sequester-deadline-looms-little-support-for-cutting-most-programs/.

Pew Research Center (2013b). Views of Government: Key Data Points. Downloaded from: http://www.pewresearch.org/2013/04/18/views-of-government-key-data-points/.

Pojman, L., & Reiman, J. (1998). *The Death Penalty: For and Against*. Lanham, MA: Rowman & Littlefield.

Robinson, M. (2009). *Justice Blind? Ideals and Realities of American Criminal Justice*. Upper Saddle River, NJ: Prentice Hall.

Sourcebook of Criminal Justice Statistics (2002). Table 2.41.2002. Respondents Indicating too Little is Spent on Selected Problems in this Country. Downloaded from: http://www.albany.edu/sourcebook/pdf/t241.pdf.

Sourcebook of Criminal Justice Statistics (2003). Table 2.48.2003. Attitudes toward the Treatment of Juveniles who Commit Violent Crimes. Downloaded from: http://www.albany.edu/sourcebook/pdf/t248.pdf.

Sourcebook of Criminal Justice Statistics (2010). Table 2.0038.2010. Respondents' Attitudes toward Making Marijuana Legally Available for Doctors to Prescribe. Downloaded from: http://www.albany.edu/sourcebook/pdf/t200382010.pdf.

Sourcebook of Criminal Justice Statistics (2010). Table 2.28.2011. Attitudes toward Approaches to Lowering the Crime Rate in the United States. Downloaded from: http://www.albany.edu/sourcebook/pdf/t2282010.pdf.

Sourcebook of Criminal Justice Statistics (2010). Table 2.49.2010. Attitudes toward the Better Penalty for Murder. Downloaded from: http://www.albany.edu/sourcebook/pdf/t2492010.pdf.

Sourcebook of Criminal Justice Statistics (2011). Table 2.0005.2011. Attitudes toward Fairness of the Application of the Death Penalty. Downloaded from: http://www.albany.edu/sourcebook/pdf/t200052011.pdf.

Sourcebook of Criminal Justice Statistics (2011). Table 2.54.2011. Attitudes toward Fairness of the Application of the Death Penalty. Downloaded from: http://www.albany.edu/sourcebook/pdf/t2542011.pdf.

Sourcebook of Criminal Justice Statistics (2011). Table 2.64.2011. Attitudes toward Laws Covering the Sales of Firearms. Downloaded from: http://www.albany.edu/sourcebook/pdf/t2642011.pdf.

Sourcebook of Criminal Justice Statistics (2012). Table 2.0021.2012. Attitudes toward the Legalization of Marijuana. Downloaded from: http://www.albany.edu/sourcebook/pdf/t200212012.pdf.

Sourcebook of Criminal Justice Statistics (2012). Table 2.51.2012. Attitudes toward the Death Penalty for Persons Convicted of Murder. Downloaded from: http://www.albany.edu/sourcebook/pdf/t2512012.pdf.

Sourcebook of Criminal Justice Statistics (2012). Table 2.67.2012. Attitudes toward the Legalization of Marijuana. Downloaded from:http://www.albany.edu/sourcebook/pdf/t2672012.pdf.

Sourcebook of Criminal Justice Statistics (2013). Table 2.0035.2013. Attitudes toward Priorities for Dealing with Illegal Immigration. Downloaded from: http://www.albany.edu/sourcebook/pdf/t200352013.pdf.

US Commission on Civil Rights (2013). *Domestic Wiretapping in the War on Terror*. New York: CreateSpace Independent Publishing Platform.

Welzel, C. (2007). Human Development View on Value Change. Downloaded from: http://www.worldvaluessurvey.org/wvs/articles/folder_published/article_base_83.

Wills, G. (1982). Introduction. *The Federalist Papers*. New York: Bantam Books.

Zinn, H. (2005). *A People's History of the United States*. New York: Harper Perennial.

3

THE CRIMINAL JUSTICE SYSTEM

[T]he entire system generally comes down hardest on those with the least amount of power and influence, and generally comes down in the most lenient fashion on those with the most power and influence.

Randy Shelden, 2007 (p. xiii)

As we argued in Chapter 2, Americans believe that they are a just people. Further, they generally believe that their system of laws and criminal justice more generally (i.e., police, courts, and corrections) operate in the interests of justice for all. Yet, as alluded to in the quote above, there are some serious scholars like Randy Shelden who question the nation's criminal justice system, suggesting that—at a minimum—it does not serve all the people equally well.

In Chapter 1, we pointed out that this book is about justice and injustice, and we stated that our goal is to identify ways in which American society generally, and criminal justice agencies in particular, strive to be just and eradicate injustice. We also wish to show ways in which both sometimes fall short of our ideals of justice, remaining and even at times reinforcing injustice, including injustice in society—the opposite of social justice.

We also showed that the meaning of justice depends on the context or circumstances and that there are varying theories of justice, including libertarianism, egalitarianism, utilitarianism, and virtue-based theories. Not surprisingly—since each theory of justice posits principles that are found in the nation's founding documents—Americans value liberty, equality, happiness, and virtue. The review of the evidence in Chapter 2 illustrates that these principles are still important to people in the United States; but the priority given to one principle or another often depends on the context or circumstances.

In this chapter, our focus is exclusively on the criminal justice system. Our focus is on the criminal law, which defines crimes against the state and federal government, as well as each of the agencies of the criminal justice system—police, courts, and corrections. The goal of this chapter is simply to reexamine in greater detail what each of the branches of criminal justice does, and also to discuss in the broadest terms ways in which each can help bring about, as well as interfere with, the realization of social justice in American society.

Law and Crime

Recall in Chapter 1 that we defined *criminal justice* as the efforts of government agencies at the local, state, and federal levels to reduce crime and achieve justice for crime victims while also protecting the due process rights of criminal defendants. That is, the criminal justice system is the tool used to achieve *crime reduction* (efforts aimed at decreasing crime) and *due process* (efforts aimed at assuring Constitutional rights are protected).

The *criminal justice system* is an enforcement mechanism that includes the police, courts, and corrections. Yet, everything these agencies do depends on the criminal law because it is the criminal law that determines what is illegal and how agencies of criminal justice must operate when processing a person through the system.

Criminal Law

Recall that the *criminal law* defines harmful acts as crimes, specifies possible punishments, and sets forth rules of due process that must be followed by police, courts, and corrections. Specifically, it is the *substantive criminal law* that defines harmful acts as crimes and specifies possible punishments and the *procedural criminal law* that specifies the rules of due process that must be followed by criminal justice agencies as they process someone through the system (Samaha, 2013).

In essence, the criminal law represents the beginning point of the criminal justice system, as shown in Figure 3.1. Since the law defines which behaviors are illegal and which are legal, without it the police would have no one to arrest. Further, the courts would have no one to try, no one to convict or acquit, no one to sentence to punishment upon conviction, and corrections would have no one to punish and/ or rehabilitate. All of this depends on the law, which is why the criminal law must be understood as the beginning point of all criminal justice (Robinson, 2009).

Here is an example: Americans generally think that killing another human being is wrong (but not always, as in the case of self-defense). Hence, lawmakers have decided that, under most circumstances, killing another person is a crime. Stated simply, a *crime* is an act that violates the criminal law; it is something that one is forbidden by law from doing. Generally speaking, killing is illegal, and it comprises crimes including murder and manslaughter. Thus, when one commits the crime of murder or manslaughter, one is arrested and processed through the criminal justice system.

Murder is defined by the Federal Bureau of Investigation (FBI, 2012b) as "the willful (nonnegligent) killing of one human being by another" where *non-negligent* refers to the absence of negligence. *Negligent homicide* is a form of killing that is generally less serious than murder because it is not committed with intent, meaning the killer did not necessarily mean to kill the victim. An example of negligent homicide would include a death resulting from a failure to do something expected or required of you, such as a worker being killed at the workplace because his or her boss did not follow safety guidelines required by the government or a person who drowned in a pool because the lifeguard on duty was not paying attention. A negligent homicide is commonly referred to as *involuntary manslaughter*, whereas *voluntary manslaughter* refers to an intentional killing committed without malice or aforethought, meaning it was provoked and/or not planned in advance.

Even though murder is generally seen as the most serious crime in America, not all forms of killing other human beings are illegal (Robinson & Murphy, 2009). For example, police are entitled to legally

FIGURE 3.1 The Criminal Justice System.

kill suspects under certain circumstances, and soldiers are expected to kill enemy combatants during times of war. Citizens are also allowed to kill in self-defense, generally when their lives or the lives of their loved ones are in jeopardy. Controversially, many states have passed so-called *Stand Your Ground laws* that allow a person to kill any person who threatens your life, whether it be in your home or elsewhere. And, of course, there is capital punishment and abortion (one of which ends a life and the other ends a potential life), both currently legal in most states. So, even killing—supposedly the most serious crime one can commit in the United States—is not always illegal. It is generally illegal but there are certain contexts or circumstances where it is tolerated.

Activity 3.1 Stand Your Ground Laws

Go online and research *Stand Your Ground* laws.

Be sure to read the article, "Racial bias and 'stand your ground' laws: what the data show" by Patrik Johnson: http://www.csmonitor.com/USA/Justice/2013/0806/Racial-bias-and-stand-your-ground-laws-what-the-data-show.

Do you think these laws are just or unjust? Use the theories of justice—utilitarianism, libertarianism, egalitarianism, and virtue-based theories—to explain.

What determines which forms of killing—the most serious harmful behavior of all—are crimes? It is the criminal law, which is created by lawmakers at the federal level of government (i.e., Congress) as well as at the state level (i.e., state legislatures).

Serious Crime

But what makes a crime serious in the first place? Under our federalist government system, all states have the right to create their own laws and definitions of serious crimes, and so there is some variation across states on these matters. Yet, generally, every state treats at least the Part 1 Index Offenses of the Uniform Crime Reports (UCR) as serious crimes. These are shown in Table 3.1.

The list of serious crimes in the table comes from the federal government, and the Federal Bureau of Investigation (FBI) has gathered data on them from each of the states since 1930. According to the FBI (2013), "the International Association of Chiefs of Police (IACP) recognized the potential value in tracking national crime statistics. The Committee on Uniform Crime Records of the IACP developed and initiated this voluntary national data collection effort in 1930." Since then, the FBI uses the UCR to collect and present "offense information for murder and nonnegligent manslaughter, forcible rape, robbery, aggravated assault, burglary, larceny-theft, motor vehicle theft, and arson [the latter crime added in 1978]." Why are just these crimes included? The FBI claims:

> These . . . are serious crimes by nature and/or volume. Not all crimes, such as embezzlement, are readily brought to the attention of the police. Also, some serious crimes, such as kidnapping, occur infrequently. Therefore, the UCR Program limits the reporting of offenses known to the eight selected crime classifications because they are the crimes most likely to be reported and most likely to occur with sufficient frequency to provide an adequate basis for comparison.

In a nutshell, the FBI views these crimes as the most harmful and the most common crimes in America (Robinson, 2009). Turns out, however, that this is simply not true; this has enormous implications for social justice in America, as we'll show below.

Other Forms of Crime

The types of crimes commonly pursued by agencies of criminal justice (and included in the Part 1 Index Offenses of the UCR) are often referred to by criminologists as *street crimes*, crimes committed on the streets of America. So, crimes such as bank robbery are considered serious and lead to a high likelihood of arrest, conviction, and incarceration. Other crimes—even crimes committed at and by banks—tend to be generally ignored by agencies of criminal justice (Robinson & Murphy, 2009).

Crimes such as *fraud*—theft of money or property through trickery or false pretenses—are examples of white-collar and corporate crime. Though the terms are related, *white-collar crime* is generally understood to refer to crimes committed by people during the course of their job, and is usually committed against the business itself (Sutherland, 1977); *corporate crime* is generally defined as crimes committed by a corporation, often against consumers and sometimes other corporations (Clinard & Yeager, 2005). Since there are no national data on the nature, prevalence, and harms associated with these crimes—no UCR for white-collar and corporate crime—estimates on their frequency and the damages they cause vary. Yet,

TABLE 3.1 Part 1 Index Offenses of the Uniform Crime Reports

Criminal homicide—(a) Murder and non-negligent manslaughter: the willful (non-negligent) killing of one human being by another. Deaths caused by negligence, attempts to kill, assaults to kill, suicides, and accidental deaths are excluded. The program classifies justifiable homicides separately and limits the definition to: (1) the killing of a felon by a law enforcement officer in the line of duty; or (2) the killing of a felon, during the commission of a felony, by a private citizen. (b) Manslaughter by negligence: the killing of another person through gross negligence. Deaths of persons due to their own negligence, accidental deaths not resulting from gross negligence, and traffic fatalities are not included in the category Manslaughter by negligence.

Forcible rape—The carnal knowledge of a female forcibly and against her will. Rapes by force and attempts or assaults to rape, regardless of the age of the victim, are included. Statutory offenses (no force used—victim under age of consent) are excluded.

Note: In December 2011, the UCR Program changed its SRS definition of rape: "Penetration, no matter how slight, of the vagina or anus with any body part or object, or oral penetration by a sex organ of another person, without the consent of the victim." The effect of this definition change will not be seen in reported crime data until after January 2013. Data reported from prior years will not be revised.

Robbery—The taking or attempting to take anything of value from the care, custody, or control of a person or persons by force or threat of force or violence and/or by putting the victim in fear.

Aggravated assault—An unlawful attack by one person upon another for the purpose of inflicting severe or aggravated bodily injury. This type of assault usually is accompanied by the use of a weapon or by means likely to produce death or great bodily harm. Simple assaults are excluded.

Burglary (breaking or entering)—The unlawful entry of a structure to commit a felony or a theft. Attempted forcible entry is included.

Larceny-theft (except motor vehicle theft)—The unlawful taking, carrying, leading, or riding away of property from the possession or constructive possession of another. Examples are thefts of bicycles, motor vehicle parts and accessories, shoplifting, pocketpicking, or the stealing of any property or article that is not taken by force and violence or by fraud. Attempted larcenies are included. Embezzlement, confidence games, forgery, check fraud, etc., are excluded.

Motor vehicle theft—The theft or attempted theft of a motor vehicle. A motor vehicle is self-propelled and runs on land surface and not on rails. Motorboats, construction equipment, airplanes, and farming equipment are specifically excluded from this category.

Arson—Any willful or malicious burning or attempt to burn, with or without intent to defraud, a dwelling house, public building, motor vehicle or aircraft, personal property of another, etc.

Source: Uniform Crime Reporting Statistics.

of one thing we can be certain—they are more common and more harmful to Americans than all street crimes combined. According to Russell Mokhiber (2007): "Corporate crime inflicts far more damage on society than all street crime combined. Whether in bodies or injuries or dollars lost, corporate crime and violence wins by a landslide."

Damages caused by white-collar and corporate crimes are generally thought to be at least one trillion dollars per year, far more than the roughly $20 billion caused in direct losses by street crime (Reiman & Leighton, 2013). Incredibly, the $1 trillion figure is likely an underestimate, given that some individual scandals cause more damage than this; one example is the recent fraud on Wall Street—identified as a financial crisis, and specifically a banking crisis by the US Government Accountability

Office (GAO)—which cost taxpayers between $12 and 22 trillion (depending on how you measure it). For example, the crisis cost the average American household about $5,800 in income ("due to reduced economic growth during the acute stage of the financial crisis from September 2008 through the end of 2009"), plus $2,050 (due to the government's "interventions to mitigate the financial crisis"), plus about $100,000 (in "loss from declining stock and home values"). Thus, the average US household lost about $107,000 because of the economic collapse (Pew, 2010).

The GAO puts the costs of the financial crisis at more than $12 trillion, roughly equivalent to more than 600 years of losses due to all property street crimes combined! And the true cost—including losses in Gross Domestic Product, large declines in employment, household wealth, and "other economic indicators"—was actually higher, at about $22 trillion. This figure is equivalent to 1,100 years of property street crime!

Activity 3.2 Causes of the Financial Crisis

Go online and research the causes of the financial crisis.

Be sure to read the article, "Causes of the financial crisis" by Mark Jickling: http://www.fas.org/sgp/crs/misc/R40173.pdf.

Who is responsible for the crisis?

What did they do?

For example, which of Jickling's factors do you think caused the crisis?

What, in your opinion, should happen to them to assure a just outcome? Explain.

But, of course, street crime physically injures and kills people, especially robbery, assault, rape, and murder. According to the Bureau of Justice Statistics, these crimes produced about 5.8 million victimizations for people ages 12 years and older in the US in 2011 (Truman & Planty, 2012). Yet, the great bulk of these victimizations—totalling about 4 million victimizations, were *simple assault* (a battery that does not involve a weapon and is not intended to produce serious bodily injury). Further, only 1.5 million people were injured by violent street crime and less than 700,000 produced a serious bodily injury (in a country with more than 300 million people). As for the most serious crime of all—murder—14,612 people were victims of murder in 2011. We show these data in Table 3.2.

Would you believe it if we told you that corporate crime leads to far more injuries and deaths than all street crimes combined? Table 3.3 shows the estimated number of deaths caused by different kinds of corporate behaviors and products, some of which are legal and others illegal.

While many of the deaths that result from the behaviors and products above cannot be considered *intentional* like murder, it is likely that the great majority of them result from the *culpable* acts of corporations, meaning the corporations are morally and legally responsible for the deaths because of negligence, recklessness, and knowing behaviors (Reiman & Leighton, 2013). As noted earlier, *negligence* refers to a failure to do something expected of you (in this case, which produces a death). *Recklessness* means acting

TABLE 3.2 Violent Victimization in the United States

Violent crime	5.8 million
Murder	14,612
Rape	244,000
Robbery	557,000
Aggravated assault	858,000
Simple assault	4.0 million
Domestic violence	1.4 million
Intimate partner violence	851,000
Violent crime involving injury	1.5 million
Serious violent crime	
Serious domestic violence	369,000
Serious intimated partner violence	263,000
Serious violent crime involving weapons	1.2 million
Serious violent crime involving injury	690,000

Source: Data are from the US Department of Justice and the Federal Bureau of Investigation.

without regard for human life or property (which in this case leads to a death). And *knowingly* simply means doing something where you know an outcome is likely (in this case a death).

Although a person can be held legally responsible for any harmful behavior committed with culpability, no one will be arrested, convicted, or punished for such behaviors unless they are identified in the criminal law as crimes. Perhaps the greatest failure of the criminal justice system is that these acts that produce the greatest harms and that are most deadly to Americans are perfectly legal, even though the harms and deaths result from culpable acts and are preventable. The social justice implications of this are discussed later in the chapter.

Police

After a crime is committed, the *police* investigate the crime and apprehend the person or people they suspect of breaking the law. Because of this, police are the entry point into the criminal justice system;

TABLE 3.3 Death Caused by Elite Deviance

Tobacco use	443,000
Medical treatment and infection	325,000
Poverty and income inequality	291,000
Adverse reactions to prescriptions	100,000
Hospital error	98,000
Air pollution	55,000
Occupational disease and injury	54,000
Lack of health insurance	45,000
Defective products	20,000

Source: Harvard University, http://news.harvard.edu/gazette/story/2009/09/harvard-medical-study-links-lack-of-insurance-to-45000-u-s-deaths-a-year; Reiman & Leighton, 2013; Robinson & Murphy, 2009.

without them, there would be no cases for the courts to hear and no clients for correctional agencies to punish and/or rehabilitate (Gaines & Kappeler, 2015).

The primary responsibilities of police officers are stated clearly in the *Law Enforcement Code of Ethics*, written by the International Association of Chiefs of Police (2001): "As a law enforcement officer, my fundamental duty is to serve the community; to safeguard lives and property; to protect the innocent against deception, the weak against oppression or intimidation and the peaceful against violence or disorder; and to respect the constitutional rights of all to liberty, equality and justice." Within this statement, we see five major roles of police officers:

1. **Law enforcer**: Police investigate alleged crimes, collecting and protecting evidence from crime scenes, apprehending suspects, and assisting the prosecution in obtaining convictions (e.g., testifying in court).
2. **Peace preserver**: Police intervene in noncriminal conduct in public places that could escalate into criminal activity if left unchecked (e.g., sporting events, roads, concerts).
3. **Crime preventer**: Police engage in various activities to stop crime before it occurs (e.g., education campaigns, preventive patrols, and community policing).
4. **Service provider**: Police perform functions normally served by other social service agencies (e.g., counseling, referring citizens for social services, assisting people with various needs, and keeping traffic moving).
5. **Rights Upholder**: Police help protect all persons' rights regardless of race, ethnicity, class, gender, and other factors (e.g., reading Miranda warnings to prevent people from incriminating themselves in violation of their Fifth Amendment rights).

The Law Enforcement Code of Ethics goes further, noting how police should carry out these duties in the ideal world:

> I will keep my private life unsullied as an example to all and will behave in a manner that does not bring discredit to me or to my agency. I will maintain courageous calm in the face of danger, scorn or ridicule; develop self-restraint; and be constantly mindful of the welfare of others. Honest in thought and deed both in my personal and official life, I will be exemplary in obeying the law and the regulations of my department. Whatever I see or hear of a confidential nature or that is confided to me in my official capacity will be kept ever secret unless revelation is necessary in the performance of my duty. I will never act officiously or permit personal feelings, prejudices, political beliefs, aspirations, animosities or friendships to influence my decisions. With no compromise for crime and with relentless prosecution of criminals, I will enforce the law courteously and appropriately without fear or favor, malice or ill will, never employing unnecessary force or violence and never accepting gratuities. I recognize the badge of my office as a symbol of public faith, and I accept it as a public trust to be held so long as I am true to the ethics of police service. I will never engage in acts of corruption or bribery, nor will I condone such acts by other police officers. I will cooperate with all legally authorized agencies and their representatives in the pursuit of justice. I know that I alone am responsible for my own standard of professional performance and will take every reasonable opportunity to enhance and improve my level of knowledge and competence. I will constantly strive to achieve these objectives and ideals, dedicating myself before God to my chosen profession. . . law enforcement.

Although this sounds great in the ideal world (and would appear to make law enforcement consistent with Americans' social justice ideals stated in the Declaration of Independence and US Constitution examined in Chapter 1, as well as those found in recent poll results discussed in Chapter 2, the real world of policing is of course different from the ideal world (Robinson, 2010).

For example, police focus their attention almost solely on street crime while ignoring white-collar and corporate crime; less than 5 percent of police officers in the US target these crimes (Robinson, 2009). Further, the police are more likely to be located in higher numbers in poor areas, especially when higher proportions of the population are comprised of people of color (Kent & Jacobs, 2005). For these reasons, the poor and people of color make up the great bulk of people stopped, questioned, detained, searched, and arrested by the police in the United States (Alexander, 2012; Tonry, 2012). A systematic review of how race and ethnicity impact criminal justice practice in the US by Samuel Walker, Cassia Spohn, and Miriam DeLone (2012) found:

- Police in some jurisdictions use race and ethnicity to *profile* people (p. 156).
- African Americans and Hispanics are more likely to be stopped, questioned, searched, and arrested by the police than whites; they are also more likely to have force used against them, including excessive force and lethal force (p. 181).

That it is only in some jurisdictions that police profiling occurs means that the criminal justice system is not plagued by *systemic discrimination* (discrimination at all places and all stages of criminal justice), but instead is characterized by *contextual discrimination* (discrimination that occurs within some contexts of criminal justice, or only in some places). The social justice implications of these realities are discussed later in the chapter.

Courts

After the point of arrest, *courts* conduct their own investigation (this is the job of the *prosecutor*, who will determine whether to press charges and which charges to press), and then ultimately determine the legal guilt of those accused of crimes. Those found guilty will be sentenced to some form and term of punishment by the courts (Neubauer & Fradella, 2010).

America's courts have two major jobs. The first is, as noted above, to determine if those who are arrested are legally guilty of the crime(s) for which they are charged. This can be done informally, as in the case of *plea bargaining* (where a defendant waives his or her right to a trial, along with all other rights such as the right to appeal) and pleads guilty in exchange for a reduction in charges and/or likely sentence. Or it can be done formally, in open court, as expected by Americans based on their Sixth Amendment right to trial.

The other job of the courts is to interpret the law to tell us what it means. Since laws tend to be broadly written and in terms not specifically defined, we need courts to tell us what the laws and terms mean by analyzing them as they apply the law to particular cases. Individual judges do this, as do appeals courts when they create case law pertaining to individual challenges to state or federal laws (Meador, Baker, & Steinman, 2001).

American courts are clearly about protecting social values that are important to Americans' social justice. As an example, take the Fifth and Fourteenth Amendments to the US Constitution, which guarantee all the right to due process of law.

The Fifth Amendment states that:

> No person shall be held to answer for a capital, or otherwise infamous crime, unless on a present-ment or indictment of a grand jury, except in cases arising in the land or naval forces, or in the militia, when in actual service in time of war or public danger; nor shall any person be subject for the same offense to be twice put in jeopardy of life or limb; nor shall be compelled in any criminal case to be a witness against himself, *nor be deprived of life, liberty, or property, without due process of law;* nor shall private property be taken for public use, without just compensation.

And the Fourteenth Amendment states:

> All persons born or naturalized in the United States, and subject to the jurisdiction thereof, are citizens of the United States and of the state wherein they reside. No state shall make or enforce any law which shall abridge the privileges or immunities of citizens of the United States; *nor shall any state deprive any person of life, liberty, or property, without due process of law;* nor deny to any person within its jurisdiction the equal protection of the laws [emphasis added].

So both the federal government and state governments *can* deprive people of life, liberty, and prop-erty, but only if that person has first been given his or her right to due process (i.e., the process one is due as a citizen, such as a criminal trial with the rights of defense and other rights guaranteed by the Bill of Rights). Given this, it is clear that, from the founding of the country, Americans valued liberty and equality, and thus, the ideals of courts are consistent with libertarianism and egalitarianism (Robinson, 2010).

Yet, there are serious problems with courts in the real world. Scholars have pointed out, for example, that America has a multi-tiered court system—commonly referred to by the metaphor of a *wedding cake model* where only the top layer of the cake (or the most serious of the cases) can reasonably expect to receive a full criminal trial but the rest of the cases are not likely at all to receive criminal trials (Walker, 2011). In this model, the upper layer of the cake is comprised of celebrity cases, high-profile cases, and the most serious of crimes; most cases are resolved via plea bargaining, meaning due process is not fol-lowed and the factual guilt of defendants is never actually established.

The review of race and ethnicity and criminal justice noted earlier (Walker et al., 2012) found, with regard to courts:

- In some places, race and ethnicity impact pre-trial decision-making including bail, charging by prosecutors, and plea bargaining in the courts (p. 231).
- People of color are, in many jurisdictions, denied the right to serve on trial juries through the use of *peremptory challenges* (where people are removed as potential jurors with no stated reason) based solely on their race (p. 273), even though this practice is explicitly illegal.
- African Americans and Hispanics who are convicted of certain types of crimes (e.g., drug crimes and violent crimes against whites) are treated more harshly than whites for those crimes (p. 274).
- Tougher sentences tend to be handed down to people of color than to whites in "borderline cases" where prosecutors and judges tend to have discretion about whether to pursue probation or a term of incarceration (p. 333).

So, just as with policing, American courts are characterized by *contextual discrimination*, meaning that in some places and at some levels of courts, disparities exist that are explained by discriminatory actions of criminal justice personnel. The social justice implications of these realities are discussed later in the chapter.

Corrections

Upon conviction in a criminal court, a person is sentenced to a form of punishment and/or rehabilitation in a correctional agency of some kind. The job of correctional agencies is simply to carry out the sentence of the courts in as humane a way as possible.

Corrections can be divided into *institutional corrections*, where offenders are housed in correctional institutions (e.g., jail, prison) for the duration of their sentences, and *community corrections*, where offenders fulfill their sentences in the communities where they live (Clear, Reisig, & Cole, 2012). Although the US leads the world both in the rate of its incarceration as well as the total number of people it locks up (which is incredible considering that much larger countries such as China actually have fewer of their citizens incarcerated), there are far more people being supervised by community corrections (e.g., probation) than institutional corrections.

Table 3.4 shows data from the Bureau of Justice Statistics about correctional populations in the US from 2011. Keep in mind that while *probation* is a sentence of the court to be served in the community under supervision by a probation officer with additional expectations for behavior of the offender, *parole* is not a sentence of the court but is instead a period of supervision to be served by an offender after he or she is released from incarceration. Also be aware that, of the 1.6 million prisoners in the US, about 1.4 million are being held by states, whereas only about 216,000 are housed in federal prisons.

Whereas the term corrections implies (or suggests strongly) that community and institutional correctional agencies are involved in *correcting* offenders, the fact is there is very little rehabilitation going on in corrections today. Instead of *rehabilitation* (where the sources of deviant and criminal behavior are identified and corrected), corrections in the US has been more about punishment as a means to achieve incapacitation and deterrence (Walker, 2011). *Incapacitation* refers to reducing crime by taking away the freedoms of offenders by locking them up or closely supervising them while they live in the community

TABLE 3.4 Correctional Populations in the US, 2011

Community Corrections	
Probation	3.9 million
Parole	854,000
Total	4.8 million
Institutional Corrections	
Prison	1.6 million
Jail	736.000
Total	2.2 million
Overall total	7 million

Source: Glaze and Parks (2011). Correctional populations in the United States. Bureau of Justice Statistics. Retrieved August 26, 2013 from: http://www.bjs.gov/content/pub/pdf/cpus11.pdf.

under probation, and *deterrence* refers to reducing crime by making an individual offender afraid of committing a future crime (*specific deterrence*) or making others afraid of committing future crimes by making an example out of other offenders (*general deterrence*).

For the past several decades starting really in the 1970s and 1980s, America has invested heavily in simply warehousing an enormous number of criminal offenders for short-term declines in street crime, with little concern for what happens to offenders upon release (Reddington & Bonham, Jr., 2011; Stuntz, 2011). The major increase in imprisonment is depicted in Figure 3.2. Though street crime did decline, perhaps as little as 25 percent of the declines were attributable to imprisonment, and most were due to factors outside of the criminal justice system (Zimring, 2008). The social justice implications of these realities are discussed later in the chapter.

Implications for Social Justice

Knowing only what has been established in this chapter about the law, police, courts, and corrections, we can draw some tentative conclusions about likely relationships between criminal justice practice in the US and social justice in broader American society. We believe that criminal justice is *ideally* aimed at goals consistent with social justice—things like protecting our life and liberties (as valued by libertarianism), public safety and happiness (as valued by utilitarianism), equality (as valued by egalitarianism), and even our values or morality (as valued by virtue-based theories). For example, criminal justice is aimed at protecting the lives of people, both by preventing crime and by apprehending and incapacitating offenders so that they cannot offend again. These actions serve libertarian and utilitarian goals.

Further, the criminal law (e.g., the Bill of Rights in the US Constitution) was set up to protect civil liberties and to provide for equality, at least on paper. American criminal justice agencies that enforce the law are thus ideally dedicated to outcomes consistent with social justice from an egalitarian perspective (e.g., due process and equal protection). And all of criminal justice can be viewed as a means to enforce the people's values or morality—or at least those that are reflected in the criminal law—making it consistent with virtue based theories of justice.

Yet, the *reality* of actual criminal justice practice puts criminal justice at conflict with social justice in many ways. As will be shown throughout this book, the law and criminal justice practice are becoming more and more in line with our ideals; yet, we still have a long way to go. The progress that has been made has only occurred due to the work, struggle, and sacrifice of those who challenged authority in order to bring about needed change. Below we briefly summarize this point by examining the law/crime, police, courts, and corrections.

Law/Crime

Starting with the Bill of Rights of the United States Constitution, the law establishes due process rights and equal protections for all citizens under the law (Orth, 2007). Thus, it can be seen as consistent with the principles of social justice posited by libertarians and egalitarians. Recall from Chapter 1 John Rawls's (1971) equal liberties principle (saying that "Each person has the same indefensible claim to a fully adequate scheme of equal basic liberties, which scheme is compatible with the same scheme of liberties for all") and David Miller's (2003) principle of equality (referring to "the social ideal that society regards and treats its citizens as equals, and that benefits such as certain rights should be distributed

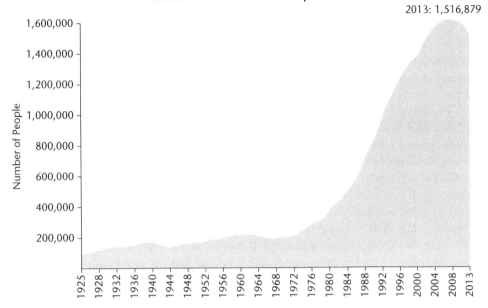

U.S. State and Federal Prison Population, 1925–2013

2013: 1,516,879

Source: Bureau of Justice Statistics *Prisoners Series*.

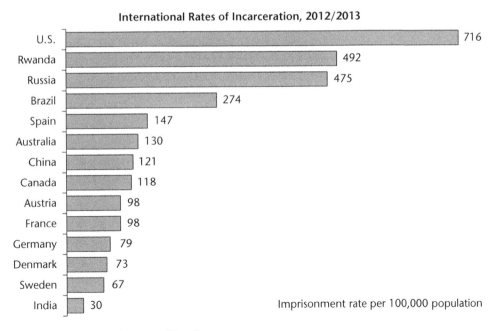

International Rates of Incarceration, 2012/2013

Country	Rate
U.S.	716
Rwanda	492
Russia	475
Brazil	274
Spain	147
Australia	130
China	121
Canada	118
Austria	98
France	98
Germany	79
Denmark	73
Sweden	67
India	30

Imprisonment rate per 100,000 population

FIGURE 3.2 American Imprisonment Trends.

Source: Walmsley, R. (2013). *World Population List*. 10th ed. Essex: International Centre for Prison Studies.

equally"). From the founding of our country, these principles have been codified—written down on paper for all to see—as a demonstration of our commitment to them.

Recall that Rawls suggested that his first principle (the equal liberties principle) applies to the "constitutional essentials." The ideal of American criminal justice as found in the US Constitution is thus on its face consistent with Rawls's first principle. Also recall that Miller's conception of equality is to be applied in matters of citizenship, suggesting that all members of a political society in modern liberal democracies be granted the same rights by law. The ideal of American criminal justice as found in the US Constitution thus appears to be consistent with Miller's equality principle. We showed in Chapter 1 that these theories perhaps come closest to capturing what Americans value, and thus the US Constitution appears to satisfy Americans' major conceptions of justice.

However, as shown in Chapter 2, historians, sociologists, and other scholars have interpreted the US Constitution differently. They have argued that the Constitution was not written behind "a veil of ignorance" (as Rawls put it) and was thus not "blind to personal preference" (as Miller would say). Instead, the founders may have acted with their own personal interests in mind when they wrote the US Constitution. Recall the arguments of Charles Beard (1913), John Harrigan (2000), and Joe Feagin (2001), for example. These scholars suggest the Constitution was really about protecting the interests of wealthy, powerful, whites—people who owned slaves and subjugated women (something clearly *not* consistent with our values today).

To the degree that the claims of these scholars are accurate, then the US Constitution was actually a rationalization of self-interest on the part of wealthy, large land holders and slave owners. This would make those parts of the US Constitution that serve limited interests inconsistent with social justice. Yet, as we will show in this book, rights granted by the Constitution have been extended to more and more people over time. This is not because of some inevitable march toward greater equality in society, but rather resulted from the work of real people, as noted earlier. Think of marriage equality as one example: historically marriage was a legal protection only afforded to heterosexual couples; today it is a right that is increasingly becoming available to any couple, heterosexual or homosexual. At the time of writing, gay marriage is legal in 37 states. Evidence suggests it is the changing values of citizens that explain this policy change, a change that reflects the struggles of tens of thousands of people over decades of time.

Oftentimes, it merely takes a new interpretation of the Constitution by the US Supreme Court to change the meaning of rights we enjoy as citizens. For example, the Fourth Amendment's freedom from unreasonable search and seizure by the police used to apply only to acts of the federal government. This changed with the decision by the US Supreme Court in the case of *Mapp v. Ohio* (1961), as noted in Chapter 2. So, from when the Bill of Rights was enacted until 1961, the Fourth Amendment precluded only the federal government from using illegally obtained evidence against criminal defendants; it took almost two centuries for this right to be used to protect an individual's Fourth Amendment rights from state government actions.

As for the criminal law, it defines crimes to maintain public order and to protect citizens from harms (Davenport, 2008). Since government protection from willful harmful acts such as crimes protects a basic human right or need (such as the need for or right to life), criminal justice efforts to pursue and apprehend criminal offenders is consistent with libertarianism (e.g., David Miller's principle of need). After all, what liberty is more important than the right to life? Recall that it is the first such right stated in the Declaration of Independence. It is also aimed at assuring happiness for people by protecting them from harmful behaviors.

Keep in mind that Miller's principle of need is meant to be applied in solidaristic communities such as families, so to the degree that all citizens are viewed as a family, protecting people from crime to assure their need to survive seems like a pretty important thing for government to do. Defining crimes to protect citizens and society is also consistent with John Rawls's notion that *primary goods* should be available to all because primary goods include the right of people to live freely and safely.

However, from the very beginning of the criminal justice practice, there is differential access to lawmaking in the form of voting and lobbying activities (Lynch, Michalowski, & Groves, 2000). The poor and people of color are underrepresented among voters and legislators themselves and are also least likely to donate money to political campaigns (Robinson, 2009). This raises the significant possibility of bias in the criminal law, the outcome being that certain groups have their voices and interests represented more than others and that certain acts will be more and less likely to be criminalized, not based on degree of harm caused but instead on other political and ideological grounds (Reiman & Leighton, 2013). Figure 3.3 shows how different lawmakers look from citizens in terms of demographic and social factors.

Differential access to the criminal law and criminalization of various harms based on differential access to the criminal law are outcomes that are inconsistent with libertarianism and egalitarianism. Specifically, Rawls's equal opportunities principle and Miller's equality principle demand that all people have equal access to the law and lawmakers; to be consistent with social justice, every citizen should have an equal chance to influence the criminal law and have his or her interests reflected in the criminalization process.

A recent study, stunning in its findings and implications, supports the above statement. The study, examining whether American lawmaking more closely resembles the consensus, conflict, or pluralist views discussed earlier, suggests that American politics more closely resembles an *oligarchy* (a government or entity ruled by a small, powerful group) rather than a democracy (Gilens & Page, 2014). According to the authors: "When the preferences of economic elites and the stands of organized interest groups are controlled for, the preferences of the average American appear to have only a minuscule, near-zero, statistically non-significant impact upon public policy" (p. 21). The authors further note:

Nor do organized interest groups substitute for direct citizen influence, by embodying citizens' will and ensuring that their wishes prevail . . . Interest groups do have substantial independent

	US population	US Senate	US House	State legislatures
Female	51%	17%	17%	24%
Male	49%	83%	83%	76%
White	78%*	96%	82%	86%
Hispanic	17%*	2%	6%	3%
Black	13%*	0%	10%	9%
Average age	37 years	62 years	57 years	56 years
Income	$27,915 per capita $52,762 per household	$174,000	$174,000	$7,000–$95,000 (85% are part-time)
Net worth	$57,000	$13 million	$6 million	not available

FIGURE 3.3 Who Makes the Law?

* People may report more than one "race" to the US Census.

impacts on policy, and a few groups (particularly labor unions) represent average citizens' views reasonably well. But the interest group system as a whole does not. Over-all, net interest group alignments are not significantly related to the preferences of average citizens. The net alignments of the most influential, business oriented groups are *negatively* related to the average citizen's wishes.

(Gilens & Page, 2014: 22)

The authors thus reject the idea that the law directly serves the people (which they refer to as *Majoritarian Electoral Democracy*) as well as the notion of pluralism that favors common, every day Americans (*Majoritarian Pluralism*).

Instead, their findings indicate support for *Biased Pluralism* (where "corporations, business associations, and professional groups predominate" (p. 3) and *Economic Elite Domination* (where "policy making is dominated by individuals who have substantial economic resources, i.e., high levels of income and/or wealth—including, but not limited to, ownership of business firms" (p. 6)). The authors thus state that:

preferences of economic elites . . . have far more independent impact upon policy change than the preferences of average citizens do. To be sure, this does not mean that ordinary citizens always lose out; they fairly often get the policies they favor, but only because those policies happen also to be preferred by the economically elite citizens who wield the actual influence.

(Gilens & Page, 2014: 22)

The conclusion of the authors is that, in America:

the majority does *not* rule—at least not in the causal sense of actually determining policy outcomes. When a majority of citizens disagrees with economic elites and/or with organized interests, they generally lose. Moreover, because of the strong status quo bias built into the US political system, even when fairly large majorities of Americans favor policy change, they generally do not get it.

(Gilens & Page, 2014: 23)

In addition, it is obvious that the rules and procedures of criminal justice are not created behind a "veil of ignorance," raising a significant possibility that criminal justice practice is not blind to personal preferences and may thus be created as rationalizations of self-interest (McGarrell & Flanagan, 1987). In fact, all criminal justice policies are lobbied for and against by powerful interests, both economic and ideological. Groups responsible for current criminal justice policy are not necessarily motivated by concerns for social justice. One likely outcome of this reality is that many forms of harmful behaviors will not be legislated as crimes and targeted by criminal justice agencies, simply because of who commits them. In fact, although the criminal law is aimed at protecting people from harmful acts, those acts that pose the greatest threats to citizens (i.e., white-collar and corporate crimes) are the ones that are least likely to be legislated as crimes and especially as serious crimes (Simon, 2007). Thus, the most dangerous criminals often do not get what they "deserve" (Robinson & Murphy, 2009). This is not consistent with Miller's concept of desert.

To reiterate, since Miller's concept of desert is most relevant for instrumental associations such as work, the application of desert to the criminalization process may not be viewed at all as entirely appropriate. However, it is well established that being labeled a "criminal" and suffering sanctions from governmental institutions such as the police, courts, and corrections will likely produce outcomes such as *felony disenfranchisement* (losing rights due to a criminal conviction) that interfere with the ability of citizens to engage in instrumental associations such as work (Sennott & Galliher, 2006). Thus, forms of punishment such as incarceration can be seen as inconsistent with social justice to the degree that they interfere with one's ability to engage in activities such as work that allow people to be rewarded for their contribution to society (Wheelock, 2005).

Simultaneously, relatively minor criminals often get far more than they "deserve" based on the harms caused by their behaviors (Meier & Geis, 1997). As one example, recall that corporate and white-collar crime cost Americans at least one trillion dollars in direct losses every year, compared to only $20 billion in losses caused by street crime. Yet, less than 5 percent of police officers are focused on the former, and about 99 percent of all people incarcerated in the United States are incarcerated for committing the latter. This is inconsistent with Miller's concept of desert. The argument is that the "worst of the worst" offenders should be subjected to the "worst of the worst" criminal sanctions. In the United States, this is simply not the case.

Further, crimes of the poor (e.g., theft) are at times aimed at satisfying basic human "needs" (Agnew, 2005). Thus, the application of the law to stop such acts can be seen as interfering with social justice, at least when the means to achieve one's goals are blocked for reasons such as discrimination, which itself is not consistent with social justice (Simons & Gray, 1989). That is, if opportunities to succeed through legal means are not truly equally available to all (as they should be according to Rawls), and some people respond through "innovation" by creating new, illegitimate (i.e., criminal) means to achieve their goals (Merton, 1938), then we can see the labeling of some behaviors as crimes as the criminalization of efforts to meet needs.

In a nutshell, to the degree that the criminal law is aimed at the crimes committed disproportionately by the poor and people of color while it simultaneously ignores the harmful and culpable acts of the powerful (e.g., wealthy whites), it is unequal, undeserved, not focused on helping people achieve their basic needs, and clearly not aimed at providing the greatest advantage to the least advantaged. Thus, it violates Rawls's and Miller's conceptions of need, equality, desert, and the difference principle. Given that Rawls's and Miller's theories are among the best examples of libertarianism and egalitarianism, it is hard to deny that the criminal law in reality is inconsistent with these two major schools of justice.

We would argue that not holding the guilty accountable for the harmful acts they commit with culpability, and defining relatively minor crimes (e.g., marijuana possession) is also inconsistent with utilitarianism because these actions do not serve to increase overall utility in society and do not result in creating the greatest happiness for the greatest number of people. In fact, as we demonstrate in this book, it is the *majority* of people in society who suffer from the current state of the criminal law, for nearly all of us are subjected to risks associated with the deviant and harmful acts of the powerful. And we all are harmed by the fact that the criminal justice system disproportionately targets acts of the poor and powerless, causing undue suffering for the poor, people of color, and especially young, poor, men of color (Shelden, 2007); this reality is inconsistent with America's ideals of equal liberty and justice for all. We would also argue that this reality is not virtuous in any way.

Finally, since police, courts and corrections enforce the criminal law (through arrest, conviction, sentencing, and punishment), any bias in the criminal law will logically be perpetuated through enforcement of that law (Reiman & Leighton, 2013; Robinson, 2009; Shelden, 2007). This is likely the greatest threat to social justice in criminal justice practice. This threat to social justice (enforcing biased law) is found in policing, courts, and corrections.

The remainder of this book will focus on how the law more generally has been used both to maintain current power arrangements in society and to resist social justice, but also to challenge power and bring about social justice. Before moving on to that, however, it is important to examine how criminal justice agencies operate and establish the relevance for social justice.

Policing

Even though there will be significant problems with policing because of enforcing biased law, there are also clear signs that policing in the ideal world is meant to insure social justice. For example, the *Code of Ethics/Law Enforcement Code of Conduct* specifies that one of the fundamental duties of police is to protect people's rights, provide important services to the community, as well as enforce the law, prevent crime, and uphold the peace (International Association of Chiefs of Police, 2008). Since all of these can be seen as "needs" of the community and basic rights of the people, the written functions or roles of police are consistent with libertarianism and egalitarianism (especially if the rights of people are respected equally).

Take David Miller's principle of need and John Rawls's conception of primary goods as examples; both of these are protected by police when they provide for public safety by enforcing the law. That is, to the degree police are successful in reducing crime—as they reportedly were in New York City, for example, by flooding the city with more cops and engaging in smarter policing (Zimring, 2011)—this provides an enormous benefit to citizens by protecting their liberty.

Further, rights protection is consistent with Miller's equality principle as well as Rawls's equal liberties principle. One good example is at the point where arrest is imminent; police officers read suspects their rights to remain silent in order to protect their Fifth Amendment right against self-incrimination (Stuart, 2008).

Yet, since officers have *discretion*, it can be abused (Alpert, Dunham, & Stroshine, 2005). When it is, it leads to differential police outcomes. For example, poor people and people of color are disproportionately likely to be stopped, searched, arrested, and have force use against them (Walker et al., 2012). They are also more likely to be victims of racial profiling (Withrow, 2005). These are outcomes that are inconsistent with Rawls's equal liberties as well as Miller's equality principle and thus are not consistent with libertarianism or egalitarianism. All citizens deserve to be treated the same by the police and other agents of government, unless their own actions lead them to "deserve" more attention. *Racial profiling* implies that certain groups in society are being targeted more based on extra-legal factors such as race rather than legal factors such as criminality (Miller, 2003).

Take New York City for an example of how rights protection and equality can suffer in a place that is zealously trying to reduce crime. In 2011, about 90 percent of those targeted by the police department through its "stop and frisk" policy were either African American or Hispanic; together, African Americans and Hispanics make up less than 53 percent of the city's population (Velez, 2013). Since few arrests resulted from these actions and weapons were rarely found, it cannot be demonstrated empirically that this policy of differential harassment helped reduce crime and thereby serve some libertarian or utilitarian goal; instead, it seems to merely conflict with the major tenet of equal treatment under the law inherent in egalitarianism.

Since criminal justice involvement can interfere with legitimate opportunities such as school and work, we could argue that being processed through the system after arrest is a threat to Rawls's "equal opportunities principle" (at least when such arrest is really not warranted). And since differential involvement with police tends to harm the least advantaged (Shelden, 2007), it is inconsistent with Rawls's "difference principle." To be consistent with Rawls's difference principle, activities of government institutions such as law enforcement agencies should be arranged to assist the least advantaged, not to hinder or hurt them.

Is all this consistent with the major tenets of utilitarianism? To draw such a conclusion, one would have to weigh the benefits of policing in America (e.g., modest reductions in street crime, assisting crime victims, providing services to the community) against the costs (e.g., financial costs, unequal enforcement, ignoring the worst harms). Whether police activity produces outcomes consistent with utilitarianism depends on whether they contribute to overall happiness in society. Our conclusion is that policing serves to both fulfill and interfere with utilitarian goals. Specifically, policing contributes to our overall happiness when it helps the people, protects their rights, and assures their safety from all culpable harms. Yet, unequal enforcement of the law producing disparities based on race and class is not in the utilitarian interests of society even if it only harms a small segment of the population.

American policing does not generally achieve utility for Americans, when the police are overly harsh on minor offenders, ignore the harmful acts of the powerful, and result in unequal and thus unjust outcomes. Because of this, we would also suggest that many police activities likely tend to conflict with American virtues, making them inconsistent with virtue-based theories of justice seen as relevant to Americans.

Courts

In courts, because of due process rights, every citizen has the right to trial, as well as other constitutional protections that are supposed to be upheld in an adversarial process whereby prosecutors and defense attorneys represent different actors in a battle to determine the truth (Neubauer, 2007). Recall the rights granted to Americans (when criminal suspects and defendants) as part of the Bill of Rights identified in Chapter 1. Assuring individual rights and equal protection under the law makes courts, in theory, consistent with libertarianism and egalitarianism. For example, due process is clearly part of Rawls's equal liberties principle as well as Miller's equality principle.

Yet, as noted earlier, many Constitutional rights, including the right to trial, are, in reality, rarely enjoyed by many Americans. Because there are so many criminal cases and not enough resources to process them in criminal trials, the courts operate on the assumption that most criminal defendants will eventually plead guilty to the charges they face without enjoying their right to trial. As noted earlier, more than 90 percent of people charged with felonies now waive all their rights in exchange for reductions in charges and/or sentences (Robinson, 2009). This is a major threat to social justice, particularly libertarianism and egalitarianism.

Still, there are measures in place to protect the weak (e.g., *indigent defense*), consistent with American social justice ideas (e.g., Rawls's difference principle) (National Association of Criminal Defense Lawyers, 2008). However, there is unequal access to *quality* defense representation in criminal cases. For example, those that can afford private attorneys are less likely to sit in jail awaiting trial and are less likely to be incarcerated upon conviction (Bureau of Justice Statistics, 2008), suggesting that the ability to pay for private defense protection does lead to differential outcomes. This is not consistent with Rawls's equal liberties or Miller's equality principle. It is also a threat to Rawls's difference principle because access to quality defense representation is not arranged for the benefit of the least advantaged.

Quality of defense can be considered incompatible with Miller's principle of desert, for some clients do not have their case adequately defended based merely on their inability to pay. Wrongful convictions, caused mostly by overzealousness on the part of police and prosecutors, as well as faulty eye-witness testimony, are obviously inconsistent with the concept of "desert" (Bell, Clow, & Ricciardelli, 2008). This is true for two reasons: first, no one deserves to be punished for acts they did not commit; second, when wrongful conviction occurs, the factually guilty do not receive the punishment they rightly deserve and are free to commit further crimes, causing even more harm to society.

The imbalance of power in the courts that exists in America is also not consistent with the values on which the court system was supposedly founded—due process and "innocent until proven guilty." Currently, the prosecution has much more power than the defense, as evidenced by more employees and a much larger budget nationwide. This threatens the ability of defendants to seek and obtain meaningful trials, which necessitates plea bargaining (Walker, 2011). Research shows that plea bargaining occurs for two main reasons: first, the police make too many arrests; second, the courts receive only about 20 percent of all resources devoted to criminal justice, meaning they do not have enough resources to justify having a trial for every one accused of even serious crimes.

The very practice of plea bargaining is not consistent with due process (Fisher, 2003), and thus is not compatible with Rawls's equal liberties principle. In essence, the right to a criminal trial is more myth than fact. Plea bargaining is also inconsistent with Miller's equality principle since plea bargaining is much more likely to occur with poor clients who are not well represented by quality defense attorneys (Padfield, 2009).

Plea bargaining also tends not to assign punishments that achieve proper desert of guilty criminals. Further, plea bargaining leads to too much punishment for those who are innocent but plead guilty anyway in the face of the coercive nature of plea bargaining (Siegel, 2005). Walker (2011) shows that both "conservatives" and "liberals" do not like plea bargaining because it satisfies neither the requirements of punitive justice nor procedural justice.

When trials (rarely) happen, they are plagued by serious threats to principles of social justice. For example, the *voir dire* process routinely results in African Americans being excused from jury service through the use of peremptory challenges (Walker et al., 2012). This is a significant threat to equal treatment, due process, and even desert (if defendants are convicted in part due to the racial composition of a jury). Research by the Capital Jury Project shows just how important the racial make-up of juries is for outcomes such as conviction and sentencing, even in death penalty cases where someone's life is literally at stake (Brewer, 2004).

When it comes to sentencing, efforts are made (e.g., through *sentencing guidelines*) to produce fair sentences based on legal variables such as offense seriousness and prior record rather than extra-legal factors such as race and gender. This is aimed at protecting egalitarianism, and is thus consistent with Miller's conception of equality (Walker, 2011).

Yet, there are problems with sentencing, including unequal outcomes based on race, ethnicity, and other demographic variables, which are a threat to our egalitarian ideals (Walker et al., 2012). The practice of *mandatory sentencing* is consistent with Miller's principle of desert when it is utilized for the worst offenders (who thus deserve the worst punishment). However, mandatory sentencing is inconsistent with the notion of desert when it is used against relatively harmless criminals who do not deserve such punishment based on the small amount of harm they cause to society. For example, "three strikes" laws have generally been used against non-violent offenders, leading to life imprisonment sentences. Meanwhile, white-collar and corporate offenders are rarely punished at all, even when serious injury or death results (Robinson, 2009). Three strikes laws have also been applied in a racially discriminatory manner, thereby threatening Miller's equality principle (Brown & Jolivette, 2005; Rand, 2005).

Activity 3.3 Three Strikes Laws

Go online and research three strikes laws.

Be sure to read the report, "Racial Divide: An Examination of the Impact of California's Three Strikes Law on African-Americans and Latinos" by the Justice Policy Institute: http://www.justi cepolicy.org/uploads/justicepolicy/documents/04-10_tac_caracialdivide_ac-rd.pdf.

Do you think three strikes laws are just or unjust?

Use the theories of justice—utilitarianism, libertarianism, egalitarianism, and virtue-based theories—to explain why.

Do you agree that race plays a role in these cases and how they tend to be resolved?

As with policing, whether court activity produces outcomes consistent with utilitarianism depends on whether they contribute to overall happiness in society. We contend that American court activities do not generally achieve utility for Americans, especially when they are overly harsh on minor offenders, ignore the harmful acts of the powerful, and result in unequal and thus unjust outcomes. Because of this, we would also suggest that court activities likely tend to conflict with American virtues, making them inconsistent with virtue-based theories of justice seen as relevant to Americans.

Corrections

Corrections is the one branch of criminal justice that has the least impact on actual policy. That is, they do not create the law, nor do they decide who is to be arrested and/or prosecuted or even sentenced to punishment. Instead, correctional agencies merely carry out the punishment imposed on offenders by courts. Thus, problems in corrections such as racial disparities in prison populations cannot be blamed on the correctional facilities themselves. Instead, they are created by either biases in the law, biased law enforcement, or biases in court procedures.

It is an undeniable fact that the poor and people of color—and especially young, poor, men of color—are disproportionately likely to be exposed to probation, jail, prison, and executions (Alexander, 2012; Barak, Leighton, & Flavin, 2006; Walker et al., 2012). To the degree that this is not due to disparate criminality of these groups, it is not consistent with social justice, especially libertarianism and egalitarianism—because it interferes with their liberty and exemplifies unequal treatment at the hands of the criminal justice system.

As it turns out, it is a fact that some groups of people in society tend to commit more of some kinds of crimes than others. For example, African Americans (and especially African American men) tend to commit roughly half the murders and robberies in the United States in any given year. In 2006, they accounted for 51 percent of those arrested for murder and 56 percent of those arrested for robbery (Sourcebook of Criminal Justice Statistics, 2008). While some use these data to suggest that African

Americans are thus more dangerous than whites (New Century Foundation, 2005), murder is but one form of culpable killing and robbery is but one form of taking property through culpable action. If one were to focus on all forms of culpable killing and property taking behaviors, the vast majority of offenders would be white, for the vast majority of white-collar and corporate offenders are white (Robinson, 2009). Thus, the disproportionate focus on African American offenders owes itself to the fact that criminal justice agencies are aimed at pursuing only certain types of criminals (the street crime variety), and this is inconsistent with the concept of desert that is key to social justice (Lynch, McGurrin, & Fenwick, 2004; Ross & Rothe, 2007; Rothe & Friedrichs, 2006). That is, criminals only tend to get what they deserve when they commit certain types of culpable harms.

Correctional agencies are, however, charged with functions that are consistent with our social justice ideals. As noted earlier with regard to the police, to the degree that corrections helps reduce crime, this serves goals consistent with libertarianism and utilitarianism. Specifically, protecting people's lives and property assures their liberty (e.g., freedom to live and thrive), and contributes to the overall happiness of society.

From the moment where offenders are processed through the correctional system, they are classified based on various criteria including their personal needs. Additionally, inmates in jails and prisons are provided care by facilities, and to some degree they are offered educational and vocational opportunities (Clear, Cole, & Reisig, 2008). This is all consistent with principles of major social justice theories, most notably Rawls's difference principle and Miller's conception of need. Yet, the limited educational and vocational opportunities available to inmates can be considered a threat to the needs of inmates (Ross & Richards, 2002). As noted earlier, contemporary correction is less about "correcting" offenders than it is about warehousing them.

For some, the bottom line with regard to corrections and social justice in America is that any and all unequal application of sanctions in America is a threat to the social justice ideals held by Americans. For example, major disparities in correctional outcomes that are not rooted in differential levels of dangerousness violate Rawls's and Miller's principles of equal liberties, equal opportunity, equality, desert, and the difference principle (Robinson, 2010). Recall that the practices of criminal justice institutions should respect the civil liberties of all citizens, should be applied in an equal fashion, should be based on desert, and should be arranged to the benefits of the least advantaged.

We would also add that the harsh conditions of prison—commonly referred to as the *pains of imprisonment*—(Sykes & Western, 2007) are also a threat to social justice. While incarceration is supposed to achieve the goal of incapacitation for the protection of society, imprisonment entails much more than mere removal of one's freedom. Inmates are routinely subjected to violence, sexual harassment and assault, and similar negative treatments by both other inmates and guards (Jones & Pratt, 2008; Wolff, Blitz, Shi, Siegel, & Bachman, 2007). This is not consistent with the notion of desert. Further, it may in the long-term result in conditions in society upon inmate release that cause further harm to citizens, something that is also not consistent with social justice.

Although most Americans are probably unaware of the realities of corrections identified here, we contend that they are not in the interests of utilitarianism. As noted earlier with regard to policing and courts, we contend that American correctional activities do not generally achieve utility for Americans, especially when they are overly harsh on minor offenders, ignore the harmful acts of the powerful, and are applied in an unequal and thus unjust way. Because of this, we would also suggest that correctional activities likely tend to conflict with American virtues, making them inconsistent with virtue-based theories of justice seen as relevant to Americans.

A Special Focus on Capital Punishment

Finally, we can show that the *death penalty*, as actually practiced, also is not consistent with social justice principles of utilitarians, egalitarians, and libertarians, and thus virtue-based arguments are hard to make in justification of the punishment (Robinson, 2011). When it comes to the death penalty, the most important question for libertarians is whether capital punishment respects liberty or freedom. The most important question for egalitarians is whether capital punishment practice is equal (i.e., applied in an equal fashion). For utilitarians, the most important question is whether capital punishment increases overall utility or happiness in society. Finally, for virtue-based theorists, the question is whether capital punishment respects and promotes our values, our moral goodness, and whether it is the right thing to do.

Supporters of capital punishment argue that executing murderers respects liberty by sending the clearest and strongest of messages about how important (innocent) life is to society; the most serious crime (murder) warrants the most serious consequence (death penalty). While this is logical, opponents point out that executions also end life and therefore greatly diminish liberty. The fundamental issue of importance here is about the rights of citizens and whether they apply to murderers. These rights include the right to life. As noted in the Declaration of Independence: "We hold these truths to be self-evident, that all men are created equal, that they are endowed by their Creator with certain unalienable Rights, that among these are *Life*, Liberty and the pursuit of Happiness" (US History, 2010, emphasis added). Clearly, US law grants every citizen the right to life. Then there is the issue of rights of any human being. Article 3 of the Universal Declaration of Human Rights posits: "Everyone has the right to *life*, liberty and security of person" (United Nations, 2010, emphasis added).

The issue over which capital punishment supporters and opponents disagree is whether the right to life espoused in US and international law should be maintained after a person commits a murder; death penalty supporters maintain that by taking a life, murderers should sacrifice their own life as a form of retribution; opponents disagree and argue that these rights cannot be sacrificed, no matter what behaviors a person commits.

Such philosophical arguments cannot be resolved with empirical evidence. Thus, we must simply examine whether capital punishment, as actually practiced in the United States, helps achieve liberty or diminishes it. Empirically, it is easy to see that capital punishment is so rarely carried out in literally every death penalty jurisdiction (including those counties and states that still practice it), that capital punishment does not help achieve or assure liberty in society. Stated simply, if an execution were necessary to help protect the liberties of potential victims, states fail citizens 98–99 percent of the time (because only 1–2 percent of murderers are executed and sentenced to death, respectively). Let's say that one liberty Americans value is freedom from serious criminal victimization. If capital punishment were necessary to incapacitate and thereby permanently deprive murderers of their ability to commit future murders—which would thereby assure the liberty of citizens from serious criminal victimization (i.e., crime prevention)—murderers would have to be convicted, sentenced to death, and executed at a much higher rate than 1–2 percent.

Finally, it is important to again acknowledge that innocent people are wrongly convicted of murder, sentenced to death, and even (apparently) occasionally executed. It is an affront to liberty when an innocent person loses his life for a crime he did not commit. The libertarian argument of capital punishment is thus that the death penalty is unjust. It is unjust because it does not help protect or assure liberty, and also because it occasionally is used against the innocent.

Free market libertarians have not written about the death penalty. Yet, it is interesting to know that capital punishment is generally more expensive than other severe sanctions including even life in prison (Bohm, 2012; Cook, 2010; Robinson, 2008, 2009, 2011). As an example, in North Carolina, where the "most comprehensive death penalty study in the country" was conducted, the cost of a death penalty case all the way to execution above adjudication and a 20-year sentence was $163,000. The extra cost per death penalty sentence was $216,000, and the total costs per execution were $2.16 million more than life imprisonment (Cook, Slawson, & Gries, 1993). Another study found that North Carolina could save $11 million annually if it did not pursue capital punishment. This figure includes dollars spent on extra defense costs for capital cases in the trial phase, extra payments to jurors, post-conviction costs, resentencing hearings, and costs of imprisonment, but does not include money spent on the Office of the Appellate Defender and the North Carolina Supreme Court, the extra time spent by prosecutors in capital cases, and the costs to taxpayers for federal appeals (Cook, 2009). And an additional study found North Carolina spends $20 million per year just on defense costs alone (North Carolina Office of Indigent Services, 2008).

It would be interesting to see what free market libertarians might say about capital punishment if they ever took the time to weigh in on it. One relevant question would be is the capital punishment system a good use of resources, given it is so rarely used. Studies now show, for example, that to maintain their capital punishment systems (whether used frequently or not), states have had to make cuts to spending on police, criminal defense, prison guards, highways, indigent care, libraries, higher education, health care, and state employee raises. They have also had to raise taxes (Death Penalty Information Center, 2010).

Clearly, there are significant racial disparities, class disparities, and gender disparities in capital punishment practice. Scholars nearly universally agree that these problems stem from systemic biases pertaining to characteristics of both defendants and victims. Thus, an undeniable conclusion of capital punishment practice is that the death penalty is applied in an unequal fashion. This should not be surprising, given that there are also very disturbing extra-legal biases in virtually all of criminal justice practice, including imprisonment (which itself is a very unpleasant experience) (Barak et al., 2006; Feagin, 2001; Reiman, 2003; Robinson, 2009; Walker, Spohn, & DeLone, 2007; Shelden, 2000).

While it is undeniably true that much, if not all, of criminal justice is biased against certain groups in society—and it is quite possibly true that such biases will be difficult if not impossible to eradicate—it is also true that capital punishment has long been viewed as different than any other sanction, best captured in the phrase, "Death is different" (Acker, 2009; Foster, 1999). According to Abramson (2004), capital punishment is "different in kind" from any other punishment, including even life imprisonment. At least two things make it different. The first is the "finality" of execution, making biased outcomes "irrevocable" and "irreversible." The second is the "severity" or "enormity" of the punishment, making biased outcomes not only uncorrectable but also more perverse.

The United States has a long history of treating some groups of people differently than others in terms of criminal punishments; one horrific example is the extra-legal punishment of lynching blacks for crimes (both real and imagined) mostly against whites (Bright, 2002; Jacobs, Carmichael, & Kent, 2005; Messner, Baller, & Zevenbergen, 2005). Zimring (2003: 66) finds that the:

> states and the region where lynching was dominant show clear domination of recent executions, while those states with very low historic lynching records are much less likely than average to have either a death penalty or execution late in the twentieth century.

(*Zimring, 2003: 66*)

Zimring finds that the median number of executions in high lynching states is 24, versus zero in low lynching states. Zimring explains that:

> The statistical contrast between these two groups of states shows that they occupy the same extreme positions on the distribution of two distinct varieties of lethal violence in the United States separated by almost a century and the formal participation of government authority in the killing.
>
> *(Zimring, 2003: 96)*

Capital punishment is now not only connected to this history but has become part of it. Thus, the egalitarian argument of capital punishment is that the death penalty is unjust.

The final issue of inequality pertains to the evidence of geographic disparities associated with capital punishment practice. While each state has the right to pursue its own laws and policies under the concept of federalism, the resulting disparities are claimed to be unjust by some egalitarian justice scholars (e.g., Miller, 2003). Their argument is that, in a nation of laws that values equality, a person should not be treated differently based simply on where he or she lives. The counterargument is that place of residence will inevitably impact risk of capital processing due to different laws as well as the discretion of prosecutors to pursue whichever cases they see fit, using the threat of any punishment they choose to use.

Does the death penalty contribute to the overall happiness of society, to the general welfare of the people? One might think that if capital punishment could achieve desirable goals for society and that if the death penalty was actually used frequently enough to achieve these goals, it might contribute to societal welfare and citizen happiness. Yet, as noted earlier, capital punishment is so rarely carried out in literally every death penalty jurisdiction (including those counties and states that still practice it), that a safe conclusion is that capital punishment does not help achieve or assure happiness or welfare. This is especially true given how expensive the punishment is and the important government functions that must be sacrificed in order to carry it out.

This is not to say that the death penalty does not achieve any benefits to society. Clearly, executions do result in some incapacitation of offenders. That is, to whatever degree murderers do not commit murders that they would have committed but cannot because of their execution, this is a benefit to society. The relevant questions here are: to what degree are murderers likely to kill again? and, is capital punishment necessary to stop such future killings? The answer to the first question is very unlikely, mostly because most people who commit murder do not reoffend. For example, a study of those inmates released as a result of the *Furman v. Georgia* (1976) decision (which outlawed capital punishment in the US and commuted the sentences of those on death row to various terms of imprisonment) found that they "lived a combined total of 1,282 years in the community while committing twelve violent offenses—approximately two violent offenses per year for the released inmates or nine violent offenses per 1,000 releases per year." Further, of the 238 paroled offenders, "only a small percentage (less than 1%) of released murderers were returned to prison for committing a subsequent homicide. For example, of 11,532 murderers released between 1971 and 1975, twenty-six committed new homicides in the first year after release from prison . . . after five years on parole, only one murderer committed a second murder while in the larger society . . . Seven (1.3%) *Furman* commuted prisoners were responsible for seven additional murders" (Marquart & Sorensen, 1997: 171–174).

Yet, a small number of murderers would kill again if not effectively incapacitated. Ironically, it is incapacitation though imprisonment that tends to stop these murderers from killing again. Thus, in answer to the second question, executions may be excessive because effective incapacitation can be achieved through life imprisonment.

Executions may also produce a small general deterrent effect, thereby lowering the murder rate in society, although the vast majority of research on this topic suggests that capital punishment does not deter murder (Bailey, 1998; Berk, 2004; Cochran & Chamlin, 2000; Cochran, Chamlin, & Seth, 1994; Donohue & Wolfers, 2005; Fagan, 2005; Goertzel, 2004; Kovandzic, Vieraitis, & Boots, 2009; Land, Teske, & Zheng, 2009; Peterson & Bailey, 1991; Sorensen, Wrinkle, Brewer, & Marquart, 1999; Stack, 1993; Thomson, 1997; Yunker, 2001).

If there is any deterrent effect, it is likely so small that it cannot even be measured (Robinson, 2008). This is, in fact, not even a controversial statement, since the following groups do not think the death penalty deters murder, according to the studies: scholars of capital punishment (Robinson, 2008); Presidents of the American Society of Criminology (ASC), the Academy of Criminal Justice Sciences, and the Law and Society Association (Radelet & Akers, 1996); ASC fellows, winners of the ASC Sutherland Award, and presidents of ASC between 1997 and 2009 (Radelet & Lacock, 2009); ASC's National Policy Committee (2001); everyday, ordinary citizens (Gallup, 2006) and law enforcement chiefs (Dieter, 1995).

The relevant question here is not really whether capital punishment deters murder but whether it deters murder more than other available, severe sanctions (such as life imprisonment without the possibility of parole). The available evidence suggests that executions produce no further deterrent effect (Robinson, 2008). A slightly different conclusion was reached by the National Research Council of the National Academy of Sciences (Nagin & Pepper, 2012). They write: "The committee concludes that research to date on the effect of capital punishment on homicide is not informative about whether capital punishment decreases, increases, or has no effect on homicide rates" (p. 2). Yet, the authors agree with our sentiment above, saying:

> the relevant question about the deterrent effect of capital punishment is the differential or marginal deterrent effect of execution over the deterrent effect of other available or commonly used penalties, specifically, a lengthy prison sentence or one of life without the possibility of parole.
>
> *(Nagin & Pepper, 2012: 2–3)*

Finally, executions undeniably provide some closure to murder victims' families (Lifton & Mitchell, 2000). Yet, it is also true that executions do not provide closure to many victims' families (Peterson, 2008), in part because of the delay between conviction, sentencing, and ultimate execution (average time span of 11 years). Vandiver explains:

> The end of the trial and sentencing may mark an end to the involvement of the victim's family with the legal system. If the defendant is sentenced to life without parole or to a very long term of imprisonment, the sentence will begin immediately, and there should be no reason for the family to have to deal with the defendant again. If the defendant is sentenced to a short term of years, or will be eligible for parole after a short time, or above all, if he is sentenced to death, then the victims' family is likely to face a prolonged engagement with the criminal justice system. . . . If the

sentence is death, the family's involvement will continue beyond the trial for three or four years at a minimum, and may go on for as many as 20 or more years.

(Vandiver, 2003: 621)

It is also true that some families do not seek or want the death penalty for killers of their loved ones and that family members of the condemned also suffer immensely, typically without the support of greater society (King, 2003, 2005; Vandiver, 1989).

And once again, the relevant question is whether capital punishment leads to a greater sense of closure than that offered by other available, severe sanctions (such as life imprisonment without the possibility of parole). Unfortunately, there is no definitive answer to this question; yet, executions are so rare that if closure requires an execution, we as a society fail to provide it to murder victims' families about 98–99 percent of the time.

To determine the relative utility of capital punishment, one must of course assess these modest benefits against the costs of capital punishment. Assessing the contribution of capital punishment to the overall welfare of society is problematic for at least a few reasons. First, although one can readily identify the costs and benefits of policies such as the death penalty, quantifying some of them is quite difficult. How, for example, does one measure the worth of the closure that some victims' families may receive when the person who murdered their loved ones is executed? Second, weighing such benefits against costs associated with the practice of capital punishment such as biases based on extra-legal factors like race, class, and gender—not to mention easily quantifiable costs such as the additional financial expense of capital punishment above and beyond other criminal sanctions such as life imprisonment—is difficult if not impossible.

Third, as should be obvious by the term "weighing," any weighing of costs and benefits involves much more than just counting them up and seeing whether there are more costs or more benefits; the weighing part requires that each benefit and each cost be prioritized more or less based on each person's own values. For example, one person may think the little bit of closure provided to victims' families by capital punishment and the possibly small crime reduction effect (through a tiny incapacitative effect and a possible general deterrent effect of executions) is worth more than extra-legal biases in the application of the punishment; this person would thus weigh the benefits more than the costs. Another person may find the risk of executing an innocent person, however small, to be such a serious cost that it outweighs any conceivable benefit of capital punishment. Such individualized opinions and preferences are affected by many factors, including race, gender, age, income level, political party and ideology, geography of residence, and religious beliefs (Young, 2002). Support for the death penalty is also partially determined by fear of crime, views of how courts treat suspects, and racial animosity (Cochran and Chamlin, 2006; Young, 2004).

In spite of all this, it is a safe conclusion that capital punishment, as actually practiced in the United States, has only modest benefits but enormous costs. Thus, the utilitarian argument of capital punishment is that the death penalty is unjust.

Finally, as for the issue of virtue, a sizable portion of Americans (roughly 66 percent) say they support capital punishment. Thus, they apparently find it moral or virtuous or at least they are willing to live with it. Yet, studies show that when Americans are given information about the realities of capital punishment (e.g., when they learn that studies show racial biases in capital punishment), support falls. Support also falls when people are given the choice of alternative sanctions such as life imprisonment without the possibility of parole (Robinson, 2011). To supporters of the death penalty, we ask a simple question: if the death penalty, as actually practiced, does not respect liberty or lead to increases in overall happiness, and is unequally applied, on what virtue can one draw to argue in favor of it?

Summary

In the ideal world, criminal justice serves to promote and protect social justice ideals found in the founding documents of the United States and currently held by Americans. That is, the law, police, courts, and corrections strive ideally to serve libertarian, egalitarian, and utilitarian goals, rooted in just and proper virtues and values.

Yet, the reality of criminal justice practice—from the law through policing, courts, and corrections—is, in many ways, inconsistent with our social justice ideals. In this chapter, we identified these ways, showing how policing, courts, and corrections generally tend to focus on certain groups of people in society, thereby creating greater burdens for some and less for others, resulting in unequal outcomes in arrests, convictions, sentences, and correctional punishments. It is, plainly stated, young, poor, minority males who suffer the most at the hands of criminal justice practice.

Our argument in this chapter is that the main reason this occurs is because of the criminal law, which tends to criminalize their harmful behaviors and treat them as more serious than even the acts of elite deviance which cause so much more damage. Thus, the law—consistent with social justice, at least on paper—can generally be seen as inconsistent with the social justice ideals actually held by Americans in the real world.

Discussion Questions

1. What is the criminal law?
2. Contrast the substantive criminal law with the procedural criminal law.
3. What is murder? Compare and contrast murder with negligent homicide and non-negligent homicide.
4. Compare and contrast voluntary manslaughter and involuntary manslaughter.
5. What makes a crime "serious?"
6. List and define the Part I Index Offenses of the Uniform Crime Reports.
7. Compare and contrast white-collar crime and corporate crime.
8. Which types of crime produce the largest amount of property crime losses—street crime or white-collar and corporate crime? Provide evidence.
9. Which types of crime produce the largest amount of injuries and deaths—street crime or white-collar and corporate crime? Provide evidence.
10. What is culpability? List and define intentional, negligence, recklessness, and knowingly.
11. Identify and define the five major roles served by police officers.
12. What are some of the major problems with policing, according to Samuel Walker and his colleagues?
13. What are the major functions of courts in America?
14. What rights are granted by the Fifth and Fourteenth Amendments to the US Constitution?
15. What is the wedding cake model?
16. What are some of the major problems with courts, according to Samuel Walker and his colleagues?

17. Compare and contrast institutional corrections and community corrections.
18. Contrast probation with parole.
19. Define rehabilitation.
20. Compare and contrast general deterrence and specific deterrence.
21. Identify the ways in which the law and definitions of crime are consistent with social justice. Also, in what ways are they inconsistent with social justice?
22. Identify the ways in which police help bring about social justice. Also, in what ways is policing inconsistent with social justice?
23. Identify the ways in which courts help bring about social justice. Also, in what ways are courts inconsistent with social justice?
24. Identify the ways in which corrections help bring about social justice. Also, in what ways is corrections inconsistent with social justice?
25. Discuss whether capital punishment is consistent with social justice. Why?

References

Abramson, A. (2004). *Death-is-Different: Jurisprudence and the Role of the Capital Jury.* Downloaded from: http://moritzlaw.osu.edu/osjcl/Articles/Volume2_1/Symposium/Abramson.pdf.

Acker, J. (2009). Actual Innocence: Is Death Different? *Behavioral Sciences & the Law, 27*(3), 297.

Agnew, R. (2005). *Why do Criminals Offend? A General Theory of Crime and Delinquency.* New York: Oxford University Press.

Alexander, M. (2012). *The New Jim Crow: Mass Incarceration in the Age of Colorblindness.* New York: The New Press.

Alpert, G., Dunham, R., & Stroshine, M. (2005). *Policing: Continuity and Change.* Long Grove, IL: Waveland.

American Society of Criminology, National Policy Committee (2001). *The Use of the Death Penalty.* Retrieved from: http://www.asc41.com/policypaper2.html.

Bailey, W. (1998). Deterrence, Brutalization, and the Death Penalty: Another Examination of Oklahoma's Return to Capital Punishment. *Criminology, 36*(4), 711.

Barak, G., Leighton, P., & Flavin, J. (2006). *Class, Race, Gender, and Crime: The Social Realities of Justice in America.* Lanham, MA: Rowman & Littlefield.

Beard D. (1913). *An Economic Interpretation of the Constitution of the United States.* New York: MacMillan.

Bell, J., Clow, K., & Ricciardelli, R. (2008). Causes of Wrongful Conviction: Looking at Student Knowledge. *Journal of Criminal Justice Education, 19,* 75–96.

Berk, R. (2004). New Claims about Execution and General Deterrence: Deja Vu all Over Again? *Journal of Empirical Legal Studies.* Retrieved from: http://preprints.stat.ucla.edu/396/JELS.pap.pdf.

Bohm, B. (2012). *DeathQuest: An Introduction to the Theory and Practice of Capital Punishment in the United States.* 4th ed. Waltham, MA: Elsevier (Anderson Publishing/Routledge).

Brewer, T. (2004). Race and Jurors' Receptivity to Mitigation in Capital Cases: The Effect of Jurors', Defendants' and Victims' Race in Combination. *Law and Human Behavior, 28*(5), 529–545.

Bright, S. (2002). Why the United States will Join the Rest of the World in Abandoning Capital Punishment. In Bedau, H., & P. Cassell (Eds.), *Debating the Death Penalty: Should America have Capital Punishment? The Experts from Both Sides Make their Case* (pp. 152–182). New York: Oxford University Press.

Brown, B., & Jolivette, G. (2005). *A Primer: Three Strikes—The Impact after More than a Decade.* Downloaded from: http://www.lao.ca.gov/2005/3_strikes/3_strikes_102005.htm.

Bureau of Justice Statistics (2008). Defense Counsel for Criminal Cases. In Robinson, M. (2005). *Justice Blind? Ideals and Realities of American Criminal Justice.* Upper Saddle River, NJ: Prentice Hall.

Clear, T., Cole, G., & Reisig, M. (2008). *American Corrections.* Independence, KY: Cengage.

Clear, T., Reisig, M., & Cole, G. (2012). *American Corrections*. Independence, KY: Cengage.

Clinard, M., & Yeager, P. (2005). *Corporate Crime*. Edison, NJ: Transaction.

Cochran, J., & Chamlin, M. (2000). Deterrence and Brutalization: The dual Effects of Executions. *Justice Quarterly*, *17*(4), 685.

Cochran, J., & Chamlin, M. (2006). The Enduring Racial Divide in Death Penalty Support. *Journal of Criminal Justice*, *34*(1), 85–99.

Cochran, J., Chamlin, M., & Seth, M. (1994). Deterrence or Brutalization? An Impact Assessment of Oklahoma's Return to Capital Punishment. *Criminology*, *32*(1), 107.

Cook, P. (2009). *Potential Savings from Abolition of the Death Penalty in North Carolina*. Downloaded from: http://www.deathpenaltyinfo.org/documents/CookCostRpt.pdf.

Cook, P. (2010). *Potential Savings from Abolition of the Death Penalty in North Carolina*. Paper presented to the annual meeting of the American Society of Criminology. San Francisco, CA. November.

Cook, P., Slawson, D., & Gillen, L. (1993). *The Costs of Processing Murder Cases in North Carolina*. Downloaded from: http://www.deathpenaltyinfo.org/northcarolina.pdf.

Davenport, A. (2008). *Basic Criminal Law: The Constitution, Procedure, and Crimes*. Upper Saddle River, NJ: Prentice Hall.

Death Penalty Information Centre (2010). *Costs of the Death Penalty*. Retrieved from: http://deathpenaltyinfo.org/costs-death-penalty.

Dieter, R. (1995). *On the Front Line: Law Enforcement Views on the Death Penalty*. Retrieved from: http://www.deathpenaltyinfo.org/front-line-law-enforcement-views-death-penalty.

Donohue, J., & Wolfers, J. (2005). Uses and Abuses of Empirical Evidence in the Death Penalty Debate. *Stanford Law Review*, *58*, 791–846.

Fagan, J. (2005). *Public Policy Choices on Deterrence and the Death Penalty: A Critical Review of New Evidence*. Testimony before the Joint Committee on the Judiciary of the Massachusetts Legislature on House Bill 3934, July 14, 2005. Retrieved from: http://www.deathpenaltyinfo.org/MassTestimonyFagan.pdf.

Feagin, J. (2001). *Racist America*. New York: Routledge.

Federal Bureau of Investigation (2012a). *Uniform Crime Reports*. UCR general FAQs.Downloaded from: http://www.fbi.gov/about-us/cjis/ucr/frequently-asked-questions/ucr_faqs.

Federal Bureau of Investigation (2012b). *Crime in the United States, 2011. Murder*. Downloaded from: http://www.fbi.gov/about-us/cjis/ucr/crime-in-the-u.s/2011/crime-in-the-u.s.- 2011/violent-crime/murder.

Federal Bureau of Investigation (2013). *Uniform Crime Reporting*. Downloaded from: https://www2.fbi.gov/ucr/ucr_general.html.

Fisher, G. (2003). *Plea Bargaining's Triumph: A History of Plea Bargaining in America*. Stanford, CA: Stanford University Press.

Foster, B. (1999). *Why Death is Different: Capital Punishment in the Legal System*. Downloaded from: http://www.burkfoster.com/DeathIsDifferent.htm.

Gaines, L., & Kappeler, V. (2015). *Policing in America*. 8th ed. Waltham, MA: Elsevier (Anderson Publishing/Routledge).

Gallup (2006). *Respondents Reporting Whether they Believe the Death Penalty Acts as a Deterrent to Murder*. Retrieved from: http://www.albany.edu/sourcebook/pdf/t2572006.pdf.

Gilens, M., & Page, B. (2014). *Testing Theories of American Politics: Elites, Interest Groups, and Average Citizens*. Downloaded from: http://scholar.princeton.edu/sites/default/files/mgilens/files/gilens_and_page_2014_-testing_theories_of_american_politics.doc.pdf.

Glaze, L., & Parks, E. (2011). *Correctional Populations in the United States. Bureau of Justice Statistics*. Downloaded from: http://www.bjs.gov/content/pub/pdf/cpus11.pdf.

Goertzel, T. (2004). Capital Punishment and Homicide: Sociological Realities and Econometric Illusions. *Skeptical Enquirer Magazine*. Retrieved from: http://www.deathpenaltyinfo.org/article.php?scid=12&did=1176.

Harrigan, J. (2000). *Empty Dreams, Empty Pockets: Class and Bias in American Politics*. New York: Addison-Wesley Longman.

International Association of Chiefs of Police (2008). *Law Enforcement Code of Ethics*. Downloaded from: http://www.theiacp.org/PublicationsGuides/ResearchCenter/Publications/tabid/299/Defau lt.aspx?id=82&v=1.

Jacobs, D., Carmichael, J., & Kent, S. (2005). Vigilantism, Current Racial Threat, and Death Sentences. *American Sociological Review, 70*, 656.

Jones, T., & Pratt, T. (2008). The Prevalence of Sexual Violence in Prison: The State of the Knowledge Base and Implications for Evidence-Based Correctional Policy Making. *International Journal of Offender Therapy and Comparative Criminology, 52*(3), 280.

Kent, S., & Jacobs, D. (2005). Minority Threat and Police Strength from 1800 to 2000: A Fixed-Effects Analysis of Nonlinear and Interactive Effects in Large US cities. *Criminology, 43*(3), 731–760.

King, R. (2003). *Don't Kill in our Names: Families of Murder Victims Speak out Against the Death Penalty*. Rutgers, NJ: Rutgers University Press.

King, R. (2005). *Capital Consequences: Families of the Condemned Tell their Stories*. Rutgers, NJ: Rutgers University Press.

Kovandzic, T., Vieraitis, L., & Boots, D. (2009). Does the Death Penalty Save Lives? New Evidence from State Panel Data, 1977 to 2006. *Criminology & Public Policy, 8*(4), 803.

Land, K., Teske, J., & Zheng, H. (2009). The Short-Term Effects of Executions on Homicides: Deterrence, Displacement, or Both? *Criminology, 47*(4), 1009.

Lifton, R., & Mitchell, G. (2000). *Who Owns Death? Capital Punishment, the American Conscience, and the End of Executions*. New York: William Morrow.

Lynch, M., McGurrin, D., & Fenwick, M. (2004). Disappearing Act: The Representation of Corporate Crime Research in Criminological Literature. *Journal of Criminal Justice, 32*(5), 389.

Lynch, M., Michalowski, R., & Groves, B. (2000). *The New Primer in Radical Criminology: Critical Perspectives on Crime, Power and Identity*. Monsey, NY: Willow Tree Press.

Marquart, J., & Sorensen, J. (1997). A National Study of the *Furman*-Commuted Inmates: Assessing the Threat to Society from Capital Offenders. In Bedau, H. (Ed.), *The Death Penalty in America: Current Controversies* (pp. 162–175). New York: Oxford University Press.

McGarrell, E., & Flanagan, T. (1987). Measuring and Explaining Legislator Crime Control Ideology. *The Journal of Research in Crime and Delinquency, 24*(2), 102.

Meador, D., Baker, T., & Steinman, J. (2001). *Appellate Courts: Structures, Functions, Processes, and Personnel*. Newark, NJ: LexisNexis.

Meier, R., & Geis, G. (1997). *Victimless Crime? Prostitution, Homosexuality, and Abortion*. New York: Oxford University Press.

Merton, R. (1938). Social Structure and Anomie. *American Sociological Review, 3*(5), 672–682.

Messner, S., Baller, R., & Zevenbergen, M. (2005). The Legacy of Lynching and Southern Homicide. *American Sociological Review, 70*(4), 633–655.

Miller, D. (2003). *Principles of Social Justice*. Cambridge, MA: Harvard University Press.

Mokhiber, R. (2007). Twenty Things you Should Know about Corporate Crime. *Alternet*, June 15. Downloaded from: http://www.alternet.org/story/54093/twenty_things_you_should_know_about_corporate_crime?paging=off.

Nagin, D., & Pepper, J. (2012). *Deterrence and the Death Penalty*. Committee on deterrence and the death penalty; Committee on Law and Justice; Division on Behavioral and Social Sciences and Education; National Research Council. Downloaded from: http://www.nap.edu/catalog.php?record_id=13363.

National Association of Criminal Defense Lawyers (2008). *Criminal Defense Issues*. Downloaded from: https://www.nacdl.org/criminaldefense.aspx?id=20169.

Neubauer, D. (2007). *America's Courts and the Criminal Justice System*. Independence, KY: Cengage.

Neubauer, D., & Fradella, H. (2010). *America's Courts and the Criminal Justice System*. Independence, KY: Cengage.

New Century Foundation (2005). *Race and Crime*. Washington, DC: New Century Foundation.

North Carolina Office of Indigent Services (2008). *FY07 Capital Trial Case Study. PAC and Expert Spending in Potentially Capital Cases at the Trial Level*. Downloaded from: http://www.ncids.org/Reports%20&%20Data/Latest%20Releases/FY07CapitalStudyFinal.pdf.

Orth, J. (2007). *Due Process of Law: A Brief History*. Lawrence, KS: University of Kansas Press.

Padfield, N. (2009). Shining the Torch on Plea-Bargaining. *The Cambridge Law Journal*, *68*(1), 11–15.

Peterson, R., & Bailey, W. (1998). Is Capital Punishment an Effective Deterrent for Murder? An Examination of Social Science Research. In Acker, J., Bohm, B., & C, Lanier (Eds.), *America's Experiment with Capital Punishment: Reflections on the Past, Present, and Future of the Ultimate Penal Sanction* (pp. 251–282). Durham, NC: Carolina Academic Press.

Peterson, W. (2008). Voices of the Victims: Capital Punishment and a Declaration of Life. *The Review of Litigation*, *27*(4), 769.

Pew (2010). *The Impact of the 2008 Economic Collapse*. Downloaded from: http://www.pewtrusts.org/en/research-and-analysis/reports/2010/04/28/the-impact-of-the-september-2008-economic-collapse.

Radelet, M., & Akers, R. (1996). Deterrence and the Death Penalty: The Views of the Experts. *Journal of Criminal Law & Criminology*, *81*(1), 1–16.

Radelet, M., & Lacock, T. (2009). Do Executions Lower Homicide Rates? The Views of Leading Criminologists. *Journal of Criminal Law & Criminology*, *99*(2), 489.

Rand Corporation (2005). *California's New Three Strikes Law*. Downloaded from: http://www.rand.org/pubs/research_briefs/RB4009/index1.html.

Rawls, J. (1971/2003). *A Theory of Justice*. New York: Belknap.

Reddington, F., & Bonham, Jr., G. (2011). *Flawed Criminal Justice Policies: At the Intersection of the Media, Public Fear, and Legislative Response*. Durham, NC: Carolina Academic Press.

Reiman, J. (2003). *The Rich Get Richer and the Poor Get Prison*. New York: Routledge.

Reiman, J., & Leighton, P. (2013). *The Rich Get Richer and the Poor Get Prison: Ideology, Class, and Criminal Justice*. Upper Saddle River, NJ: Prentice Hall.

Robinson, M. (2008). *Death Nation: The Experts Explain American Capital Punishment*. Upper Saddle River, NJ: Prentice Hall.

Robinson, M. (2009). *Justice Blind? Ideals and Realities of American Criminal Justice*. Upper Saddle River, NJ: Prentice Hall.

Robinson, M. (2010). Assessing Criminal Justice Practice Using Social Justice Theory. *Social Justice Research*, *23*, 77–97.

Robinson, M. (2011). *The Death Penalty in North Carolina: A Summary of the Data and Scientific Studies*. Downloaded from: http://libres.uncg.edu/ir/asu/f/Robinson_Matt_2011_The_Death_Penalty.pdf.

Robinson, M., & Murphy, D. (2009). *Greed is Good: Maximization and Elite Deviance in America*. Lanham, MD: Rowman & Littlefield.

Ross, J., & Richards, S. (2002). *Convict Criminology*. Beverly Hills, CA: Wadsworth.

Ross, J., & Rothe, D. (2007). Swimming Upstream: Teaching State Crime to Students at American Universities. *Journal of Criminal Justice Education*, *18*(3), 460.

Rothe, D., & Friedrichs, D. (2006). The State of the Criminology of Crimes of the State. *Social Justice*, *33*(1), 147–161.

Samaha, J. (2013). *Criminal Law*. Independence, KY: Cengage.

Sennott, C., & Galliher, J. (2006). Lifetime Felony Disenfranchisement in Florida, Texas, and Iowa: Symbolic and Instrumental Law. *Social Justice*, *33*(1), 79–94.

Shelden, R. (2000). *Controlling the Dangerous Classes*. Boston, MA: Allyn & Bacon.

Shelden, R. (2007). *Controlling the Dangerous Classes: A History of Criminal Justice in America*. Boston, MA: Allyn & Bacon.

Siegel, A. (2005). Moving Down the Wedge of Injustice: A Proposal for a Third Generation of Wrongful Convictions Scholarship and Advocacy. *The American Criminal Law Review*, *42*(4), 1219–1237.

Simon, D. (2007). *Elite deviance*. Upper Saddle River, NJ: Pearson.

Simons, R., & Gray, P. (1989). Perceived Blocked Opportunity as an Explanation of Delinquency among Lower-Class Black Males: A Research Note. *The Journal of Research in Crime and Delinquency*, *26*(1), 90.

Sorensen, J., Wrinkle, R., Brewer, V., & Marquart, J. (1999). Capital Punishment and Deterrence: Examining the Effect of Executions on Murder in Texas. *Crime and Delinquency, 45*(4), 481–493.

Sourcebook of Criminal Justice Statistics (2008). Table 4.1. *Arrests by Offense Charged, Age Group, and Race, United States, 2006*. Downloaded from: http://www.albany.edu/sourcebook/pdf/t4102006.pdf.

Stack, S. (1993). Execution Publicity and Homicide in Georgia. *American Journal of Criminal Justice, 18*(1), 25–39.

Stuart, G. (2008). *Miranda: The Story of America's Right to Remain Silent*. Tucson, AZ: University of Arizona Press.

Stuntz, W. (2011). *The Collapse of American Criminal Justice*. Harvard, MA: Belknap Press.

Sutherland, E. (1977). White-Collar Criminality. In Geis, G., & Meier, R. (Eds.), *White-Collar Crime: Offenses in Business, Politics, and the Professions*. New York: The Free Press.

Sykes, G., & Western, B. (2007). *The Society of Captives: A Study of a Maximum Security Prison*. Princeton, NJ: University of Princeton Press.

Thomson, E. (1997). Deterrence Versus Brutalization: The Case of Arizona. *Homicide Studies, 1*(2), 110–128.

Tonry, M. (2012). *Punishing Race: A Continuing American Dilemma*. New York: Oxford University Press.

Truman, J., & Planty, M. (2012). Criminal Victimization, 2011. Downloaded from: http://www.bjs.gov/content/pub/pdf/cv11.pdf.

United Nations (2010). Universal Declaration of Human Rights. Downloaded from: http://www.un.org/en/documents/udhr/index.shtml.

Vandiver, M. (1989). Coping with Death: Families of the Terminally Ill, Homicide Victims, and Condemned Prisoners. In Radelet, M. (Ed.), *Facing the Death Penalty: Essays on Cruel and Unusual Punishment* (pp. 123–138). Philadelphia, PA: Temple University Press.

Vandiver, M. (2003). The Impact of the Death Penalty on the Families of Homicide Victims and of Condemned Prisoners. In Acker, J., Bohm, B., & C. Lanier (Eds.), *America's Experiment with Capital Punishment: Reelections on the Past, Present, and Future of the Ultimate Penal Sanction* (2nd ed.) (pp. 613–646). Durham, NH: Carolina Academic Press.

Velez, N. (2013). NYPD Releases Stop-and-Frisk Data for First Time. *New York Post*, February 5. Downloaded: http://www.nypost.com/p/news/local/nypd_releases_stop_frisk_data_whf644ouNc8P7dP 8u7NPcJ.

Walker, S. (2011). *Sense and Nonsense about Crime, Drugs, and Communities*. Belmont, CA: Wadsworth.

Walker, S., Spohn, C., & DeLone, M. (2012). *The Color of Justice: Race, Ethnicity, and Crime in America*. Belmont, CA: Wadsworth.

Wheelock, D. (2005). Collateral Consequences and Racial Inequality: Felon Status Restrictions as a System of Disadvantage. *Journal of Contemporary Criminal Justice, 21*(1), 82.

Withrow, B. (2005). *The Racial Profiling Controversy*. Flushing, NY: Looseleaf Law.

Wolff, N., Blitz, C., Shi, J., Siegel, J., & Bachman, R. (2007). Physical Violence Inside Prisons: Rates of Victimization. *Criminal Justice and Behavior, 34*(5), 588.

Young, R. (2004). Guilty until Proven Innocent: Conviction Orientation, Racial Attitudes, and Support for Capital Punishment. *Deviant Behavior, 25*(2), 151–167.

Yunker, J. (2001). A New Statistical Analysis of Capital Punishment Incorporating U.S. Postmoratorium Data. *Social Science Quarterly, 82*(2), 297–311.

Zimring, F. (2003). *The Contradictions of American Capital Punishment*. New York: Oxford University Press.

Zimring, F. (2008). *The Great American Crime Decline*. New York: Oxford University Press.

Zimring, F. (2011). *The City that Became Safe: New York's Lessons for Urban Crime and its Control*. New York: Oxford University Press.

4

SOCIAL CONSTRUCTION OF DIFFERENT GROUPS

The only freedom which deserves the name is that of pursuing our own good, in our own way, so long as we do not attempt to deprive others of theirs, or impede their efforts to obtain it.

John Stuart Mill, 1859

In the first section of this book, we discussed the interrelatedness between social justice and criminal justice, we provided an overview of this country's founding documents and guiding principles, and we outlined the basic functions of the criminal justice system. This section of the book will focus on how both the law and the criminal justice system have been used to protect as well as to repress the rights of different groups of people. As John Stuart Mill (1859) argues in the quote above, our role as a democratic society is to ensure that all members of society are afforded the ability to pursue the important tenets of life, liberty, and the pursuit of happiness. Our freedom to do so is diminished the moment that we, as a society, impede the rights of some of our members.

In this regard, the most important questions to ask ourselves are: (1) does everyone in the United States have equal rights? (2) why or why not? In answering these questions, it is important that we understand how we have come to create certain *categories of difference* that serve as a divide between various subgroups of our citizens. As such, tracing the history of different subgroups of people is an important and necessary step in learning how the rights outlined in the Declaration of Independence and in the United States Constitution have been applied to American citizens over the last several centuries.

While it is true that our founding fathers stated that all people are created equal, the history of this country shows that we apply different standards of treatment to different groups of people. This is partly explained by the fact that American society is structured in a manner consistent with *social stratification* where categories of people are arranged in a hierarchy with those at the top garnering more relative power than those at the bottom (Mills, 1959). Recall from Chapter 2 that this social stratification may have been created with the full knowledge of the founding fathers in an attempt to protect their own position and power. The system of social stratification that is still in existence today contributes to a system of inequality inherent in our society and is based on the belief of *essentialism*—that human behavior is based on biological or genetic differences and as such, is not subject to change (Grewal, 2006). This essentialism is maintained by *hegemonic*, or culturally dominant, beliefs in our culture and generally supports rigid definitions of what behaviors are "natural" (Marx & Engels, 1848).

What's interesting is that while there are biological differences between different groups of people (e.g., men and women), the associated stereotypes and prejudices attributed to these differences are almost entirely socially constructed (Ore, 2011). This chapter will examine how we have historically created these social differences and subsequently have come to accept them as facts.

Creating Categories of Difference

When human beings are born, individuals have no sense of who they are in relation to anyone else. They don't know what it means to be a girl or a boy and they don't ascribe different attributes to people of different skin color or religion. These differences, along with most behaviors, must be learned. Not surprisingly, these lessons will vary both by the culture that one is born into as well as the time in which someone is born. For example, a person born in San Francisco, California in 1970 may have a completely different viewpoint than someone born in Birmingham, Alabama in 1930. His or her race/ethnicity, sex, and gender will also influence his or her life experiences and upbringing. In other words, a black female and a white male born on the same day in the same city may also experience fundamentally different life lessons. What we believe to be true about society and its members is formed in various contexts, which we will cover next.

The Institutional Context

We will begin by discussing the broadest, but perhaps most influential, of the contexts that inform the creation of categories of difference—the *institutional context*. According to Ore (2011: 8), "an institution is the set of rules and relationships that govern the social activities in which we participate to meet our basic needs." There are a number of social institutions that influence us all:

- the family
- the education system
- peer groups
- religion
- the media
- the government
- the economy.

The Family

The *family* is the primary social institution responsible for imparting information concerning a host of lessons including acceptable social behavior, personal care and grooming, and interpersonal skills. In the first decade of life, there is perhaps no institution more significant than that of the family. Family also helps children define their sense of identity. We learn, for example, whether we are male or female; rich, poor, or middle-class; white, black, Latino, or other; etc., and with each of these parts of our identities, we learn certain behaviors that are appropriate and inappropriate to these identities.

Part of our identities is learning right from wrong and separating moral behaviors from immoral behaviors. In accordance with the doctrine of social learning theory, individuals "are taught how to behave, or misbehave in a social context" (Brown, Esbensen, & Geis, 2007). Drawing on the principles of *differential association theory*, this learning process varies in "frequency, duration, priority and intensity" (Sutherland & Cressey, 1974). As stated by Akers (1998: 216),

> those associations that occur earlier (priority), last longer and occupy more of one's time (duration), take place most often (frequency), and involve others with whom one has the more important or closer relationship (intensity) will have the greater effect on behavior.

It is worth noting that parents convey lessons about morality, among other things, both through their words *and* through their own decisions and behavior. We have all heard the epitaph, "Practice what you preach." This lesson is in direct contrast to the "do as I say, not as I do" model of parenting. A parent can tell their children to treat all people the same, but if that same parent locks their car doors when an African American youth walks by the car, what message is that sending the children? According to a study by Hofferth and Sandberg (2001), parents spend on average less than 30 minutes a day talking to their school-aged children. While this amount of time may vary widely from family to family, it stresses the point that children learn more from their parents' actions than their words.

Parents also impart lessons and knowledge through their use of *discipline*, a term that refers to teaching that occurs through rewarding prosocial behavior and punishing antisocial behavior. It's worth noting that the lack of discipline and correction is as important as when it's invoked. Children understand what is acceptable behavior based on whether they're permitted to engage in a certain behavior or voice a certain opinion. If a child says something in front of his or her parents that is derogatory about a racial or ethnic minority or a person of the opposite sex and this behavior isn't corrected, it sends a message of reinforcement about the voiced opinion or action. Above all else, family dynamics and the messages received set the tone for the belief system that children hold. While it is possible to alter one's beliefs over the life course, these early lessons set the stage for future interactions.

The Education System

For most people, the next social institution of importance is the *education system*. Particularly in an era where curriculums are standardized and teachers are increasingly restricted in the content that they teach, schools help shape what children believe to be true. Whereas parents are the child's first teacher, school teachers take over where parents leave off (and often spend more time with our children during the day than we do). When children leave the home to attend schools, teachers and peers act as second parents and supplement the lessons from home. Other than teaching basic educational skills such as reading, writing and math, schools also shape social interactions between students.

Oftentimes, the information that children receive from their parents about how to interact with different types of people can be less than egalitarian in nature. When that's the case, the burden falls on the school to teach equality and respect for others. While there is some resistance to the idea that educators should act with a value-laden agenda, research shows that they already do. Kohl (1991) argues that students learn a particular set of lessons based on the teacher's behavior, the choice of textbooks and supplemental readings used, the order in which lessons are presented and even the tone of voice used in the lesson. In other words, teaching style and classroom management style are as important to the curriculum as the information presented. In the event that children have a positive and supportive home environment, a similarly positive school environment simply reinforces the lessons from home. Considering that most children will spend eight hours a day in primary school over the course of 12 years, the role of the education system in shaping values is central to the institutional context.

Peer Groups

As childhood gives way to adolescence, *peer groups* provide the primary social context for teenagers. During adolescence, the importance of peers increases and teens often look to their peer group for reinforcement on how to dress, what to think, and how to behave. According to Meldrum and colleagues, "Reinforcement is dependent, however, on the individual's ability to encode and interpret social cues from their peer group" (Meldrum, Miller, & Flexon, 2013: 106). In other words, some kids are more conforming than others. Studies have found that increased susceptibility to peer influence can result in higher engagement of delinquent and risky behaviors (Miller, Malone, & Dodge, 2010).

Social-psychological factors also appear to affect the degree to which an individual is susceptible to peer influence. Research demonstrates that teens that place a high value on being a member of a group are increasingly vulnerable to the influence of peers (Kiesner, Cadinu, Poulin, & Bucci, 2002). Also, adolescents who place high importance on their social status are similarly at risk for peer pressure (Cillessen & Mayeux, 2004). More recently, Trucco, Colder, and Wieczorek (2011) found that youth with strong communal, or shared, goals showed increased susceptibility to the influence of their peers.

Lest it sound like individuals of a certain age always follow the herd, it is important to note that, alas, teenagers do not always simply do what their peers tell them to. There is a two-way pull between wanting to please their peers and finding their own identity. Adolescence is also the time where teens begin to understand that the difference between right and wrong is also not wrought in absolute terms. One must also take into account context, intentions, abilities and motivation before making a judgment. This is also the time when individuals begin to understand that laws and authority figures are not indisputable. Rules are often challenged and individuals may begin to make up their own minds and determine their own paths of behavior. With that said, peers become their primary sounding board and there is a shift away from believing that parents are the ultimate authority on every subject.

Criminological research shows that, whereas peers can influence the behavior of a child, children tend to seek out like peers—"birds of a feather flock together." In this way, children with certain values and behaviors will seek out and befriend other children with similar values and behaviors; these friendships will reinforce existing predispositions. So, for example, deviant kids tend to seek out friends who are deviant, and these friendships make further deviant behavior more likely to occur (Robinson & Beaver, 2009).

> ## Activity 4.1 Corporate Crime
>
> Go online and research corporate crime, particularly how it is learned within the culture of the corporation.
>
> Be sure to read the article, "Understanding 'Criminogenic' Corporate Culture: What White-Collar Crime Researchers Can Learn from Studies of the Adolescent Employment–Crime Relationship," by Robert Apel & Raymond Paternoster: http://www.link.springer.com/chapter/10.1007%2F978-0-387-09502-8_2#page-1.
>
> How is crime learned and justified in the context of corporations?
>
> Do you agree with the authors that the white-collar crime is learned in social groups similar to street crime?
> Explain.

Religion

The United States of America is unique in both the level of religiosity displayed by citizens—from atheist to fundamentalist—as well as in the plethora of different types of religions practiced. Our nation's borders are home to people who practice Buddhism, Islam, Judaism, Paganism and many more. Even with Christianity, the dominant *religion* in the United States, there is not a single denomination with majority-group membership.

Most religions have a particular *ideology*, which is a set of beliefs and values about the way the world ought to be and the way that individuals ought to act (Tracy, 1817). Inherent in this ideology is the idea of what is right versus what is wrong. Many people often refer to this designation of right and wrong as *morality*. What complicates the issue is that morality can mean different things to different people. Take, for example, the issue of homosexuality. As Figure 4.1 shows, the support for same-sex marriage varies by the level and type of religiosity of the respondent. One religious ideology may purport that homosexuality is sinful and wrong, or immoral, whereas a different religious ideology may believe that we are all God's children—regardless of sexuality—and it is immoral to judge the behavior of others. But how do we know who is correct? This is similar to the issue of whose virtues do we follow when we assess an issue using virtue-based theories, as noted in Chapter 1.

Therein lies the difficulty of living in a country with numerous different ideologies. Every single group feels that their beliefs are right and that others not living according to the same beliefs are living the wrong way. For many people, religion—as an institution—can trump the influence of other institutions like education, the media and the government. This is because of at least two different reasons: many religions use thousands of years of doctrines and teachings as their foundation, which is a lot more concrete than the ever-changing nature of the other institutions mentioned; and many religions believe that not living in accordance with their teachings can have dire consequences, which may last an eternity! In general, people who identify as religious tend to have more conservative views about issues that are considered moral questions (gay marriage, abortion, drug use, prostitution). To legislate

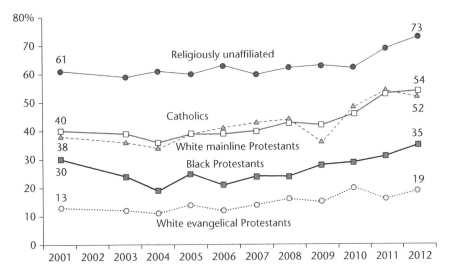

FIGURE 4.1 Views of Same-Sex Marriage by Religious Affiliation.

Source: Aggregated data from Pew Research Centre polls conducted in each year.

these types of behaviors is to legislate morality, along the lines of virtue-based theories of justice. While this country has Judeo-Christian roots, our founding fathers went to great lengths to support both religious freedom and to hold separate the church and the state. Recall from Chapter 2 that our First Amendment right includes the phrase, "Congress shall make no law respecting an establishment of religion, or prohibiting the free exercise thereof." This separation of church and state was intentional. There was, and still is, a huge division of permissible behaviors between different religions and denominations. If the state and government were given free rein to legislate on morality, whose morality was to be used as the standard?

Our legal system, discussed at length in Chapter 3, is organized towards the end of removing the human dimension of morality and emotion so that disputes can be settled on logical grounds. As we saw in Chapter 3, it is the state that brings legal action against the defendant in the criminal justice system, and not the party that was wronged. Even so, all of the players involved—the officers, the lawyers, the judges, the victim, the family members of both parties, the jurors—are bringing into the courtroom their own set of morals and justice. For devout religious followers, it is not possible to separate the beliefs from the person. In essence, religion is the foundation for both their actions and reactions to how they view the world.

The Media

In an era of increasing technology and accessibility to instant news sources, the media's role as a provider of information has grown exponentially. While we often use the term *media* as if it were a single, collective group operating with one agenda, the media comprise thousands of different information sources. Much like society is in reality the combined opinions, beliefs and attitudes of individuals, media is the plural form of the word medium, which refers to a method of communicating entertainment or information. A *medium* can be television, the Internet, radio, newspapers, books, or any other communication source. With regard to sharing news and current events, people generally get their information from the *mass media*, which refers to information sources that communicate with large numbers of people.

One of the most important functions of the media is serving as a gatekeeper to decide which stories and issues receive attention. While the media generally cannot tell the general public what to think, they can focus their attention on what to think about. Part of this decision-making process is driven by profit (Bagdikian, 2004; Herman & Chomsky, 2002; McChesney, 2004). After all, the vast majority of media outlets are commercial ventures that generally make their money by selling advertising space. The more people visit a media outlet, the more people see the advertisements, the more profits are generated. Because of this, Americans are bombarded with constant messages reinforcing consumerism and other values consistent with free market libertarianism, often equating money and consumer goods with happiness.

According to the American Time Use Survey (2013) collected by the Bureau of Labor Statistics, Americans spend an average of 3.9 hours a day watching television and 3.8 hours a day online outside of work. That means that almost one third of every day (and half of our waking hours) is spent engaging with some type of media. With this much media consumption, it is easy to see how media can influence beliefs about different groups of people or support certain stereotypes.

One aspect of mass media that has received a fair amount of attention is the inherent biases of choosing to watch or subscribe to one media outlet over another. While media providers may claim to be unbiased or fair and balanced, this is often not the case. After all, someone at the outlet needs to make decisions about what the viewers will find interesting enough to read or watch. Stories don't write themselves so there is often a political leaning—to the right or the left—in both the nature of the stories that are picked up and in how those stories are written. As such, individuals tend to pick the media source that reinforces their personal beliefs and opinions. Further, certain media organizations are explicitly biased in favor and against particular political ideologies (e.g., Fox News in favor of Conservative and Republican ideologies) (Brock & Rabin-Havt, 2012).

The Government

In Chapter 2, we discussed the various documents that define our rights as American citizens. The United States *government* has the responsibility of supporting those rights, creating new laws and managing the welfare of all that live within our country's borders. When the United States government was created, it was designed in such a way that no one individual or group should be able to seize too much power. This division of power is also supported by the concept of *federalism*, which is shared power between states and the federal government; federalism makes realizing social justice more difficult, as in the case of states conflicting with the federal government over civil rights.

As illustrated by Table 4.1, the United States federal government is broken up into three branches: the Executive Branch, the Legislative Branch, and the Judicial Branch.

Each state also has a similar division of power with the Governor acting in an executive capacity and elected officials serving the role of House and Senate participants so that all parts of the state are represented. States also have an extensive court system that handles all state-level disputes. Almost all of the roles and laws outlined in Chapter 3, the criminal justice system, are handled on the state level.

TABLE 4.1 Branches of Government

The Executive Branch	The President of the United States is the elected leader of the executive branch of government. The President's responsibilities include acting as Commander-In-Chief of our military and running the government and its various agencies.
The Legislative Branch	Acting through Congress, the legislative branch of government creates and modifies laws. Congress is divided into the Senate and the House of Representatives. While each state has two elected Senators, their representation in the House of Representative varies by the population of each state.
The Judicial Branch	Comprised of the nation's extensive court system, the judicial branch of government is responsible for making sure that the rest of the government follows the law. Other duties include interpreting the United States Constitution and settling disputes between different groups of people. The United States Supreme Court has the final say regarding federal law and their decisions become law.

This is because most criminal statutes vary state to state. Offenders are most often arrested by local law enforcement, prosecuted by district attorneys and sentenced to correction or supervision with agencies that represent the county or state.

While government regulation spans all topics and areas, for the purposes of this chapter, the importance of the government as an entity is in the control and regulation of what behaviors are legal and illegal. Oftentimes, the behaviors that we criminalize disproportionately affect a particular group of people. For example, nowhere is this disparate treatment more clear than in the laws governing the possession of crack cocaine versus powder cocaine. The crack cocaine laws passed during the war on drugs era of the 1980s determined that an offender would have to possess 100 times the amount of powder cocaine to receive the same sentence as someone in possession of crack. The Anti-Drug Abuse Act of 1986, as well as other drug laws, was used to disproportionately target minority offenders who were the majority of the arrests for crack cocaine and contributed to the mass incarceration of young, black men (Mauer & Huling, 1995).

Interestingly, after literally decades of research and experience demonstrated racially disparate outcomes in drug sentencing, Congress was ultimately forced to modify the law, and in 2010 it passed the Fair Sentencing Act that eliminated five year mandatory sentences for possession of crack cocaine and reduced the sentencing disparity between crack cocaine and powder cocaine from 100:1 to 18:1. This serves as evidence that egalitarian values remain important to us. As we will see in the remainder of this book, the government is thus also the entity charged with correcting inequities once they have been discovered. Oftentimes, it takes a great deal of time and social pressure to balance such inequities.

The Economy

The *economy*, and those that control the distribution of it, is responsible for regulating the use and expenditure of material resources. While it is often said that we live in society rooted in *capitalism* where, according to Karl Marx (1867), a small group of people with vast resources (or capital) make the most important economic decisions, that is not entirely accurate. The United States economic structure is more accurately described as a *mixed economy*, with the government playing an important role alongside private enterprise. The most basic elements of our economic system are:

1. *Natural resources*—the resources available on and through American land, air, and water.
2. *Labor*—the individuals who turn natural resources into goods.
3. *Managers*—those responsible for coordinating labor efforts and responding to signals from global markets.
4. *Corporations*—the stockholders, or members, of a corporation provide the financial support to start businesses or expand current ones.

While the laws of supply and demand typically rule in a pure capitalist state, in a mixed economy, the government is primarily responsible for the administration of a number of industries, including the criminal justice system, education, national defense and infrastructure. Recall the purposes of the government according to the United States Constitution. In the US, the government controls important aspects of the economy such as interest rates and taxes, and it also provides welfare and unemployment benefits to individuals who are unable to support themselves and medical care for senior citizens and those who live in poverty. Now it is involved in the issue of access to health care in the form of the Patient Protection and Affordable Care Act (or "Obamacare").

The strength of the economy and the availability of jobs can heavily influence the other institutions. For example, when the economy is strong, there are more available taxes to provide support for schools and students. When the economy is weak and the unemployment rate rises, the number of people below the poverty line increases and there may be more stress on the family structure. Messner and Rosenfeld (1994) argue that pressure for individuals to succeed in their pursuit of the *American Dream* can cause a great deal of *strain* or frustration, which is known to be a source of crime. The *American Dream* places emphasis in this country on appearing successful through material possessions (e.g., a nice car, a nice house, designer clothes) and not on the process through which those goods are obtained (e.g., hard work, saving). The result is *anomie*, often defined as a sense of normlessness but in this case meaning a strain on the norm of law-abiding behavior. The bottom line is that, in the United States, our goals are driven by economic achievement. As such, the welfare of the economy dominates other social institutions, which are then forced to make accommodations based on the health and wealth of the US economy; this too is thought to be a source of crime (Robinson & Murphy, 2009).

It should be clear by now that every system in the institutional context is influenced by the other systems. Each of our institutions plays an important role in our societal structure, but they all seem to operate on the same wavelength. For example, when the economy is strong, the government appears to be productive and supportive, schools have adequate funds to fulfill their missions, families are employed and not reliant on assistance for food, and the media report on prosperity. When the economy is bad, it dominates the news headlines and a feeling of unease filters down to the most basic levels of our daily life; happiness even declines, as we showed in the last chapter.

Institutional Context and Categories of Difference

The institutions described are instrumental in creating and maintaining *categories of difference*. Much like a parent chooses whether or not to discipline a child, the government has the ability to discipline the choices and lifestyles of individuals. For example, the government determines the tax structure—how much of your income do you pay, who pays more, who pays less, and why. This directly impacts not only how much money people have left over after they pay taxes but also how they feel about what it is moral to pay for government services for oneself (e.g., roads, police and fire protection), for one's family (e.g., public education), and for others (e.g., social security, Medicare). Taxes today are at near-record lows and yet many people still feel over-taxed, especially free market libertarians.

Another example is marriage equality; when gay marriage is illegal in a particular state, it is clearly sending the message that same sex relationships are wrong, at least according to that state's law. Each of the institutions examined in this chapter informs society's *norms*—or the "expectations for behavior" of people living in a society. Norms are learned in interactions with others in our homes, schools, religious institutions, from the media, etc. From these sources we learn what behaviors are normal and which are not, including how to treat people like us as well as those who are different than us.

The Interpersonal and Internal Contexts

The next step is to identify how those norms affect us as individuals. At its core, the interpersonal context is defined by an individual's interactions with others. On a daily basis, individuals get feedback, both verbal and non-verbal, on what is desirable and "normal" or undesirable. This feedback can come from family and friends or from strangers that they come across randomly. This feedback from others is constant and can be about someone's appearance, speech, choice of friends or relationships, etc. It can be influenced by skin color or tone, sex, assumed sexual preference, age and a host of other defining characteristics that are visible to others.

Taking the feedback that is given in the interpersonal context and fusing with the lessons and norms put forth in institutional contexts, individuals internalize those values and beliefs. These internalized beliefs alter future behavior and begin to be the lens through which we all see the world. *Social construction theory* argues that what we know as *real* is the combined result of all of these interactions (Berger & Luckmann, 1966). These cultural products, or lessons, are then taken for granted and ultimately, taken for fact. For example, think of the dozen of stereotypes that might come to mind about different groups of people: Muslims are militant, Mexicans are here illegally, Asians are good at math, Jews are stingy, homosexuals wear pink, and the stereotypes go on and on. Ask yourself, what is the root of these stereotypes? Even if some individuals in any given group act according to these stereotypes, how do the actions of a few come to define an entire group of people?

Activity 4.2 Stereotypes

Do some research into common stereotypes in America.

Make a list of these stereotypes.

Then, discuss which of them you think are accurate and inaccurate, and why.

Most importantly, try to determine where you learned these stereotypes and where they emerged in the first place.

Figure 4.2 depicts how an individual is impacted by these different institutions, including the family, the education system, peer groups, religion, the media, the economy, and the government. The effects of any one institution will vary across the course of a person's life. For example, some will impact a person earlier in life beginning in infancy (such as families). Others will impact them a bit later in late childhood and adolescence (such as friends and the education system). Still others will impact people across the entire span of a person's life (such as the media, the economy, and the government). And others may or may not directly impact people, depending on how they are raised (such as religion). But the point is that we are impacted by all of these institutions at some point in our lives.

Only through critically analyzing what we think we *know* to be true and dissecting the history behind these truths can we start to deconstruct the prejudices and biases that are taken as fact. This is an important and necessary step because, sometimes, these biases and prejudices are the basis for the enactment of laws that affect us all. Now that we've discussed how lessons, beliefs and "reality" are created and shared, let's take a closer look at the history behind the social construction of race/ethnicity, social class, sex, gender, and sexual preference.

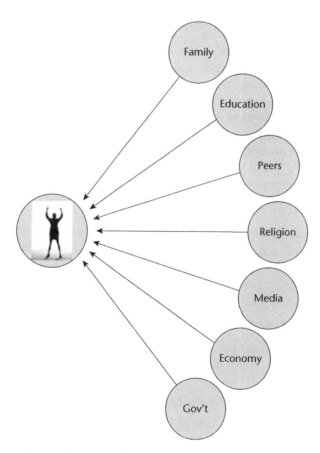

FIGURE 4.2 The Impact of Institutions on Individuals.

Social Construction of Race/Ethnicity

While race and ethnicity are often used as interchangeable terms, they are two distinct concepts. *Race* is a descriptive term using to refer to a group of people that share, or are perceived to share, common hereditary traits such as skin color, hair texture or eye shape. *Ethnicity* is more broadly defined as shared cultural traits like language, food, religion, customs and traditions (Ore, 2011). While there are distinct traits for eye shape, skin color and hair texture, these traits are entirely independent of each other. What that means is that scientists have established there is no genetic basis for race. Furthermore, there is more genetic differentiation within a local community than there is between different communities. In other words, two unrelated Russians are as unlikely to be genetically similar as a Japanese with a Russian. Sticking with this train of thought, it is also common knowledge in the scientific community that the trait for skin color is completely unrelated to athletic ability and intelligence.

So if intelligence and physical ability are not genetically determined by race, from where do our racial stereotypes arise? The answer to that question has a lot to do with the initial colonization of North America. The first piece of the puzzle rests in the relationship between European settlers and Native Americans. While this relationship will be covered in detail in Chapter 7, a primary point worth noting in the current chapter is that, once the settlers no longer needed to rely on the indigenous population for knowledge of food sources and general mapping of the topography of North America, they used the obvious physical and cultural differences between themselves and the indigenous population to support their belief that the Native Americans were a primitive and less evolved group. Following this justification, racial and ethnic differences were codified into law and used as the reasoning for taking lands away from the Native Americans and relocating them to the least desirable parts of the country. In other words, the law was used to inhibit equality and thus social justice, based on a category of difference created by white settlers.

If you'll recall from Chapter 2, one of the grievances filed in the Declaration of Independence was that England's government had "plundered our seas, ravaged our coasts, burnt our towns, and destroyed the lives of our people." These same charges could be levied at the Revolutionaries themselves when examining their relations with the Native American tribes. This contradiction offers a glimpse about how they viewed themselves as being worthy of better treatment while not giving the same consideration to the Native Americans.

Another part of the race puzzle deals with the settlers' initial reliance on slave labor to support the local economy. Keeping in mind that the purpose of the discovery of new lands was to produce agricultural goods for sale and trade, a large and competent labor force was perceived as a necessary part of colonization. The earliest American colonials used indentured servants for their labor needs, an obvious violation of libertarianism and social justice. In the system of *indentured servitude*, a laborer would make the journey to the Americas under contract and would be required to work for a set number of years before eventually earning his freedom (Higginbotham, 1980). This system was lucrative for the settlers because under the harsh conditions of the new world, the indentured servants rarely lived long enough to be free. While there were also slaves during these early years, the laws that governed them were few and far between and the only difference between the slaves and the indentured servants was that the slaves were under permanent contract.

Once both settlers and laborers became more comfortable with the means of survival in America, indentured servants began living long enough to earn their freedom and gain landholdings for themselves.

These newly freed servants shared interests and loyalty with the slaves instead of with the plantation owners from which they were freed. Tensions grew and in 1676, the event known as *Bacon's Rebellion* became a turning point for the codification of establishing difference races. Nathaniel Bacon, a wealthy Virginia landowner, was in conflict with William Berkeley, the governor of Virginia, over Indian relations and land rights in the western part of the colony. Bacon brought a small army to Jamestown, the colonial capital, and promised that he would grant freedom to the slaves and indentured servants who joined his assault on Jamestown.

While Bacon did fire and seize control of the colonial capital temporarily, his victory was short-lived and he died shortly thereafter. While his followers were executed, Bacon's tactics and the response from the labor class sent waves of panic to the wealthy plantation owners who realized that class rebellion and uprisings were very real possibilities. Combined with the reduced use of indentured servants (they were living too long to remain useful as a labor source) and the increased use of Africans as slaves, Virginia enacted a formal *slave code* to limit the rights, associations and mobility of the slaves. Between these laws and the use of Africans as slave labor, race emerged as a visible and tangible difference between landowners and those who were owned; all of this violates the major tenets of libertarianism, egalitarianism, and social justice.

The distinct physical appearance of the Africans, combined with their lack of command over European languages and non-Christian origins, began being used as a justification for their continued enslavement. After a number of generations, both the slaves born in the Americas and the landowners who *owned* them forgot their African heritage and both groups operated under the assumption that the institution of slavery was natural. The social history and circumstances that created the institution was forgotten and differences between races emerged as a hierarchy upon which the United States of America was created. And so it was that when the Declaration of Independence asserted that life, liberty and the pursuit of happiness was our natural and God-given right, the crafters of that famous document were primarily thinking of their own rights and not of every individual on North America soil (certainly not Native Americans and African slaves). That is, America was not truly founded on social justice principles of liberty and quality for all.

How We Measure Race Today

While immigrants have historically flocked to the United States from more than a hundred different countries, we typically measure race and ethnicity with five or six different designations seen in Table 4.2. This is primarily due to the creation and implementation of the US Census. In Article 1, Section 2 of the United States Constitution, it states:

> Representatives and direct Taxes shall be apportioned among the several States which may be included within this Union, according to their respective Numbers . . . The actual Enumeration shall be made within three Years after the first Meeting of the Congress of the United States, and within every subsequent Term of ten Years, in such Manner as they shall by Law direct.

And so, beginning in 1790, we began accruing a count of the people living in each state. As part of this counting process, we also recorded the sex, gender, and status (either free or slave) of each inhabitant.

Initially, the census considered only whites and non–whites, but, by 1890, the following instructions were included with the section on race:

> Write white, black, mulatto, quadroon, octoroon, Chinese, Japanese, or Indian, according to the color or race of the person enumerated. Be particularly careful to distinguish between blacks, mulattoes, quadroons, and octoroons. The word "black" should be used to describe those persons who have three-fourths or more black blood; "mulatto," those persons who have from three-eighths to five-eighths black blood; "quadroon," those persons who have one-fourth black blood; and "octoroon," those persons who have one eighth or any trace of black blood.

This process of categorization was important because, according to the *Three-Fifths Compromise* reached during the Philadelphia Convention, slaves were only considered three-fifths of a person for the purposes of taxation and representation. With such a historical precedence of ranking white males as the superior group, blacks, Hispanics and all other non-whites have been saddled with inferior treatment, negative stereotypes, and unequal treatment in the criminal justice system. Again, this history offers further support that the documents that we hold as progressive—the Declaration of Independence and the Constitution—were perhaps not meant to be equalizing and liberating, but instead were intended to secure the position of white, wealthy male landowners in this new republic.

Social Construction of Social Class

Social class is the term used to describe access to economic, social and/or lifestyle resources. Establishing the social class of any given individual is more complicated than simply adding up his or her income and wealth and comparing it to the poverty threshold, which is considered to be the official divide between the middle and lower classes. With that said, economic resources are an important indicator of social class and we will begin there.

TABLE 4.2 Definitions of Race and Ethnic Groups Measured in the United States

White	A person having origins in any of the original peoples of Europe, the Middle East, or North Africa
Black	A person having origins in any of the Black racial groups of Africa
American Indian or Alaska Native	A person having origins in any of the original peoples of North and South America (including Central America) and who maintains tribal affiliation or community attachment
Asian	A person having origins in any of the original peoples of the Far East, Southeast Asia, or the Indian subcontinent including, for example, Cambodia, China, India, Japan, Korea, Malaysia, Pakistan, the Philippine Islands, Thailand, and Vietnam
Native Hawaiian or Other Pacific Islander	A person having origins in any of the original peoples of Hawaii, Guam, Samoa, or other Pacific Islands

Source: The United States Census Bureau, http://www.census.gov/population/race/about/.

Economic Resources

Economic resources are often discussed in terms of income and wealth. *Income* is defined as money earned on a regular basis through work and investments whereas *wealth* is more broadly defined as the ownership of all property that has a monetary value (minus one's debt) (Yntema, 1933). To help illustrate the difference between the two, an individual can have a great deal of wealth, particularly in real estate, with no income of which to speak. Going back to the relationship between income and social class, the government regulates the poverty threshold, which, as previously stated, is the line of demarcation between the lower and middle-classes. According to the Federal Register, the poverty threshold is currently $23,550 for a family of four. The significance of this is that if you fall below this line, you are eligible for a number of benefits and assistance, some of which are explained in Table 4.3.

This figure of $23,550 is a source of debate because the formula for its creation was drafted in 1964. At the time of the original formulation, expenditures like transportation and childcare were not taken into account because they were not regular and reoccurring expenses for most families. Interestingly, the formula used for developing these thresholds and guidelines has not been modified to account for the changing lifestyles of Americans. As such, the individuals most affected by this threshold are those who fall just above it. They have neither the benefit of receiving assistance nor the monetary cushion of the true middle-class. This introduces the issue of whether or not Americans are able to earn a *living wage*, or the minimum amount necessary to pay for basic expenses, without using government assistance (Martin, 2001). An accurate calculation of a true living wage takes into consideration the variable cost of living in a particular city and estimates the hourly wage that an individual must earn to be able to survive without assistance. The living wage takes into account items such as childcare and transportation that were left off of the poverty threshold formulation.

Activity 4.3 Living Wage

Do some research into the "living wage."

Define it and discuss how it is measured.

Then, try to find out a living wage for your town or a nearby city.

Would it be possible to pay this living wage for everyone working full-time in your community, for every job?

What might it take to achieve this goal?

And is it worth it?
Explain.

Additionally, wealth in a capitalist society is a cumulative process—the more resources that individuals and groups have, the more wealth they can accumulate. In this sense, poverty is more often than not multi-generational. If someone's parents were born into poverty and died the same way, the subsequent

TABLE 4.3 Benefits for Individuals who Fall Below the Poverty Threshold

Department of Health and Human Services:

- Community Services Block Grant
- Head Start
- Low-Income Home Energy Assistance Program (LIHEAP)
- PARTS of Medicaid
- Hill-Burton Uncompensated Services Program
- AIDS Drug Assistance Program
- Children's Health Insurance Program
- Medicare – Prescription Drug Coverage (subsidized portion only)
- Community Health Centers
- Migrant Health Centers
- Family Planning Services
- Health Professions Student Loans — Loans for Disadvantaged Students
- Health Careers Opportunity Program
- Scholarships for Health Professions Students from Disadvantaged Backgrounds
- Job Opportunities for Low-Income Individuals
- Assets for Independence Demonstration Program

Department of Agriculture:

- Supplemental Nutrition Assistance Program (SNAP) (formerly Food Stamp Program)
- Special Supplemental Nutrition Program for Women, Infants, and Children (WIC)
- National School Lunch Program (for free and reduced-price meals only)
- School Breakfast Program (for free and reduced-price meals only)
- Child and Adult Care Food Program (for free and reduced-price meals only)
- Expanded Food and Nutrition Education Program
- Department of Energy:
- Weatherization Assistance for Low-Income Persons

Department of Labor:

- Job Corps
- National Farmworker Jobs Program
- Senior Community Service Employment Program
- Workforce Investment Act Youth Activities
- Department of the Treasury:
- Low-Income Taxpayer Clinics

Corporation for National and Community Service:

- Foster Grandparent Program
- Senior Companion Program

Legal Services Corporation:

- Legal Services for the Poor

generation is more likely to remain in poverty as well. In contrast, if a parent accumulated property or savings and passed that wealth onto the children, they have the ability to build on that wealth for the next generation if they decide to do so.

Social Resources

Income and wealth are not, however, the only indicators of social class. *Social resources* refer to the degree to which groups can exercise cultural authority or political influence (Ore, 2011). This is measured by the ability to shape popular consciousness through access to mass media, education, or other platforms of public communication found in the institutional context.

Probably the most important social resource indicator is *social capital*. *Social capital* refers to the connections within and between social networks (Routledge & Amsberg, 2002). With regard to gaining acceptance into a particular school or gaining employment in a competitive job market, *who* you know is sometimes more important than what you know. In this respect, social capital is an important dimension of social class because individuals in the middle and upper classes have social connections to people that can help individuals network.

Lifestyle Resources

Oftentimes, presumptions about the social class that someone belongs to are made solely based on how someone dresses or speaks. *Lifestyle resources* refer to the degree to which group-based patterns of behavior and belief are valued or devalued within our society (Ore, 2011). These lifestyle resources include styles of dress, modes of speech and even expressed attitudes and beliefs. Not all manners of dress and speech are equally valued in this society. Cohen (1955) coined the term *middle-class measuring rod* to describe the standard against which all youth are compared. Middle-class white children, who are considered well dressed, well spoken and well behaved, exemplify this standard. In other words, the less an individual looks, speaks and dresses like a middle-class white, the less likely he or she is to be given the same value in our society. There clearly remain many negative stereotypes about the poor in the US today; these stereotypes are passed down from generation to generation and tend to maintain categories of difference.

Social Construction of Sex and Gender

While sex, or the biological determination of being male or female at birth, seems like a cut and dried designation, the construction of gender is not nearly so concrete. *Gender* refers to the social roles expected of males and females and falls along a continuum with masculinity on one end and femininity on the other. As Judith Lorber describes:

> Most people find it hard to believe that gender is constantly created and re-created out of human interaction, out of social life, and is the texture and order of that social life. Yet gender, like culture, is a human production that depends on everyone constantly "doing gender."
>
> *(Lorber, 1994: 13)*

This process of "doing gender" begins from birth. From the color of a baby blanket to the piercing of infants' ears, from the name chosen to the style of dress—we are constantly giving social clues as to what gender both we and our offspring are. Similarly, boys and girls are encouraged to act in a manner consistent with their assigned gender. By encouraging girls to "act like a lady" or telling boys to "man up," we start the cycle of gender conditioning to make sure that those boys and girls grow up into men and women who know their social role. Much as we described earlier in this chapter, this process of conditioning involves three steps: learning what is expected, emulation of those ideals, and receiving enforcement (both positive and negative) for how well those expectations are met (Lorber, 1994).

The current gender stereotypes can be traced back to the beliefs about how women should act in the nineteenth century, which is considered the Victorian Era. Prior to the nineteenth century, the majority of people lived and worked on farms where both men and women contributed to the labor necessary to keep the farm operational. With the coming of the Industrial Revolution, men began working outside of the home and women remained at the homestead to manage the house and raise the children. This division of labor forced men and women to adapt to different environments and roles than they were accustomed to. As these new roles evolved, a new value system emerged which Barbara Welter (1966) dubbed "The Cult of Domesticity and True Womanhood." This new value system, which was outlined in great depth in both religious literature and women's magazines, stated that women should judge themselves on four cardinal virtues associated with femininity: piety, purity, submissiveness and domesticity.

The first virtue—*piety*—originated with the prevailing belief that women's tender sensibilities were more suited to religious studies. If a woman were pious, it would assist her in maintaining the second virtue, which was *purity*. *Virginity* was synonymous with femininity during the Victorian era and, while women were generally seen as being uninterested in sex, they were considered vulnerable to seduction. Interestingly, men were not considered nearly as pious or virtuous, but their association with a "True Woman" could elevate them in this regard (Welter, 1966). This insistence on the purity and subsequent monogamy of women is tied to reproduction. While women are 100 percent certain that the children they birth are their own, men have no such guarantees. Subsequently, the sexual activity of women, particularly outside of wedlock, was—and still is—often judged far more harshly than the promiscuity of men.

The third virtue of the Cult of True Womanhood was *submissiveness*. Women were expected to be timid, dependent on men and weak. Women were encouraged to seek out strong, forceful men to take the lead in the family group. The fourth virtue, *domesticity*, was intimately connected with submissiveness. Women were to be concerned with domestic affairs, which included making a home and raising children. Since the argument was that a "True Woman" embodied these four virtues, a woman who failed to do so was considered somehow less, spoiled and unfeminine.

So now the question is, are women still being measured against these standards or have we progressed beyond these narrow boundaries? Clearly, the social roles of men and women began to change in the 1960s. The *Women's Liberation Movement*, which will be described in detail in Chapter 9, made incredible strides towards increasing the relative value, power and worth of women both in the home and in the workplace. Today, women have a great deal more freedom than they did 200 years ago, but even so, structured gender roles do still exist.

It is important to point out that the gender roles themselves are not the issue. Instead, it is the relative value associated with each particular gender that is problematic. In a patriarchal society like the United States, the masculine archetype is still dominant over the feminine. That is to say masculine traits are valued over feminine ones. This is exemplified by the way that we see hegemonic masculinity portrayed in our cultural norms of what is acceptable. Women can wear pants, but men cannot wear skirts. Women can go without lipstick, but men cannot wear it. Girls can play with cars, but boys can't play with dolls. These social cues supporting this hierarchy can be seen in daily interactions. When a boy is told to "act like a man" or "stop running like a girl," the messages being sent are that girls are inferior and weak.

Much like in the situation of the *middle-class measuring rod* (where we encourage all members of society to speak, dress and act like our middle-class, white standard), everyone—males and females alike—is encouraged to exhibit masculine traits if they want to succeed. When you examine the work force, the most successful women are those who have mastered the balance of exhibiting desirable masculine traits, such as being non-emotional and strong, without crossing the line and being *too* masculine. In this sense, women have a broader range of gender that they can exhibit in a socially acceptable manner than men do. After all, if men exhibit a singular feminine attribute, such as crying or favoring the color pink—particular during their adolescence—they are likely to experience comments and bullying from their peers and possibly even their families. With that said, there is still a great deal of gender stereotyping with regard to which jobs and careers men and women fill. For example, the halls of lower-grade elementary schools are dominated by female teachers much like the halls of Congress are overwhelmingly filled with men.

When gender differences result in structural inequalities, women have less power, status and economic rewards than men (often for the same jobs). This inequality in power is clear when you examine how men dominate positions of authority and leadership in government, the criminal justice system, the military and religion. The combined message sent from all of these different examples of the gender power differential is that women are not seen as capable of being leaders.

Social Construction of Sexuality

There is great deal of overlap between our creation of gender roles and the perceived sexuality of individuals. As a society, we have historically recognized two sexual orientations: *straight* and *gay*. Even the term *straight* is indicative of society's general view of the rightness or wrongness of someone's sexual preference. If something is not straight, it is crooked, broken, bent. This imagery indicates that it's a condition that warrants fixing. In these two narrow designations of sexuality, we cast suspicion on anyone who has had a thought or interaction that was anything but purely heterosexual in nature. These rigid guidelines for our thoughts and feelings often lead to *alienation*, which is a sense of not fitting in with the greater community. Youth often go through a period of identity crisis where they are trying to figure out why they are having bad thoughts. This might also lead to *self-alienation*, which is a "hatred for one's own position and oneself" (Ore, 2011: 13).

The reality is that there are not just two sexual orientations. The *LGBT* (Lesbian, Gay, Bisexual, Transgender) community has been battling dogmatic beliefs about sexuality in the United States since the 1950s. While homosexuality has been seen in cultures worldwide since the beginning of documented history, it did not receive much attention in a formal sense until the nineteenth century. While some countries, such as England, were less tolerant of various sexual orientations, other great powers were relatively open and supportive, such as Germany. The famous psychotherapist Sigmund Freud was sympathetic to the natural occurrence of homosexuality and bisexuality and the scientist Magnus Hirschfield founded Berlin's Institute for Sexual Science. The Institute was Europe's best resource for materials on gay culture and history, but it was burned down during the Nazi regime in 1933.

While the history of the LGBT community in the United States varies by region and urbanity, it wasn't until Senator Joseph McCarthy's inquest in the 1950s into homosexual federal employees that sexuality took center stage. Senator McCarthy, best known for his witch-hunt for communists within American borders, was convinced that the "homosexual underground" was assisting the communist cause. These accusations moved gay federal employees to the top of the national agenda. President Eisenhower, who ran his campaign on an agenda of eradicating communists and strengthening national security, signed Executive Order 10450 in 1953, which prohibited the employment of gays and lesbians by the federal government. This began an era of open discrimination against gays and lesbians who took to the court system to try and gain equal rights. This battle is still ongoing and will be discussed in further detail in Chapter 10.

Within this category of difference, we again see that one group—*heterosexuals*—is valued above all others. Particularly within certain branches of the religious community, homosexuality is looked upon as an abomination and a sin. While there is evidence that sexual preference is as much a part of the individual as eye color or hair color, in a large number of communities, it is still unacceptable in many parts of the country to be openly gay. In broader American society, recent public opinion polls show that a majority of Americans see homosexuality *not* as a lifestyle choice but instead "just the way people are." A majority of Americans are also now not only tolerant of homosexuality but also supportive of gay marriage; support is highest among the young and Democrats and the lowers among the older and Republicans.

What Is the Purpose of Creating Categories of Difference?

You may be asking yourself, what could be the purpose of a campaign to convince women that they need to seek out four virtues to be considered "True Women?" Or to create an arbitrary definition of what it means to be poor? Or to institutionalize a system of slavery where an entire group of people is born into a class of powerless laborers? Or to devalue relationships that aren't explicitly between a man and a woman? The answer lies in the need to create a *negative ideology*, or false consciousness (Marx, 1866). You'll recall that, earlier, we defined *ideology* as a set of beliefs and values about the way the world ought to be and the way that individuals ought to act. Negative ideology is when this set of beliefs is created in an effort to hide the essence of what the power structure in society really is, which is beneficial to the ruling class at the time.

The crux of a successful negative ideology is getting the citizenry to buy into the ideology being presented as reality. For example, if African Americans think it is their natural position to remain enslaved, they will not rebel. If poor people believe it is their fault that they live in poverty, they will not make demands on government or business for help. If women believe that they are naturally weak, submissive, and that their position is in the home, they will not seek out education and gainful employment. And so forth.

Today, where slavery is no longer legal or practiced within the US, what is relevant is the larger issue of how people of color—including African Americans and Latinos—are seen by those who hold on to negative ideologies about race and ethnicity. Further, how are poor people, women, and homosexuals perceived by those who hold on to negative ideologies about class, gender, and sexuality? Evidence exists that significant institutions in society, including lawmaking and the media, produce negative ideologies about relatively powerless groups in society, thereby serving the interests of those in power (Reiman & Leighton, 2013). This is a major barrier to realizing social justice, one that will be revisited throughout the rest of the book.

You will notice that the process of negative ideology set the stage for allowing the ruling class of the 1700s—the white, male landowners—to remain mostly unchallenged in their seat of power. Interestingly, these same people still rule today, and they do this by making the law, owning and operating the mainstream media, running major corporations, etc. (Robinson, 2011).

Why the Social Construction of Difference Matters in the Criminal Justice System

We've established that social justice examines issues of equality and inequality in society and that, for social justice theorists, the pursuit of justice is often the pursuit of equal treatment. Turning our attention now to the criminal justice system, social justice theorists ask whether there are either systematic inequalities and/or discriminatory behaviors present in the criminal justice system with regard to race, ethnicity, social class, gender, or sexuality.

There has been extensive debate among scholars over the better part of the last century as to whether discrimination exists in the criminal justice system. Part of the contentiousness of this debate may have more to do with the breadth of the term *discrimination* and the many ways that it could potentially be manifested in the criminal justice system. *Discrimination*, or the differential treatment of individuals based on a physical or non-physical attribute that they possess, comes in many forms with varying degrees of seriousness. Walker, Spohn, and DeLone (2012) offer four types of discrimination potentially present in every society. They are shown in Table 4.4.

Regardless of the source or type of inequality present in our society, its mere existence indicates that we are not living in a just society. The fact remains that our perception of different sub-groups of people fundamentally alters how they are perceived and processed by the criminal justice system. What makes the criminal justice system and its actors unique from the other institutions discussed is that it operates in a manner that allows *discretion*. *Discretion* is defined as the ability of people to act according to their own professional judgment (Goldstein, 1960). What this means is that there is the possibility for a criminal justice professional's own code of morality (i.e., what behaviors and actions are right and what behaviors and actions are wrong) to influence their decisions at work.

There are dozens of ways that morality and judgment may interject into the criminal justice system. From the decision to criminalize certain behaviors over others, to deciding which individuals to pull over, to choosing which cases are prosecuted and with what offenses, there is a large margin of personal discretion present in all branches of the criminal justice system. As a result, the values we assign to different groups of people based on their race, ethnicity, sex, gender or other defining attributes have very real implications for how those groups are treated. When examining the intersection of criminal justice and social justice, we must keep going back to the following questions:

TABLE 4.4 Types of Discrimination

Systematic	Discrimination at all stages of the criminal justice system, at all times and places
	e.g., when a particular race, gender, age, ethnicity, or lifestyle group encounters discrimination in every stage of the criminal justice process, in every part of the country, and without variation
Intitutionalized	Racial and ethnic disparities in outcomes that are the result of the application of racially neutral factors such as prior criminal record, employment status, demeanor, etc.
	e.g., when courts sentence people to longer sentences because they commit more serious crimes (which is determined by the law) and have longer criminal records (which is determined by the police)
Contextual	Discrimination found in particular contexts or circumstances
	e.g., when African Americans and poor people are sentenced more harshly at the federal level for drug offenses; when killers of whites are sentenced more harshly than killers of people of color
Individual	Discrimination that results from the acts of particular individuals but is not characteristic of entire agencies or the criminal justice system as a whole
	e.g., when a racist police officer or prosecutor plants or fabricates evidence to convict someone because he is presumed guilty based on the color of his skin

Source: Walker, Spohn, and DeLone (2012).

- What makes a fair, just and equitable society?
- When an injustice is detected, how do we fix it?
- Are there systematic inequalities or discriminatory behaviors that lead to unequal benefits, which can in turn lead to injustices?
- How large a role do stereotypes and prejudices play in our creation of the law?

Only through critically analyzing and reanalyzing our laws can we move towards the goal of achieving a just society. The remaining chapters in this section will do just that in an effort to outline the history of how our law has been used both to maintain oppression and to examine how we have corrected some of these inequities over time, each of which has clear social justice implications.

Summary

Americans often think of our society as a living and breathing entity all of its own. People frequently begin their commentary with phrases such as, "society thinks . . . " or "American culture says . . . " but what do they really mean by this? In this chapter, we analyzed the different contexts that comprise what we think we know to be true and how we have learned these societal and cultural messages. From the many institutions in our lives to how we internalize these messages, we're left with a belief system that we accept as fact.

Digging beneath the surface of these facts, we briefly touched on the history that contributed to the creation of the categories of difference that still exist today. From the roots of slavery and the creation of social class, from the tenets of being a "True Woman" to the vilification of homosexuality—creating and maintaining categories of difference has very real consequences for us all. These social facts have implications from what behaviors are criminalized to who is prosecuted in the criminal justice system.

Discussion Questions

1. What is social stratification?
2. Define the term essentialism. After reading the chapter, is America socially stratified and is this maintained by any hegemonic beliefs?
3. What is the institutional context of categories of difference in the US?
4. Identify and define seven categories of difference in the US.
5. Define the family and discuss its role in helping to establish beliefs of children.
6. Define the educational system and discuss its role in helping to establish beliefs of children.
7. Define peer groups and discuss their role in helping to establish beliefs of children.
8. Define religion and discuss its role in helping to establish beliefs of children.
9. What is meant by the term ideology in the context of religion?
10. What is the media and how does it impact the beliefs of people in society?
11. What is the government and what role does it take in impacting the beliefs of people in society?
12. Define federalism and the three major branches of government in the US.
13. Define economy and discuss whether America has a capitalist economy or a mixed economy.
14. How does the economy produce anomie and strain?
15. What is a norm? Provide an example. How do norms impact our behaviors?
16. What is race? Ethnicity? How are these concepts socially constructed?
17. What is social class? How is this concept socially constructed?
18. Define economic resources, and contrast income with wealth.
19. What is a living wage?
20. Define social resources and social capital.
21. What are lifestyle resources?
22. Contrast sex and gender and discuss how these concepts are socially constructed.
23. Identify and discuss four cardinal virtues associated with femininity.
24. Contrast the sexual orientations of straight and gay. How are these concepts socially constructed?
25. What is negative ideology and what role does it play in helping to maintain categories of difference in society?
26. What is discrimination? List and define the major types of discrimination that can occur in criminal justice.
27. What is discretion? How can it lead to abuse in criminal justice?

References

Akers, R. L. (1998). *Social Learning and Social Structure: A General Theory of Crime and Deviance.* Boston: Northeastern University Press.

Bagdikian, B. (2004). *The New Media Monopoly.* Boston: Beacon Press.

Berger, P., & Luckmann, T. (1966). *The Social Construction of Reality: A Treatise in the Sociology of Knowledge.* Garden City, NY: Doubleday.

Brock, D., & Ravin-Havt, A. (2012). *The Fox Effect: How Roger Ailes Turned a Network into a Propaganda Machine.* New York: Anchor Books.

Brown, S., Esbensen, F., & Geis, G. (2007). *Criminology: Explaining Crime and its Context.* New York: Routledge.

Bureau of Labor Statistics. (2013). *American Time Use Survey* [press release]. Retrieved from http://www.bls.gov/news.release/pdf/atus.pdf.

Cillessen, A., & Mayeux, L. (2004). From Censure to Reinforcement: Developmental Changes in the Association Between Aggression and Social Status. *Child Development, 75*(1), 147–163.

Cohen, A. (1955). *Delinquent Boys: The Culture of the Gang*. Glencoe, Ill: Free Press.

Goldstein, Joseph (1960). *Police Discretion Not to Invoke the Criminal Process: Low-Visibility Decisions in the Administration of Justice*. Faculty Scholarship Series. Paper 2426. Retrieved from http://digitalcommons.law.yale.edu/fss_papers/2426.

Grewal, I. (2006). *An Introduction to Women's Studies: Gender in a Transnational World* (2nd ed.). Boston: McGraw-Hill Higher Education.

Herman, E., & Chomsky, N. (2002). *Manufacturing Consent: The Political Economy of the Mass Media*. New York: Pantheon Books.

Higginbotham, A. (1980). *In the Matter of Color: The Colonial Period*. New York: Oxford University Press.

Hofferth, S., & Sandberg, J. (2001). How American Children Spend Their Time. *Journal of Marriage and Family, 63*(2), 295–308.

Kiesner, J., Cadinu, M., Poulin, F., & Bucci, M. (2002). Group Identification in Early Adolescence: Its Relation with Peer Adjustment and its Moderator Effect on Peer Influence. *Child Development, 73*, 196–208.

Kohl, H. (1991). *I Won't Learn from You: The Role of Assent in Learning*. Minneapolis, Minn: Milkweed Editions.

Lorber, J. (1994). *Paradoxes of Gender*. New Haven, CT: Yale University Press.

Martin, I. (2001). Dawn of the Living Wage: The Diffusion of a Redistributive Municipal Policy. *Urban Affairs Review, 36*, 470–496.

Marx, K. (1867). *Capital: A Critique of Political Economy*. Oxford, UK: Oxford University Press.

Marx, K. (1866). *Capital Volume One: A Critique of Political Economy*. New York: Dover Publications.

Marx, K., & Engels, F. (1848). *Manifesto of the Communist Party*. New York: International.

Mauer, M., & Huling, T. (1995). *Young Black Americans and the Criminal Justice System: Five Years Later. The Sentencing Project*. Retrieved from http://www.sentencingproject.org/doc/publications/rd_youngblack_5yrslater.pdf.

McChesney, R. (2004). *The Problem of the Media: U.S. Communication Politics in the Twenty-First Century*. New York: Monthly Review Press.

Meldrum, R., Miller, H., & Flexon, J. (2013). Susceptibility to Peer Influence, Self-Control, and Delinquency. *Sociological Inquiry, 83*(1), 106–129.

Messner, S., & Rosenfeld, R. (1994). *Crime and the American dream* (2nd ed.). Belmont, CA: Wadsworth Pub.

Mill, J. (1859). *On Liberty*. London: Longman, Roberts & Green.

Miller, S., Malone, P., & Dodge, K. (2010). Developmental Trajectories of Boys' and Girls' Delinquency: Sex Differences and Links to Later Adolescent Outcomes. *Journal of Abnormal Child Psychology, 38*(7), 1021–1032.

Mills, C. (1959). *The Sociological Imagination*. New York: Oxford University Press.

Ore, T. (2011). *The Social Construction of Difference and Inequality: Race, Class, Gender, and Sexuality* (2nd ed.). Boston, MA: McGraw-Hill.

Reiman, J., & Leighton, P. (2013). *The Rich Get Richer and the Poor Get Prison: Ideology, Class and Criminal Justice* (10th ed.). New York: Wiley.

Robinson, M. (2011). *Media Coverage of Crime and Criminal Justice*. Durham, NC: Carolina Academic Press.

Robinson, M., & Beaver, K. (2009). *Why Crime?: An Interdisciplinary Approach to Explaining Criminal Behavior* (2nd ed.). Durham, NC: Carolina Academic Press.

Robinson, M., & Murphy, D. (2009). *Greed is Good: Maximization and Elite Deviance in America*. Lanham, MA: Rowman & Littlefield.

Routledge, B., & Amsberg, J. (2002). Social Capital and Growth. *Journal of Monetary Economics, 50*(1), 167–193.

Sutherland, E., & Cressey, D. (1974). *Criminology* (9th ed.). Philadelphia: Lippincott.

Tracy, A. (1817). *A Treatise on Political Economy: To Which is Prefixed a Supplement to a Preceding Work on the Understanding, or Elements of Ideology: With an Analytical Table and an Introduction on the Faculty of the Will*. Georgetown, DC: Joseph Milligan.

Trucco, E., Colder, C., & Wieczorek, W. (2011). Vulnerability To Peer Influence: A Moderated Mediation Study of Early Adolescent Alcohol Use Initiation. *Addictive Behaviors*, (36), 729–736.

Walker, S., Spohn, C. & DeLone, M. (2004). *The Color of Justice: Race, Ethnicity and Crime in America* (3rd ed.). Belmont, CA: Thomson/Wadsworth. Retrieved October 5, 2009, from University of Phoenix, CJA423-Culturual Diversity in Criminal Justice rEsource website.

Welter, B. (1966). The Cult of True Womanhood: 1820–1860. *American Quarterly*, *18*(2), 151–174.

Yntema, D. (1933). Measures of the Inequality in the Personal Distribution of Wealth or Income. *Journal of the American Statistical Association*, *28*(184), 423–433.

5

RACE, ETHNICITY, AND SOCIAL JUSTICE

I wish I could say that racism and prejudice were only distant memories. We must dissent from the indifference. We must dissent from the apathy. We must dissent from the fear, the hatred and the mistrust . . . We must dissent because America can do better, because America has no choice but to do better.

Thurgood Marshall, 1992

In Chapter 4, we explained how race was a social myth rather than a biological determinant. While being different in society is not inherently bad, race and ethnicity in our society were constructed in such a manner that made racial and ethnic minorities not only different from European Americans, but ultimately seen as less than them as well. In this chapter, we will examine two things: (1) how the law has been used to codify oppression of people of color; and (2) how we have over time made strides to remedy this grievance.

As the Honorable Thurgood Marshall asserted in his quote above, we must acknowledge how fear and mistrust of those different from society's elite lead to oppressive legislation and, more importantly, we must continue to make strides to remedy the issue of racial and ethnic inequality that has wormed its way so deeply into our collective conscience. This chapter illustrates that, while America has made progress toward achieving social justice, we still have some way to go before American practice matches our ideals.

Minority Group Membership

Table 5.1 illustrates the racial and ethnic composition of the US in 2012. As you can see, whites make up a large majority of all Americans, at 77.9 percent of the population. African Americans make up 13 percent of the population, and Hispanics make up 16.9 percent of the population.

This chapter will cover three different racial and ethnic minority groups—blacks, Latinos, and Native Americans—but before we begin, let's address the use of the term *minority group*. A minority

TABLE 5.1 Demographics of the US Population

White	77.9%
White alone (not Hispanic)	63.0%
African American	13.1%
Asian	5.1%
American Indian/Alaska Native	1.2%
Native Hawaiian/Pacific Islander	0.2%
Two or more races	2.4%

Source: Data from the United States Census Bureau, http://quickfacts.census.gov/qfd/states/00000.html.

group is not determined by what percentage of society they comprise—they can be outnumbered by the dominant group members and often are. Instead, *minority group* refers to a distinct racial or ethnic group that has significantly less power or privilege than the members of the dominant or majority group (Schaeffer, 2011). Schaeffer names five characteristics that define whether a group is a minority. They are shown in Table 5.2.

The primary problem with having a dominant group in dialectic with minority groups is that the process of *socially constructing* race clearly benefits the dominant group members as they are the catalysts that define who is privileged and who is not (Schaeffer, 2011). Here, the classic criminological theory *culture conflict* is relevant. Thorsten Sellin (1938) posited that different groups in society often have different *conduct norms*, or expectations for behavior that specify how one behaves in given situations. Two unique cultures will often conflict over different conduct norms, resulting in *primary cultural conflicts*. Additionally, different subcultures within a heterogeneous culture such as America will often disagree about what behaviors are normal and which are abnormal, resulting in *secondary cultural conflicts*. When it comes to race, it is generally the "white race" that determines which conduct norms are reflected in the laws, thereby creating advantages for whites and disadvantages for people of color. A significant example shown in Chapter 3 was that it is largely whites who make and fund the criminal law (and own the mainstream media).

While it is true that there are many different personality and behavioral differences between people, the danger lies in associating specific personality or mental characteristics with distinct physical characteristics. This process of assuming that a person who looks a certain way will act a certain way is the core of *stereotyping* (Ore, 2011). *Stereotypes* are generalizations about all members of any given group without allowing for individual differences. Generally speaking, stereotypes come about when a specific subset of a group act in a certain way. For example, while only a small percentage of Latinos working in this country are here illegally, the generalization becomes that if someone comes across a manual laborer speaking Spanish, he must be an illegal immigrant. Similarly, some feminists identify as homosexual and this fact is generalized into "all feminists are gay."

Taking stereotyping one step further, *prejudice* involves negative attitudes, beliefs and thoughts about an entire group of people (Fiske, 1998). When dealing specifically with racial and ethnic minorities, *racism* is when these implied differences lead someone to believe that a minority group member is inferior to a majority group member. Finally, when prejudice and racism are acted upon, this is called *discrimination*, and obviously discrimination is a threat to equality and social justice. To connect each of these terms about racial groups, stereotypes about racial groups often lead to racism, and ultimately

TABLE 5.2 Characteristics of Minority Groups

1. *Unequal treatment.* Members of minority groups often have fewer opportunities for education, wealth, success, and power than members of dominant groups. They also have less power over their own lives. This is primarily due to discrimination, prejudice, segregation, and isolation, which perpetuate social, economic, and political inequality.

2. *Distinguishing physical or cultural traits.* Minority group members possess physical traits (skin color, hair texture, eye shape) or cultural traits (language, religion) that differentiate them from members of the dominant group. The distinguishing characteristics that are most important in defining dominant group membership are unique to each society and are further mediated by time and place.

3. *Involuntary membership.* An individual cannot choose whether he or she belongs to a dominant or minority group. Instead, people are involuntarily born into the group.

4. *Awareness of subordination.* Members of minority groups are aware of their level of "otherness" from the dominant group. They have a strong sense of solidarity within the group and the longer the prejudice and discrimination continues, the more concrete their feeling of outsider status.

5. *In-group marriage.* Primarily, in-group marriage occurs because a member of the dominant group does not want to decrease their social status by joining themselves with a member of the minority group. Secondly, minority group members are encouraged to marry within their own group to maintain the social solidarity of the group.

Source: Schaeffer (2011).

discrimination. Thus, eliminating prejudice, racism, and discrimination will likely require overcoming stereotypes pertaining to different races.

African Americans and the Law

You'll recall that, in Chapter 4, we discussed the process of colonization that created the link between slavery and race that was unique to America. This association of viewing blacks as *chattel*, or property, started our country down a path of systematic and institutionalized discrimination. What we will see as this chapter unfolds is that this discrimination shifted from overt to covert means, particularly with regard to our legislation. That is to say that, while we have historically discriminated against others explicitly, discrimination today is often masked or couched in less obvious ways. We will also show how progress is rarely linear. It ebbs and flows; gains ground and loses it. Without further ado, let's begin our look into the institution of slavery because, in essence, it has defined the relationship between whites and blacks for centuries.

Slavery

While most people associate slavery with the South—which, by 1830, was the primary region of the country that relied on slavery—some of the first colonies to legalize slavery were actually in the North. Massachusetts became the first colony to legalize the institution of slavery in 1641 and was followed by Connecticut in 1650 and New York and New Jersey in 1664 (Meltzer, 1993). While the most common depiction of slave labor is that of working large plantations, slaves were used on small farms, cities big and small, inside homes and for transportation (Clinton, 1982). Once it was codified into law, slavery was a clearly delineated institution of labor and, while it took many forms, the root conditions were the same.

Noel (1972) outlined the five basic tenets that defined the institution of slavery. First and foremost, slavery was a permanent condition. A person born into slavery was considered a slave regardless of where he traveled. Second, the status of slave was inherited through the maternal line—if a mother was a slave, her children were also considered slaves regardless of who fathered them. This condition was to protect the landowners who impregnated their slaves from having to claim or provide for their offspring. Third, slaves were property of their owners. As such, slave owners could do pretty much whatever they wanted to their slaves. This included punishment and, on a rare occasion, death. Fourth, slaves were not afforded rights. As we will discuss shortly, *slave codes* dictated every aspect of a slave's life from whether they could marry to where they could travel. Fifth and finally, the system of slavery was maintained through coercion, for it was not only slaves who were punished, but also whites that spoke out against the institution of slavery or dared to educate their slaves (Aptheker, 1951).

If you'll recall from Chapter 4, Bacon's Rebellion of 1676 led to stricter slave codes, which primarily emerged to protect landowners from a slave rebellion. While *slave codes*, or laws that dictated the behavior of slaves, varied from state to state—and from year to year—they all shared some similar restrictions. Table 5.3 shows examples of some of those restrictions.

The most common method of dealing with an infraction was whipping, but mutilation and branding were not unheard of (Franklin & Moss, 1994). The adherence to the slave codes became even tighter if there was even a whisper of a slave insurrection. The insurrection—either rumored or real—was often met by white vigilante groups that set out to quell any thoughts of rebellion in the area (Schaeffer, 2011).

In Chapter 4, we discussed the role of religion as an institution through which values and beliefs were taught. During the time of slavery, the slaves were allowed to practice Christianity. We know through the writings of W. E. B. Du Bois (Wilson, 1970) that it was a type of Christianity that stressed obedience to their owners and reward in the afterlife for this steadfast obedience. In contrast, questioning the institution of slavery, or God's will, would almost certainly result in eternal damnation. By communicating to slaves that "the harder the cross, the brighter the crown," owners were in effect encouraging slaves to embrace their hardships and suffering towards a greater reward in the afterlife

TABLE 5.3 Slave Codes

1. A slave cannot enter into a contract of any kind (including marriage)
2. A slave cannot legally buy or sell anything except by special arrangement of their owner
3. A slave cannot speak harshly to or squabble with whites
4. A slave cannot leave a plantation without documentation of their destination and time of return
5. A slave must abide by established curfews
6. A slave cannot participate in gambling
7. A slave cannot possess property except as warranted by their owner
8. A slave is barred from learning to read or write
9. A slave cannot own a book (including the bible)
10. A slave cannot possess weapons or liquor
11. A slave cannot testify in a court of law except against another slave
12. Slaves cannot gather without a white present

Source: Wilson (1970).

(Jones, 1998). Figure 5.1 illustrates a slave code from the state of Alabama. As you see, this slave code was simply a part of the state law, a law that flies in the face of today's conceptions of social justice (but that was justified by a virtue-based conception of social justice in nineteenth-century America).

It should be obvious that the practice of slavery is inconsistent with the ideals on which America was founded. That is, it did not promote liberty and thus is inconsistent with libertarianism. It was also clearly unequally applied based on race, making it inconsistent with egalitarianism. Thus, slavery clearly violated the major principles of John Rawls's theory of *justice as fairness* as well as David Miller's *pluralistic theory of justice* reviewed in Chapter 1. That is, the practice of slavery stands in direct opposition to *equal liberties*, *equal opportunities*, the *difference principle*, as well as *equality* in matters of citizenship.

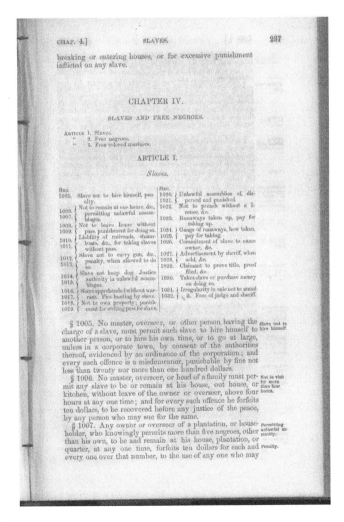

FIGURE 5.1 Slave Codes.

And even though slavery violates our sense of virtue now, it was not ultimately seen as without virtue at the time, which explains why many of America's founders owned slaves! This, of course, does not mean that slavery offered only negatives to the country. In fact, there is the argument that, without slavery, the country could not have been fully economically developed. Thus, some may argue that the practice of slavery contributed to the overall happiness of the country and therefore might be justified based on utilitarian principles. But this does not change the fact that it violates our contemporary preferences for liberty and equality.

Abolition

By the end of the American Revolution, slavery was on the decline in the North. As Revolutionaries demanded the right to life, liberty, and the pursuit of happiness, they were forced to more closely examine their own actions of enslaving others while seeking a free society. The Declaration of Independence not only freed the colonies from Britain, it also served as the catalyst for social change in the North. Vermont became the first state to abolish slavery in its 1777 state constitution. By 1804, every Northern state had voted to abolish slavery. The process of making emancipation a reality was gradual and slaves were released from bondage when they reached a specific age or the end of a work cycle. The end of the slavery era in the North was a trigger, though certainly not the only one, of the onset of the Civil War.

Meanwhile, resistance to slavery in the South came in two forms: criticisms from the outside and rebellion from the slaves themselves. Approximately 40,000 to 100,000 slaves escaped from the South. While some slaves found their own way to freedom, others were assisted by the famed *Underground Railroad*, which comprised a network of abolitionists who helped slaves once they made it as far as a free state. *Abolitionists*, or those individuals who advocated against slavery, included both whites and free blacks. Antislavery societies had been active since before the American Revolution, but the language included in the United States Constitution severely limited the Abolitionists' ability to fight slavery through the courts. As was discussed in Chapter 4, a slave was only counted as three-fifths of a person in calculating the population for appropriate representation in the House of Representatives. While this three-fifths compromise was primarily written in to appease the South, it legitimized slavery as an acceptable institution in the fledgling United States of America.

The fight against slavery was further hampered by the Supreme Court's ruling in the 1857 case of *Dred Scott v. Sanford*. Dred Scott was an army surgeon's slave who had left Missouri to live in Illinois and Wisconsin, both free states/territories, for several years. Upon his return to Missouri, where slavery was still legal, Scott sued for his freedom on the grounds that he had been living in free lands for an extended period of time. Unfortunately for Scott and others like him, the Supreme Court ruled that traveling through free states—for however long—did not make him free once he returned to a slave state. Further, since Scott was a black man, he was excluded from United States citizenship and could not exercise the amendments that would allow him to bring suit.

As it was explained in the Supreme Court opinion, blacks had not been part of the "Sovereign People" who drafted the Constitution. As such, they were not entitled to protection under the US Constitution. What's more, the Court also ruled that Congress did not and does not have the right to prohibit slavery in any territory since any such ban was a violation of the Fifth Amendment, which prohibits denying property rights without due process of law. This was a damning blow to the fight against slavery, but it was not a surprising verdict given that five of the nine Justices on the Supreme Court had been slave owners prior to their appointment.

The Dred Scott case served to further divide the states and territories and caused tension between politicians struggling with the interpretation of both the Declaration of Independence and the US Constitution. Abraham Lincoln was one such politician and approximately three years before he was elected the sixteenth President of the United States, he had this to say in response to the Supreme Court's ruling on Dred Scott:

> Chief Justice Taney, in his opinion in the Dred Scott case, admits that the language of the Declaration is broad enough to include the whole human family, but he and Judge Douglas argue that the authors of that instrument did not intend to include negroes, by the fact that they did not at once, actually place them on an equality with the whites. Now this grave argument comes to just nothing at all, by the other fact, that they did not at once, or ever afterwards, actually place all white people on an equality with one or another. And this is the staple argument of both the Chief Justice and the Senator, for doing this obvious violence to the plain unmistakable language of the Declaration. I think the authors of that notable instrument intended to include all men, but they did not intend to declare all men equal in all respects. They did not mean to say all were equal in color, size, intellect, moral developments, or social capacity. They defined with tolerable distinctness, in what respects they did consider all men created equal—equal in "certain inalienable rights, among which are life, liberty, and the pursuit of happiness." This they said, and this meant. They did not mean to assert the obvious untruth, that all were then actually enjoying that equality, nor yet, that they were about to confer it immediately upon them. In fact they had no power to confer such a boon. They meant simply to declare the right, so that the enforcement of it might follow as fast as circumstances should permit. They meant to set up a standard maxim for free society, which should be familiar to all, and revered by all; constantly looked to, constantly labored for, and even though never perfectly attained, constantly approximated, and thereby constantly spreading and deepening its influence, and augmenting the happiness and value of life to all people of all colors everywhere. The assertion that "all men are created equal" was of no practical use in effecting our separation from Great Britain; and it was placed in the Declaration, not for that, but for future use. Its authors meant it to be, thank God, it is now proving itself, a stumbling block to those who in after times might seek to turn a free people back into the hateful paths of despotism. They knew the proneness of prosperity to breed tyrants, and they meant when such should re-appear in this fair land and commence their vocation they should find left for them at least one hard nut to crack.
>
> *(Lincoln, June 26, 1857)*

And so it became that while the outbreak of the Civil War in 1861 began as a struggle to preserve the Union and not as a battle over the preservation of slavery, many in both the North and the South saw it as a means of settling both issues. Fortunately for those enslaved, the North prevailed and on December 6, 1865—a mere eight months after the end of the Civil War—the United States passed and adopted the *Thirteenth Amendment* to the Constitution, which outlawed the institution of slavery.

Although the Civil War did not end until 1865, President Lincoln issued the *Emancipation Proclamation* in 1863 (depicted in Figure 5.2). While it did not free any slaves—since the Confederate Army still had

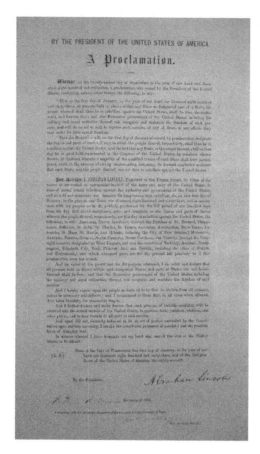

FIGURE 5.2 Emancipation Proclamation.

control of the slave states—it was a promise of what was to come after the Union was reformed. It also served as evidence that America in practice was becoming more consistent with its ideals of liberty and equality specified in the Declaration of Independence and the US Constitution.

The period immediately following the Civil War was called the *Reconstruction* period. The purpose of the Reconstruction was to bridge the differences between the North and South and to re-forge a stronger Union. President Lincoln was assassinated shortly after the official end of the Civil War and while the Thirteenth Amendment was indeed ratified, the Union fell to now President Andrew Johnson's leadership. Unfortunately, it was not a smooth transition for slaves to live as free men.

The Midwestern states were among the first states to pass *black codes* in order to discourage freed slaves from moving to their area. Soon adopted by all former Confederate states, black codes were quite similar to the slave codes they replaced in that they controlled blacks socially, politically and economically. Ironically, Mississippi passed a law entitled, "An Act to Confer Civil Rights on Freedmen, and for Other Purposes," which was quite misleading. While blacks could now marry and enjoy other privileges, they were by no means considered equal to whites. In the same Act listed above, Mississippi deemed that a black person who committed the crime of marrying a white person could be sentenced to life in prison for such an offense. This is an example of a more covert discriminatory law that was mentioned earlier in the chapter—it seemed to say one thing, but was in fact more of the same type of freedom-limiting legislation that the South was used to.

Progress Through Legislation

Congress responded to these black codes by passing additionally restorative legislation. First, Congress passed the *Civil Rights Act of 1866*, which granted citizenship and the same rights enjoyed by whites to everyone "without distinction of race or color, or previous condition of slavery or involuntary servitude." Interestingly, President Johnson vetoed the bill, but a two-thirds majority in both houses of Congress overruled his veto and so it became the law of the land. Even so, the division of power between the federal government and each state allowed individual states to continue to enact oppressive legislation. To close this loophole, Congress passed the *Fourteenth Amendment* in 1867, which stated:

> All persons born or naturalized in the United States, and subject to the jurisdiction thereof, are citizens of the United States and of the state wherein they reside. No state shall make or enforce any law which shall abridge the privileges or immunities of citizens of the United States; nor shall any state deprive any person of life, liberty, or property, without due process of law; nor deny to any person within its jurisdiction the equal protection of the laws.

The passing of the Fourteenth Amendment was intended to put to rest questions of which rights newly-freed slaves were entitled to—the same as everyone else—and as such, it became known as the *Equal Protection Clause*. It also set the standard that individual states cannot abridge each and every citizen's inalienable rights. In essence, the Fourteenth Amendment extended the rights of the Fifth Amendment to citizens of states, meaning Americans' right to due process now applied to state governments and not just the federal government. This is further evidence that rights tend to be extended to more and more people over time through passage of laws, as noted earlier in the book, and that realizing social justice takes time as well as struggle.

The final Amendment passed during the Reconstruction period was the *Fifteenth Amendment*, which granted male citizens of color the right to vote:

> The right of citizens of the United States to vote shall not be denied or abridged by the United States or by any State on account of race, color, or previous condition of servitude.

What the Fifteenth Amendment didn't do was extend the right to vote to women, white or otherwise. As we will see in Chapter 7, women had to wait another 50 years to gain the right to vote themselves. And so, inequality persisted in US society. The three Reconstruction Amendments seemed to be a turning of the tides for racial inequality in this country. Slaves were set free, granted citizenship, and black men were included in the right to vote. The disenfranchisement of blacks, however, would continue for another 100 years with the passage of Jim Crow laws. It would seem that, even though slavery was at an end, the newly formed Union would be reformed based on white supremacy.

Jim Crow

Beginning in the 1890s, Southern states passed laws inhibiting the ability of blacks to achieve equality. These statutes, collectively known as *Jim Crow laws*, were enforced until the 1960s. The first thing that these laws achieved was severely limiting the newly won right to vote. By requiring literacy tests, passing poll taxes, creating elaborate registration systems, and moving poll locations, politicians were maneuvering to keep blacks from the polls and thus out of office. The laws were incredibly effective. In Louisiana, where 130,000 blacks had registered to vote by 1896, that number had dropped to a mere 1,342 by 1904 (Basseti, 2012). These laws also set the standard for segregation. Black and white children had to go to different schools, sit in different sections of movie theaters, drink from separate water fountains, order food from different counters, live in different parts of town, use different libraries. The list goes on and on. In effect, blacks continued to be treated as second-class citizens; equality and social justice were still not realities.

When blacks turned to the courts to help uphold their constitutional rights, they were disappointed to find out that the Supreme Court determined that segregation was lawful. In the landmark case of *Plessy v. Ferguson* in 1896, the highest court in the land ruled that separate facilities, so long as they were equal, were not a violation of the Constitution. Putting it bluntly, segregation was not discriminatory.

Compounding the fact that the courts were upholding Jim Crow laws and Black Codes, disgruntled whites were pursuing their own type of ill-conceived justice. The *Ku Klux Klan* was founded in Pulaski, Tennessee in 1866. Through fear and brutality, these groups attempted to intimidate both blacks and local politicians into maintaining the status quo. By 1920, the KKK was a politically powerful force that was intolerant of many different groups including Catholics, Jews, and immigrants. Lynchings and other forms of brutal violence were utilized to maintain current arrangements in society, and whites were encouraged to obtain and use weapons to keep order.

Hate crimes committed during this time were actually not violations of the law, and high-ranking politicians, as well as lawmen, were part of the KKK. Today, crimes motivated by racial hatred are included as violations of the federal law as *hate crimes*, and hate groups are tracked by groups such as the Southern Poverty Law Center. Specifically, federal law defines hate crimes as willfully causing or attempting to cause

> bodily injury to any person or, through the use of fire, a firearm, a dangerous weapon, or an explosive or incendiary device . . . because of the actual or perceived race, color, religion, or national origin of any person . . . [and/or] because of the actual or perceived religion, national origin, gender, sexual orientation, gender identity, or disability of any person.
>
> *(18 US Code, Section 249)*

Activity 5.1 Hate Map

Go to the website of the Southern Poverty Law Center and examine their hate map: http://www.splcenter.org/get-informed/hate-map.

What kinds of hate groups exist in the US?

Why do you think so many exist?

Not willing to be broken, black lawyers began strategizing in the 1930s to challenge segregation in the same legal system that upheld it just decades before. By the early 1950s, lawyers for the *National Association for the Advancement of Colored People* brought forth a class action lawsuit on behalf of the families of school children in Delaware, Kansas, South Carolina, and Virginia. This class action lawsuit asked the courts to allow black students to attend the superior white schools because black schools were not, and would never be, equal to the white schools. These legal and political challenges culminated in a victory that turned the tide of racial segregation. That victory was *Brown v. Board of Education*—one of the class action cases—which resulted in a landmark reversal of the *Plessy v. Ferguson* decision. In 1954, the Supreme Court held that racial segregation in public schools did, in fact, violate the Equal Protection Clause of the Fourteenth Amendment thus ending 50 years of sanctioned segregation. In the *Brown* case, the Court overturned its precedent in *Plessy*, calling it "conceived in error."

What followed was a series of deliberate, peaceful actions of civil disobedience to keep the attention on inequality and the pressure on the legislature. *Civil disobedience*, or the deliberate disobeying of law under specific circumstances, was not a new tactic. In fact, the rebellion against Great Britain during the Revolutionary War was an example of civil disobedience. In that sense, it could be said that this country was founded on that principle. While civil disobedience sounds a lot like simply breaking the law, Dr Martin Luther King, Jr. turned rebellion into a systemic protest. He distinguished between laws to be disobeyed and laws to be followed by employing the following logic: "A just law is a man-made law of God. An unjust law is a code that is out of harmony with the moral law" (King, 1963: 82). King added, in his *Letter from a Birmingham Jail*, that "an unjust law is no law at all."

Dr King explicitly outlined his strategy (1958: 101–107). Some elements included are shown in Table 5.4. You see, passively accepting injustice is intolerable, and yet acting out violently will not yield results. For an example of what civil disobedience looks like, we need look no further than Rosa Parks. In 1955, Ms. Parks famously refused to move to the back of a crowded bus in Montgomery, Alabama when asked to do so in accordance with bus policy. She was arrested and became the tinder that ignited a series of boycotts and sit-ins. Dr Martin Luther King, Jr. spoke out about the boycotts and said:

> We are tired . . . of being segregated and humiliated . . . For many years we have shown amazing patience . . . But we come here tonight to be saved from that patience that makes us patient with anything less than freedom and justice.
>
> *(Turck, 2000: 27–28)*

It is important to understand that this occurrence created the opportunity for King to later become a great civil rights leader. He was elected President of the *Montgomery Improvement Association* (MIA),

TABLE 5.4 Dr King's Strategy

1. Actively, but non-violently, resist evil.
2. Do not seek to humiliate or defeat opponents, but instead, win their understanding and friendship.
3. Focus on challenging the forces of evil rather than the people doing the evil.
4. Accept suffering without retaliating.
5. Refuse to hate your opponent.
6. Act with the conviction that the universe is on the side of justice.

Source: King (1960 in Williams, Page, & Petrosky, 2014).

which led the bus boycott for more than a year. King was thus a product of the Civil Rights Movement as much as he was an initiator of it. In fact, Rosa Parks herself, like other prominent members of the movement, had earlier trained in peaceful civil disobedience alongside both whites and blacks at the Highlander Folk School in Monteagle, Tennessee, a school that had been in existence for decades. The lesson here is that people—known but also unknowns—are always working behind the scenes to achieve social justice.

As can be imagined, *Brown v. Board of Education* was not met with enthusiasm. In a follow up to the *Brown* decisions, referred to as *Brown II*, the Supreme Court had commanded that states integrate their schools with "all deliberate speed." Arkansas's governor and legislature had other ideas and proceeded to pass laws and constitutional amendments undermining the mandate to integrate. This conflict came to a head on September 4, 1957, when Arkansas's governor Orval Faubus ordered the Arkansas National Guard to prevent a group of nine black students from enrolling in Little Rock's Central High School. The incident became known as "The Little Rock Nine" and ended with President Dwight D. Eisenhower sending in federal National Guard troops to protect the nine students while they successfully enrolled. Figure 5.3 shows an image of these black students attending school under the protection of federal officials. Here, social justice practice had to be accomplished at the barrel of a gun—in this case by the federal government against state officials in the south supposedly standing up for "states' rights."

The Supreme Court enforced integration by their ruling in the *Cooper v. Aaron* case in 1958, which stated that states could not pass legislation to undermine the *Brown v. Board of Education* decision. While the *Brown* and *Cooper* decisions did not signify the start of the Civil Rights Movement, they did serve to keep the momentum going.

FIGURE 5.3 Little Rock Nine.

By the early 1960s, the Civil Rights Movement was in full effect. Lunch counter-sit-ins, public swimming pool wade-ins, white church kneel-ins and movie theater protests were occurring with increasing regularity. In August of 1963, a march was planned in Washington DC to stress the need for a new Civil Rights Bill. With over 250,000 people in attendance, Dr Martin Luther King Jr. gave his famous "I Have a Dream" speech that remains a pinnacle of the quest for equality. Incredibly, the "I Have a Dream" speech was unplanned and off the cuff. King's written speech was dryer and less emotional, and as he gave it, a woman on the stage (a famous singer from the time) behind him yelled that he should "tell them about the dream!" And so he did, off the top of his head.

King's efforts, along with the thousands of activists who fought tirelessly beside him, had paid off. Congress passed the *Civil Rights Act of 1964* to effectively end segregation in all public places and to ban employment discrimination on the basis of race, color, religion, sex, or national origin. The law was originally proposed by President John F. Kennedy, but was ultimately signed into law by President Lyndon B. Johnson following President Kennedy's assassination.

Even so, the fight was not over. In 1965, King Jr. participated in a march of 30,000 activists who walked from Selma, Alabama to Montgomery, Alabama. Their cause was bringing attention to the continuing difficulties of blacks who wanted to exercise their right to vote. Almost 100 years after the passage of the Fifteenth Amendment, blacks were still facing poll taxes and harassment in an attempt to prevent them from exercising their voting rights. Congress responded by passing the Voting Rights Act of 1966, which bans racial discrimination in voting practices by both the federal government and state and local governments.

While riots and civil unrest were not invented in the 1960s, they did garner far more attention than they had in previous decades thanks to the advent of the television. What became clear through the pictures broadcast in black and white was that not everyone was sold on the idea of peaceful protest, particularly when the protesters were so frequently brutalized by both police and angry bystanders alike. Incredibly, images of violence and clashes with police were used by state and federal politicians to scare whites into voting for Republican politicians running for governor, Congress, and even President, as part of the intentional *Southern Strategy*. The Southern Strategy was a coordinated plan by Republican party leaders to win back the South for the purposes of gaining power and eroding social welfare programs. According to Michelle Alexander:

> The success of law and order rhetoric among working-class whites and the intense resentment of racial reforms, particularly in the South, led conservative Republican analysts to believe that a "new majority" could be created by the Republican party, one that included the traditional Republican base, the white South, and half the Catholic, blue-collar vote of the big cities. Some conservative political strategists admitted that appealing to racial fears and antagonisms was central to this strategy, though it had to be done surreptitiously.
>
> *(Alexander, 2012: 44)*

It was Richard Nixon who was behind the Southern Strategy, and his advisors and strategists later admitted that this plan was explicitly about subtly using race to encourage whites to vote Republican. Republican strategist Kevin Phillips, for example, wrote that a new Republican majority could be achieved if candidates ran on issues of race but using "coded antiblack rhetoric" (Alexander, 2012: 45).

Earlier, Barry Goldwater used terms like "states' rights" to try to appeal to white supremacist voters (Tonry, 2011: 108).

Martin Luther King, Jr. may have been the public face of the Civil Rights Movement, but he wasn't the only major player in the game during the 1950s and 1960s. Malcolm Little, also an outspoken activist, is better known by his adopted name—Malcolm X. He dropped his surname in a rejection of his "slave" name and became a force within the *Nation of Islam*, a religious organization, as well as the Black Nationalism movement. Malcolm X took a decidedly different approach than Martin Luther King, Jr. Instead of advocating peaceful protests, he urged blacks to defend themselves by "any means necessary." Also, integration was not one of his goals. Instead, Malcolm X wanted the black community to define their identity through the creation of separate schools and churches. The Black Nationalism movement firmly believed that white America had erased blacks' cultural identity and, as a result, the leaders within this group fought strongly against assimilation.

In retrospect, it isn't difficult to see why Martin Luther King, Jr. and Malcolm Little advocated such different perspectives. Dr King was born to middle-class parents who were influential within Atlanta's black community. He had a normal and happy childhood, despite the limitations imposed by Jim Crow laws in the South. He went to college in Atlanta and, later, to graduate school in Boston, which is where he met his college-educated wife, Coretta Scott. Armed with hope, optimism, and a degree in theology, Dr King saw love and peaceful resistance as the only means to enact lasting social change. Comparatively speaking, Malcolm Little's childhood was decidedly more somber. While both Dr King and Malcolm X were born to preacher fathers, Malcolm's first memories were of white aggression. When he was four years old, local KKK members smashed all of the family's windows. Malcolm's father decided to move them to Omaha Nebraska, but the harassment continued. Less than a year after their move, a racist mob lit their house on fire and Malcolm's family watched as the all-white firefighters who responded to the scene refused to offer aid or assistance.

Two years later, Malcolm's father, Earl Little, was found dead on the municipal street car tracks. His death was classified as a suicide even though Malcolm and his family strongly felt that he was most likely murdered by white supremacists. To add insult to injury, by labeling it a suicide, the Little's could not claim the life insurance policy that Earl Little had taken out in order to provide for his family in the event of his death. Malcolm was an excellent student and very bright, but he was cynical and jaded following his exposure to violence in his short life. He dropped out of school at the age of 15 and, shortly thereafter, was sentenced to ten years in prison on burglary charges. He became familiar with the Nation of Islam during his incarceration and came out of prison an educated man, ready to fight for his version of equality.

Sadly, Malcolm X shared another similarity with Dr King. He was assassinated in February of 1965—both men were 39 years old when they were killed. Even after his death, his influence fueled the Black Power movement of the late 1960s and 1970s. *Black Power*, or embracing and celebrating a black cultural identity, resonated within the urban black communities that felt disenfranchised and frustrated by the lack of progress being made towards equality. It's no wonder that his message resonated with urban black communities who so often felt the hate instead of the love from their white brothers and sisters.

It is hard not to note the irony that whereas Malcolm X became more passive in his final years, travelling to Mecca and walking with people of all races and ethnicities, Martin Luther King became more revolutionary, anti-war, and founded the *Poor People's Movement* to benefit all disaffected people regardless of race; shortly before his death he promised to shut down Washington, DC, and was planning the event at the time of his death.

Post-Civil Rights Life

Once the courts mandated desegregation, the next battle for blacks came under the auspices of affirmative action. *Affirmative action* was the term used for policies put into place to increase the representation of those who have suffered discrimination. The phrase originated in 1961 with President John F. Kennedy's executive order that called on the federal government to increase the hiring of blacks. By the mid-1970s, affirmative action was in place in higher education as well as in state agencies. There was a cry of *reverse discrimination*—discrimination against whites resulting from preferences for minorities codified into the law or practice. Of course, such a reality would only be possible had society made enormous progress from the days of systematic discrimination against people of color.

A recent US Supreme Court ruling in the case of *Shelby County v. Holder*, 12-96 (decided June 25, 2013) is suggestive of the amount of progress that has been made in US society. In the case, the Court struck down Section 4 of the 1965 Voting Rights Act that was created to address entrenched racial discrimination in voting. Although Section 2 of the law (which bans any "standard, practice, or procedure" that "results in a denial or abridgment of the right of any citizen . . . to vote on account of race or color") remains in effect, Section 4's "coverage formula" was struck down. The formula in question basically identified areas of the country where racial disparities in voting were common and at least in the past stemmed from discriminatory practices that made it more difficult for people of color to vote.

In striking down Section 4 as unconstitutional, the Court held by a 5–4 vote that:

> Nearly 50 years later, things have changed dramatically. Largely because of the Voting Rights Act, "[v]oter turnout and registration rates" in covered jurisdictions "now approach parity. Blatantly discriminatory evasions of federal decrees are rare. And minority candidates hold office at unprecedented levels." . . . The tests and devices that blocked ballot access have been forbidden nationwide for over 40 years.

The Court reasoned that the country is no longer divided upon racial lines and thus formulas to decide if states discriminate based on race are no longer relevant. Further, the Court wrote that when Congress recently reenacted the law, it "did not use that record to fashion a coverage formula grounded in current conditions. It instead reenacted a formula based on 40-year-old facts having no logical relation to the present day."

Incredibly, states such as Texas passed laws (e.g., voter ID laws) prior to the ruling that are predicted to greatly reduce minority voting, and after this ruling numerous other states (mostly in the South) passed similar laws, as well as others that greatly restrict voting. The US Department of Justice is suing at least two states (i.e., Texas and North Carolina). With regard to the North Carolina law, the Justice Department is challenging four provisions of North Carolina's law, including:

> the elimination of the first week of early voting, which reduces the total number of days of early voting (from 17 days to 10 days); the elimination of same-day voter registration during the early

voting period; the prohibition on counting certain provisional ballots; and the failure to provide adequate safeguards for voters who lack the limited types of acceptable photo identification cards that will be required in future elections.

Each of these provisions is predicted to "have a discriminatory impact on minority voters" (US Department of Justice, 2013). This battle between the federal government to eliminate racial discrimination in voting and states who want to decide their own fate and direction is illustrative of the reality that federalism often makes realizing social justice more difficult, as well as of the constant struggle to make actual practice match American ideals. Further, it is evidence that we're yet to achieve a society characterized by equal liberties and social justice as envisioned by justice scholars such as Rawls and Miller, whose theories were reviewed in Chapter 1.

Activity 5.2 Martin Luther King

Go online and study the last two years of Martin Luther King's life.

Why are his actions including his Poor People's Campaign largely ignored in the media?

Based on his work to help poor people of all races and his calls for redistribution of wealth, was King a civil rights leader or something else?

The Study of Social Control

Since the turn of the twentieth century, the majority of theoretical formulations explaining crime and deviance have included either micro- or macro-elements of social control, albeit in a different manner. The *conflict perspective of criminology* is one of the various theoretical perspectives that inform the study of social control. While conflict-oriented theories date back to the late nineteenth century, critical discourse on crime and criminality emerged en masse during the 1960s and early 1970s.

Conflict theorists view the criminal justice system as a social control apparatus used by dominant groups to maintain their position in society (Spitzer, 1975; Turk, 1969). As the sentencing branch of the system, the courts are viewed as a powerful tool for supporting those interests. Through the use of *discretionary sentencing*, threatening groups are controlled towards a larger goal of maintaining social order (Akers, 1997; Quinney, 1970). According to the conflict perspective, an analysis of sentencing decisions within the criminal courts should yield evidence of differential decisions imposed on the basis of the social position of the defendant independent of the effects of objective legal variables such as offense seriousness and prior criminal record; social position is generally associated with demographic variables such as gender, age, and race/ethnicity.

Richard Quinney (1970) suggests that, while a framework for sentencing decisions is outlined by the law, *extra-legal factors* can affect sentencing decisions within these boundaries. Chambliss and Seidman (1971) support this point by arguing that many extra-legal characteristics about the offender are allowed to enter in sentencing decisions. Our review of court data in Chapter 3 supports this argument; recall that evidence suggests that race, class, and gender are found to impact criminal sentences in some cases at some times, suggestive of *contextual discrimination* (Walker, Spohn, & DeLone, 2004).

The foregoing discussion is premised on the assumption that the power struggle between competing groups in society is an integral element of social and political life. Legal sanctions put forth through legislation and enforced by the actors in the criminal justice system indicate an official response to behaviors or defendants that are perceived as threatening by the dominant group. Blalock (1967) developed this systematically in a sociological analysis of the power imbalance and competition between dominant and minority groups in society.

Blalock's Formulation of Social Threat and Social Control

Hubert Blalock (1967) presented a comprehensive theoretical framework discussing macro-level factors that may affect a social control response. Referred to as the *power threat hypothesis*, Blalock's analysis explored the association between the presence and growth of minority groups and various social control mechanisms. Blalock hypothesized that minority groups may be perceived as threatening by dominant groups and that, specifically, growth in minority group populations may amplify this threat.

Blalock (1967) outlined three different manifestations of minority group threat: status, economic, and power or political threat. *Status threat* is described as the acquisition of social position, rank, or status. Minorities are viewed as a hindrance to the dominant group's acquisition of status goals by competing for the resources necessary to obtain these objectives (Blalock, 1967). According to Blalock, status threat is the only one of the three categories of threat that is neither related to the exact size of the minority population nor positively related to social control. Instead, it is the social rank of the minority population in relation to the social position of the dominant group that determines the level of perceived status threat.

The dominant group generally responds to status threat through discrimination, avoidance, and displaced aggression. *Discrimination* is most likely to be used as a social control measure when the minority group status is low, since interacting with low-status minorities may result in a loss of status for members of the dominant group (Blalock, 1967: 70). Similarly, dominant group members may avoid interacting or socializing with minority group members, since such interaction may be viewed as encumbering their pursuit of a higher status. *Avoidance* is most common when dominant group members are cognizant of the social arrangements both between and within social groups, have a high level of status consciousness, or when the gap between the social position of the dominant group and minority group is sizeable. Finally, *displaced aggression* is the use of violence as a means of alleviating social frustration on a person or group that is a substitute target for the direct source of frustration, which may not be known (Blalock, 1967: 42).

Minorities may be perceived as presenting an *economic threat* by competing with the dominant group for economic resources. Blalock (1967) stated that the social control techniques used to respond to economic threat are dependent on various factors, including the way in which resources are distributed across competing groups; the manner of reward distribution; the number of competitors vying for the same reward; and the value of the reward for both the individual and the group. Based on this logic, Blalock (1967) asserted that a positive nonlinear relationship should exist between the intensity of economic threat and the discriminatory social control response. That is, when the minority presence is small, it poses little economic competition and the dominant group is not very motivated to mobilize control efforts. The social control response will rise in turn with increasing economic threat until the minority group reaches a certain level (i.e., a sizeable minority approaching a majority), at which point the positive relationship is hypothesized to stabilize or level off.

Power threat refers to the possession of political influence by minority groups. Blalock conceptualized "power" as the combination of the ownership of resources and the ability to mobilize those resources for the group's benefit. The four factors outlined as influencing the power struggle are: minority group resources; minority group mobilization; dominant group resources; and dominant group mobilization (Blalock, 1967: 111). Blalock described the relationship between power threat and discriminatory social control as curvilinear. That is, when minorities are not perceived as threatening to the political hegemony of the dominant group, little discriminatory response is necessary; however, as their "power" increases, the dominant group must intensify their social control response to maintain their position. Some common discriminatory social control practices engaged in response to power threat include the restriction of minority political rights, symbolic forms of segregation, and ritualistic forms of violence.

A complex set of interacting circumstances determine whether the threat is perceived as being status, economic, or political. Those circumstances include social conditions and the size and composition of both the dominant and minority groups (Blalock, 1967). Blalock (1967) argued that, while multiple types of threat may be present, a single threat type will emerge as the dominant factor, particularly during periods of economic or political instability. The social control response of the dominant group is conditioned by the specific type of threat perceived. Dominant group members respond to this threat by deploying discriminatory social control measures to maintain their dominance in the social order. In this way, we can see discrimination as a means to maintain status quo power arrangments in US society arranged around race and other social statuses, an argument that goes all the way back to the US Constitution.

Blalock's theory utilized both macro- and micro-level processes in his explanation of the discriminatory social control measures employed by dominant group actors that result in racial inequality. He acknowledged the inherent complexities in attempting an integrated model noting:

> One of the most challenging problems that continually arise in almost all substantive fields within the social sciences is that of just how one translates back and forth between the macro level, where groups are the units of analysis, and the micro level where the focus is on individuals. The problems are both conceptual and empirical: there are questions of definition, aggregation, and the practical limitations . . . of gathering data on both levels.
>
> *(Blalock, 1967: 21)*

In formulating a causal theory to explain the intricate relationship between racial threat and social control, Blalock focused his explanation on the macro-level processes, specifically using a threat measure of percent nonwhite. That is, a high percentage of nonwhites in the population in any area will be perceived as threatening to white majorities. He proceeded to incorporate individual-level processes that might influence the use of social control mechanisms. This causal process was distilled into four interrelated propositions. The first proposition stated that exposure to a large population of minority group members was a "forcing" variable, which was threatening to individual members of the dominant group (Blalock, 1967: 28). Blalock argued in the second proposition that the threat posed by the minority population interacted with different personality traits within the individual to produce varying levels of motivation to discriminate.

In the third proposition, it is stated that similarly motivated members of the dominant group will interact with each other in a manner that fosters discriminatory actions. In the fourth and final proposition, Blalock asserts that, "discriminatory behavior, when aggregated in some way, leads to lowered (aggregate) minority levels" (1967: 28). The diverse social control measures available to the dominant group suggest several conceptualizations of the process through which minority populations are decreased in number. One possibility is through the use of coercive controls, such as arrest or incarceration. In this causal process, the levels of minority presence and the fluctuations in those levels are the key determinants of social control.

Blalock's formulation of the minority threat hypothesis expanded the study of social control beyond a single dimension analysis and introduced the importance of examining complex race relations using a multi-level approach. His influence as a pioneer in the social threat and social control literature is evidenced by the broad expansion of his theory to other groups and other types of threat by subsequent theorists. Recent theorists have transformed the study of social threat and social control to include other types of threat and additional techniques of control.

Reformulations of Blalock's Concepts

Lofland (1969) expanded Blalock's initial conceptualization of social threat. His focus was not merely on the presence of a threatening group, but also included the level and distribution of that threat. Broadly speaking, Lofland stated that the concept of *deviance* is created when conflict exists between social groups. He hypothesized that the application of deviant labels occurs when dominant group members feel threatened by and are afraid of another segment of society, consistent with the notion of culture conflict introduced earlier. He listed several important factors in identifying groups that may be perceived as threatening. These variables include: the size of the population; the level of organization; the relative amount of power of the minority group; the relative amount of power and organization of the threatened group. Lofland felt that in order to identify the level and distribution of threat as well as the subsequent social control response, these aggregate characteristics must be examined.

Liska (1992) examined the "impact of social threat on the pattern and shape of deviance and crime control institutions, organizations, programs, and policies" (p. 1). He described institutional controls as initiatives authorized by a unit of the government aimed at either directly or indirectly reducing crime. These formal government controls are a specification of Blalock's more general social control. Additionally, Liska introduced a new threat type—*criminal threat*—to describe the perceived danger posed by minorities. Liska discussed the various social control mechanisms that are used in response to specific threat groups including fatal, coercive and beneficent controls. Each of these is discussed below.

First, there are *fatal controls as a mechanism of social control*. Fatal or lethal controls can come in the form of both formal and informal social controls. The use of the death penalty is an example of a formal fatal control while *vigilantism* would be considered an informal social control. *Lynching* and *police use of deadly force* are typically the focus of studies exploring the relationship between racial threat and fatal controls.

Tolnay and Beck (1992) examined fatal forms of social control in their research investigating whether the social threat hypothesis was a plausible explanation of lynching as a social control tool in the Deep

South between 1900 and 1930. During that time period, in excess of 3,000 blacks were lynched, with more than half of those occurring in the Deep South. With regard to status threat, they discussed how race was synonymous with social status, since the prevailing belief at that time was that whites were considered superior to blacks in a myriad of characteristics and as such were considered to be of a higher social status. Particularly for lower-class whites, the maintenance of the caste line was important for the preservation of what little social status they had. For example, numerous cases were cited of blacks being lynched simply for being disrespectful to whites.

Tolnay and Beck (1992) also noted that blacks posed a real power threat due to the fact that whites were the numerical minority in various parts of the region. They stated that it is plausible to argue that some members of this region used lynching as a mechanism to dissuade blacks from exercising their political rights, but that overall, findings were inconclusive in regards to whether the power threat hypothesis explained the use of lynching.

Ayers (1984) argued that lynching might have been more feasibly used in response to economic threat rather than as a response to political threat, since other control measures such as disenfranchisement and Jim Crow laws were utilized to limit the political involvement of blacks. Additionally, economic competition skyrocketed for poor southern whites since blacks were technically considered free to pursue economic advancement during this period and were willing to do so for lower wages (Tolnay & Beck, 1992). The economic competition between poor whites and blacks was manipulated by white elites who enjoyed increased profits when wages were driven down, but who simultaneously feared that a partnership might form between the two economically inferior groups in order to demand greater compensation. In other words, poor whites might have used lynching in response to a direct economic threat posed by blacks, whereas white elites utilized lynching as a primary tool of social control to maintain the caste system.

Tolnay and Beck (1992) were hesitant in concluding whether enough evidence existed to support the social threat hypothesis for various reasons. One of the primary reasons they cited was the difficulty in isolating the specific type of threat to which lynching was employed in response. The overlap between status, power and political threat has made the empirical assessment of a social control response to a single threat type difficult. Additionally, they stated that further research is necessary to examine the mediating effect that non-lethal controls may have in determining the level of fatal social control used in response to racial threat.

Several studies have been conducted examining the use of deadly force by the police as a fatal control in response to racial threat. Generally speaking, these studies have found that, after controlling for relevant variables, percent minority in the population is causally related to police use of deadly force (Chamlin, 1989; Jacobs & O'Brien, 1998; Sorenson, Marquart, & Brock, 1993). Liska and Yu (1992) investigated a slightly different hypothesis and theorized that the relationship between fatal controls and racial threat is the result of a perceived association between minorities and threatening acts, instead of perceiving minorities as a threat in and of themselves. Their results showed that, after controlling for relevant variables including crime rates, police homicides rose significantly as the percent of nonwhites increased. Clearly, these outcomes are inconsistent with social justice, particularly equal liberties.

Second, there is *coercive controls as a mechanism of social control*. Liska defined coercive controls as social controls used to "physically constrain peoples' behavior" (Liska & Yu, 1992: 21). Coercive controls can include arrest, imprisonment, and nonlethal police intervention. Chamlin and Liska (1992) investigated the relationship between racial composition of neighborhoods and police response in the form of arrest rates. *Arrest* is a powerful social control tool, considering that it is the necessary first point of entry into the criminal justice system. Once an individual is arrested, his or her personal information becomes a permanent record in the system, regardless of whether he or she is actually prosecuted and/or convicted of a crime.

Contrary to the findings that they anticipated, results demonstrated that the nonwhite arrest rate declined as the percent of nonwhites in the population increased. One suggestion given for this finding is that, in nonwhite neighborhoods, crime is mainly restricted to intraracial offending (i.e., within the same race). Chamlin and Liska discovered an important interaction between race and *crime threat*. Results showed that elevated crime rates increased both the arrest of whites and nonwhites, but the positive effect of crime rates was more prominent for nonwhite defendants. They argue that, as a result, it is the cumulative threat of race and crime rates that results in a significant increase of social control for minorities. This likely explains why police presence is generally higher in areas with high minority presence and high levels of calls for police service (Robinson, 2002).

Police use of non-lethal force is considered another type of coercive control. Holmes (2000) investigated civil rights complaints involving excessive use of force against minorities as a social control response to populations considered threatening. Results indicated that, after controlling for variables including region, city population and crime, the percent black was positively related to charges of police brutality. An additional finding was that, in the southwest region of the country where Hispanics are a sizeable minority, percent Hispanic was also positively related to police brutality. Smith and Holmes (2003) replicated this study and, upon finding the same results, they concluded that minority group presence increases law enforcement's perception of minority threat and in turn amplifies their use of coercive controls in response to the perceived threat.

A third type of coercive control is the allocation of police expenditures and resources. Several studies have established a positive relationship between racial composition and both law enforcement expenditures and deployment (Chamlin, 1990; Greenberg, Kessler, & Loftin, 1985; Jackson, 1989). Jackson (1992) stated that law enforcement serves the role of regulating minority groups and that funding for various departments should vary by the level of the socially threatening population in their charge. In regards to racial threat, Sever (2001) examined police deployment in cities with a population of at least 25,000 between 1980 and 1990. Results showed a positive significant relationship between percent black and police deployment, another outcome inconsistent with social justice.

Incarceration is possibly one of the most important forms of coercive control. The *imprisonment binge* of the previous four decades and its disproportionate effect on the minority population has been well documented (Irwin & Austin, 1994). One explanation is that the increase in incarceration rates and subsequent correctional expenditures have been motivated by a response to racial threat. Numerous studies have found a significant and positive relationship in this regard (Beckett & Western, 2001; Bridges, Crutchfield, & Simpson, 1987; Myers, 1990). In their study of incarceration rates from 1971 to 1991, Greenberg and West (2001) found that percent black was positively and significantly associated with increased incarceration rates in state prisons, also inconsistent with key concepts of libertarianism and egalitarianism. They also found that states with higher welfare expenditures tended to have lower incarceration rates, leading them to believe that beneficent controls were used in place of coercive controls.

Third, there are *beneficent controls as a mechanism of social control*. Beneficent controls are described as those that appear to aid the threatening population, but in reality serve as a behavioral constraint (Liska, 1992). Beneficent controls generally come in the form of *welfare* to assuage economically threatening groups or in the use of *asylums* as a method of rehabilitation. Foucault (1965) has shown that mental asylums were used as early as the seventeenth century to control individuals. Szasz (1970) suggested that the mental health system is a more effective tool of social control than the criminal justice system due to the fact that it is not constrained by the rule of law.

Arvanites (1992) also explored the relationship between threatening groups and institutionalization. He stated that social control operations function independent of one another and, as a result, as one type of control declines, the frequency with which other types are used should increase. He argued that the *deinstitutionalization* movement (where state mental hospitals were closed) was an example of this type of shift, pointing to evidence that suggests that mentally ill individuals have been arrested at a higher rate since deinstitutionalization.

In one of the most comprehensive analyses of this issue, Piven and Cloward (1993) investigated the relationship between threatening populations and beneficent controls. They conducted an historical analysis examining periods of increased relief and surmised that the increase in the use of beneficent controls can be understood as a response to insurgent movements and are granted in the name of preserving economic and political order. They argued that periods of increased civil disorder served as a catalyst for an outpouring of relief that was quickly diminished or removed once social order was restored. For example, the extensive urban rioting, which preceded the passage of the Civil Rights Act of 1964 and the Voting Rights Act of 1965, increased the level of political threat presented by the minority population and contributed to the use of beneficent controls, in the form of *Great Society* programs; Great Society programs were aimed at reducing poverty and racial inequality by investing in the nation's infrastructure.

Blalock provided the framework for analyzing the effects of aggregate threat measures and the subsequent mobilization of social control at the macro or social level. Liska and others discussed above expanded Blalock's conceptualizations to include other types of threat and social control responses. While aggregate levels of social threat are an integral part of the race and social control discourse, it is only one dimension in the complex relationship. On the micro level, other theorists have examined the effect an individual's race or ethnicity may have on social control outcomes.

Individual Threat and Social Control

While Blalock made the assertion that micro processes are an integral part of the social threat and social control relationship, he does not grant individual-level discrimination much attention in his work. This gap has been filled by recent theorists who, through their research on the effect of race and ethnicity on sentencing outcomes, shed light on social control responses to individual members of threatening groups.

Individual-level theoretical formulations of social control typically focus on the association between an individual's minority status and presumed negative attributes (e.g., stereotypes). Albonetti (1991) examined the discretionary nature of judicial decision making in her theory of *bounded rationality*. She argued that judges attempt to make rational decisions even when presented with incomplete information and uncertainty, particularly concerning potential future criminality. Judicial decision makers form patterned responses on the basis of prejudices, stereotypes, and past experience (Clegg & Dunkerley, 1980). These stereotypes and prejudices are used as rationalizations to justify the sentence imposed on a defendant. The problem that arises for minority defendants is that they are often the target of negative stereotypes and attributes and consequently receive harsher sentences than Whites.

A similar theoretical framework outlined by Steffensmeier, Ulmer, and Kramer (1998) argued that three *focal concerns* are present in judicial decision making. These three elements include practical constraints, protection of the community, and blameworthiness. The focal concern of *practical constraints* encompasses both organizational and individual elements. *Organizational concerns* include the maintenance of the courtroom workgroup and caseload, while *individual concerns* focus on offender-related characteristics such as the offender's health and ability to serve out a correctional sentence. Another primary concern in the development of sentencing decisions is the focal concern of *protection of the community*, which centers on the concepts of deterrence and incapacitation of offenders. *Blameworthiness* focuses on the level of injury to the victim and addresses an individual's culpability. *Offense seriousness* and *prior record* are also considered as part of blameworthiness and have frequently been cited as important dimensions in sentencing decisions.

The interplay of these three focal concerns is complex, particularly since the judge is often making decisions with incomplete information. This information gap creates a "perceptual shorthand" that allows personal attributes of the offender, such as race, to influence judicial decision making. In interviews with judges, Steffensmeier and associates (1998) reported that judges frequently characterize minority defendants as more dangerous and culpable than other groups of defendants. Spohn and Beichner (2000) also theorized that judges rely on stereotypes of minority defendants to complement the incomplete information used to assess blameworthiness. They specifically discussed the willingness of judges to define minority defendants as predatory offenders who engage in recidivistic behavior.

Kalven and Zeisel's (1966) *liberation hypothesis* explored another element of decision making in a sentencing process replete with uncertain information. The liberation hypothesis states that racial disparity in sentencing decreases as the seriousness of the case increases. In their study of jury behavior, it was argued that the jury considered their own beliefs and values in cases where the evidence implicating the defendant was either contradictory or weak.

In a variation of the liberation hypothesis, Unnever and Hembroff examined the degree to which a defendant's race or ethnicity influenced sentencing outcomes depending on the level of dispositional certainty or uncertainty present in the case (1987: 57). They measured the degree of uncertainty by including a number of attributes about the case, such as seriousness of the offense, prior record, and number of charges presented. Unnever and Hembroff (1987) hypothesized that sentences would have increased certainty when the attributes of the case consistently pointed to either incarceration or probation. In testing their hypothesis on drug offenders convicted in Miami, results showed that, as the degree of uncertainty increased in the case, the effect of race on the sentencing outcome also increased in turn. This means race impacts cases when it can, consistent with lots of other evidence (Walker et al., 2012).

In their test of the liberation hypothesis, using a sample of defendants convicted of violent felonies in Detroit, Spohn, and Cederblom (1991) found support for the hypothesis in regards to the decision to incarcerate. The authors argued that in cases where the charges are less serious and the appropriate sentence is less obvious, judges are "liberated from the constraints imposed by law, by other members of the courtroom workgroup, and by public opinion, and are free to take into account extra-legal considerations such as race" (Spohn & Cederblom, 1991: 323). Thus, discrimination in sentencing occurs when it is possible for it to occur; as crime seriousness increases, judicial discretion in sentencing decisions decreases, making discrimination less possible. This is consistent with the evidence shown in Chapter 3.

Steffensmeier and Demuth (2000, 2001) most notably expanded the minority threat issue to include Hispanics in a series of sentencing studies. They highlighted several possible explanations for increased judicial discrimination towards Hispanic populations. The first of these explanations focused on the stereotypes associated with Hispanic populations, which include an association with drug trafficking and drug-related violence, thus increasing the perception of threat. Additionally, the authors argued that Hispanics are less able than other groups to resist discrimination and that the historical context of Hispanic Americans might emphasize the belief that Hispanics are dissimilar to other racial or ethnic groups.

Criminal Justice as a Social Control Mechanism

Given all this discussion about social control in the courts and correctional facilities, is it possible that criminal justice practice serves as a social control mechanism to keep people of color oppressed? Michelle Alexander answers yes, arguing that criminal justice is a mechanism intended to control African Americans. Specifically, she sees mass imprisonment of especially African American males as an intentional *racial caste system*, which she says denotes "a stigmatized racial group locked into an inferior position by law and custom" (2012: 12). Her argument is based on the fact that America has always had racial caste systems—from slavery to the current day—and she says such systems do not end, they are just redesigned or change forms over time.

Alexander examines US history and suggests that, when slavery was abolished, a new form of racial caste system eventually emerged called *Jim Crow*. As shown earlier, the heart of the Jim Crow system was the notion of "separate but equal," where blacks would supposedly have equal access to societal institutions, but this access must remain separate from that of whites. After the Jim Crow system was finally defeated legally as a result of the Civil Rights Movement—meaning the nation's institutions would finally have to be desegregated so that, among other things, blacks could attend the same schools as whites—America's racial caste system would have to change again. This time, according to Alexander, it was the criminal justice system that would step in to take the lead (just as police maintained Jim Crow by enforcing the criminal laws at the time). So today, where it is not legally permissible to discriminate using race in America's "colorblind society," we instead use the "legitimate" or "race neutral" factor of "criminality" to control minorities. To Alexander, *black* is synonymous with *criminal*.

How did this happen, according to Alexander? The "law and order" approach to crime control that started in the 1960s was born in response to the Civil Rights Movement, which was depicted by southern politicians as a breakdown in law and order. That is, the acts of civil disobedience engaged in by groups such as the National Association for the Advancement of Colored People, Student Nonviolent Coordinating Committee, Congress on Racial Equality, and Martin Luther King, Jr.'s Southern Christian Leadership Conference were often depicted by national, state, and local politicians as criminal behaviors in need of criminal justice intervention. As noted by Katherine Beckett and Theodore Sasson:

In an effort to sway public opinion against the civil rights movement, southern governors and law enforcement officials characterized its tactics as "criminal" and indicative of the breakdown of "law and order." Calling for a crackdown on the "hoodlums," "agitators," "street mobs," and "lawbreakers" who challenged segregation and black disenfranchisement, these officials made rhetoric about crime a key component of political discourse in race relations.

(Beckett & Sasson, 2000: 49)

And, of course, participants as well as leaders in the movement were arrested by police, hosed down by firefighters, attacked by police and police dogs, as well as assaulted and murdered.

It did not help that riots in the streets and images of lawlessness were widely depicted in the news and meaningfully connected to civil disobedience and the civil rights movement itself. And, even though studies would eventually show that many riots were actually initiated by the police through excessive use of force against innocent and peaceful marchers, politicians were able to frame these events as examples of threats to life, liberty, domestic tranquility, and the general welfare of society—the very values that Americans enshrined in the Declaration of Independence and US Constitution. At the very least, the civil rights movement became seen by many as a serious threat to the status quo of American society and the racial caste system that has always been part of it.

When Jim Crow laws were overturned, something else had to take the place of Jim Crow; Alexander claims it is America's current system of mass imprisonment. So perhaps it is not a coincidence that America's boom in imprisonment began just five years after the murder of the man who stood at the center of the Civil Rights Movement's work for equality, Dr Martin Luther King, Jr. King was assassinated in April 1968 and increases in imprisonment began in 1973. That is, it took only five years from the death of the nation's most important civil rights leader for the nation to begin its transition to mass imprisonment, a phenomenon that has most severely impacted African Americans.

According to Alexander, such a development does "not require racial hostility or overt bigotry to thrive" (2012: 14) only indifference to the suffering of millions of Americans who are seen simply in the eyes of Americans as criminals. As noted by Alexander, "Today, mass incarceration defines the meaning of blackness in America: black people, especially black men, are criminals. That's what it means to be black" (2012: 197). So today, to many Americans, *black* and *crime* are synonymous and thus imprisoning people viewed as dangerous appears perfectly normal.

Just how bad is it for African Americans in America today? According to Alexander, there are more black people in prison today in the US than there were in South Africa during Apartheid. And "a black child born today is less likely to be raised by both parents than a black child born during slavery" (2012: 180). This is true even though blacks are not actually more dangerous than whites (this issue will be further discussed later in the chapter).

Criminal justice bias, according to Alexander, occurs in two stages:

The first step is to grant law enforcement officials extraordinary discretion regarding whom to stop, search, arrest, and charge for drug offenses, thus assuring that conscious and unconscious racial beliefs and stereotypes will be given free rein. Unbridled discretion inevitably creates huge racial disparities. Then, the damning step: Close the courthouse doors to all claims by defendants and private litigants that the criminal justice system operates in a racially discriminatory fashion.

Demand that anyone who wants to challenge racial bias in the system offer, in advance, clear proof that the racial disparities are the product of intentional racial discrimination—i.e., the work of a bigot.

(Alexander, 2012: 103)

Alexander focuses attention on the drug war as the primary culprit that explains mass incarceration of young black men in America. And in her summary of this new racial caste system, she writes that it works like this:

- Phase one—police round up large numbers of young black men as part of the drug war;
- Phase two—courts deny these people meaningful legal representation and coerce them to plead guilty; and
- Phase three—correctional facilities house them, largely invisibly, until their release dates, after which the stigma of conviction follows and harms them for the rest of their lives.

(Alexander, 2012: 185–186)

The *drug war* is a term that summarizes America's approach to fighting drug producers, growers, manufacturers, sellers, possessors, and users in order to reduce drug use. Why do we fight a drug war? Because of the criminal law, which first determined that certain drugs are illegal and that second called for strict criminal penalties for producing, growing, manufacturing, selling, possessing, and using drugs. So, according to Alexander's argument, the law really is the problem. And the law is thus still an impediment to realizing social justice, even as it has been used to help move the nation toward racial equality, as shown in this chapter.

Activity 5.3 Race and Offending

To what degree does race actually explain differences in offending?

Do some research online and see what arguments exist that might explain why African Americans are overrepresented among arrestees.

To the degree Alexander's idea of a racial caste system is correct, criminal justice practice today can be seen as a major impediment to America's ideals of libertarianism, egalitarianism, and even utilitarianism (especially with regard to the happiness of those subjected to increased crime control). Similarly, to the degree conflict approaches are accurate, criminal justice practice (e.g., police use of force, longer criminal sentences) is not consistent with the ideals of criminal justice.

Summary

America is a diverse nation, but it is one still largely dominated by whites and the wealthy. As such, members of many racial groups remain members of minority groups, as they have less privilege and power in society. Further, prejudice, racism, and ultimately discrimination still exist in American society, in spite of laws that explicitly aim to eliminate discrimination within institutions such as the economy (e.g., employment, hiring), citizenship (e.g., voting), education (e.g., college admissions), etc.

Some prejudice and discrimination in America owes itself to stereotypes that persist to this day, in spite of numerous efforts over the decades to overcome false notions about groups of people based on the behaviors of individuals. Yet, some prejudice and discrimination in American society has been institutionalized, meaning it has become entrenched within institutions in society such as the law and in agencies of criminal justice.

Here, conflict criminology is useful in helping us understand how the rights and interests of whites and the wealthy are often better served than those of people of color and the poor. In essence, threats are assigned and/or perceived that are affiliated with different racial groups in society, most notably African Americans. It is suggested that African Americans are depicted and seen as more threatening, and, thus, they are suppressed to protect citizens, thereby maintaining current arrangements in society in line with the interests of the powerful and in violation of our principles of liberty and equality.

Discussion Questions

1. What is a minority group?
2. Differentiate primary and secondary culture conflicts.
3. What is a stereotype? And how does it lead to prejudice, racism, and discrimination?
4. Outline the ways in which slavery and slave codes maintained power differentials in US society.
5. In your opinion, how could a nation that was founded on principles of liberty and equality participate in slavery?
6. Identify the earliest efforts in American society to assure equality in society by abolishing slavery and/or stating equal rights for all citizens.
7. What is Reconstruction and how did it fall short of assuring equality in America?
8. What were Jim Crow laws and how were they overcome?
9. In your opinion, is civil disobedience acceptable? Why, or why not?
10. What laws were passed in the 1960s to assure equality in American society? What did these laws do?
11. Discuss the Southern Strategy and outline the role that race played in it.
12. Discuss the main tenets of the conflict perspective in criminology.
13. What is the power threat hypothesis? What evidence is there in criminal justice that suggests it still exists?
14. Differentiate between different social control mechanisms that are used in response to specific threat groups, according to Liska.
15. Identify and define individual sources of social control.
16. How does criminal justice operate as a social control mechanism, according to Alexander?

References

Akers, R. (1997). *Criminological Theories: Introduction and Evaluation* (2nd ed.) Los Angeles: Roxbury.

Albonetti, C. A. (1991). An Integration of Theories to Explain Judicial Discretion. *Social Problems, 38*(2), 247–266.

Alexander, M. (2012). *The New Jim Crow: Mass Incarceration in the Age of Colorblindness* (Rev. ed.). New York: The New Press.

Aptheker, H. (1951). *American Negro Slave Revolts*. New York: International.

Arvanites, T. (1992). The Mental Health and Criminal Justice Systems: Complementary Forms of Social Control. In Allen Liska (Ed.) *Social Threat and Social Control*. Albany, NY: SUNY Press.

Ayers, E. (1984). *Vengeance and Justice: Crime and Punishment in the 19th Century American South*. New York: Oxford University Press.

Bassetti, V. (2012). *Electoral Dysfunction: A Survival Manual for American Voters*. New York: The New Press.

Beckett, K., & Sasson, T. (2000). *The Politics of Injustice: Crime and Punishment in America*. Thousand Oaks, CA: Sage.

Beckett, K., & Western, B. (2001). Governing Social Marginality: Welfare, Incarceration, and the Transformation of State Policy. In Garland, D. (Ed.), *Mass Imprisonment: Social Causes and Consequences*. London: Sage Publications.

Blalock, H. (1967). *Toward a Theory of Minority-Group Relations*. New York: Wiley.

Bridges G., Crutchfield R., & Simpson E. (1987). Crime, Social Structure and Criminal Punishment: White and Nonwhite Rates of Imprisonment. *Social Problems, 34*, 345–361.

Chambliss, W., & Seidman, R. (1971). *Law, Order, and Power*. Reading, MA: Addison-Wesley Pub.

Chamlin, M. B. (1989). Conflict Theory and Police Killings. *Deviant Behavior, 10*, 353–368.

Chamlin, M. B. (1990). Determinants of Police Expenditures in Chicago, 1904–1958. *Sociological Quarterly, 31*, 485–494.

Chamlin, M. B. & Liska, A. E. (1992). Social Structure and Crime Control Revisited: The Declining Significance of Intergroup Threat. In Liska, A. E. (Ed.) *Social Threat and Social Control*. Albany, NY: SUNY Press.

Clegg, S., & Dunkerley, D. (1980). *Organization, Class and Control*. London: Routledge and Kegan Paul.

Clinton, C. (1982). *The Plantation Mistress: Woman's World in the Old South*. New York: Pantheon Books.

Fiske, S. T. (1998). Stereotyping, Prejudice, and Discrimination. In Gilbert, D. T., Fiske, S. T., & Lindzey, G. (Eds.), *The Handbook of Social Psychology* (4th ed., Vol. 2, pp. 357–411). New York: McGraw-Hill.

Foucault, M. (1965). *Madness and Civilization: A History of Insanity in the Age of Reason*. New York: Pantheon Books.

Franklin, J., & Moss, A. (1994). *From Slavery to Freedom: A History of African Americans* (7th ed.). New York: McGraw-Hill.

Greenberg, D., & West, V. (2001). State Prison Populations And Their Growth, 1971–1991. *Criminology, 39*(3), 615–654.

Greenberg, D. F., Kessler, R. C., & Loftin, C. (1985). Social Inequality and Crime Control. *Journal of Criminal Law and Criminology, 76*, 684–704.

Holmes, M. (2000). Minority Threat and Police Brutality: Determinants of Civil Rights Criminal Complaints in U.S. Municipalities. *Criminology, 38*(2), 343–368.

Irwin, J., & Austin, J. (1994). *It's About Time: America's Imprisonment Binge*. Belmont, CA: Wadsworth Pub.

Jackson, P. I. (1989). *Minority Group Threat, Crime, and Policing: Social Context and Social Control*. New York: Praeger.

Jackson, P. I. (1992). Minority Group Threat, Social Context, and Policing. In Liska A. E. (Ed.), *Social Threat and Social Control*. Albany, NY: State University of New York.

Jacobs, D., & O'Brien, R. M. (1998). The Determinants of Deadly Force: A Structural Analysis of Police Violence. *American Journal of Sociology, 103*, 837–862.

Jones, W. (1998). *Is God a White Racist? A Preamble to Black Theology*. Boston: Beacon Press.

Kalven, H., & Zeisel, H. (1966). *The American Jury*. Boston: Little, Brown.

King, M. (1958). *Stride Towards Freedom: The Montgomery Story*. New York: HarperCollins.

King, M. (1963). *Letter from the Birmingham Jail*. In King, M. (Ed.), *Why We Can't Wait*, (pp. 77–100). New York: Signet.

Liska, A. (1992). *Social Threat and Social Control*. Albany, NY: State University of New York Press.

Liska, A. E., & Yu, J. (1992). Specifying and Testing the Threat Hypothesis: Police Use of Deadly Force. In Liska, A. E. (Ed.), *Social Threat and Social Control*. Albany, NY: State University of New York.

Lofland, J. (1969). *Deviance and Identity*. Englewood Cliffs, NJ: Prentice-Hall.

Meltzer, M. (1993). *Slavery: A World History*. New York: Da Capo.

Myers, M. A. (1990). Black Threat and Incarceration in Postbellum Georgia. *Social Forces, 69*, 373–393.

Noel, D. (1972). *The Origins of American Slavery and Racism*. Columbus, OH: Merrill.

Ore, T. (2011). *The Social Construction of Difference and Inequality: Race, Class, Gender, and Sexuality* (2nd ed.). Boston, MA: McGraw-Hill.

Piven, F., & Cloward, R. (1993). *Regulating the Poor: The Functions of Public Welfare* (Updated ed.). New York: Vintage Books.

Quinney, R. (1970). *The Social Reality of Crime*. Boston: Little, Brown.

Robinson, M. (2002). *Justice Blind? Ideals and Realities of American Criminal Justice*. Upper Saddle River, NJ: Prentice Hall.

Schaefer, R. (2011). *Racial and Ethnic Groups* (12th ed.). Boston: Prentice Hall.

Sellin, T. (1938). Culture Conflict and Crime. *American Journal of Sociology*, *44*(1), 97–103.

Sever, B. (2001). The Relationship Between Minority Populations and Police Force Strength: Expanding our Knowledge. *Police Quarterly*, *4*(1), 28–68.

Smith, B. W., & Holmes, M. D. (2003). Community Accountability, Minority Threat, and Police Brutality: An Examination of Civil Rights Criminal Complaints. *Criminology*, *41*, 1035–1063.

Sorensen, J. R., Marquart, J. W., & Brock, D. E. (1993). Factors Related to Killings of Felons by Police Officers: A Test of the Community Violence and Conflict Hypotheses. *Justice Quarterly*, *10*, 417–440.

Spitzer, S. (1975). Toward a Marxian Theory of Deviance. *Social Problems*, *22*, 638–651.

Spohn, C., & Beichner, D. (2000). Is Preferential Treatment of Female Offenders a Thing of the Past? A Multisite Study of Gender, Race, and Imprisonment. *Criminal Justice Policy Review*, *11*, 149–184.

Spohn, C., & Cederblom, J. (1991). Race and Disparities in Sentencing: A Test of the Liberation Hypothesis. *Justice Quarterly*, *8*, 305–327.

Steffensmeier, D., & Demuth, S. (2000). Ethnicity and Sentencing Outcomes in U.S. Federal Courts: Who is Punished More Harshly. *American Sociological Review*, *65*(5), 705–729.

Steffensmeier, D., & Demuth, S. (2001). Ethnicity and Judges' Sentencing Decisions: Hispanic–Black–White comparisons. *Criminology*, *39*(1), 145–178.

Steffensmeier, D., Ulmer, J., & Kramer, J. (1998). The Interaction of Race, Gender, and Age in Criminal Sentencing: The Punishment Cost of Being Young, Black, and Male. *Criminology*, *36*(4), 763–798.

Szasz, T. (1970). *The Manufacture of Madness: A Comparative Study of the Inquisition and the Mental Health Movement*. New York: Harper & Row.

Tolnay, S., & Beck, E. (1992). Racial Violence and Black Migration in the American South, 1910 to 1930. *American Sociological Review*, *57*, 103–116.

Tonry, M. (2011). *Punishing Race: A Continuing American Dilemma*. New York: Oxford University Press.

Turck, M. (2000). *The Civil Rights Movement for Kids: A History with 21 Activities*. Chicago, Ill: Chicago Review Press.

Turk, A. (1969). *Criminality and Legal Order*. Chicago: Rand McNally.

Unnever, J., & Hembroff, L. (1987). The Prediction of Racial/Ethnic Sentencing Disparities: An Expectation States Approach. *Journal of Research in Crime and Delinquency*, *25*, 53–82.

US Department of Justice. (2013). Retrieved from: http://www.justice.gov/opa/pr/justice-department-file-lawsuit-against-state-north-carolina-stop-discriminatory-changes.

Walker, S., Spohn, C., & DeLone, M. (2004). *The Color of Justice: Race, Ethnicity and Crime in America* (3rd ed.). Belmont, CA: Thomson/Wadsworth.

Williams, K., Page, R., & Petrosky, A. (2014). Nonviolence and Marketing. *Journal of Academic and Business Ethics*, *9*.

Wilson, W. (Ed.). (1970). *The Selected Writings of W. E. B. Du Bois*. New York: New American Library.

6

LATINOS AND SOCIAL JUSTICE

Not like the brazen giant of Greek fame, with conquering limbs astride from land to land; Here at our sea-washed, sunset gates shall stand a mighty woman with a torch, whose flame is the imprisoned lightning, and her name Mother of Exiles. From her beacon-hand glows world-wide welcome; her mild eyes command the air-bridged harbor that twin cities frame. "Keep, ancient lands, your storied pomp!" cries she with silent lips. "Give me your tired, your poor, your huddled masses yearning to breathe free, the wretched refuse of your teeming shore. Send these, the homeless, tempest-tost to me, I lift my lamp beside the golden door!"

Emma Lazarus, 1883

In the United States, no other status is as important as that of *citizenship*, a status of a person as a citizen of a country that guarantees him or her certain rights and privileges, as well as duties. While the United States has historically been a nation of immigrants—even the Founding Fathers were immigrants at one point—no single issue is currently as contentious as immigration reform. The irony here is that historically, seeking the *American Dream* of prosperity, security, and success was one of the reasons that all immigrants eventually came to our shores. We need look no further than the plaque engraved and mounted inside of the Statue of Liberty—proudly displaying a sonnet written by Emma Lazarus—which is the featured quote at the beginning of this chapter. During the height of immigration in the early 1900s, many of our immigrants were individuals who had exhausted their options for prosperity in their homelands and came to the United States looking for a fresh start.

One could argue that this reasoning and logic remains today, as a large portion of Americans want even illegal immigrants to have some means available to them to stay in the country permanently; however, public hostility towards immigrants is growing. Recall that we showed in Chapter 2 a good bit about what Americans value. There, we did not address the issue of public opinion polls dealing with citizenship and immigration issues. In this chapter, we will illustrate what Americans generally think about these issues; polls generally show a willingness to accept immigrants into the country and to help them succeed here. We also examine issues of unauthorized immigration into the US, focusing on issues of ethnicity and social justice as they relate to Latinos.

Unauthorized Immigration

The total foreign-born population in the US in 2011 was 40.4 million, comprising 13 percent of the US population (Hipsman & Meissner, 2013). About 42 percent of these are naturalized citizens, 31 percent are permanent residents, and 27 percent are unauthorized immigrants. *Unauthorized immigrants* include people who sneak into the country illegally, people who overstay their visas, and people who are admitted on the basis of fraudulent documents (Wasem, 2013). When you think of immigration in the US, it is likely that you think of Mexican immigration.

Of the 40 million immigrants living in the US in 2012, 11.4 million were Mexican immigrants. Of these, 51 percent are illegal immigrants, 32 percent are permanent residents, and 16 percent are naturalized citizens (Gonzalez-Barrerra & Krogstad, 2014). Mexicans make up the largest portion of illegal immigrants in the US (Light, Lopez, & Gonzalez-Barrerra, 2014), and Latinos comprise three-fourths of that.

A main reason why many Mexicans immigrate into the US illegally is because legal immigration is so greatly restricted. *Per-country limits* on legal immigration specifically restrict the total portion of immigrants coming from any country at 7 percent, meaning that no more than 7 percent of all *legal immigrants* coming into the US can come from any one country, including Mexico. This imposes a greater burden on people from countries with larger populations who want to come into the US than it does on countries with smaller populations; those countries with the largest number of immigrants coming to the US are Mexico, India, and China, all with large populations. Further, legal immigration from Mexico is now capped and the estimated waiting time for a green card is now 10 years. Immigrants from Mexico generally come to the US in pursuit of higher wages and greater freedom. And roughly 46 percent of them are thought to have small children (Hippsman & Meissner, 2013). Yet, keep in mind that not all Latinos and not all Mexicans are unauthorized immigrants. In 2012, there were almost 34 million Latinos of Mexican origin living in the US, including 11.4 million immigrants born in Mexico and 22.3 million Mexicans born in the US. Mexican immigration into the US began to increase in the 1930s but really took off starting in the 1970s.

Latino Groups in the United States

According to the 2012 Census, 16.9 percent of individuals living in America self-identify as Hispanic or Latino. This figure confirms that Latinos are now the largest minority group in the United States— African Americans currently comprise 13.1 percent of our nation's demographic. With that said, it's important to note that individuals from many different ethnic backgrounds are classified as Latinos. As we noted in Chapter 5, while ethnic minorities are differentiated from the dominant group on the basis of cultural differences such as language, customs, and food preferences, there can be numerous differences between individuals included within that ethnic minority group, as will be shown in this chapter. In this chapter, we will discuss the history of each of the specific Latino groups mentioned above before addressing Latino rights in the twentieth and twenty-first centuries as a whole. We will also discuss that, for Latinos, the status of their citizenship is ambiguous at best.

When we look at the Latino population in the United States, 63 percent of the total Latino population identifies as Mexican, 9.2 percent as Puerto Rican, 3.5 percent as Cuban and 24.3 percent as "other." These data are shown in Table 6.1. While there are certainly commonalities, such as a shared language, each of these countries has a varied and rich history.

Below we address different histories and experiences of Cuban Americans, Puerto Rican Americans, and Mexican Americans. As you read about each group, consider that, although each is very different in many ways, each is included as part of the Latino population.

Cuban Americans

The Republic of Cuba, an island in the Caribbean Sea, is a mere 100 miles from the coastline of Florida. Cuba was one of the islands that Christopher Columbus stumbled upon when he was said to have "discovered America" and was established as a Spanish settlement in the early 1500s. The native population was hostile towards the settlers almost immediately because they had received word of the mistreatment of other indigenous groups in the neighboring islands. After the Spanish settlers quelled the rebellion, and decimated the local population, Spain introduced black slaves onto the island to work the land and develop towns. By 1740, the city of Havana was an agricultural epicenter that dealt in tobacco and sugar, among other crops. Cuba continued to operate under Spanish rule until the end of the nineteenth century.

The ties between the United States and Cuba go back to 1898 and the end of the Spanish–American War. The United States declared war on Spain after the US warship, the *Maine*, exploded and sank near Havana, Cuba. While the definitive cause of the explosion remains unknown, the United States held Spain accountable and, after only a few months of fighting, Spain signed a peace treaty. As part of this peace treaty, the Spanish government signed over the rights to its territories—namely Cuba, Puerto Rico and Guam. While the United States granted Cuba its independence with the stipulation that the US could intervene in Cuban affairs if necessary, that condition was later rescinded. The second condition was that the United States be granted perpetual lease of Guantanamo Bay, the American naval base located in southeastern Cuba (used currently to house *enemy combatants* in America's *war on terror*).

During the first half of the twentieth century, travel and trade between Cuba and the United States was wide open. In fact, the United States owned 60 percent of the land in Cuba and 75 percent of the sugar industry. Towards the middle of the century, one event would change the course of Cuban–American relations for good. At the conclusion of World War II, the countries of the world were essentially divided along two different forms of government—countries that practiced democracy and countries that practiced communism.

TABLE 6.1 Latino Groups in the US

Mexican	63%
Puerto Rican	9.2%
Cuban	3.5%
Other	24.3%

Source: Census Quick Facts Dataset. http://quickfacts.census.gov/qfd/states/00000.html.

Prior to the 1960s, Cubans were not very well represented in the United States—the 1960 Census showed that fewer than 80,000 people of Cuban descent lived in the US That all changed, however, with Fidel Castro's rise to power during the Cuban Revolution of 1959. Under Castro's leadership, Cuba became the first Communist state created in the Western Hemisphere. While the United States government originally recognized Castro as the new Cuban dictator, they withdrew that support when the leader nationalized US assets on the island.

Roughly 200,000 Cubans fled in the first three years after Castro's ascension to power. In an ill-fated plan, called the *Bay of Pigs Invasion*, the CIA trained 1,400 of these Cuban exiles and sent them back to Cuba to oust Castro. The plan failed when it became immediately apparent that the invaders were grossly outnumbered and they surrendered less than 24 hours after the fighting began. The Soviet Union responded to this attack by placing nuclear weapons in Cuba, aimed at the United States. This standoff became known as the *Cuban Missile Crisis*, which ended with the Soviet government removing the weapons in exchange for a promise from the United States that they would not invade Cuba. This was the closest the US ever came to all-out nuclear war.

The American government put a trade embargo into place shortly after the Bay of Pigs invasion in the hopes that isolating Cuba economically would undermine the Communist regime and deprive it of necessary resources. Since 1960, American citizens have been barred from traveling to, trading with, or investing in Cuba. Prior to 1991, the embargo was supported as a national security measure, since Fidel Castro maintained close ties to the Soviet Union. That national security threat ended with the fall of Soviet Communism in 1991. The loss of Soviet support has left Cuba without resources and in poverty, but the United States has maintained, and even increased the sanctions and embargo, for over 50 years.

One of the primary effects of the embargo is that, for decades, Cuban Americans and Cuban citizens in exile in the United States could not easily travel back and forth to Cuba. When Fidel Castro overthrew the Cuban government, the first wave of immigrants to arrive in the United States was the wealthiest. These professionals and businessmen abandoned their culture, money, and political connections with the knowledge that their country would soon be in a state of upheaval. The second wave of immigrants to follow was the less wealthy relatives and friends of the first wave of elite Cubans and they settled in the large urban communities of South Florida.

Interestingly, this second wave of immigration was aided greatly by the United States government. President Lyndon Johnson ran weekly "freedom flights" to help oppressed Cubans get to safety in America. While these first two waves of Cubans quickly integrated into the United States and found jobs for their skills, two things became clear: there was little room left in South Florida for poor and/or minority Cubans looking for refuge; with the exodus of the skilled and professional labor force from Cuba, the country's future looked increasingly bleak. Once the freedom flights stopped running their route in the 1970s, Cubans looking to flee to the United States took it upon themselves and began attempting the 100-mile trip by boat. By 1980, the media were covering story after story of Cubans washing up on the shores of Miami. Lacking the skill and funds of the elite Cubans who were by this point well established in Florida, these new refugees were portrayed as criminals and undesirables who were perceived as nothing more than a drain on American resources.

The fourth and final wave of Cuban immigrants took place during the 1990s. With the implementation of the 1995 revision of the *Cuban Adjustment Act of 1966*, the United States instituted what became informally known as the "wet foot/dry foot" policy. What this meant was that, if the United States Coast Guard intercepted Cuban exiles at sea en route to Florida, they would return the exiles to Cuba. If, however, the Cuban exiles made it to land, they could seek refuge within the United States. For those exiles that did not successfully make it all the way to US soil, the Cuban government agreed in 1994 not to take action against returning refugees. The refugees that did successfully make the trip were eligible to apply for a change in legal status that made them eligible for an immigrant visa, permanent residence, and, eventually, United States citizenship.

Interestingly, this policy regarding undocumented aliens applies only to those fleeing Cuba. Undocumented refugees from Haiti or the Dominican Republic are not similarly eligible for immigrant visas. Without a doubt, Miami and New York City are the two American hubs that have seen the largest change as a result of the exodus. When Fidel Castro handed over power in 2008 to his brother Raul Castro, travel became somewhat less restricted. In 2009, the Obama administration allowed Cubans with family on the island to make unlimited trips.

It should be obvious to you that none of this was motivated by a desire to bring about social justice, but instead by US foreign policy objectives which are so often devoid of any serious social justice considerations. If any social justice implications were considered, they pertained to concerns of free market libertarians wanting to maximize wealth by protecting US capitalistic interests.

Puerto Rican Americans

Puerto Rico is another country that was "discovered" by Christopher Columbus. While it was originally documented under the name of San Juan Bautista, it was soon known as "Puerto Rico," or rich port, thanks to the gold found in the river. Once Puerto Rico was established as a Spanish colony, the capital city took the name San Juan instead, and the island was soon transformed into an important military post for the Spanish government.

Much like the history of Cuba, the indigenous Taino and Carib Indians already inhabited Puerto Rico prior to the Spanish colonization of the island. Slaves were brought in to farm the land for cattle, sugar cane, coffee, and tobacco. While numerous attempts were made by the French, Dutch, and British to conquer the island, Puerto Rico remained in Spanish hands until the Treaty of 1898, which passed possession over to the United States government. Under American rule, the island was transformed from an agricultural economy to an industrial one. The combination of cheap labor and favorable tax laws attracted American companies and by the middle of the twentieth century, Puerto Rico's economy was grounded in manufacturing and tourism.

The people of Puerto Rico were granted US citizenship in 1917, and in 1952, Puerto Rico became a US Commonwealth; that status remains. In Puerto Rico today, Spanish and English are both official languages and the currency is the US Dollar. Still, many Americans on the mainland are perhaps unaware of the citizenship status of Puerto Ricans. According to the Census, an estimated 4.9 million Latinos of Puerto Rican origin currently reside on the United States mainland. That is actually greater than the population of Puerto Rico, which is currently at 3.7 million people. Much like Cubans, individuals who identify as Puerto Rican are mainly located in New York and Florida.

Interestingly, while Puerto Ricans living in Puerto Rico are indeed US citizens, they do not have the right to vote nor do they have any voting representation in Congress. While the issue of Puerto Rico becoming the fifty-first state of the United States has been raised numerous times over the last century, the people of Puerto Rico have historically elected to keep their current status. In 2012, however, a referendum was issued in which the majority of Puerto Ricans stated opposition to continuing as a US territory and favored becoming a state over the other available options. With that support, Senator Heinrich (D, NM), a member of the Senate Committee on Energy and Natural Resources—which has jurisdiction over the issue of Puerto Rico's political status—filed the Puerto Rican Status Resolution Act during the 2014 Congressional session. Senator Heinrich said:

> In 2012, 54 percent of Puerto Ricans rejected their current relationship with the United States. We have a responsibility to act on that referendum, and this step is critical in that effort. My home state of New Mexico spent 66 years as a territory before gaining statehood in 1912—the longest of any state. Puerto Rico has spent nearly 116 years as an American territory. That's long enough. The debate over Puerto Rico's status needs to be settled once and for all so that its people can focus on fostering a more prosperous future (*In Historic Step, Puerto Rico Statehood Admission Bill Is Introduced in U.S. Senate*. 2014 news release. Retrieved: October 6, 2015).

In the same press release, Senator Wyden of Oregon added,

> For a nation founded on the principles of democracy and the consent of the governed, how much longer can America allow a condition to persist in which nearly four million US citizens do not have a vote in the government that makes the national laws which affect their daily lives?

This is a great example of the inconsistencies between American practice and American ideals. In Chapter 2, we showed that Americans value liberty and equality, yet our immigration policy in some ways conflicts with these principles.

Mexican Americans

With regard to the relationship between Mexico and the United States, war plays a prominent role—doesn't it always? When the Spanish began colonizing Mexico in the 1500s, they had two major victories that spurred their continuing interest in the Americas. First, Spanish conquistador Herman Cortes conquered the Aztec Empire in 1519 by taking the city of Tenochtitlan and capturing Cuauhtemoc, the Aztec emperor. Then, Francisco Pizarro overthrew the Incas of Peru in 1532. These lands were wealthy in gold and silver, and, while the Spanish continued to explore for even more wealth, conflicts with indigenous people prevented any sizable settlement from occurring until the 1700s. While Santa Fe was founded in 1609 in what is now New Mexico, it was not until 1749 that Spain established the first civilian town in what is now Texas; twenty years later, settlements began to crop up in what is now California.

Over the next half-century, American revolutionaries would declare their independence from Britain. The Spanish colonies followed suit in the early part of the nineteenth century during the Spanish–American wars of independence. They were able to do so thanks to Napoleon's invasion of Spain in 1807, which provided enough of a distraction for the colonists to begin skirmishes. By 1821,

Spain formally recognized Mexico's independence. New Mexico, Texas, and parts of California became known as the new Mexican republic, as shown in Figure 6.1. The bulk of the population who inhabited these lands was of Mexican, Native American, European, and African mixed lineage. This mixed bloodline was called *mestizo* and they were the ancestors of the current Latinos living on those lands.

In reviewing Figure 6.1, we hope the irony that this land used to belong to Mexico is not lost on you. Consider, for example, that many Americans today see high population of Latinos (including Mexicans) in these same states as a sign that America's traditions are being eroded by immigrants, perhaps a serious threat to some people's morals or virtues and thus their sense of social justice. That those same people are often motivated to deny equal rights to Latinos is, however, inconsistent with principles of libertarianism and egalitarianism reflected in the theories of John Rawls and David Miller introduced in Chapter 1, as well as our nation's founding documents. Table 6.2 shows Mexican populations within different US states.

In a bit of foreshadowing, the United States had been trying to purchase Texas for years. Presidents John Quincy Adams and Andrew Jackson had both made offers to Mexico. The desire to purchase Texas stemmed from agricultural interests. Cotton and cattle were both plentiful on the Texas plains

FIGURE 6.1 The Mexican Republic.

TABLE 6.2 Mexicans in the US (2010)

State/Territory	Mexican American Population (2010 Census)	Percentage
Alabama	122,911	2.6
Alaska	122,911	3.0
Arizona	1,657,668	25.9
Arkansas	138,194	4.7
California	11,423,146	30.7
Colorado	757,181	15.1
Connecticut	50,658	1.4
Delaware	30,283	3.0
District of Columbia	8,507	1.4
Florida	629,718	3.3
Georgia	519,502	5.4
Hawaii	35,415	2.6
Idaho	148,923	9.5
Illinois	1,602,403	12.5
Indiana	295,373	4.6
Iowa	117,090	3.8
Kansas	247,297	8.7
Kentucky	82,110	1.9
Louisiana	78,643	1.7
Maine	5,134	0.4
Maryland	88,004	1.5
Massachusetts	38,379	0.6
Michigan	317,903	3.2
Minnesota	176,007	3.3
Mississippi	52,459	1.8
Missouri	147,254	2.5

(continued)

TABLE 6.2 *(continued)*

State/Territory	Mexican American Population (2010 Census)	Percentage
Montana	20,048	2.0
Nebraska	128,060	7.0
Nevada	540,978	20.0
New Hampshire	7,822	0.6
New Jersey	217,715	2.5
New Mexico	837,171	44.5
New York	457,288	2.4
North Carolina	486,960	5.1
North Dakota	9,223	1.4
Ohio	172,029	1.5
Oklahoma	267,016	7.1
Oregon	369,817	9.7
Pennsylvania	129,568	1.0
Rhode Island	9,090	0.9
South Carolina	138,35	3.0
South Dakota	13,839	1.7
Tennessee	186,615	2.9
Texas	7,951,193	31.6
Utah	258,905	9.4
Vermont	2,534	0.4
Virginia	155,067	1.9
Washington	601,768	8.9
West Virginia	9,704	0.5
Wisconsin	244,248	4.3
Wyoming	37,719	6.7
Total US	31,798,258	10.3

Source: Data from the US Census Bureau.

and many Anglo settlers moved into the area for this reason. The primary conflict between the Mexican government and the Anglos was that Mexico had abolished slavery. This was to the detriment of the Anglo settlers living in Texas, because they could not bring their slaves in to help them farm lands. The secondary issue was that Mexico had customs laws that regulated trade with the United States, but the Anglo cotton farmers wanted free trade with the US.

The issue was settled once and for all through the Mexican–American War. Earlier in this chapter, we discussed how the Mexican–American War resulted in the United States acquiring Puerto Rico. At the conclusion of the same war, Mexico and the United States signed the *Treaty of Guadalupe Hidalgo*, which stated that Mexico would cede Texas, California, and most of New Mexico and Arizona for the sum of $15 million. After the treaty was signed, the 75,000 Mexican nationals that chose to remain on the annexed land were automatically given US citizenship.

While the Mexican nationals originally welcomed the United States' protection against local Native American tribes, they quickly realized that their true status was that of second-class citizens. Mexican landholders were told that they would keep possession of their lands after the treaty took effect. Shortly thereafter, tax laws and land-use laws were passed to make it virtually impossible for the Mexican landowners to do so. When the Mexican landowners tried to fight these laws, the language barrier and corrupt lawyers made their efforts futile. Additionally, while the newly minted Mexican–Americans legally had the right to vote, literacy tests, and poll taxes—all created by US law—kept them from exercising this right. To add insult to injury, when the Mexican–Americans did lose their lands, they were often hired on as laborers by the very people who acquired it through corrupt means. What resulted was a system of colonial labor, using Latinos as the primary labor force. Without a doubt, Latinos during this time experienced a severe downward economic mobility (Healy, 2003).

Robert Blauner (1972) argues that the experience of Africans and Mexicans in the United States has been one of the key factors that differentiated them from European immigrants and contributed to the system of racial and ethnic stratification. Building on this thought, David Montejano (1977) used the concept of *labor repression* to define the experiences of Latinos workers in the southwest. He also focused on the use of coercion and legal restrictions, such as those mentioned above, to limit the degree of freedom that Latinos had, relative to non-minority laborers. By limiting their ability to move up the social hierarchy or gain political power through the voting process, ethnic minorities were at the mercy of those willing to employ them.

Recall the discussion of different conflict theories in criminology from Chapter 5. Efforts to restrict rights and privileges of Latinos by powerful interests in the US are consistent with claims made by conflict theorists, and not at all consistent with the major tenets of libertarianism and egalitarianism.

Activity 6.1 Mexican Immigration

Go the website of the Migration Policy Institute and read "Mexican Immigrants in the United States" here: http://www.migrationpolicy.org/article/mexican-immigrants-united-states-0.

Why do you think so many Mexicans reside in border states and especially California and Texas?

The Rise of Immigration as a Social Justice Issue

During the course of the twentieth century, *migration, industrialization,* and *urbanization* changed the landscape of the southwest. As the United States began to prosper at a rate far exceeding its Latino neighbors, immigration into the US continued at an accelerated rate. Figure 6.2 shows the rate of growth of the US population over time; about one-third of population growth over the past decade is due to immigration.

Interestingly, a large majority of Americans (73 percent) favors providing a way for illegal immigrants to stay in this country, yet almost half (46 percent) think those who are here illegally should be allowed to apply for citizenship. Americans are evenly divided about whether the recent increase in deportations is a "good thing" or a "bad thing"—45 percent of Americans are in each category (Pew, 2014). According to Pew (2014), Republicans and whites are much more supportive of deportations than Democrats and Latinos. And only liberal Democrats generally favor allowing illegal immigrants to become citizens (66 percent). This is a good reminder of the contextual nature of social justice—responses often depend on the issue and who is being asked.

Further, just about half (49 percent) of Americans say new immigration legislation is important, yet proposed legislation is stalled in Congress for political reasons. Although such legislation is more important to liberals than to conservatives, and to Latinos than to whites or African Americans (Pew, 2014), the point is that many Americans seek a long-term solution to our problem of illegal immigration.

At the same time, corporations in the United States invested in—or exploited—Mexican labor in two ways to contribute to this reality. First, many companies moved production to Mexico to take advantage of the cheaper cost of labor. Second, corporations would bring Mexican laborers into the US as undocumented workers to farm the lands and would dismiss them without a means of returning to Mexico when they no longer needed them (Guerin-Gonzales, 1994). This is a practice that continues today, particularly in states such as North Carolina, which are far away from the Mexican border.

During the Great Depression in the 1930s, the United States government passed a series of measures aimed at reducing the number of Mexicans seeking jobs. They created a program called *repatriation,* which was the deportation of Mexicans back to Mexico. While the program was billed as constitutional because it focused on the deportation of illegal immigrants, the reality was that American citizens of Mexican descent were also caught up in this net of deportation (Balderrama & Rodriguez, 2006). Unconstitutional as this was, in reality, most deported citizens did not have the means to fight the deportation.

By the end of World War II—and with a depleted labor pool—Mexican laborers once again became a hot commodity. The United States and Mexico reached an agreement to allow contract laborers, called *braceros,* to enter the US to fill this labor need. This program continued until 1954 when the United States government implemented stricter immigration quotas for Mexicans. These quotas did not stop the flow of immigration from Mexico; it simply changed the immigration status of the individuals coming into the US from legal to illegal.

During the following decade, the Civil Rights Movement was in full effect and with it came the passage of the *Immigration Act of 1965.* Under the previous immigration control structure, each country was allotted a quota of immigrants that were granted entry into the United States. Worth noting is that, under the quota system, 70 percent of all immigrant slots were reserved for just three countries—United Kingdom,

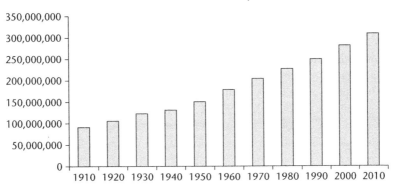

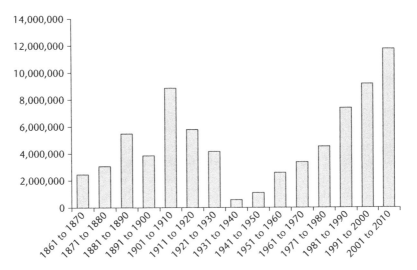

FIGURE 6.2 US Population Growth.

Ireland, and Germany. The new legislation was based instead on a system that focused on family reunification and needed skills. During the signing ceremony, President Lyndon Johnson criticized the old immigration system by saying:

> This system violates the basic principle of American democracy—the principle that values and rewards each man on the basis of his merit as a man. It has been un-American in the highest sense, because it has been untrue to the faith that brought thousands to these shores even before we were a country.

> *(Johnson, 1966: 1037–1040)*

Note the term *merit* in the quote above. Consistent with virtue-based theories of justice, Johnson was suggesting that Americans value rewarding people for their contribution to society, consistent with the utilitarian notion of desert laid out by Miller and discussed in Chapter 1.

At its core, the Immigration Act of 1965 became the basic structure of today's immigration law. As was previously mentioned, it abolished the national origin quota system while attempting still to moderate the rate of immigration into the United States. This new law allocated 170,000 new visas to countries in the Eastern Hemisphere and 120,000 to those in the Western Hemisphere, thus effectively increasing the ceiling of immigrants from 150,000 to 290,000. Keep in mind that spouses, minor children, and parents of US citizens over the age of 21 years were not counted in this quota. The most important change in the new immigration bill is that it was supposed to end discrimination. By removing a system of preferential treatment for some countries at the expense of others, the idea was that the *American Dream* would be accessible to everyone who was motivated to relocate to the States for a better life—this is thus also an effort to legislate our value of equality. Over the next 20 years, immigrants from Asia and Latin America would comprise the vast majority of new immigrants into the country.

By the 1980s, it was clear that there was not an adequate number of visas for the immigrants seeking to enter this country, and public opinion was moving towards a place of intolerance with regard to immigration issues. A primary complaint—and fear—was that the new immigrants would mean more mouths to feed and more bodies to compete in the job market. With the limited number of available visas (and the bureaucratic difficulties in obtaining them), an increasing number of immigrants were entering the country illegally. In 1986, the *Immigrant Reform and Control Act* was passed in an attempt to combat and deter this illegal immigration. This was done in two ways. First, it provided amnesty and temporary status to all illegal immigrants who had lived in the United States continuously since before January 1, 1982. This particular act also extended a separate and more lenient amnesty to farmworkers. More importantly, new sanctions were imposed on employers who knowingly hired illegal immigrants. These sanctions were levied against individuals who hired, recruited, or referred (for a fee) immigrants with a known illegal status. The hope was that, by providing amnesty for those immigrants who had already settled in the United States and by punishing employers who encourage illegal immigration, we could start anew with trying to curb the entry of illegal immigrants.

Yet, Congress also passed the *Immigration Act of 1990* in order to admit more highly skilled and educated immigrants into the US. As the labor market boomed in the 1990s, immigration including illegal immigration grew in New York, New Jersey, Florida, Texas, Illinois, and California, as well as in many other states (Hippsman & Meissner, 2013).

In 1996, *The Illegal Immigration Reform and Immigrant Responsibility Act* was passed into law. The purpose of this follow up Act was to increase the penalties against illegal immigration, streamline the deportation process and, finally, curb the ability of terrorists to use the immigration process to enter and operate in the United States. Once the "t" word was invoked, the Act authorized the following:

- 5,000 additional Border Patrol agents;
- a 14-mile-long fence in San Diego, California;
- expanded programs aimed at fingerprinting illegal immigrants apprehended nationwide;
- facilitated deportation of criminal aliens;
- required states to phase in drivers' licenses and state-issued ID documents.

By linking immigration to terrorism, government officials made it easier to pass such bills into law, a method used regularly in the nation's drug war going back as far as the 1980s!

Other laws from the 1990s that had implications for immigration include the *Personal Responsibility and Work Opportunity Reconciliation Act* (which denied access to federal benefits for some immigrants), the *Illegal Immigration Reform and Immigrant Responsibility Act* (which stepped up immigration enforcement, increased penalties for crimes related to immigration, sped up removal of noncitizens, and more), and the *Anti-Terrorism and Effective Death Penalty Act* (which made it easier to arrest and deport noncitizens) (Hippsman & Meissner, 2013).

This "get tough" on immigration rhetoric continued into the twenty-first century with the passage of laws such as the *Enhanced Border Security and Visa Entry Reform Act of 2002* (which increased visa screenings, border inspections, and tracking of some foreign-born persons), as well as the *REAL ID Act* from 2005 (which prohibits states from issuing forms of identification to unauthorized individuals) and the *Secure Fence Act of 2006* (which authorized a 700-mile fence along the border with Mexico).

The state of Arizona became the forerunner in oppressive immigration policy with the passing of SB 1070, also known as the *Support Our Law Enforcement and Safe Neighborhoods Act*. The main elements of the act are shown in Table 6.3.

The United States filed suit against Arizona shortly after the passage of the law. The federal government argued that the Bill encroached on the federal government's jurisdiction to create and enforce immigration legislation and to manage foreign policy, under Article 1, section 8, clause 4 of the US Constitution, which empowers Congress to regulate naturalization of foreign-born citizens.

The United States correctly identified that Arizona's intent on passing the Act was strictly punitive. As such, it would undermine the United States' careful balancing of immigration enforcement with foreign diplomacy. The United States government (US, 2010) additionally noted that:

> It will cause the detention and harassment of authorized visitors, immigrants, and citizens who do not have or carry identification documents specified by the statute, or who otherwise will be swept into the ambit of S.B. 1070's "attrition through enforcement" approach. It will conflict with longstanding federal law governing the registration, smuggling, and employment of aliens. It will altogether ignore humanitarian concerns, such as the protections available under federal law for an alien who has a well-founded fear of persecution or who has been the victim of a natural

TABLE 6.3 Support Our Law Enforcement and Safe Neighborhoods Act

- Requires officers to make a reasonable attempt to determine the immigration status of a person stopped, detained, or arrested if they possess "reasonable suspicion" that the person is unlawfully present in the United States, and requires the verification of the immigration status of any person arrested prior to releasing that person (Section 2(B));
- Criminalizes noncitizens' failure to apply for or carry alien registration papers (Section 3);
- Bars unauthorized aliens from soliciting, applying for, or performing work (Section 5(C)); and
- Authorizes the warrantless arrest of noncitizens where there is probable cause to believe the person has committed a public offense that makes the person removable from the United States (Section 6).

Source: Federation for American Immigration Reform, Support Our Law Enforcement and Safe Neighbourhoods Act, Summary of Arizona SB 1070 as Enacted, April 27, 2010, http://www.fairus.org/site/DocServer/ariz_SB1070_summary.pdf?docID=4761.

disaster. And it will interfere with vital foreign policy and national security interests by disrupting the United States' relationship with Mexico and other countries.

In layman's terms, the Complaint filed by the government indicated that Arizona's law constituted discrimination and would encourage profiling and harassment, all of which is inconsistent with Americans' ideals of liberty and equality.

The Supreme Court, the final arbiters where issues of constitutionality are concerned, issued a ruling on this case in 2012; the case was *Arizona v. United States*, 567 US (2012). While the Supreme Court deemed several of the provisions unconstitutional, it upheld the most controversial provision in the Bill. The Justices stated that it is constitutional for an officer to make a reasonable attempt to determine the immigration status of a person stopped, detained or arrested if there is reasonable suspicion that the individual is in the country illegally. For the other provisions, the Supreme Court indicated that Arizona would need to contact the office of *Immigration and Customs Enforcement* (now a part of the *Department of Homeland Security*) prior to initiating deportation proceedings. Emboldened by Arizona's draconian law, five states—Alabama, Georgia, Indiana, South Carolina, and Utah—passed similar laws in the years that followed.

Arizona officials reported that their motivation for passing this law was because the federal government was not effectively carrying out its responsibility to secure the nation's border with Mexico; Arizona, is after all, a border state. That is, this law, and all the others passed since the 1990s, were not motivated by social justice concerns. There were clearly free market concerns addressed, such as the right of corporations to profit from immigration.

Shockingly, the idea for Arizona's law came from private, for-profit companies. The bill was introduced and sponsored by legislators who received financial donations from those same companies, and signed into law by a governor with close connections to the companies as well. It started in a meeting between Arizona legislators and corporate officials from the *American Legislative Exchange Council* (ALEC), which included members of the *Corrections Corporation of America* (CCA).

CCA's plan was to build and operate prisons for illegal immigrants, including both adults and children, and they sold this plan to Arizona as a positive gain for the community in terms of jobs. Reports by CCA show they believed illegal immigration to be the next big financial market for their company. So they helped draft the model bill that became Arizona's immigration reform law.

Ultimately, 36 legislators joined to co-sponsor the bill, and two-thirds of them were members of ALEC or were at the meeting with ALEC when the bill was drafted. As the bill was being considered, CCA was lobbying the legislature to assure passage. Of these 36 co-sponsors, 30 received donations from prison lobbyists or companies within six months of the passage of the bill. Governor Jan Brewer then signed the bill into law. It turns out that two of her top advisers used to be lobbyists for private prison corporations.

The lesson of this story is simple: if private companies wrote this law, because they thought it would benefit them financially, then they clearly do not really want illegal immigration to go away. How do we know? Because they are in the business of making money, they would not write and push a law that would lead to monetary loss. Translation: as long as there is illegal immigration, private prisons will make money. If illegal immigration is stopped, they will not make money. That is the clearest proof that the Arizona immigration law (written by the private prison industry) will not reduce illegal immigration into the country, and that this was not its assumed purpose (in spite of claims by state officials). And, clearly, the law thus promotes free market libertarianism rather than any other conception of justice.

Clearly these actions violate the major principles of John Rawls's theory of *justice as fairness* as well as David Miller's *pluralistic theory of justice* reviewed in Chapter 1. That is, legislating on immigration for profit stands in direct opposition to *equal liberties*, *equal opportunities*, the *difference principle*, as well as *equality* in matters of citizenship, especially when policies are enacted to the detriment of one group for the benefit of another.

The irony is that, under President Obama, more than 1.9 million immigrants have been deported from America (Cassata, 2014). This is more than any other presidential administration in US history (Horsley, 2014). Under President Obama, roughly 400,000 unauthorized immigrants a year have been deported (Light, 2014). Further, a record 419,384 were deported in 2012 (Pew, 2014). Yet, the President did create the Deferred Actions for Childhood Arrivals (DACA) program in June 2012. DACA grants deferred action, meaning no deportation, as well as authorization to work to young immigrants who came to the US as children, have pursued education, have not committed serious crimes and do not pose a national security threat to the US (Hippsman & Meissner, 2013).

Just when it seemed like our policy regarding immigration was becoming increasingly strict and intolerant, the Development, Relief, and Education for Alien Minors Act (also known as the *Dream Act*) was introduced into Congress. Although supported by President Obama, the bill has not been passed and signed into law. According to the National Immigration Law Center (2014), the Dream Act would allow certain immigrant students who have grown up in the US to apply for temporary legal status and, if they go to college or serve in the US military, to later apply for permanent legal status and become eligible for US citizenship. It would also eliminate federal penalties to states who provide in-state tuition to some immigrants.

Activity 6.2 The DREAM Act

Go online and read about the DREAM Act.

Outline the major arguments for it and the major arguments against it.

Then decide if you think the bill should become law.

Why or why not?

Further, restorative legislation was passed in the form of the Deferred Action for Childhood Arrivals (DACA) Act. Passed in 2012, DACA was passed for those undocumented immigrants who: entered the country prior to their sixteenth birthday; have lived continuously in the United States for at least five years; have not been convicted of a felony or significant misdemeanor; and are currently in school. The individuals who fall into this group are typically youth who were brought into the United States early on in life. They often are not aware of their undocumented status until they try to apply for a driver's license or college and realize that they do not have the necessary paperwork to do so.

The problem for the estimated two million juveniles who fall into this category is that they are culturally American and generally have few ties to their home country. Under the previous immigration legislation, they were at risk of deportation to a country that they may know little to nothing about. Additionally, with an inability to attend college or gain legal employment, these individuals had few available alternatives. To remedy this issue, this Act provides a pathway to citizenship through either a college education or military service. While the individuals wouldn't be eligible for federal education grants, they would be allowed to enroll in college and obtain student loans.

Symbolic Racism

For the last several pages, we've discussed the extensive legislation put into place to control Latino immigrants. What's curious is that, typically, Americans do not exhibit the same type of xenophobic reaction to, say, an immigrant from England or Germany. This begs the question: what is it about Latinos that Americans find so threatening? To answer this question, we must pull from the messages that we are getting from both political and popular discourse in the contemporary United States, which has made the term *immigrant* virtually synonymous with the term *criminal*, particularly with regard to the Latino population; this is similar to Michelle Alexander's claims about *blackness* being conflated with *crime*, discussed in the last chapter.

This convergence of terms has brought about a *moral panic*, which is defined as a condition, episode, person or group of persons who are perceived as being a threat to societal values and interests (Cohen, 1971). As Leo Chavez (2008) points out, the American public perceives Latino immigrants as the "quintessential illegal aliens" and, subsequently, their social identity carries the stigma of this perceived illegality. To follow this line of thought, if one thinks of Latino immigrants as illegal, it is not a stretch to view the immigrants as illegitimate members of our society. Figure 6.3 provides an example of what a moral panic can look like—in this case, a protest in Washington, DC over proposed immigration reform. More recently, hordes of Americans, carrying signs and banging US flags on the ground, ambushed buses carrying children and teenagers who had recently entered the US illegally in an effort to flee serious violence in Central American countries.

Immigrants and refugees are often characterized as "enemies at the gate" who are attempting to invade Western nations (Lynn & Lea, 2003). Depictions such as these further fuel the moral panic and lead the public to believe that immigrants pose a physical, economic, and cultural threat, consistent with predictions made by the conflict perspective in criminology. This uncertainty about the potential threat of immigrant populations is often turned into crisis proportions once the news agencies play on these fears. For example, Chavez (2001) analyzed magazine covers from 1965 to 1999 and found that the images were increasingly negative and depicted immigrants as invaders. The resulting dehumanization of immigrants may appeal to members of the public because it further serves to justify the status quo, strengthens ingroup–outgroup boundaries, and defends against perceived threats to the ingroup's status in society (Haslam, 2006).

This process of *dehumanization* involves the denial of full humanness to others (Haslam, 2006). In an examination of the psychological literature on dehumanization, one important way in which people consider the "humanness" of others is the degree to which they have risen above their animal origins in an evolutionary sense. An important issue here is trying to understand why some individuals are particularly likely to dehumanize members of other groups, particularly groups like refugees and immigrants. As

FIGURE 6.3   Moral Panic in Washington DC?

noted above, one possibility is that people dehumanize other groups because they want to protect their privileged position and keep other groups from encroaching on their status and resources. Indeed, we discussed in Chapter 4 how the process of racial stratification classifies ethnic minorities as both "other" and "less than" for the purposes of justifying their treatment as second-class citizens. One need look no further than the *English First Movement* to see an example of this stratification. On the English First website, the mission statement is as follows:

> Did you know that English is not the official language of the United States of America? It's not. Not only do we have an assault of political correctness coming from all fronts, but we are pay-ing dearly with our tax dollars to accommodate people who've not taken the time to learn the English language. The top of the Constitution says "We the people . . . " in English, not multiple languages. English first is a national, nonprofit grassroots lobbying organization founded in 1986 and based in Springfield Virginia, just outside of Washington DC. As the only pro-English group to testify against bilingual ballots in 1992 and the only pro-English group to lead the fight against bilingual education in 1994, it is natural for English First to lead the charge for federal ballots, making English the official language of the United States and providing protection from frivolous lawsuits and money losing mandates due to political correctness. English First's sole purpose is to pass legislation making English the official language of the United States.

After reading the above statement, one would presume that the vast majority of Latino immigrants and their families do not speak English. Research shows that this is not the case. In a study conducted by Pew Hispanic (2012), 61 percent of Latino adults in the United States report speaking English very well. When measuring the language proficiency of second-generation Latino-Americans—that is, the children of immigrants—that figure increases to 92 percent because, as one might expect, the longer a group stays in the US, the more likely it will assimilate and become more similar to American citizens.

Additionally, many first-generation immigrants relocate to areas that are considered *ethnic enclaves*, or neighborhoods where a concentration of immigrants from the same country can be found. What this means is that Latino immigrants with only a rudimentary grasp of the English language often live in close proximity to other Latinos who can be of assistance to them as they navigate American bureaucracy.

Interestingly, English was not the native language of America. As we will discuss in Chapter 7, there were millions of Native Americans living here before Europeans colonized the eastern seaboard. The very first immigrants to this country would be considered undocumented by today's standards.

Also, while English is not the native language of America, it actually is the native language of the United Kingdom, which—the last time we checked—is located on the other side of the Atlantic Ocean. It appears that the sole purpose of the English First propaganda is to continue to perpetuate the established hierarchy of white America at the expense and humiliation of all others living here. This is clearly not consistent with American social justice ideals of libertarianism and egalitarianism.

Latino Ethnicity, Crime, and Criminal Justice

While the public and political perception is certainly that immigration increases crime, it is important to note that there is a scholarly consensus that the opposite is true. What's more, research has consistently shown that increased immigration may actually help to reduce the crime rate (Hagan & Palloni, 1999; Ousey & Kubrin, 2009; Sampson, Morenoff, & Raudenbush, 2005). This relationship holds true for both documented and undocumented immigrants, both of whom have been vilified as being crime-prone and law breaking.

There are many reasons for why this might be happening. Some theories include that Latinos may actively try to stay off of the police's radar for fear of being deported or that they may be working long hours, which does not leave much time for criminal behavior. Studies also find that first generation immigrants are less crime prone than their second-generation children or third-generation grandchildren (Rumbaut & Ewing, 2007). That is, the longer people stay here, the more they become like Americans (including committing crimes). According to Morin (2014), the reason crime increases among second-generation immigrants is because they "are just 'catching up' with the rest of us." In essence, the longer people spend in the country, the "more susceptible to temptation and harmful influences" they become.

Activity 6.3 Latinos and Crime

Read the Bureau of Justice Statistic's report, "Felony Defendants in Large Urban Counties, 2006—Statistical Tables."

Examine table 5. For which crimes are Latinos overrepresented among criminal defendants in the nation's largest counties?

What explains this?

First-generation immigrants also have more to lose, especially if they are here illegally (e.g., deportation), so their crime rates are much lower than those of native-born Americans; crime rates of second-generation Americans soar and are basically identical to native-born Americans. Second-generation Americans become more susceptible to the risk factors that increase criminality in others, including having delinquent peers or friends in gangs. As Sampson points out: "Cities of concentrated immigration . . . are some of the safest places around" (2008: 30).

It's easy to see why people aren't aware of the fact that immigration does not drive up the crime rate, because, when the literature is examined, Latinos are consistently sentenced more harshly than whites. Here is a sampling of that literature:

- Holmes and colleagues (1996) analyzed the effect of race and ethnicity on sentence severity in two Texas counties. Their data included a random sample of felony indictments adjudicated from 1987 to 1989. Results indicated that Hispanic defendants received significantly harsher sentences than whites after controlling for relevant legal and extra-legal characteristics.
- Albonetti (1997) examined 14,189 drug offenders sentenced from 1991 to 1992 in federal courts where Tobit modeling was applied to examine the race and ethnicity effects on the length of imprisonment. Similar to the findings presented in her earlier research, this study showed that Hispanic defendants received harsher sentences than white defendants.
- Felony offenders convicted in Kansas City and Chicago during 1993 were the focus of the study conducted by Nobiling, Spohn, and DeLone (1998) examining the effects of race and unemployment on sentencing outcomes. Results showed that white defendants were significantly less likely than Hispanic defendants to be incarcerated in Chicago.
- Engen and Steen (2000) examined the effect of race on sentencing outcomes using drug offense sentencing data collected from Washington State in 1992. The authors reported that black and white defendants had similar odds of incarceration; however, Hispanic defendants were significantly more likely than white defendants to be incarcerated. The odds of receiving a longer sentence length were also increased for Hispanic defendants when compared with white defendants.
- Chicago and Kansas City were selected along with Miami as the research sites for a study conducted by Spohn and Beichner (2000) examining the effect of race and ethnicity on the decision to incarcerate. Results indicate that Hispanic defendants had an increased likelihood of incarceration in Chicago.
- Mustard (2001) investigated the effect of race and ethnicity on sentence length using US Federal Courts data for 77,236 cases. He included a control for sentencing district along with other legal and extra-legal factors. Results demonstrated that Hispanic defendants received significantly longer sentence lengths than their white counterparts. Federal sentencing data were also used by Everett and Wojtkiewicz (2002) and included all defendants sentenced from 1991 to 1993. Hispanic defendants received significantly longer sentences than similarly situated whites.
- Drug offenders were the focus of research conducted by Kautt (2002) in her investigation of the effects of race and ethnicity on length of sentence for federal drug trafficking cases. Hispanic offenders received longer prison sentences than whites.
- Sentencing outcomes for Hispanic, black and Asian violent and sex offenders were compared in the study of 65 large US counties conducted by Maxwell, Robinson, and Post (2003). Hispanic defendants had an increased likelihood of incarceration compared to their white counterparts, but received

shorter sentences once incarcerated. Asian defendants also received shorter prison sentences than white defendants.

- Demuth and Steffensmeier (2004) researched the relationship between race/ethnicity and sentencing in their study, which used data from the State Court Processing Statistics gathered for 1990, 1992, 1994 and 1996. The authors found that Hispanic defendants received harsher sentences than comparable white defendants.

Add onto this the studies such as those mentioned in Chapter 2 illustrating *racial profiling* in some jurisdictions by police against people of color (including Latinos), and the results of these studies are consistent with claims made by Walker, Spohn, and DeLone (2012) about the presence of *contextual discrimination* in the courts, including sentencing. A review of correctional populations shows that Latinos are overrepresented, as shown in Table 6.4.

These outcomes are not consistent with American social justice principles of liberty and equality, and they violate the social justice theories of Rawls and Miller that were discussed in Chapter 1. It'd also be hard to justify them using the argument that they contribute to our happiness (i.e., utilitarianism) or that they are virtuous or right.

It is important to point out that increases in illegal immigration, stepped up enforcement by federal agencies (such as *US Customs and Border Protection*), and changes in policy such as no longer releasing those apprehended at the border to return without penalty to Mexico) have led to a growing burden on agencies of criminal justice. According to Michael Light (2014): "Dramatic growth over the past two decades in the number of offenders sentenced in federal courts has been driven primarily by enforcement of a particular immigration offense—unlawful entry into the United States." Incredibly, between 1992 and 2012, the number of people sentenced in federal courts for unlawful reentry convictions rose from 690 cases to 19,463 cases, a 28-fold increase; this increase accounts for about 48 percent of the growth in defendants sentenced in federal courts, and the second fastest-growing offense category during this time was drug offenses at 22 percent. Given this reality, it is not surprising that the proportion of Latinos sentenced in federal courts also increased during this time, from 23 percent of sentenced offenders in 1992 to 48 percent in 2012. Further, the proportion of offenders who were not US citizens grew from 22 percent to 46 percent during these years (Light, 2014).

Back in 1992, only 5 percent of all federal offenders were people who had committed immigration offenses, and by 2012 this had risen to 30 percent! Further, unlawful entry offenses were the

TABLE 6.4 Latinos and Correctional Populations

Prison (2010)	22%
Jail (2012)	15%
Probation (2010)	13%
Parole (2010)	18%
Death row (2014)	13%

Sources: Data from: US Department of Justice, Bureau of Justice Statistics, Prisoners in 2010, Bulletin NCJ 236096 (Washington, DC: US Department of Justice, December 2011), p. 26, Appendix Table 13; p. 27, Appendix Table 15; Bureau of Justice Statistics, Jail Population Increases after Three Years of Decline, http://www.albany.edu/sourcebook/pdf/t6332010.pdf; Death Penalty Information Center.

second-highest offense category in 2012, making up 26 percent of all federal criminal sentences; this is up from 2 percent in 1992. One should not thus be surprised that immigration offenses are producing federal prison terms. From 1998 to 2010, 56 percent of the growth in federal prison admissions was attributable to immigration offenses (Mallik-Kane, Parthasarathy, & Adams, 2012). Since 92 percent of unlawful reentry offenders were Latino in 2012, Latinos now make up a large proportion (48 percent) of all federal offenders.

We must ask ourselves, if Latino immigrants do not increase the crime rate, why then are they the targets of punitive crime policies? Ian Haney-López (2010) discusses four ways in which punitive crime policies contribute to racial stratification and subsequent racial and ethnic exclusion. The four dimensions are *profit*, *politics*, *degradation*, and *population control*. Beginning with the process of how criminalization yields *profit*, the increased punitiveness of immigration policy has created an "immigration industrial complex," which is characterized by laws and policies that benefit both corporate elites and government (Golash-Boza, 2009). The latest figures show that there are 400,000 immigrants detained annually (Department of Homeland Security, 2011). Half of these immigrants are housed in for-profit private prisons, which has become a booming industry as a result. In fact, the two largest private prison corporations in the world have spent millions of dollars to support candidates who will propose and pass strict immigration legislation (Kirkham, 2012).

Recall the example of Arizona's "show me your papers" law, discussed earlier. With regard to the government, agencies that focus on the policing of immigrants receive far more funding than those who attempt to provide social services (Welch, 2000). This trend is seen consistently in our national budgets. We regularly slash the funding that we allocate to schools, but rarely do so for national defense or corrections.

The second dimension is the *politics of criminalization*. In Chapter 5, we discussed Blalock's racial threat hypothesis, which outlined how rising minority populations—coupled with economic decline—yield anxiety in the white majority. The combination of an increasing unemployment rate, generally brought about by market factors such as demanufacturing, deinvestment, and globalization, and an increase in immigration creates a political climate ripe for anti-immigration rhetoric. The criminalization of Latino immigrants allows politicians to shift the anxiety of the white majority away from failing economic policy and towards these *law breakers* (Beckett & Godoy, 2008), very similar to the strategies such as the Southern Strategy used to increase concern in white voters over blacks. What results is that white workers are encouraged to direct their anger and aggression at immigrant laborers instead of at the true source of their economic hardship—for example, the corporations who are using the cheapest labor they can find, be it undocumented immigrants or factories in third-world countries.

The third dimension, *degradation*, highlights how anti-immigrant policies fuel resentment and manifest in discrimination on all levels. When someone belonging to a minority group experiences discrimination and degradation, the humiliation that they feel reinforces their subordinate status (Longazel, 2013). It is important to note that this degradation is not just directed at undocumented immigrants. In fact, the majority of individuals who are treated with suspicion or humiliated for "looking Mexican" are, in fact, American citizens (Cervantes, Khokha, & Murray, 1995). These policies that tout the principles of public safety, crime prevention, and upholding the rule of law create a dynamic where all individuals are perceived as being potentially illegal and subsequently treated as second-class citizens.

Finally, the dimension of *controlling immigrant populations* speaks to the unrelenting fear of harassment and deportation that individuals experience on a daily basis as a result of the zero-tolerance immigration policies that have been passed. The majority of immigrants express anxiety about daily tasks such as driving a car or walking down the street (Garcia & Keyes, 2012). This fear also extends to an unwillingness to report crimes to the police, which unwittingly results in Latinos becoming increasingly susceptible to criminal victimization. This fear is not limited to undocumented immigrants. A large number of migrant workers live in "mixed" households where there are both documented and undocumented individuals living together. The fear then becomes that the documented immigrants may somehow inadvertently contribute to the deportation of their friends and family if they come to the attention of the police.

All of this means that US immigration policy is not motivated by rational concerns rooted in social justice such as utilitarianism or virtue. Instead, these overly punitive responses are often driven by profit concerns and irrational motivations such as fear.

Until recently, the vast majority of studies in the substantial body of literature covering race and sentencing dichotomized race/ethnicity into white and nonwhite or white and black. This dichotomization assumed that (1) all minority groups receive equal treatment in relation to whites; and (2) that all minority groups share certain defining characteristics (Zatz, 1984). While some scholars proposed that such ignorance of ethnic differences was the result of bias (Hawkins, 1993), the primary reason for the exclusion was based on lack of available data (Demuth & Steffensmeier, 2004). Most sentencing studies relied on official data collected by the state. Historically, Latinos have been absorbed into the white category. This is the result of their ties back to Spain, which was the country that initially conquered and colonized parts of Puerto Rico, Cuba, and Mexico, among other countries. You'll recall that earlier in this chapter, we discussed how the individuals living in the southwestern lands of North America, which were annexed by the United States as a result of the Mexican–Americans War, were given citizenship (at least on paper) and all the rights that that citizenship entailed. This categorization as whites was not to their benefit because, as a result, Latino-Americans did not have the ability to file discrimination suits on the basis of race/ethnicity.

Summary

America has a long and sordid history of dealing with Latino populations, both within and outside of the United States. From the earliest days of the country, Latinos have been harmed and exploited for the benefit of the dominant groups in society—generally wealthy whites. Yet, as illustrated in this chapter, America is becoming increasingly heterogeneous, and Latinos now make up the largest group of any ethnic or racial minority in America.

The Latino population is actually made up of individuals from numerous countries, each of which has their own unique customs. Thus, thinking of them as one single group is inaccurate and can lead to misunderstandings about what people of Mexican, Cuban, Puerto Rican, and other backgrounds experience in America. Still, collectively they are facing enormous challenges, including threats from the federal and state governments, as they pursue new immigration policies that often result in deportation of one family member, thereby breaking up families.

To some degree, efforts to restrict immigration and oppose measures such as the Dream Act are based on the false belief that Latinos (and immigrants in particular) are responsible for more than their fair share of criminality. Even though this is *not* true, there is evidence both in law enforcement and the courts of discrimination against Latinos, suggestive that America is not quite living up to its ideals of liberty and equality when it comes to criminal justice practice.

Discussion Questions

1. What is citizenship?
2. How would you define the "American Dream" and why do you think people leave their home country to come to the US to try to obtain it?
3. Identify the major Latino populations in the US.
4. Compare and contrast different Latino populations in the US.
5. In your opinion, does US policy toward Cuba make sense in the modern day? Explain.
6. In your opinion, should Puerto Rico be a US state? Explain.
7. What do you think is the solution to illegal immigration coming from Mexico? Why?
8. Identify and discuss the major federal laws that have attempted to halt immigration.
9. Will Arizona's "Support Our Law Enforcement and Safe Neighborhoods Act" actually halt illegal immigration into the US? Explain.
10. What is symbolic racism? Explain how attempts to halt Latino immigration in to the US may exemplify symbolic racism.
11. What is a moral panic? And how might recent American immigration policy be consistent with a moral panic?
12. Are Latinos more criminal than other ethnic groups in the US? Provide evidence in support of your answer.
13. Is there discrimination against Latinos in American criminal justice? Provide evidence in support of your answer.

References

Albonetti, C. A. (1997). Sentencing under the Federal Sentencing Guidelines: Effects of Defendant Characteristics, Guilty Pleas, and Departures on Sentence Outcomes for Drug Offenses. *Law and Society Review, 31*, 789–822.

Balderrama, F., & Rodriguez, R. (2006). *Decade of Betrayal: Mexican Repatriation in the 1930s* (Rev. ed.). Albuquerque, NM: University of New Mexico Press.

Beckett, K., & Godoy, A. (2008). Power, Politics, and Penality: Punitiveness as Backlash in American Democracies. *Studies in Law, Politics and Society, 45*, 139–174.

Blauner, R. (1972). *Racial Oppression in America.* New York: Harper & Row.

Cassata, *The Huffington Post.* (2014). *Republicans Still Distrust Obama Despite Aggressive Deportations.* Retrieved: October 6, 2015.

Cervantes, N., Khokha, S., & Murray, B. (1995). Hate Unleashed: Los Angeles in the Aftermath of Proposition 187. *Chicano-Latino Law Review, 17*, 1–23.

Chavez, L. (2008). *The Latino Threat: Constructing Immigrants, Citizens, and the Nation.* Stanford, CA: Stanford University Press.

Chavez, L. R. (2001). *Covering Immigration: Population Images and the Politics of the Nation.* Berkeley, CA: University of California Press.

Cohen, S. (1971). *Images of Deviance.* Harmondsworth, UK: Penguin.

Demuth, S., & Steffensmeier, D. (2004). Ethnicity Effects on Sentence Outcomes in Large Urban Courts: Comparisons Among White, Black, and Hispanic defendants. *Social Science Quarterly, 85*(4), 994–1011.

Department of Homeland Security. (2011). *U.S. Immigration and Customs Enforcement Statistics.* http://www.ice.gov/removal-statistics.

Engen, R. L., & Steen, S. (2000). The Power to Punish: Discretion and Sentencing Reform in the War on Drugs. *American Journal of Sociology, 105,* 1357–1395.

English First. (n.d.). Retrieved April 3, 2015, from http://englishfirst.org.

Everett, R., & Wojtkiewicz, R. (2002). Difference, Disparity, and Race/Ethnic Bias in Federal Sentencing. *Journal of Quantitative Criminology, 18*(2), 189–211.

Garcia, A., & Keyes, D. (2012). *Life as an Undocumented Immigrant: How Restrictive Local Immigration Policies Affect Daily Life.* Report from the Center for American Progress.

Golash-Boza, T. (2009). The Immigration Industrial Complex: Why We Enforce Immigration Policies Destined to Fail. *Sociology Compass, 3*(2), 295–309.

Gonzalez-Barrera, A., & Krogstad, J. M. (2014). *U.S. Deportations of Immigrants Reach Record High in 2013.* Washington, DC: Pew Research Center.

Guerin-Gonzales, C. (1994). *Mexican Workers and American Dreams Immigration, Repatriation, and California Farm Labor, 1900–1939.* New Brunswick, NJ: Rutgers University Press.

Hagan, J., & Palloni, A. (1999). Sociological Criminology and the Mythology of Hispanic Immigrant Crime. *Social Problems, 46,* 617–632.

Haney-López, I. (2010). Post-Racial Racism: Racial Stratification and Mass Incarceration in the Age of Obama. *California Law Review, 98*(3), 1023.

Haslam, N. (2006). Dehumanization: An Integrative Review. *Personality and Social Psychology Review,* 10, 252–264.

Hawkins, D. F. (1993). Crime and Ethnicity. In Forst, B. (Ed.), *The Socio-Economics of Crime and Justice* Armonk, NY: M. E. Sharpe.

Healey, J. (2003). *Race, Ethnicity, Gender, and Class: The Sociology of Group Conflict and Change* (3rd ed.). Thousand Oaks, CA: Pine Forge Press.

Hipsman, F., & Meissner, D. (2013). *Immigration in the United States: New Economic, Social, Political Landscapes with Legislative Reform on the Horizon.* Washington, DC: Migration Policy Institute.

Holmes, M., Hosch, H., Daudistel, H., Perez, D., & Graves, J. (1996). Ethnicity, Legal Resources, and Felony Dispositions in Two Southwestern Jurisdictions. *Justice Quarterly, 13*(1), 11–30.

Horsley, NPR.org. (2014). *President Obama Announces Executive Action On Immigration.* Retrieved: October 6, 2015.

Kautt, P. (2002). Location, Location, Location: Interdistrict and Intercircuit Variation in Sentencing Outcomes for Federal Drug-Trafficking Offenses. *Justice Quarterly, 19*(4), 633–671.

Kirkham, C. (2012). Private Prisons Profit From Immigration Crackdown, Federal and Local Law Enforcement Partnerships. *Huffington Post.* [Online]. Retrieved on July 10, 2012 from: http://www.huffingtonpost.com/2012/06/07/private-prisons-immigration-federal-law-enforcement_n_1569219.html.

Light, M. T., Lopez, M. H., & Gonzalez-Barrera, A. (2014). *The Rise of Federal Immigration Crimes.* Washington, DC: Pew Research Center's Hispanic Trends Project, March.

Longazel, J. (2013). Subordinating Myth: Latino/a Immigration, Crime, and Exclusion. *Sociology Compass, 7*(2), 87–96.

Lynn, N., & Lea, S. (2003). A Phantom Menace and the New Apartheid: The Social Construction of Asylum-Seekers in the United Kingdom. *Discourse and Society, 14*(4), 425–452.

Mallik-Kane, K., Parthasarathy, B., & Adams, W. (2012). Examining Growth in the Federal Prison Population, 1998 to 2010. Urban Institute Justice Policy Center Research Report.

Maxwell, C. D., Robinson, A. L., & Post, L. A. (2003). The Impact of Race on the Adjudication of Sexual Assault and Other Violent Offenses. *Journal of Criminal Justice, 31*(6), 523–538.

Montejano, D. (1977). *Race, Labor Repression, and Capitalist Agriculture: Notes from South Texas, 1920–1930.* Berkeley, CA: University of California, Institute for the Study of Social Change.

Morin (2014). *Crime Rises Among Second-Generation Immigrants as they Assimilate*. Retrieved April 3, 2015, from http://www.pewresearch.org/fact-tank/2013/10/15/crime-rises-among-second-generation-immigrants-as-they-assimilate/.

Mustard, D. (2001). Racial, Ethnic, and Gender Disparities in Sentencing: Evidence from the U.S. Federal Courts. *The Journal of Law and Economics*, *44*, 285–314.

Nobiling, T., Spohn, C., & DeLone, M. (1998). A Tale of Two Counties: Unemployment and Sentence Severity. *Justice Quarterly*, *15*, 459–485.

Ousey, G., & Kubrin, C. (2009). Exploring the Connection Between Immigration and Violent Crime Rates in U.S. Cities, 1980–2000. *Social Problems*, *56*(3), 447–473.

Pew. (2014). *On Immigration Policy, Deportation Relief Seen As More Important Than Citizenship*. (December 18). Retrieved April 3, 2015, from http://www.pewhispanic.org/2013/12/19/on-immigration-policy-deportation-relief-seen-as-more-important-than-citizenship/.

Pew Hispanic. (2012). *Language Use among Latinos*. http://www.pewhispanic.org/2012/04/04/iv-language-use-among-latinos/. Retrieved October 6, 2015.

Rumbaut, R., & Ewing, W. (2007). *The Myth of Immigrant Criminality and the Paradox of Assimilation*. Washington, DC: Immigration Policy Center.

Sampson, R. (2008). Rethinking Crime And Immigration. *Contexts*, *7*(1), 28–33.

Sampson, R., Morenoff, J., & Raudenbush, S. (2005). Social Anatomy of Racial and Ethnic Disparities in Violence. *American Journal of Public Health*, *95*(2), 224–232.

Spohn, C., & Beichner, D. (2000). Is Preferential Treatment of Felony Offenders a Thing of the Past? A Multisite Study of Gender, Race, and Imprisonment. *Criminal Justice Policy Review*, *11*(2), 149–184.

Walker, S., Spohn, C., & DeLone, M. (2012). *The Color of Justice: Race, Ethnicity, and Crime in America*. Belmont, IN: Wadsworth Pub.

Wasem, R. (2013). *U.S. Immigration Policy: Chart Book of Key Trends*. Washington, DC: Congressional Research Service.

Welch, M. (2000). The Role of the Immigration and Naturalization Service in the Prison Industrial Complex. *Social Justice: A Journal of Crime, Conflict & World Order*, *27*(3), 73–88.

Zatz, M. S. (1984). Race, Ethnicity, and Determinate Sentencing: A New Dimension to an Old Controversy. *Criminology*, *22*, 147–171.

7

NATIVE AMERICANS AND SOCIAL JUSTICE

> We invite the United States to acknowledge the justice of our claim. The choice now lies with the leaders of the American government—to use violence upon us as before to remove us from our Great Spirit's land, or to institute real change in dealing with the American Indian. We do not fear your threat to charge us with crimes on our land. We and all other oppressed peoples would welcome spectacle of proof before the world of your title by genocide. Nevertheless, we seek peace.
>
> *Richard Oakes, 1969, during the Occupation of Alcatraz*

The commonly used term, *American Indians*, says more about the Europeans who colonized North America than it does about the natives they found living there. The term was first used to incorrectly label the natives because the explorers had thought that they had finally found the Indies, which were in the Pacific Ocean near the continent of Asia. Upon first seeing the native residents, Christopher Columbus declared them "the people of India." Since the beginning, Native Americans have been stereotyped, misrepresented and simplified. They have also been hunted, massacred, and displaced. None of this, of course, is consistent with America's social justice ideals.

Richard Oakes, a Native American activist, wrote the words that opened this chapter in an effort to bring attention to the unyielding assault against Native American lands, culture, and autonomy that has taken place since the first footfalls of Europeans explorers on North American soil and that has endured until the present day. While most of the stereotypes of the "drunken Indian" or the "noble savage" are a fallacy created to justify the treatment of the indigenous people, what we *do* know to be true is that, for thousands of years, Native Americans roamed the vast lands of North America. Hunters and gatherers, they were adept at living in the complex physical environments of the North American continent.

While we will use the term *Native Americans* in this chapter, most tribal members prefer their tribal affiliation as a means of identification. The reasoning for this is simple—members of different tribes view themselves as distinct from one another. While there are some commonalities between the tribes, confusing a Cherokee with an Apache is much like confusing a Frenchman and a German; separate cultures yield separate identities. Currently, there are an estimated 2.4 million Native Americans and Alaskan Natives living in the United States.

Today, more than a third of Native Americans live on 557 reservations in 33 states. These reservations account for roughly 2 percent of the land in the United States (Ogunwole, 2006). Ultimately, the reservation system resulted in the marginalization of Native Americans. As Perry so eloquently writes, "The historical legacy of colonialism persists in the social and physical isolation experienced by so many residents of these rural enclaves" (2009: 401). Each of the 565 federally recognized tribes have their own history, cultural identity, and language.

While it is beyond the scope of this chapter to describe each tribe in detail, we embark upon this chapter with the understanding that there are many nuances between distinct tribes that will be inadvertently glossed over by the generic term of Native Americans. Also, an individual's self-identification as a Native American may be different from either the tribal recognition of that person as having the lineage to be included as a tribal member or from the Bureau of Indian Affairs federal recognition of that person and/or tribe. Beyond the cultural significance of self-identifying as a Native American, being a "card-carrying" and federally recognized Native American is a necessary component for receiving services and protections from the United States government. This federal recognition came about after an arduous legal battle, which will be discussed in detail later in this chapter, where the tribes fought to maintain autonomy from the growing threat posed by the newcomers to the North American continent.

Activity 7.1 North American Tribes

Go online and look into the different types of tribes that exist in the United States.

What are their major similarities and differences?

In this chapter, we will discuss America's history with Native Americans, and identify the social justice implications of this history. We first discuss the changing nature of the relationship between the Native Americans and the colonists, before highlighting the role that the law played in turning this relationship from one of amity to one of hostility. We also discuss the current state of Native American tribes and end with an examination of Native Americans in the criminal justice system today.

Native Americans in US History

The number of Native Americans in 1500 was believed to be in excess of ten million people. There was extensive warfare between tribes, but, by all accounts, they were a thriving people. Over the next several hundred years, which coincided with the arrival of settlers, Native Americans fell victim to measles, smallpox, and influenza. These diseases decimated the population and reduced the natives to about 600,000 in 1800. After another 100 years, the population was further reduced to 250,000. In contrast, the population of the settlers grew from just over 2,000 in 1620 to over five million in 1800 and ten million by 1820. To say that the arrival of the European settlers was catastrophic to the native population would be an understatement.

Social Darwinism was one of the primary ideologies used to justify the treatment—and mistreatment— of the Native Americans. *Social Darwinism* argues that the principles of survival of the fittest apply to people and that the strong will naturally survive. The settlers took the devastation of the native population by European diseases as proof that Europeans were superior to Native Americans. In other words, the Europeans assumed that the natives were simply biologically inferior and did not consider the possibility that native ways of life—and their existence—had intrinsic value.

As we will see in this chapter, the eradication of the Native Americans qualitatively shifted from *genocide* to *ethnocide*. *Genocide* refers to explicit violence intended for the eradication of a group of people. *Ethnocide* refers to the social violence and other tactics intended to deculturate a group of people and resocialize them to values of the dominant group. In other words, genocide is killing a group of people while ethnocide is killing that group's way of life. Over time, Native Americans would be "Americanized," meaning they would have to adopt the norms and values of those who would colonize and ultimately come to dominate the North American continent. This reality is captured in Figure 7.1, a photo taken in South Dakota showing the undeniable influence of European settlers on native populations.

Even with these realities, it's important to correct the historical record that often paints a picture of the natives as hapless victims who were too trusting or too unsophisticated to defend themselves against the invading white horde. The truth is that, in the early interactions between the natives and the settlers, the colonists looked to the natives for guidance with regard to many aspects of survival.

Additionally, some European commodities changed the Native American way of life for the better. The tribes originally hunted and traveled on foot, so the introduction of horses by the Spanish fundamentally changed every aspect of how the natives lived. They became better hunters and more adept at travel. It was only slowly that this relationship between the colonists and the natives shifted to one of aggression and then domination, but, in truth, the introduction of European diseases did more damage to the Native American people than guns and warfare ever could have.

Native American Relations with Settlers

In order to understand Native American involvement in the criminal justice system, we must first understand the complex relationship between Native American tribes and the United States government. Prior to European contact, Native American tribes had their own economic systems, spiritual ideology, laws, and methods of controlling deviant members. Their justice system was completely distinct from the European system to which they were later introduced. The tribal system of justice most closely resembles our modern day restorative justice practices. In its simplest form, *restorative justice* includes mediation, reparations, and acceptance of responsibility by lawbreakers, before ultimately reintegrating the offender back into the community. While banishment and death were also possible punishments, they were often used as a last resort (Dumont, 1993).

The arrival of the English—as well as Spanish, French, Dutch, and other groups who were eager to colonize the new continent—changed every aspect of Native American life. There was a shift in population demographics, ecology, technology, politics, and finally, the introduction of a new type of law that was completely foreign to the natives. The relationship between the Natives and the Europeans, like those discussed in the previous chapters, has roots deep in *colonialism*. Colonialism affected millions of people who inhabited the lands that the Europeans "discovered." Colonialism is defined as the invasion

FIGURE 7.1 Americanization of Native Americans.

and takeover of the political authority of a geographic area—and its inhabitants—by outsiders. While this complex relationship will include a discussion of political power (and the lack thereof), issues of land ownership, and the fight for the preservation of culture, it's worth noting that the initial contact was one not fraught in conflict.

There are several distinct historical periods that shaped the jurisdictional and legal history of the federal government's involvement with the Native American tribes (Myers, 2002). These historical eras are summarized in Table 7.1. Interestingly, many treaties and statutes that were passed prior to 1890 still control Native American policy. In particular, there are three Supreme Court cases commonly known as the *Marshall Trilogy*. This trio of cases will be discussed at length later in this chapter, but they effectively shaped the way that the federal government viewed and treated natives on US land. Going back to the various historical periods, we will briefly summarize them here.

TABLE 7.1 Major Periods in Native American History

1500s–early 1800s	Discovery, Conquest
Mid 1800s	Removal
Late 1800s–early 1900s	Removal
Mid 1990s	Reorganization
1960s–present	Self-determination

Historical Periods in Relations with Native Americans

The first period, which spanned from the mid-1500s to the early 1800s, was one of discovery and conquest. During this first stage, Native Americans and the colonists lived together more or less in a cooperative manner. The colonists did not have a sizeable presence, as of yet, so their numbers were not a threat to the natives. More importantly, the colonists sought out peaceful interactions with the tribes because they were in dire need of assistance. The colonists had no knowledge of this new land and, by all accounts, they were starving. In many of the earliest American settlements, more than half of those who survived the voyage across the Atlantic did not survive their first winter. While there were some early conflicts between the settlers and the natives, the settlers made a temporary peace with some of the Native American tribes and, in turn, learned valuable skills such as where to look for game, the optimal time for planting, and how to build adequate shelter. While the first several decades were difficult, the colonists soon adapted to the new land and by the middle of the seventeenth century, they began to prosper.

It is also worth noting that the ideology behind land ownership was fundamentally different between the colonists and the natives. The European laws of discovery were simple: if you came across a land with no clear landowner present, you stuck your flag in that piece of land and claimed it for your own. Conversely, the Native American philosophy of land was also simple: humans cannot own land; they can simply live off of her bounty and leave her unmarked. As one would imagine, these two philosophies came to a head quite quickly. While the Native Americans clearly occupied the land, they did not claim ownership over it and so the early colonists went about trying to establish boundaries and create treaties to ensure that their own newly claimed land rights were protected.

Here, it is important to call attention to the importance of liberty, including that conception of liberty posited by free market libertarians. Although European settlers were motivated by their own desire to own and control as much land as they could, they clearly did not extend this conception of freedom to Native populations. Thus, taking lands from Native Americans through numerous means, including treaties and hostile actions, is inconsistent with what is now an American ideal of justice. These actions were also clearly unequal in their outcomes—helpful for settlers and harmful for Native Americans—and thus inconsistent with the American principle of equality. They were deemed as virtuous or right in the minds of settlers, who pursued their own liberty—economic freedom in this "new" land.

The first recognized treaty signed between a Native American tribe and the US government was in 1778. Since that time, there have been in excess of 500 treaties negotiated. As Myers (2002) points out, these treaties were "negotiated" via the military. As can be expected, the necessity of using the military to negotiate the treaties increased as the years in this period advanced. The early treaties were more or less negotiated peacefully since the colonists were still in a relative position of weakness.

Yet, as the colonists gained strength and numbers, the second stage became one of coercion. The origins of an anti-Indian Movement began here in earnest. The rationale was clear:

> When you set about to dispossess a people of their land and source of livelihood, unless you have no conscience at all, one must find an excuse to safely hide from the truth of the pain and suffering you are inflicting on innocent peoples. If, indeed, these people were human beings, then they were in fact a lesser type of humanity who had no rights to life, land, or liberty. They could not use the land like Anglos, so they had no right to it; they had no civilizations, so they had no right to their own political institutions; their lives were not worth that of an Anglo, so they had no right to life.
>
> *(Jimson, 1992: 2)*

While it is hard to pass judgment on European settlers and colonists based on "American values" of liberty, equality, and happiness that were later codified in the Declaration of Independence and the US Constitution, it is imperative that we identify how treatment of Native Americans by those earliest white Americans conflicts with the ideals on which America was supposedly founded. Clearly, treatment of the native peoples of the Americas is inconsistent with the tenets of libertarianism and egalitarianism, although it might be justified by utilitarians who might see it as in the interests of the greater good, at least as far as white settlers were concerned. Free market libertarians likely would also justify the horrendous treatment of Native Americans because, under the tenets of *Manifest Destiny*—the doctrine that Europeans had the God-given right and, indeed, the duty to expand their territory and cultural influence throughout North America—the subjugation and extermination of Native Americans was necessary for white dominance (Loewen, 2007).

During this stage, the treaties made between the colonists and the natives were punctuated by military campaigns and massacres. In the early nineteenth century, the newly formed United States government established a policy of not antagonizing the Native Americans without cause. While we will discuss legislation at length later in the chapter, it is worth noting here that, by 1800, the federal government declared that it was the only entity that was allowed to make treaties with the various Native American tribes. These treaties were negotiated first by the Secretary of War and, later, were facilitated through the *Bureau of Indian Affairs*, which was created in 1824 and situated within the Department of War. While the initial emphasis was on maintaining peace along the frontier, it was clear that tribes who entered into treaties with the federal government would be dealt with more fairly than those who did not. Regardless, in all situations, if the needs of the whites conflicted with the need of the tribes, the whites viewed their claims as superior. This became evident as settlers moved westward, thus increasingly encroaching on lands that were inhabited by the natives.

During this era, even the well-meaning colonists ultimately damaged the integrity of the tribes' cultural traditions. Reformers and missionaries visited many tribes in an effort to impose upon Native Americans what they assumed to be superior European culture, language, religion, and social structure. Instead of recognizing that Native American tribes had established cultural roots that spanned centuries, the reformers often viewed the natives as naïve and infantile in their civility. In other words, they simply needed to be taught better ways. One example of this was the American boarding schools in which native children were enrolled (against the will of their parents). They were taught the English language and a concerted effort was made to replace their native traditions with new ones. This *assimilation*, or the process by which a group of people adopt the social and psychological characteristics of the dominant group, was widespread and resulted in the extinction of many languages and customs.

The courts became heavily involved with Native American policy during this era. In 1817, Congress passed the *Federal Enclaves Act*, which granted the federal government jurisdiction over non-Native Americans for crimes they committed on tribal lands. The federal government also claimed jurisdiction over the right to try Native Americans for certain offenses committed against non-Native Americans. Per the Act: "The general laws of the United States as to the punishment of offenses committed in any place within the sole and exclusive jurisdiction of the United States . . . [extend] to the Indian Country" (Title 18 U.S.C.A 1152). The exceptions to the Federal Enclaves Act were that it did not apply to crimes by Native Americans against other Native Americans; crimes by Native Americans that are punished by their tribe; or crimes by which Native American tribes have exclusive jurisdiction per a standing treaty.

The problem with the Federal Enclaves Act was that some criminal acts committed on these so-called "federal enclaves" were covered by state law, but not by federal law. To correct this oversight, Congress passed the *Assimilated Crimes Act of 1825*, which made state criminal law applicable to any offense not covered by federal law.

This was also the time of landmark Supreme Court decisions that would cement the relationship status of the United States government and the Native American tribes. Two of these particular Supreme Court cases involved the state of Georgia. By way of background, in the 1820s and 1830s, the Cherokee held territory in North Carolina, Tennessee, Alabama, and Georgia. The Georgia government spent the better part of these decades attempting to remove the Cherokee people from their borders. The Cherokee responded to this threat by creating their own constitutional government and declaring that, since they were a sovereign nation, they could not be removed without their explicit consent. The state of Georgia disagreed with this assessment and went about legislating the annexation of Cherokee land for the purpose of seizing it and redistributing it to the white citizens. The Cherokee refused to leave their lands and instead filed suit with the United States Supreme Court challenging the constitutionality of Georgia's new laws.

The Marshall Trilogy

The *Marshall Trilogy*, which received its name due to the leadership of Chief Justice John Marshall, would ultimately define tribal sovereignty and establish what protections tribes might expect to receive from the federal government. The first case of the Marshall Trilogy was *Johnson v. McIntosh* in 1823. In the earliest years of European settlement, individual citizens had traded with Native American tribes for the purchase of land. The case of *Johnson v. McIntosh* said that these individual treaties were invalid. The reasoning for this decision was that, as the successor to Great Britain, the original discoverer of the North American continent, the United States government had gained the preemptive right to obtain Native American land through conquest or purchase according to the *Doctrine of Discovery*. In other words, the federal government must be involved in all land exchanges involving Native American tribes.

Activity 7.2 Tribal Sovereignty

Read the "Fundamental Principles of Tribal Sovereignty" from the American Indian Policy Center here: http://www.americanindianpolicycenter.org/research/st98fund.html.

Then discuss how, even after the Marshall trilogy, treaties are supposed to favor American Indians.

One of the primary issues that became apparent in the dealings between the United States government and the Native American tribes is that, while the government viewed the natives as a single entity, that was not how the natives viewed themselves. In fact, many of the tribes had been at war with each other for hundreds of years. This meant that the US government had to negotiate with each tribe separately. This became clear in the case of *Cherokee vs. Georgia*, which is the second case of the Marshall Trilogy. In the early 1800s, gold was discovered in Georgia. As we mentioned earlier, Georgia extended its own laws into Cherokee country that were in direct conflict with existing Cherokee laws governing the same land. The Cherokee filed suit against Georgia in federal court to prevent them from encroaching upon lands that were guaranteed under the *Treaty of Hopewell* (signed in 1785 by the federal government).

While the Court was split in their decision on whether Georgia was encroaching on Cherokee lands, Chief Justice Marshall dismissed the case on jurisdictional grounds. His argument was that the Cherokee were not a foreign government and, thus, the federal government could not hear the case under their authority of mediating disputes between states and foreign states. He stated:

> While the Cherokee had an unquestionable right to the land they occupied unless it was ceded voluntarily to the federal government, it may well be doubted, whether those tribes which reside within the acknowledged boundaries of the United States can, with strict accuracy, be denominated foreign nations. They may, more correctly, perhaps, be denominated domestic dependent nations. They occupy a territory to which we assert a title independent of their will, which must take effect in point of possession, when their right of possession ceases. Meanwhile they are in a state of pupillage. Their relation to the United States resembles that of a ward to his guardian.
>
> *(Cherokee Nation v. Georgia, at 17)*

With this newly designated status as *domestic dependent nations*, the Supreme Court reaffirmed the tribes' status as sovereign entities, while avoiding a constitutional confrontation between the federal government and states' rights. You'll recall from Chapter 2 that the newly formed federal government was very careful not to appear to abridge the rights of each state since part of the impetus for the break from British rule was an aversion to a far-reaching government. Additionally, the US Constitution has an *Indian Commerce Clause* (Article 1, 8, clause 3), which states that Congress is recognized as having the power to "regulate commerce with foreign Nations and among the several states and with the Indian tribes." Even so, it is clear from Chief Justice Marshall's verbiage that the United States government viewed the Native Americans as children that needed watching and protecting. Taking it a step further, Congress frequently legislated on the lives of the natives well beyond their allowed issues of commerce and did so with the mentality that the natives, like children, don't always know what is best for them.

In this role of guardianship, the Bureau of Indian Affairs created and fostered the services offered to federally recognized tribes, including access to Indian Health Care Services, housing, food supports, and education. Again, it is important to note that at the inception of this domestic dependent nation status, the federal government chose the services that they thought the natives should receive. These services were offered without a cultural sensitivity to Native American culture, but instead with the intention of Christianizing and reforming natives to European sensibilities. As a result, Native Americans were very suspicious of the services offered and, to this day, will often not accept services offered by those outside of their reservation community.

In the third and final case of the Marshall Trilogy, *Worcester v. Georgia* (1832), the Supreme Court addressed the issue of whether the state of Georgia could impose criminal penalties on white missionaries who were living on Cherokee lands without having first obtained a license to do so from the governor of Georgia. The Supreme Court ruled that state law had no bearing on tribal lands because states could not interfere with the relationship between the federal government and individual tribes. The previous cases in the Marshall Trilogy established that, while the tribes were not recognized as foreign nations, they did have distinct sovereign powers. As such, the federal government argued that each tribe was receiving the protection of an even more powerful nation—i.e., the federal government—and that states had to recognize that protection.

Indian Removal in the Nineteenth Century

Another period of historical significance, during the mid-1800s, was marked by the removal and relocation of the eastern Native American tribes. The goal became to relocate tribes to land west of the Appalachian Mountains. While it may seem like the Marshall Trilogy was a victory of sorts, and that this movement was in direct conflict to the recently recognized sovereignty, the federal government justified the relocation of the natives from their aboriginal lands by citing their own needs for more land on the east coast (Tsosie, 2001). Oklahoma was determined to be the newly established "Indian Territory." The reservation system was also created as a means to further facilitate the assimilation of the tribes into mainstream white society. The selection of the least fruitful lands for reservations was tactical in nature. While the Native Americans had typically roamed the breadth of North America in search of game, this way of life was completely counter to the white ideas of land ownership and farming. William Medill, a nineteenth-century Indian Commissioner, explained:

> The policy already begun is, as rapidly as it can safely and judiciously be done, to colonize our Indian tribes beyond the reach, for some years . . . confining each within a small district of country so that, as the game decrease and becomes scarce, the adults will gradually be compelled to resort to agriculture and other kinds of labor.
>
> *(Medill, 1848)*

And so it came to pass in 1830 that the federal government enacted the *Indian Removal Act*, which called for the relocation of all Eastern tribes across the Mississippi River. The Removal Act passed with flying colors because it opened the way for Manifest Destiny, discussed earlier. The Cherokee, Chickasaw, Choctaw, and Creek tribes were among the largest groups resettled in Oklahoma. The resettlement, which in reality lasted more than a decade, became known as the *Trail of Tears* due to the massive loss of life that occurred during the movement. The tribes were forced off of their ancestral homelands during the harshest time of the year and many thousands perished prior to making it to the final destination. Loss of property and death are both inconsistent with tenets of libertarianism as well as egalitarianism.

Even with the resettlement, the Native Americans once again found themselves in the path of the settlers who pushed west at a quickening pace following the Civil War. The bottom line is that Americans seemingly had no place for Native populations—no matter where they were sent, they remained in our way—social justice be damned. Figure 7.2 illustrates the path taken by various tribes as they were relocated to the western United States.

By the latter part of the nineteenth century, most Native Americans had been resettled on reservations. In 1884, the *Court of Indian Offenses* was created so that Native Americans could resolve criminal matters that occurred on their own lands. Just one year later, however, Congress passed the *Major Crimes Act of 1885*. The Major Crimes Act granted the federal government primary jurisdiction over certain felonies committed in tribal lands and included crimes by one Native American against another—a situation that was previously the purview of the tribe. It also covered crimes committed by Native Americans against people of other ethnicities. The initial set of felonies that were turned over for federal prosecution, are shown in Table 7.2.

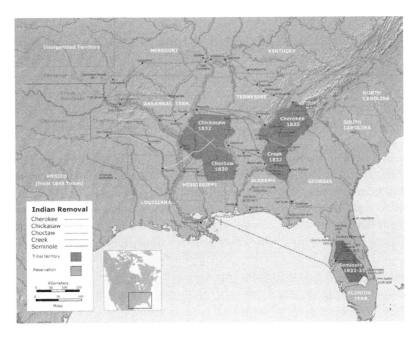

FIGURE 7.2 Trail of Tears.

TABLE 7.2 Major Crimes Act of 1885

Murder
Manslaughter
Rape
Assault with intent to commit murder
Arson
Burglary
Larceny

The Major Crimes Act further eroded the sovereignty of the tribes. By not allowing the tribes to try and punish their own serious offenders, the tribes lost the ability to deal with these offenders by their own customs and standards, a key violation of the tenets of *autonomy* (i.e., the freedom to determine your own fate) and thus libertarianism. Once again, they were forced to deal with the federal government against their will. In summary—and for the purposes of clarity—the jurisdictional issues were resolved in the following manner: the Federal Enclaves Act, Assimilative Crimes Act, and Major Crimes Act granted the federal government exclusive jurisdiction to prosecute crimes committed on tribal lands as federal crimes. States were granted jurisdiction over crimes committed on tribal lands that fell within their borders when non-Native American victims and defendants are involved. Finally, tribes have jurisdiction over misdemeanors committed on tribal lands where both the victim and the offender are Native American.

Land Allotment and Assimilation

The third period of significance occurred between 1887 and 1928. This period was punctuated by land allotment and assimilation. In 1887, the early boundary of this period, Congress argued that the tribes still had too much land. More importantly, Congress asserted that Native lands were still preventing further US growth into the western states. As a result, the *General Allotment Act* effectively reduced tribal lands from 138 million acres to 48 million acres. In order to quicken the assimilation of Native Americans into white society, the Allotment Act granted lands directly to Native American families. The intention was that the natives would create a homestead in a manner similar to a white settler and, as such, there was a provision attached to the Act that prohibited the native families from selling the land for 25 years. This, again, interfered with the rights of Native Americans of self-determination.

The problem from day one of land ownership was that the natives were given neither the tools nor the knowledge to make the land productive. As a result, much of the land granted in the Allotment Act was eventually given over to white ownership. While the land could not be sold, it could be leased through the Bureau of Indian Affairs, who would serve as a trustee for the revenue. Needless to say, the families who leased the land saw none of the resulting profit that was eventually generated through mining, oil, and timber (Deloria & Lytle, 1983). This is inconsistent with even free market libertarianism.

Then, in 1907, the tribes that were forced into Oklahoma were required to move again. The federal government now wanted to make Oklahoma a state. It was quickly becoming clear that the government had the goal of absorbing the natives into the now dominant American society so that they would not need to honor the concessions they made in the early years. In an effort to hasten this merger, Congress granted United States citizenship to all Native Americans through the *Indian Citizenship Act of 1924*. Finally, there was, on paper, a chance to stand up for the principles that Americans supposedly hold, such as John Rawls's theory of justice as fairness as well as David Miller's pluralistic theory of justice, reviewed in Chapter 1. That is, giving Native Americans citizenship allows them access to equal liberties and equal opportunities.

Even with the granting of citizenship, the failure of the assimilation policies was obvious. In the 1920s, the US Secretary of the Interior hired a team of investigators to examine and inspect the current living conditions of Native Americans in the United States. The results were published in 1928 and the document, known as the *Meriam Report*, outlined the substandard living conditions on most reservations. That is, there was serious inequality in society, inconsistent with the principles of egalitarianism. It was finally being brought to light that the legislative and policy changes enacted by the federal government had affected the quality of life of the Native Americans and those changes were not for the better. The Meriam Report also outlined the need for more funding and called for the end of the allotment policies. The tribes were here to stay and it was clear that they needed to be allowed to self-govern.

Indian Reorganization

The fourth era, one of Native American reorganization, lasted for the middle part of the twentieth century. While the early efforts of the colonists and, later, of the United States government, were focused on separating individuals from their tribes in an effort to teach them "better" ways, by the mid-1930s government officials realized that tribal identity is an inherent part of Native American identity. The *Indian Reorganization Act of 1934* created the ability for tribes to adopt a written constitution and elect tribal councils and tribal leaders. Tribal leaders had the authority to represent the best interests of the tribes when dealing with the local, state, and federal governments. While it recognized the right of Native Americans to approve or reject actions that affected them, it still forced the tribes to deal with the American government on the government's terms. Initially, many tribes were fearful that the passing of the Act was simply another assimilation tactic, but it was in actuality the first step towards the creation of tribal courts, Native American law enforcement agencies, and tribal legislative bodies.

Self-Determination

The fifth era, from the 1960s to the present, is the era of self-determination. During the Civil Rights Movement of the 1960s, the federal law that had governed Native American rights was reformed. For example, the *Indian Civil Rights Act of 1968* extended the protections of the United States Bill of Rights to tribal members from tribal government actions. The Indian Civil Rights Act, however, differs from the Bill of Rights in two ways: due to the varying resources available to each tribe, the right to counsel for criminal defense is deemed to be at "his or her own expense"; and there is no express separation of church and state for tribal government. This second provision is due to the inherent importance of traditional religious beliefs in ceremonies of every kind.

These gains of the Indian Civil Rights Act provided fuel for a secondary movement, the *American Indian Movement*, in the late 1960s. The Movement was founded to renew the spiritual strength of the Native American people so that, though they are scattered throughout the North American continent, they can finally act as one people united to continue to gain sovereignty and strength. Perhaps the most visible action of the American Indian Movement was the takeover of Alcatraz Island in 1969. On November 20, 1969, a group of Native American college students headed to Alcatraz, the sight of the abandoned federal penitentiary. The initial group of 79 Native Americans swelled to 400 people at the height of the 19-month occupation. The original purpose of the takeover of Alcatraz was to turn the abandoned penitentiary into a center for Native American Studies, but it became clear that the occupation turned into something more. A sign from that occupation is shown in Figure 7.3. On July 8, 1970, President Nixon publicly stated, "Self-determination among Indian people can and must be encouraged without the threat of eventual termination."

While the protesters dwindled as the siege wore on and ultimately ended in June 1971, the occupation of Alcatraz had a direct effect on federal Indian policy. Spurred on by the attention and emboldened by some victories, the activism associated with the American Indian Movement moved from peaceful protest to anger and retaliation. In 1972, angered by the lack of logistical support that was promised by government officials, Native American activists took over the Bureau of Indian Affairs headquarters in Washington DC and took many confidential files while causing 2.2 million dollars in damage in the process. Shockingly, the Nixon administration provided the activists almost $70,000 in transportation money in exchange for peacefully ending the occupation.

From here, the protests expanded to the tribal lands themselves. Highlighting the tension between the traditional Native Americans still living on the reservation and the Native Americans who were living in urban city centers, the conflict came to a head at a ten-week siege on the Pine Ridge Reservation in the Oglala Lakota Sioux lands of South Dakota. The issue at hand was the impeachment of the tribal

FIGURE 7.3 Occupation of Alcatraz.

chairman, Richard Wilson, over issues of corruption. While this might seem like a small matter, the standoff included tribal police, the FBI, representatives from the Bureau of Indian Affairs, and the tribal leaders themselves. When all was said and done, two Native Americans and one FBI agent were killed, and the media had broadcast the entire standoff to the country at large.

Results of the American Indian Movement

The results of the American Indian Movement were two-fold. First, there was a *cultural revitalization*, or a push to rediscover and reinstitute cultural traditions, ceremonies, languages, and social structures that were damaged as a result of colonization. This does not assure liberty, equality, and certainly not happiness, at least with regard to Native Americans. Sadly, a great deal of knowledge was lost as the result of the decimation of the population in the early years of white settlement, but tribes are actively trying to uncover that knowledge to further strengthen their current customs. Along with the cultural revitalization, there has been a move towards *self-determination*, or a movement to regain the right of Native American Nations to control their own social institutions, such as education, health, social services, health services, and criminal justice.

This brings us to the second result of the American Indian Movement: positive legislation. The *Indian Self-Determination and Education Assistance Act of 1975* mandated the Secretary of the Interior to work together with the tribes to plan and administer programs. One example of how this changed tribal operations was that it allowed tribes to contract with outside vendors for services that had previously been provided by the federal government. Another important piece of legislation during this era was the *Indian Child Welfare Act of 1978*. Congress put federal rules in place to ensure that Native American children who are removed from their homes are placed with other Native American families whenever possible, so that their cultural heritage and language can be preserved. This was an incredibly important step, given the concerted efforts of the previous centuries to separate native children from their families and their culture. While this remedy seems too little too late, it was restorative legislation that recognized important cultural distinctions between Native Americans and the surrounding non-Native American communities.

One of the issues closely tied to the cultural revitalization movement was a need to generate tribal income. One of the greatest misconceptions about Native Americans is that their entire lives are subsidized by government funds. Contrary to popular belief, the only Native Americans who receive government assistant checks are those who are either veterans or disabled. Additionally, Native Americans may receive social security income like other American citizens. The fact remains that Native Americans do not receive government checks simply for being indigenous to this country.

Since many reservations are in remote locations and unemployment is high, the tribes needed to find ways to survive. One idea for a profitable use of tribal lands came in the 1970s after the Supreme Court ruled that, based on the *Worcester v. Georgia* case, state courts could neither tax Native Americans living on the reservation nor could they regulate what the tribes built on their own lands. Shortly thereafter, the Seminole tribe of Florida built a Bingo building on their South Florida reservation. Their right to do so was supported by Congress when the *Indian Gaming Regulatory Act* was passed in 1988. This Act stated that, due to tribal sovereignty, tribes had the right to build casinos so long as they understood that the federal government had the power to regulate the gaming. This would ideally promote happiness among members of Indian tribes, consistent with utilitarianism, and give them a better ability to determine their own fate, consistent with libertarianism. The Act also required that tribes enter into Tribal–state contracts in order to engage in casino-style gaming activities. The Act outlined three classifications of gaming on Native American reservations, shown in Table 7.3.

Of the almost 600 federally recognized tribes, only 223 tribes have casinos. While it is up to the tribal councils to decide how the funds are spent, only a fraction of those tribes have money left over after expenses are paid to provide a cash payout to tribal members. A cash payout is when casino profits are split among tribal members and distributed to members for their personal use. Even in the scenarios when cash payouts are not possible, they do create jobs on the reservation.

TABLE 7.3 Indian Gaming Regulatory Act

Class I

Includes (1) traditional Indian gaming, which may be part of tribal ceremonies and celebrations, and (2) social gaming for minimal prizes. Regulatory authority over class I gaming is vested exclusively in tribal governments and is not subject to IGRA's requirements.

Class II

The game of chance commonly known as bingo (whether or not electronic, computer, or other technological aids are used in connection therewith) and, if played in the same location as the bingo, pull tabs, punch board, tip jars, instant bingo, and other games similar to bingo. Class II gaming also includes non-banked card games, that is, games that are played exclusively against other players rather than against the house or a player acting as a bank. The Act specifically excludes slot machines or electronic facsimiles of any game of chance from the definition of class II games.

Tribes retain their authority to conduct, license, and regulate class II gaming so long as the state in which the Tribe is located permits such gaming for any purpose, and the Tribal government adopts a gaming ordinance approved by the National Indian Gaming Commission (NIGC). Tribal governments are responsible for regulating class II gaming with Commission oversight. Only Hawaii and Utah continue to prohibit all types of gaming.

Class III

Includes all forms of gaming that are neither class I nor II. Games commonly played at casinos, such as slot machines, blackjack, craps, and roulette, clearly fall in the class III category, as well as wagering games and electronic facsimiles of any game of chance. Generally, class III is often referred to as casino-style gaming. As a compromise, the Act restricts Tribal authority to conduct class III gaming.

Before a Tribe may lawfully conduct class III gaming, the following conditions must be met:

- The Particular form of class III gaming that the Tribe wants to conduct must be permitted in the state in which the tribe is located.
- The Tribe and the state must have negotiated a compact that has been approved by the Secretary of the Interior, or the Secretary must have approved regulatory procedures.
- The Tribe must have adopted a Tribal gaming ordinance that has been approved by the Chairman of the Commission.

The regulatory scheme for class III gaming is more complex than a casual reading of the statute might suggest. Although Congress clearly intended regulatory issues to be addressed in Tribal–state compacts, it left a number of key functions in federal hands, including approval authority over compacts, management contracts, and Tribal gaming ordinances. Congress also vested the Commission with broad authority to issue regulations in furtherance of the purposes of the Act. Accordingly, the Commission plays a key role in the regulation of class II and III gaming.

Native Americans, Crime, and the Criminal Justice System

Earlier in the chapter, we demonstrated the degree of segregation for Native Americans living in reservations. Nowhere is segregation more purposive than in Native American country, where the lines of demarcation between the reservation and the surrounding county are clearly delineated. The reservation system also made it difficult for the Native American tribes to organize politically. By allocating remote and isolated lands for the reservation, the natives were not seen and were virtually forgotten, especially as the generations went on. That was part of what drove the American Indian Movement. The Native Americans felt that they needed to remind the government and the rest of the country that they were still here, scattered though they may be. While a number of tribes eventually moved back to their ancestral lands, the available space was minimal after a century of United States industry and settlement. The historical practices discussed for much of this chapter have restricted the opportunities for Native Americans to be productive and have, literally, left them on the economic, social, and political edges of American society. This is compounded by the fact that 70 percent of tribal lands are located in rural parts of the country.

A secondary result of this marginalization is that approximately 60 percent of Native Americans live off of tribal lands. A large number of the Native Americans living in urban areas live in poverty and experience increased involvement with the criminal justice system. Factors such as poverty, social isolation, drug and alcohol abuse, and high rates of unemployment have all been linked to crime in literally decades of research in fields such as criminology and sociology (Armstrong, Guilfoyle, & Melton, 1996; Grobsmith, 1989; Koss, Yuan, Dightman, Prince, Polacca, Sanderson, & Goldman, 2003). Like other minority groups, Native Americans are currently overrepresented in the criminal justice system.

Native Americans aren't only overrepresented in their numbers—when contrasted to their percentage in the general population—but they also generally receive longer sentences and serve a higher percentage of those sentences than similarly situated whites. These outcomes are due to both legal factors (e.g., offense seriousness and prior record) and extra-legal factors (e.g., ethnic discrimination).

Activity 7.3 Tribal Crime and Justice

Read "Tribal Crime and Justice" from the National Institute of Justice here: http://www.nij.gov/topics/tribal-justice/Pages/welcome.aspx.

Why do Native Americans experience more violent victimization than other groups in society?

Yet, Native American issues and offenders are far less studied than the other minority populations discussed in this book. There are several explanations for this:

1. Native Americans comprise a smaller percentage of the population than do blacks and Latinos. Additionally, Native Americans are highly concentrated in certain parts of the North American continent and are completely absent from others.

2. Native populations are not included in the immigration discussion that has gripped the national stage and, as a result, receive less attention in scholarly research. They are, in many ways, a minority among minorities.

3. Almost all of the research that we have regarding Native American offending and incarceration is for offenses that fall under the federal government's jurisdiction. This is, in large part, due to the inherent distrust of non-Native American scholars by tribal councils. It is difficult to gain access to data that reveals what the offending, victimization, and conviction rates are of tribal members on tribal lands.

Due to the protected status of Native American tribes, their information, for the most part, is not subject to public records requests. This makes research difficult. What we do know, particularly for Native American offenders who are charged with felonies in federal courts, is that those individuals will typically receive harsher sentences than their non-Native American counterparts who are charged with the same crime in state courts (Wilmot & DeLone, 2010; Everett & Wojtkiewicz, 2002). As noted earlier, this is due to both legally permissible factors such as offense seriousness and prior record and legally impermissible factors related to discrimination. Thus, part of the reason Native Americans receive longer sentences is because they are committing more serious crimes and/or because they have longer criminal records. For example, Williams (2012) notes:

> The country's . . . Indian reservations have violent crime rates that are more than two and a half times higher than the national average, according to data compiled by the Justice Department. American Indian women are 10 times as likely to be murdered than other Americans. They are raped or sexually assaulted at a rate four times the national average, with more than one in three having either been raped or experienced an attempted rape.

Unfortunately, crime differences do not fully explain criminal justice disparities; there is still discrimination based on race and ethnicity. Such practice is inconsistent with the American ideals of libertarianism and egalitarianism, and it clearly does not contribute to the happiness of Native Americans and their families.

As we highlighted earlier in the chapter, the unique status and sovereignty of tribes results in the criminal justice system operating differently on the tribal lands than in the rest of the country. Currently,

TABLE 7.4 Native Americans in the Criminal Justice System

- Native Americans are arrested at 1.5 times the rate of Whites, with even higher disparities for some violent (six times higher) and public order offenses (more than ten times higher).
- Native Americans are 1.4 times more likely to be on probation than Whites.
- The incarceration rates (i.e., in jails and prisons) is more than twice as high for Native Americans than Whites.
- Native Americans have prison admission rates that are more than four times higher than Whites.
- Rates of parole are twice as high for Native Americans than Whites.
- Rates of residential placement for Native American juveniles are three times higher than for White youth.
- Rates of prison placement for Native American juveniles is more than two times higher than for White youth.

Sources: Hartney, C., & Vuong, L. (2009). *Created Equal: Racial and Ethnic Disparities in the US Criminal Justice System*. National Council on Crime and Delinquency, http://www.nccdglobal.org/sites/default/files/publication_pdf/created-equal.pdf.

there are over 175 tribal law enforcement agencies in 28 states throughout the United States. These agencies often have cross-deputization agreements with neighboring non-tribal agencies to further streamline enforcement on the local level. The largest tribal law enforcement agency, the Navajo Police Department, employs almost 400 full-time officers to serve tribal lands in Arizona, New Mexico, and Utah. In addition to these tribally operated agencies, the Bureau of Indian Affairs also operates 42 agencies that provide law enforcement services to reservations. Jurisdiction over offenses that occur on tribal lands may lie with federal, state, or tribal agencies, depending on the type of offense, location of the offense, and the racial or ethnic identification of both the offender and the victim.

The *Tribal Law and Order Act of 2010* was passed to grant tribal courts a broader range of sentencing options. Prior to this Act, tribal courts were only allowed to prosecute misdemeanors and the sentences handed down could not exceed one year of incarceration. Now, tribal courts have the option of prosecuting less serious felonies themselves, since these cases are typically not pursued by federal prosecutors—the entity previous charged with managing all felony cases that occurred on tribal grounds. This is an important change because, for decades, federal prosecutors declined to pursue an excessive number of criminal cases. Statistics show that 52 percent of violent cases and 40 percent of nonviolent cases were declined for prosecution by federal prosecutors between 2005 and 2009 (US Department of Justice Declinations of Indian Country Criminal Matters, GAO-11-167R, Dec 13, 2010). Additionally, the new sentencing structure allows tribal courts to extend a sentence of up to three years per count—up to nine years per case—and includes a $15,000 cap on fines.

A secondary problem with regard to sentencing is that Native American tribal lands typically have limited facilities to house incarcerated offenders. Under the *Tribal Law and Order Act*, offenders sentenced in tribal courts can now be housed in a federal facility at the federal government's expense. The Federal Bureau of Prisons must also now notify tribal authorities when an inmate convicted of a violent crime, drug trafficking, or a sex offense is released onto tribal lands. Previously, this notification was only extended to state and local governments. Finally, the Tribal Law and Order Act grants additional tools to tribal law enforcement by providing them access to the National Crime Information Center, which is a nationwide database maintained by the FBI and containing federal intelligence information.

Summary

The people that would ultimately become known as Americans enjoyed their earliest interactions with native peoples on the North American continent; in fact, they relied on them for their survival. Yet, as colonists sought to establish a permanent place in what would become the United States, they took whatever means were necessary to essentially wipe Native Americans off the face of the Earth (at least as far as America is concerned).

Although American behaviors toward Native Americans might be justified based on utilitarian grounds (after all, without clearing them out of the country, it would not have been possible for the US of today to come into existence), the actions of colonists as well as early Americans cannot be justified on either libertarian or egalitarian grounds. Indeed, the very notions of Social Darwinism, Manifest Destiny, and the doctrine of discovery are likely revolting to contemporary Americans, not at all consistent with present-day virtues.

Fortunately, there have been efforts to assist Native American populations to both assimilate into US culture and maintain their own traditional cultures. Yet, the net effect of US policy toward Native people has been largely socially unjust, and, today, Native Americans are also disproportionately involved in criminal justice system interventions.

Discussion Questions

1. To whom does the term Native American refer?
2. How many Native Americans exist in America today, in how many tribes, and where within the US do they tend to live?
3. What means were used by European settlers to remove and eliminate Native Americans as part of their Colonialist efforts?
4. Discuss the concepts of Social Darwinism, Manifest Destiny, and the doctrine of discovery as they pertain to European interactions with Native Americans.
5. Compare and contrast the terms genocide and ethnocide.
6. Discuss each of the five major eras in Native American history dealing with settlers and Americans.
7. What is the Marshall trilogy and what is its significance for understanding Native Americans in the US?
8. When did the anti-Native American movement begin? What were its outcomes?
9. When did the Native American Movement begin? What were its outcomes?
10. Using the theories of justice, libertarianism, and egalitarianism, in what ways have our actions as a people been consistent and inconsistent.
11. Identify the major laws used to strip Native Americans of their lands. Which laws protected Native American rights?
12. Identify the major treaties used to protect Native American rights. In what ways were they violated?
13. How does the concept of domestic dependent nations allow the US government to deal with Native American tribes?
14. Describe the *Trail of Tears* and discuss its significance for social justice.
15. Discuss to what degree Native Americans are involved in criminal justice today.

References

Armstrong, T. L., Guilfoyle, M. H., & Melton, A. P. (1996). *Native American Delinquency: An Overview of Prevalence, Causes, & Correlates*. In Nielsen, M. O., & Silverman, R. A. (Eds.), *Native Americans, Crime, & Justice*. Boulder, CO: Westview Press.

Deloria, V., & Lytle, C. (1983). *American Indians, American Justice*. Austin, TX: University of Texas Press.

Dumont, J. (1993). *Aboriginal people and the justice system*. Ottawa, Canada: Ministry of Supply and Services.

Everett, R., & Wojtkiewicz, R. (2002). Difference, Disparity, and Race/Ethnic Bias in Federal Sentencing. *Journal of Quantitative Criminology*, *18*, 189.

Grobsmith, E. S. (1989). The Relationship Between Substance Abuse and Crime Among Native American Inmates in the Nebraska Department of Corrections. *Human Organization*, *48*(4), 285–298.

Jimson, T. (1992). *Reflections on Race and Manifest Destiny*. Olympia, WA: Center for World Indigenous Studies. www.cwis.org/fwdp/Americas/manifest.txt.

Koss, M. P., Yuan, N. P., Dightman, D., Prince, R. J., Polacca, M., Sanderson, B., & Goldman, D. (2003). Adverse Childhood Exposures and Alcohol Dependence among Seven Native American Tribes. *American Journal of Preventive Medicine*, *25*(3), 238–245.

Loewen, J. (2007). *Lies my Teacher Told me*. New York: Touchstone.

Medill, W. (1848). Toward a New Policy: Concentrating Indians on Reservations. *House Executive Document, No. 1, 30th Cong., 2d sess., serial 537*, 585–589. Retrieved from: http://www.digitalhistory.uh.edu/disp_textbook.cfm?smtid=3&psid=680.

Myers, J. (2002). *Critical Issues in Federal Indian Law*. Washington, DC: National Indian Justice Center.

Ogunwole, S. (2006). *We the People: American Indians and Alaska Natives in the United States*. Report for the United States Census Bureau.

Perry, B. (2009). There's Just Places ya' Don't Wanna Go: The Segregating Impact of Hate Crimes Against Native Americans. *Contemporary Justice Review, 12*, 401–418.

Tsosie, R. (2001). Land, Culture and Community: Envisioning Native American Sovereignty and National Identity in the 21st Century. *Hagar: International Social Science Review, 2*, 183–200.

Williams, T. (2012, February 21). High Crime but Fewer Prosecutions on Indian Land. *New York Times*, A14.

Wilmot, K., & Delone, M. (2010). Sentencing of Native Americans: A Multistage Analysis Under the Minnesota Sentencing Guidelines. *Journal of Ethnicity in Criminal Justice, 8*(3), 151–180.

8

SOCIAL CLASS AND THE LAW

> Corporate crime inflicts far more damage on society than all street crime combined. Whether in bodies or injuries or dollars lost, corporate crime and violence wins by a landslide.
>
> *Russell Mokhiber*

America as a nation has generally been, throughout much of its history, obsessed with crime. Yet, it is only some forms of crime that seem to be of major concern to citizens and the government alike. In fact, since the 1930s, when the Federal Bureau of Investigation created a list of *serious crimes*—those crimes thought to occur the most frequently and create the most harm—we've focused almost exclusively on *street crimes*, those crimes committed disproportionately by the poor (Robinson, 2014).

So, it should not be surprising that for most of our nation's history, we've used criminal justice agencies to control certain classes of people, including, most notably, the poor. In fact, as we'll show in this chapter, there are serious scholars who argue that the criminal justice system is actually designed to control the poor, whereas others suggest it serves this function without that necessarily being intended.

One form of bias present in criminal justice today is that we largely ignore acts of white-collar and corporate crime—so that the powerful people who commit these very harmful acts rarely are arrested, convicted, and sentenced to prison—even though they cause far more damage than street crime, as suggested by the opening quote of this chapter. Incredibly, other forms of bias also exist within agencies of criminal justice, including in policing and courts. For example, there is evidence that police tend to focus their attention on the poorest areas and that courts are harsher against the poor than other groups in society, as we noted earlier in the book (Walker, Spohn, & DeLone, 2011).

In this chapter, each of these issues is examined. First, we discuss the possible bias in criminal justice that stems from the criminal law. Then, we turn to evidence of possible biases against the poor within agencies of criminal justice. This chapter illustrates that American practice is still very inconsistent with American ideals of utilitarianism, libertarianism, and egalitarianism.

Criminal Justice Bias Against the Poor?

According to Jeffrey Reiman and Paul Leighton (2013), the criminal justice system is biased against the poor at all stages of the process. This includes policing, courts, and corrections. Reiman and Leighton show that American criminal justice fails to effectively reduce crime and suggests that this failure amounts to a victory for the powerful, because they benefit from this failure.

In a nutshell, the argument of Reiman and Leighton is that the interests of the powerful are served when we focus so heavily on street crimes rather than other types of harmful behaviors, including white-collar crimes, corporate crimes, and even governmental deviance. As a result of our focus on street crime, we have for decades been rounding up young, poor, minority males and subjecting them to government-controlled institutions like jail or prison or community alternatives such as halfway houses and boot camps. This amounts to a form of population control used to keep the poor in their place. This population control serves the interests of the powerful because we are not focused on the harmful behaviors that they commit.

This occurs because, in the United States, the labels of *crime* and *serious crime* are applied to acts of the poor when they commit street crimes such as theft, robbery, assault, etc. Extremely dangerous acts committed by the wealthy and powerful are either not illegal or are illegal but are not pursued by criminal justice agencies. Examples of harmful behaviors committed by the powerful that are either not illegal or not pursued by criminal justice agencies are maintaining unsafe workplaces, producing environmental pollution, conducting unnecessary surgery, and prescribing unnecessary prescriptions. Then there are legal products such as tobacco and alcohol which together kill more than 500,000 Americans every year (versus fewer than 15,000 murders), as well as defective products, etc.

According to Reiman and Leighton (2013: 4), "when crimes are defined in the law, the system concentrates primarily on the predatory acts of the poor and tends to exclude or deemphasize the equally or more dangerous predatory acts of those who are well off." They add that the label of crime "is not used in America to name all or the worst of the actions that cause misery and suffering to Americans. It is reserved primarily for the dangerous actions of the poor" (2013: 66).

By reviewing scores of studies of white-collar and corporate crime, Reiman and Leighton show that behaviors such as occupational disease and injury, unnecessary medical care, misuse of prescription drugs, environmental pollution, and more, injure and kill far more Americans than street crime (2013: 95), as well as cause far more property loss than street crime (2013: 131). Table 8.1 shows data from the analysis of Reiman and Leighton, comparing costs of white-collar and corporate crime with those of street crime. As you can see, the costs of the harmful acts of elites—what Reiman and Leighton refer to as "excluded harms" because they tend to be excluded from the criminal law—far surpass the costs of street crime.

TABLE 8.1 Costs of Street Crime versus White-Collar and Corporate Crime

	Property loss	*Injuries*	*Deaths*
Street crime	$17 billion	861,000	17,000
White-collar and corporate crime	$486 billion	2,100,000*	54,000*

Source: Modified from Reiman and Leighton (2010).

* Only includes occupational disease and injury.

Reiman and Leighton argue that the criminal justice system is designed to function in a way that "aims its weapons against the poor, while ignoring or treating gently the rich who prey upon their own fellows"—that it is designed to fail "to protect Americans from predatory business practices and to punish those well-off people who cause widespread harm" (2013: xvii). In other words, criminal justice is a tool of the powerful to control the powerless.

Activity 8.1 Street Crime versus White-Collar and Corporate Crime

Do you agree with the argument of Reiman and Leighton?

Explain why or why not.

If this is true, why do some many people of color end up victimized by the criminal justice system, as we showed in Chapters 5 and 6? It is partly because African Americans and Latinos have lower incomes than whites, less overall wealth, and are more likely to suffer from unemployment, poverty, child-poverty, and so on (Walker et al., 2011). We illustrate this reality in Table 8.2. But, Reiman and Leighton also agree that there are racial and ethnic biases in criminal justice as well, so that the "typical criminal" according to criminal justice officials is male, young, urban, poor, and black: "Poor, young, urban, (disproportionately) black males make up the core of the enemy forces in the crime war" (2013: 69).

Why does this happen? Reiman and Leighton write:

> [W]e are not maintaining that the rich and powerful intentionally make the system fail to gather the resulting benefits. Our view is rather that that the system has grown up piecemeal over time and usually with the best of intentions. The unplanned and unintended overall result is a system that not only fails to substantially reduce crime, but also does so in a way that serves the interests of the rich and powerful. One consequence . . . is that those who could change the system feel no need to do so. And thus it keeps on rolling along.
>
> *(2013: 6)*

TABLE 8.2 Race, Ethnicity, and Economic Outcomes

	White	*Black*	*Latino*
Unemployment rate (2010)	8%	13%	11%
People below poverty (2009)	12%	26%	25%
Children below poverty (2009)	17%	35%	33%
Median household income	$55,412	$32,229	$38,624
Net worth (2011)	$89.537	$6,314	$7,683

Sources: Data from the United States Census Bureau, http://www.census.gov/prod/2012pubs/p60-243.pdf http://www.census.gov/compendia/statab/2012/tables/12s0712.pdf http://www.census.gov/people/wealth/files/Wealth_Tables_2011.xlsx http://www.census.gov/compendia/statab/2012/tables/12s0627.pdf.

With regard to those "best intentions," Reiman and Leighton suggest policy makers "are sincerely doing what they believe is right" (2013: 178) based on a view of crime that dates back to pre-industrial times. This view of crime is built on myths of harmful behaviors created by the law and reinforced by the way media depicts crime, both of which suggest that poor street criminals are who we should fear.

A similar argument is made by Randy Shelden, who claims that the criminal justice system is a tool used to control the *dangerous classes*—poor, young minorities. Shelden also does not posit a conspiracy theory "among the 'ruling class' . . . to use the law and the legal system to trample on the rights of ordinary citizens, especially the poor." Instead, he says that if you examine

> *the results* of the law in general and the daily operations of the criminal justice system—that is the outcomes of legal decision—the entire system *generally* comes down hardest on those with the least amount of power and influence, and *generally* comes down in the most lenient fashion on those with the most power and influence.
>
> *(Sheldon, 2007: xiii)*

Shelden shows that major disparities in criminal justice based on race and class are consistent with the idea that one function of criminal justice is controlling these segments of the population.

Although there are real and meaningful impacts of race on criminal justice, Shelden suggests it is *social class* that helps determine "which behaviors come to be defined as 'criminal' and thus subject to their enforcement" by criminal justice agencies; "*who* is to be defined as 'criminal'"; "how far into the criminal justice system a particular case is processed"; and "the final sentence of a criminal case" (2007: 3–4).

Social class is understood to mean the median level of wealth and income in the US. In 2012, median household income was about $51,000, so people making around that amount were to be considered middle-class (Kamp, 2013). In fact, households earning between $25,500 and $76,500 are considered middle-class. According to Elwell (2014), around 44 percent of families make this amount of income, but only about 20 percent of households are the middle level of incomes (between $39,736 and $64,553).

According to the US Department of Health and Human Services, for a person to qualify as "poor" he or she must earn less than $11,770 per year for a family of one, less than $15,930 for a family of two, $20,090 for a family of three, less than $24,250 for a family of four, and so on. In 2013, roughly 14.5 percent of families earned so little that they were considered poor by the US government.

Shelden argues that lawmakers are more likely to define behaviors of the powerless as crimes, that powerless people are most likely to be depicted as criminals in the media, that criminal justice agencies more vigorously pursue their crimes than the harmful acts of the powerful, and that the criminal justice system tends to come down much harder on the poor than the wealthy. In this way, the criminal justice system can be seen as a system used to maintain status quo arrangements in society based on social class.

The main way this occurs, according to Shelden, is that criminal justice largely ignores the harmful acts of the powerful. This is true even though:

> Statistically speaking, the gravest threats to us are not from robbers, burglars, rapists, and the like; rather, they are from those who wear suit and tie to work, or a white medical coat, or who

occupy plush offices in corporate headquarters or powerful positions within the government. Their weapons are ballpoint pens, scalpels, computers, or their voices (as when they decide to go to war).

(Shelden, 2007: 6)

And Shelden provides evidence that corporate crime—things like fraud, hazardous working conditions, defective products, unnecessary medical procedures, and similar behaviors—are far more damaging than the street crimes on which we focus.

That the criminal law generally ignores such acts in favor of more dramatic and visible crimes like murder, robbery, carjacking, and similar acts, "reflects the interests of the ruling class" by "deflect(ing) attention from the crimes committed by their own class" (2007: 13). Thus, the major bias against the poor comes from the criminal law. This should not be surprising when you consider who makes the law and who funds the law—very wealthy, older, white people (Robinson, 2014).

Figure 8.1 compares lawmakers at the state and federal level with the American population. As you can see, whites and males are overrepresented among lawmakers whereas African Americans, Latinos, and women are underrepresented among lawmakers. Further, the average income and wealth of lawmakers is much higher than the general population (Robinson, 2014).

The law, according to Shelden, is written both to reflect the interests of the powerful and to maintain status quo arrangements in society. And he shows that "the management of the dangerous classes is not a recent phenomenon" but instead that control of the poor has always been a primary function of criminal justice (2007: 18). Perhaps it is thus not surprising that, today, prisons and jails have been referred to by many criminologists, sociologists, historians, and other social scientists as the poorhouses of the twentieth and twenty-first centuries (Herivel & Wright, 2003). In fact, Reiman and Leighton (2013) show that prisons have always been reserved for the poor (2007: 118).

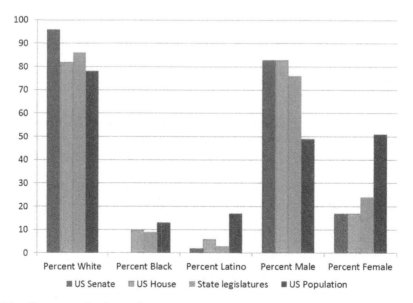

FIGURE 8.1 Non-Representative Lawmakers.

For a real-life and recent example of how the rich and powerful often get away with even extremely harmful acts, consider the recent economic recession of 2008 caused by greed and fraud in big banks and on Wall Street; this was identified as a *financial crisis*, and specifically a *banking crisis* by the US Government Accountability Office (GAO), and it cost taxpayers $12–22 trillion (depending on how you measure it). As described in Chapter 3, the crisis cost the average American household about $5,800 in income ("due to reduced economic growth during the acute stage of the financial crisis from September 2008 through the end of 2009"), plus $2,050 (due to the government's "interventions to mitigate the financial crisis"), plus about $100,000 (in "loss from declining stock and home values"). Thus, the average US household lost about $107,000 because of the economic collapse (Pew, 2010).

The GAO puts the costs of the financial crisis at more than $12 trillion, roughly equivalent to more than 600 years of losses due to all property street crimes combined! And the true cost—including losses in Gross Domestic Product, large declines in employment, household wealth, and "other economic indicators"— was actually higher, at about $22 trillion. This figure is equivalent to 1,100 years of property street crime!

How many people were arrested, convicted, and imprisoned for the frauds that caused this damage? None! This is a clear example of a bias in American criminal justice, one in favor of the wealthy and against the poor. A system that restricts the liberty of some people when they violate the rights of other people through harmful acts but not others when they do the same is not equal, making its operation inconsistent with egalitarianism; nor does it operate in the interests of the people since all of us are victimized by such fraud, making it inconsistent with utilitarianism. And we find it hard to imagine the virtues that can be served by ignoring such crimes, other than those of free market libertarianism.

Activity 8.2 Financial Crisis

Why do you think none of the powerful people who caused the financial crisis of 2008 have been prosecuted?

Read "Why Isn't Wall Street in Jail" here: http://www.rollingstone.com/politics/news/why-isnt-wall-street-in-jail-20110216.

Then provide your answer.

Further, the reality that the law is made by the wealthy and powerful reminds us of the conflict theories reviewed earlier. Recall that the *conflict perspective* argues that the criminal law (and thus its enforcement) serves the interests of the powerful over the people. Since the criminal law is made by the powerful (as well as funded by them), it is reasonable to assume that the criminal law serves their interests over those of the people; if true, a logical inference is that the criminal justice system will also serve their interests first and foremost. If so, we should expect there to be serious problems in criminal justice related to social class.

None of the outcomes discussed thus far are consistent with any conception of social justice. That is, they do not promote or respect liberty, equality, happiness, or virtue. And they clearly violate the major principles of John Rawls's theory of justice as fairness as well as David Miller's pluralistic theory of justice reviewed in Chapter 1. That is, subjugation and oppression of the poor stands in direct opposition to equal liberties, equal opportunities, the difference principle, as well as equality in matters of citizenship.

Importance of Legal Representation

As discussed in Chapter 2, the Bill of Rights is more than just an historical document. It lays out the fundamental rights afforded to all citizens, rich or poor. These rights, which are spelled out in the first ten amendments of the United States Constitution, impact every aspect of the criminal justice system. From initial contact with police to criminal sentencing, the millions of people processed through the criminal court system every year rely on these protections to offer them a modicum of protection regardless of their social status. Because about eight in ten criminal defendants are *indigent*—meaning too poor to be able to afford a private attorney—the protections afforded to US citizens are especially important.

When discussing criminal prosecution, the Sixth Amendment, in particular, is probably most important. It states:

> In all criminal prosecutions, the accused shall enjoy the right to a speedy and public trial, by an impartial jury of the state and district wherein the crime shall have been committed, which district shall have been previously ascertained by law, and to be informed of the nature and cause of the accusation; to be confronted with the witnesses against him; to have compulsory process for obtaining witnesses in his favor, and to have the assistance of counsel for his defense.

As you can see, the Sixth Amendment grants you the right to: (1) a speedy trial; (2) a public trial; and (3) an impartial jury. You also have the right to: (4) be informed of the charges against you; (5) confront witnesses against you; (6) call witnesses on your behalf; and (7) be defended by an attorney. These protections make up part of what we refer to as *due process*, or the protections you are afforded as a citizen of the United States.

While it is generally agreed that the framers of the Constitution initially meant that the right to obtain counsel would be at the defendant's own expense, the interpretation of this particular clause has evolved over time. The necessity of this evolution was apparent, considering that those who had the least power and influence were the ones most likely to find themselves facing criminal prosecution.

The first major Constitutional challenge came during the 1930s, which were the height of the *Jim Crow* laws in the South. In Alabama, nine young black men jumped aboard a freight train. When they were joined by a group of young white men, a fight ensued and all but one of the white men was thrown from the train. The men thrown from the train managed to send a message ahead to the town of Scottsboro to report the incident. When the local sheriff and a group of citizens stopped the train near Scottsboro, two young white women stated that the black men aboard the train had raped them.

A trial on these charges commenced a mere 12 days later and, on the eve of the trial, an attorney had not yet been identified to serve as counsel. The youth were illiterate and unable to assist in their defense. Ultimately, two attorneys—a real estate attorney from Tennessee who confessed ignorance about Alabama criminal law and an elderly attorney who hadn't tried a case in decades—offered their assistance to the boys. The trials started immediately and lasted a total of three days. The results of the trial, a life sentence for a 12-year-old boy and death sentences for the other eight defendants, became the basis for *Powell v. Alabama* (1932).

With the assistance of a lawyer who volunteered to file the appeals, the United States Supreme Court ruled that inadequate counsel had violated the due process rights of the defendants. The opinion stated that the right to counsel is one of the

> fundamental principles of liberty and justice which lie at the base of all of our civil and political institutions . . . There are certain immutable principles of justice which inhere in the very idea of free government which no member of the Union may disregard.
>
> *(Powell v. Alabama, 287 U.S. 45)*

While the Powell decision only extended the necessity for counsel in capital cases, it set the stage for the incorporation of the fair trial rights that were guaranteed by the Sixth Amendment applicable to the states. This is clearly about equality, and this case, as well as the general struggle for equal protections when it comes to criminal justice, illustrates that social justice is important to Americans and yet very difficult to obtain.

The next major case to expand the right to counsel for indigent defendants was *Gideon v. Wainwright* (1963). Clarence Gideon, shown in Figure 8.2, was charged with breaking and entering with the intent to commit a misdemeanor (which is a felony in Florida, the state where the crime occurred). In court, Gideon requested that counsel be appointed to him because he could not afford to hire a lawyer himself. The judge denied this request citing the *Powell v. Alabama* ruling. Gideon did not face a sentence of death and was therefore not entitled to an attorney. Gideon represented himself as best he could, but was found guilty and sentenced to five years in prison.

FIGURE 8.2 Clarence Gideon.

His initial appeal to the Florida Supreme Court was denied, but the United States Supreme Court decided to hear his case and bring resolution to the question of whether states are required to provide an attorney for non-capital cases. The Court held that, even in felony cases in state courts, the Sixth Amendment requires that a defendant enjoy the right of assistance to counsel. In their decision, the Justices stated that, "reason and reflection require us to recognize that in our adversary system of criminal justice, any person hauled into court, who is too poor to hire a lawyer, cannot be assured a fair trial unless counsel is provided for him" (*Gideon v. Wainwright*, 372 U.S. 335). One can hardly envision a better example of an effort to finally make criminal justice consistent with the major principles of John Rawls's theory of justice as fairness as well as David Miller's pluralistic theory of justice reviewed in Chapter 1. That is, providing defense for the indigent helps protect equal liberties as well as the difference principle.

With the momentum created by *Gideon v. Wainwright*, the next case to further clarify the right of indigent representation was decided with *Argersinger v. Hamlin* (1972). Jon Argersinger had been charged with carrying a concealed weapon, a misdemeanor that carried with it a possible penalty of six months imprisonment and a $1000 fine. Much like the Gideon case, he requested an attorney due to his indigent status. His request was denied and he was subsequently found guilty and sentenced to 90 days in jail. On appeal, the US Supreme Court finally, and explicitly, determined that any and all crimes that carry the possibility of imprisonment qualify an indigent defendant for an attorney. The new rule became that no individual may be incarcerated unless that individual was either represented by counsel at trial or had validly waived his or her right to counsel.

These court cases are particularly important for the lower classes since, historically, the majority of people processed through the criminal justice system are prosecuted for low-level misdemeanors. Incredibly, 50 years after the *Gideon* case, evidence shows cities and states are still having a hard time providing defense for the poor, largely due to large caseloads and budget shortfalls (Blume & Johnson, 2013).

There is further evidence that, as court fees increase to help defer the costs of adjudication, it is the poor who pay the most. This is because:

- In at least 43 states and the District of Columbia, defendants can be billed for a public defender.
- In at least 41 states, inmates can be charged room and board for jail and prison stays.
- In at least 44 states, offenders can get billed for their own probation and parole supervision.
- In all states except Hawaii, and the District of Columbia, there's a fee for the electronic monitoring devices defendants and offenders are ordered to wear.

(Shapiro, 2014)

So, again we see the discrepancies between our ideals—even those protected by Supreme Court decisions—and the realities of American criminal justice.

Other Biases Against the Poor

There have also been several important changes that have changed the long-term impact of criminal prosecutions. First and foremost, *zero-tolerance policing* and prosecution policies have eliminated the ability of police officers, prosecutors, and judges to exercise *discretion* for specific crimes. This change has pulled an increasing number of people into the criminal justice system.

The second change is that the collateral consequences of a misdemeanor conviction have increased substantially. While these consequences will be discussed in greater detail later in this chapter, they include civil restrictions, custodial rights, and immigration consequences. The reason why these collateral consequences are increasingly troubling is due to the fact that the criminal justice system is set up in a way that discourages people from exercising their Sixth Amendment rights. In *The Process is the Punishment*, Malcolm Feeley (1979) provides a historical description of the misdemeanor process wherein defendants are sorted into two groups: first are those willing to plea bargain, accept guilt and a seemingly minor punishment; and, second, are those defendants who choose to exercise their Sixth Amendment rights, which may mean facing a trial months in the future with the possibility of jail time if the misdemeanor charges result in a conviction. This is one major reason so many people plead guilty for crimes—even those they did not commit—another form of bias against the poor, who cannot afford to mount a quality defense against even routine and/or false charges (Walker, 2012).

An additional factor that may sway a defendant into a guilty plea is that many jurisdictions provide either *diversion programs* or *deferred adjudication*. While those programs carry no possibility of incarceration, they also do not entitle the defendant to the appointment of counsel. While deferring adjudication may seem like a good short-term solution at the time, it could have long-term implications with regard to the consequences mentioned above. As such, choosing the route of going to trial—and potentially awaiting that trial in a jail cell if a defendant is not offered or cannot afford bail—becomes a punishment in and of itself. This burden, for both groups, becomes all the greater when a defendant is indigent and cannot afford to hire a lawyer for advisement.

Such outcomes are all inconsistent with American principles of social justice, most notably libertarianism and egalitarianism, promoted by theorists such as Rawls and Miller, and contained within the founding documents of our country. They violated the major principles of John Rawls's theory of justice as fairness as well as David Miller's pluralistic theory of justice reviewed in Chapter 1. That is, such practices that disproportionately harm the poor stand in direct opposition to equal liberties, equal opportunities, the difference principle, as well as equality in matters of citizenship.

Legal Representation and the Death Penalty

A survey of capital punishment experts—scholars who teach and write about the death penalty—found that a large percentage of experts (84 percent) believed that capital punishment is biased against the poor (Robinson, 2007). The most significant problem identified by the experts was a lack of quality defense representation historically in death penalty cases. That is, low-quality legal representation has been not only a leading cause of wrongful conviction in capital cases (Cohen, 2003; Lytle, 2008; Radelet & Bedau, 1994), but also a significant source of social class bias when it comes to the death penalty.

Interestingly for the purposes of this book, the experts reasoned that capital punishment has to be plagued by social class biases since all of criminal justice practice is. They indicated this by saying things such as "The criminal justice system knows who pays for it and nowhere is that the poor" and "It's called capital punishment because those without the capital get the punishment" (Robinson, 2007).

Table 8.3 shows the states that have led in the number of executions since 1977, when executions resumed in the US after a five-year moratorium. In the other column, you see that state's ranking in poverty nationwide in 2007 (the higher the number, the worse its poverty rate). As you can see, six of the top ten most active death penalty states ranked in the top ten in rates of poverty that year. So, while there is not a perfect relationship between poverty and capital punishment, executions tend to be highest in states that have high rates of poverty (these states also tend to have higher rates of murder!).

Collateral Consequences

Collateral consequences refer to all of the civil restrictions that follow from a criminal conviction (Demleitner, 1999). These consequences are sometimes referred to as *status-generated penalties* since it is the individual's status as a convicted criminal that is the impetus for these sanctions imposed outside of the judicial process itself. State sex offender registries are one example of such a collateral consequence. The requirement to register as a sexual offender or predator with local law enforcement is not tied to the length or type of criminal sanction. In many states, someone convicted with a qualifying sex offense will be included on the sex offender registry—and be required to update his or her address with every move—regardless of whether their criminal sentence was probation or incarceration.

Many argue that this collateral consequence is oftentimes a more serious form of punishment than the judicial sentence imposed, particularly since some states require sex offenders to register for life. It is important to keep in mind that many different types of behaviors may qualify someone as a sex offender, including indecent exposure or statutory rape. Consider, if you will, that a 15-year-old engages in consensual intercourse with an 18-year-old. If charges are filed and a conviction results, the 18-year-old may very well find himself or herself having to register as a sex offender.

A second type of collateral consequence, and one closely related to minority groups, is the possibility of deportation. Crimes involving moral turpitude and those classified as an aggravated felony carry the secondary consequence of deportation. These criminal categories include crimes such as shoplifting, driving under the influence of alcohol, and possession of drugs—many of which rarely carry a jail sentence. This expansive set of deportable offenses has caused the number of deportations

TABLE 8.3 States with the Most Executions Since 1977 and Rank in Poverty

State	*Executions*	*State Poverty Ranking*
Texas	515	9
Oklahoma	111	10
Virginia	110	41
Florida	87	25
Missouri	75	21
Alabama	56	6
Georgia	54	13 (tie)
Ohio	53	19
North Carolina	43	13 (tie)
South Carolina	43	12

Sources: Data from the Death penalty Information Center and the United States Census Bureau, http://www.deathpenaltyinfo.org/number-executions-state-and-region-1976 http://www.census.gov/statab/ranks/rank34.html.

resulting from a criminal conviction to skyrocket. In 2004, 42,510 noncitizens were deported due to these types of offenses. That figure jumped up to 216,698 offenders in 2011 (Office of Immigration Statistics, 2011).

Sentencing enhancements, which have been increasingly popular in the last three decades, are a third type of collateral consequence for low-level offenses. Today, a prior conviction of any kind can result in a drastic increase in punishment for any subsequent convictions. In the case of *Nichols v. United States* (511 U.S. 738), the Court stated that even an uncounseled misdemeanor conviction could be used when factoring sentencing enhancements. This could mean that, even though the initial low-level misdemeanor did not result in jail time, the subsequent conviction might have years added onto a sentence of incarceration as a result of the existence of a previous offense.

Criminal history is also a potentially relevant factor when someone is trying to obtain employment. With today's technology, criminal background checks can be done easily and cost-effectively. Businesses can do a national background check in minutes and may deny employment to someone who had a petty offense in years past. This is a particularly salient consequence when the unemployment rate is high. All other factors being equal, an employer is far more likely to choose a candidate with a spotless record. If one looks at the totality of potential collateral consequences, the inability to secure legal representation, even for the pettiest of offenses, can have devastating long-term consequences. When examining the most marginalized groups, these consequences can affect entire communities. To say nothing of the informal stigma associated with a criminal conviction, formal restrictions today can include many losses, shown in Table 8.4.

Felony Disenfranchisement

Felony disenfranchisement, or prohibiting persons who would otherwise be eligible to vote if not for their criminal conviction, is perhaps one of the most troubling collateral consequences. The historical basis for felon disenfranchisement goes back to the English colonists. There was a common law practice called *civil death* that included the revocation of the right to vote. American lawmakers codified disenfranchisement and, in fact, in the years following the Civil War, 29 states had such laws on the books (Liles, 2007).

There is a simple explanation for this sudden interest in disenfranchisement. With the Fifteenth Amendment granting blacks the right to vote, a criminal conviction was all that was needed to once again revoke that right. As we discussed in Chapter 4, the lower classes have historically faced a heightened

TABLE 8.4 Lost Rights Associated with a Criminal Conviction

- to possess a firearm
- to serve in the military
- to live in public housing
- to receive student financial aid
- to receive government benefits
- to drive a car legally
- to adopt a child
- to vote.

scrutiny by law enforcement officials and have a higher likelihood of finding themselves in criminal justice processes. During the post-Reconstruction era, Southern states tailored their disenfranchisement policies to target offenses believed to be most heavily engaged in by black males.

Today, almost six million Americans are prohibited from voting as a result of felon disenfranchisement laws. Figure 8.3 shows the growth in the number of people being disenfranchised due to a felony conviction over time. While these laws vary state by state—only Maine and Vermont do not restrict anyone's voting rights—the states with the most extreme disenfranchisement laws restrict voting rights long after probation or imprisonment has been completed. Typically, individuals have to appeal for the restoration of their rights after a specific period of time has elapsed. When one examines the racial composition of our current prison population, it is clear that these policies have a disproportionate effect on the poorest communities, which are often minority communities. In fact, blacks are four times more likely to lose their voting rights (Sentencing Project, 2013). In Florida, Kentucky, and Virginia, more than one in five black adults is disenfranchised.

Activity 8.3 Felony Disenfranchisement

Do some research into how felony disenfranchisement impacted the 2000 Presidential election in the state of Florida.

Document whether it changed the outcome, and then discuss its implications for US politics ever since.

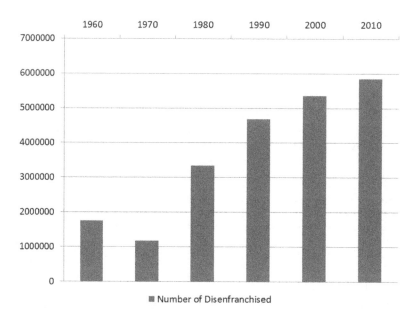

FIGURE 8.3 The Growth of Felony Disenfranchisement.

Due to the protected nature of voting rights, there have been numerous legal challenges about the constitutionality of disenfranchisement policies. In the case of *Richardson v. Ramirez*, three individuals who lost their voting rights as a result of their felony convictions sued for the restoration of those rights (418 U.S. 24). The legal challenge was focused on the Fourteenth Amendment. The defense argued that, per Section 1 of the Fourteenth Amendment, a state cannot legally restrict voting rights unless a compelling state interest is demonstrated. Even so, the United States Supreme Court found that felon disenfranchisement laws were indeed constitutional due to Section 2, which allowed the denial of voting rights for participation in rebellion or other crimes.

The Justices indicated that the Equal Protection Clause of the Fourteenth Amendment was not intended to prohibit these types of disenfranchisement policies. Their rationale was that Section 2 was intended to protect the voting rights of the newly freed slaves from any attempts by states to disenfranchisement them and, as such, was not applicable to felon disenfranchisement. Not to be deterred, civil rights groups initiated a new set of challenges in the late 1990s. Recognizing that the Courts were not particularly sympathetic, activists turned to state legislatures to initiate reform. These efforts were markedly more successful. Since 2000, 23 states have expanded voter eligibility resulting in an additional 800,000 individuals regaining their right to vote.

Are these outcomes warranted? One could argue they are if they are owing to harmful, criminal behaviors of those being disenfranchised. In this case, they are *deserved*, consistent with at least one view of social justice. Yet, this practice undeniably harms the least advantaged and thus is not consistent with the idea of the difference principle and thus another view of social justice. It also promotes further inequality and may do more harm than good, thereby violating tenets of egalitarianism and utilitarianism.

Prison Industrial Complex

During the economic crisis of the last decade, unemployment had climbed to 8.4 percent for all Americans and to a catastrophic 40 percent for African American males. Running parallel to this economic crisis was something that Thompson (2012) called a "carceral crisis"—referring to a massive increase in incarceration. Decades of aggressive crime policies resulted in the imprisonment of over two million people. It is common knowledge that the United States incarceration rates far surpass those of any Western nation.

Importantly, the US incarceration rate of 700 per 100,000 people is not evenly distributed among all Americans. African American males are over six times more likely to be imprisoned than whites. This changes the very fabric of communities that are often disproportionately poor. In *Punishment and Inequality*, Bruce Western (2006) discusses how incarceration has become a primary vehicle for maintaining inequality. The collateral consequences of the incarceration binge can be seen in the rising rates of single-parent families, rising unemployment, and record levels of urban poverty. Longitudinal studies have shown that, for impoverished families, having a parent arrested leads to economic strain due to income loss and a broken home, both of which are risk factors for children in those families.

Criminologists have been pushing for criminal justice policy reform for decades. With studies consistently showing that mass incarceration breaks up families, creates new generations of crime-prone children, and generally does more harm than good—all while not reducing the crime rate—we must ask ourselves, why do we continue to do it? The answer is relatively simple: prisons are profitable, very profitable. Considering that the group that passes the laws is beholden to corporate interests, it behooves them to keep the attention firmly affixed to the lower classes so that the public is firmly in support of maintaining our mass incarceration in spite of the cost to tax payers and poor communities.

This is not a new story. Companies for centuries have been trying to hold down the price of labor. Prison industries had been a major source of competition for free-market labor since the 1800s. Looking back to the creation of the penitentiary, both the Pennsylvania system and the Auburn system required inmates to partake in craft- or factory-oriented work. The goods produced were available for sale in the open market. This was also the era of chain gangs that worked on roads, canals, and prison construction. In fact, it was actually inmates who built Sing Sing, which was New York's second prison. During this time, inmates were also contracted out to work in stone quarries, coal mines, and also in private-sector businesses such as furniture and textiles, which are closely tied to prison industries even today. The practices of sending inmates off to work in quarries and mines was known as *convict leasing*, which was essentially the labor force used to replace slaves. This should not be surprising given that the language of the Thirteenth Amendment was, "Neither slavery nor involuntary servitude, except as a punishment for crime whereof the party shall have been duly convicted, shall exist within the United States, or any place subject to their jurisdiction."

This use of convict labor continued until the 1930s when New Deal Legislation temporarily prevented states and the federal government from accessing prison labor. This legislation came in the form of three pieces of legislation. First, the *Hawes-Cooper Act* allowed states to prevent the importation of prison goods. Then, the *Ashurst-Sumners Act* both prohibited the interstate transport of prison-made items to states where such goods were prohibited and required that prison-made products sold in interstate commerce be labeled. The third piece of legislation, the *Walsh–Healy Act* of 1936, prohibited the use of inmate labor to fulfill government contracts in excess of $10,000.

The primary driver of these legislative initiatives was that making inmate-produced goods available to the public negatively affected the price the free market could garner. This moratorium was lifted in 1979 with the passage of the *Justice System Improvement Act*. This system opened the door for prison privatization and also allowed for the transport of prison goods across state lines. This marriage of corporate interests and conservative politicians was the results of lobby efforts by the American Legislative Exchange Council. What followed the passage of the *Justice System Improvement Act* was an increasing trend towards mandatory sentencing practices, truth in sentencing statutes and three strikes laws.

Having a large group of offenders serving long prison sentences created a readily available source of cheap labor. If you're wondering how cheap, here are some comparisons. Thompson writes that most inmates make between $0.12 and $1.15 per hour. That means that businesses contracting with the 18 federal prisons that make furniture are avoiding the $13.04 per hour labor costs that furniture factory workers make in the free market. Similarly, there are 22 federal prisons that specialize in textiles and the average textile worker earns $10.95 in the free market. At the state level, even when states command the minimum wage of $7.25 for prison labor, loopholes in the law mean that the state can keep the majority of these wages for other business-related expenses such as constructing work facilities within prison grounds.

It goes without saying that prison labor, with its 600,000 to 1 million inmates working full-time while incarcerated, has had a direct impact on manufacturing jobs in the free world (Zatz, 2008). When manufacturing companies that produce goods lose out on contracts to prison industries, job losses are inevitable. In support of this, Thompson pointed out that, while unemployment was rising, "exporting of jobs to low-wage countries has undercut the American labor movement over the last forty years, [while] corporate success at growing prisons and accessing their enormous captive labor force has . . . proved highly detrimental to poor and working-class Americans" (Thompson, 2012: 40).

There are those would argue that mass incarceration produces a number of benefits for society. Some of these stated benefits are that building prisons creates jobs in small towns and that inmates who work while incarcerated leave prison with marketable job skills. While those claims sound good in theory, they are not founded. With regard to prisons providing jobs for rural communities, a single prison actually does not provide noticeable job growth when comparing towns where prisons are built to towns without prisons. Additionally, correctional officers typically make less than agricultural or manufacturing jobs would pay, to say nothing of the high level of stress that comes with the job. Limited prison budgets also result in not increasing the number of correctional officers even as prison populations grow.

Switching our focus to the inmates, the claim that inmates are gaining marketable skills might be true if anyone were actually willing to hire convicted felons. If we were so motivated, prisons would be an ideal setting for educating, vocationally training, and preparing convicted offenders for a productive life after their period of incarceration ends. We will discuss the collateral consequences of being processed through the criminal justice system later in this chapter, but suffice it to say that, regardless of the job skills that an individual possesses, the stigma of a criminal conviction results in former inmates being one-half to one-third as likely as non-offenders to be considered by employers (Pager, 2003). Additionally, as county-level incarceration rates grow, unemployment rates for African Americans living in those counties also grow (Sabol & Lynch, 2003).

The prison industrial complex, justified perhaps only by free market principles, violates conceptions of social justice rooted in liberty, equality, happiness, and virtue. It also clearly violates the major principles of John Rawls's theory of justice as fairness as well as David Miller's pluralistic theory of justice reviewed in Chapter 1. That is, incarceration of the poor and people of color—who are *not* more dangerous than the wealthy and whites—stands in direct opposition to equal liberties, equal opportunities, the difference principle, as well as equality in matters of citizenship.

Drug Testing of Welfare Recipients

As we discussed in Chapter 4, federal government welfare programs have been formally part of government spending since the Great Depression in the 1930s (Martin, 2001). During the Great Depression Era, it is estimated that the unemployment rate was as high as 25 percent. The government responded to the national hardship with the passing of the *Social Security Act*. The Act created a number of programs including unemployment compensation and *Aid to Dependent Children*, which was aimed at preventing family disruption due to poverty.

The welfare system came under fire during the 1976 presidential campaign when Ronald Reagan made his first bid for that office. The myth of the "welfare queen" was born while he was on the campaign trail. In one speech, Reagan told his supporters,

> In Chicago, they found a woman who holds the record. She uses 80 names, 30 addresses, 15 telephone numbers to collect food stamps, Social Security, veterans' benefits for four nonexistent decreased veteran husbands, as well as welfare. Her tax-free cash income alone has been running $150,000 a year.
>
> *(Levin, 2013)*

Even though the woman he discussed in Chicago was a fictional character, the seed had been planted. Reagan's story contributed to the belief that welfare fraud was an epidemic and that America's poorest people were lazy and trying to defraud hardworking Americans of their tax dollars. This sentiment lingered and culminated in the 1996 welfare reform law—the *Personal Responsibility and Work Opportunity Act*—which overhauled many welfare programs to reduce federal spending. In addition to reductions in food stamps and supplemental security income, the law imposed a citizenship requirement for many benefits. This additional requirement opened the door for states to seek additional special conditions to qualify for benefits, including the drug testing of applicants and current recipients of TANF, or *Temporary Assistance for Needy Families*.

By 2009, more than 20 states had proposed legislation that would mandate drug testing for public assistance programs. None of these proposals advocating for random drug testing became law due to *Marchwinski v. Howard*, which found that subjecting welfare recipients to drug testing without reasonable suspicion was unconstitutional. Since that ruling, ten states have passed laws that require screening in the event that suspicion of drug use exists. The caveat to these laws is that refusal to submit to a drug test is grounds for denial of benefits.

Is drug testing of welfare recipients warranted? One could argue it is if it is because welfare is not a right but instead a special benefit to the poor (who may end up spending their government assistance on drugs). Yet, this practice undeniably harms the least advantaged and thus is not consistent with the idea of the difference principle and thus a view of social justice consistent with American ideals. It also promotes further inequality and may do more harm than good, thereby violating tenets of utilitarianism, especially when states that have enacted such measures end up spending millions of dollars and find almost no one who uses drugs!

Summary

As this chapter shows, America still has serious problems with regard to social class and criminal justice practice. Specifically, there is strong evidence of a bias against the poor in the criminal law. This is perhaps the greatest threat to social justice within criminal justice, for we tend to ignore the harmful acts of the wealthy and powerful.

Further, there is evidence of other forms of bias against the poor within criminal justice. For example, there is the issue of low-quality legal representation for the poor. And then studies show significant problems with regard to felony disenfranchisement in terms of how it hurts the poor and especially poor people of color.

All of this has deeply troubling social justice implications. Criminal justice is supposed to be blind not only with regard to factors such as race and ethnicity, but also to other factors such as social class. As this chapter shows, this is clearly not the case. Thus, we still have not assured equal liberties and protections for the most vulnerable among us; indeed, the criminal justice system may very well be a tool of the powerful to keep the powerless in their place, as predicted by conflict theorists.

Discussion Questions

1. What is serious crime?
2. What is street crime? Contrast street crime with white-collar crime and corporate crime.

3. How is criminal justice used to control the poor?

4. In what way does social class bias start with the criminal law?

5. Summarize the main argument of Reiman and Leighton, and then explain whether you agree with it.

6. Summarize the main argument of Shelden, and then explain whether you agree with it.

7. What is the relationship between social class and race and ethnicity? Why do you think African Americans and Latinos are generally more disadvantaged than whites?

8. Which is more dangerous? Street crime or white-collar and corporate crime? Explain, using evidence.

9. Define the term indigent.

10. Why do poor people have the right to criminal defense? Which part of the US Constitution and which Supreme Court cases guarantee them this right?

11. Summarize the case of *Powell v. Alabama*.

12. Summarize the case of *Gideon v. Wainwright*.

13. Summarize the case of *Argersinger v. Hamlin*.

14. What are collateral consequences of criminal convictions?

15. What are some of the rights sacrificed when you are convicted of a crime?

16. What is meant by the term felony disenfranchisement?

17. How many people have lost the right to vote because of a criminal conviction? What are the implications of this for citizenship and democracy?

18. Compare and contrast the due process model and crime control model of criminal justice.

19. Discuss how the *Personal Responsibility and Work Opportunity Act* changed welfare in America.

20. How do you feel about drug testing people on welfare? Explain.

21. Is the death penalty biased against the poor? Explain.

References

Blume, J., & Johnson, S. (2013). Gideon Exceptionalism? *Yale Law Journal, 122*, 2126–2148.

Cohen, S. (2003). *The Wrong Men: America's Epidemic of Wrongful Death Row Convictions*. New York: Carroll & Graf.

Demleitner, Nora. (1999). Preventing Internal Exile: The Need for Restrictions on Collateral Sentencing Consequences. *Stanford Law and Policy Review, 11*, 153–162.

Elwell, C. (2014). *Congressional Research Service. The Distribution of Household Income and the Middle Class*. Retrieved from: https://fas.org/sgp/crs/misc/RS20811.pdf.

Feeley, M. (1979). *The Process is the Punishment: Handling Cases in a Lower Criminal Court*. New York: Russell Sage Foundation.

Herivel, T., & Wright, P. (2003). *Prison Nation: The Warehousing of America's Poor*. New York: Routledge.

Kamp, K. (2013, September 20). *By the Numbers: The Incredibly Shrinking American Middle Class*. BillMoyers. com. Retrieved April 23, 2015, from http://billmoyers.com/2013/09/20/by-the-numbers-the-incredibly-shrinking-american-middle-class/.

Levin, J. (2013, January 1). *The Real Story of Linda Taylor, America's Original Welfare Queen*. Retrieved April 23, 2015, from http://www.slate.com/articles/news_and_politics/history/2013/12/linda_taylor_welfare_queen_ronald_reagan_made_her_a_notorious_american_villain.html.

Liles, W. W. (2007). Challenges to Felony Disenfranchisement Laws: Past, Present, and Future. *Alabama Law Review, 58*(3), 615–629. Retrieved from www.sentencingproject.org/doc/. . ./fd_research_liles.pdf.

Lytle, L. (2008). *Execution's Doorstep: True Stories of the Innocent and Near Damned*. Boston: Northeastern University Press.

Martin, I. (2001). Dawn of the Living Wage: The Diffusion of a Redistributive Municipal Policy. *Urban Affairs Review, 36*(4), 470–496.

Office of Immigration Statistics (2011). *2011 Yearbook of Immigration Statistics.* Washington DC: Department of Homeland Security.

Pager, D. (2003). The Mark Of A Criminal Record. *American Journal of Sociology, 108*(5), 937–975.

Pew (2010). *The Impact of the 2008 Economic Collapse.* Downloaded from: http://www.pewtrusts.org/en/research-and-analysis/reports/2010/04/28/the-impact-of-the-september-2008-economic-collapse.

Radelet, M., & Bedau, H. (1994). *In Spite of Innocence: Erroneous Convictions in Capital Cases.* Boston: Northeastern University Press.

Reiman, J., & Leighton, P. (2010). *The Rich Get Richer and the Poor Get Prison: A Reader.* Boston, MA: Allyn & Bacon.

Reiman, J., & Leighton, P. (2013). *The Rich Get Richer and the Poor Get Prison: Ideology, Class, and Criminal Justice.* Upper Saddle River, NJ: Prentice Hall.

Robinson, M. (2007). *Death Nation: The Experts Explain American Capital Punishment.* Upper Saddle River, NJ: Prentice Hall.

Robinson, M. (2015). *Criminal Injustice: How Politics and Ideology Distort American Ideals.* Durham, NC: Carolina Academic Press.

Sabol, W., & Lynch, J. (2003). Assessing the Longer-Run Consequences of Incarceration: Effects on Families and Employment. In Hawkins, D., Myers, S., & Stone, R. (Eds.), *Crime Control and Social Justice: The Delicate Balance.* Westport, CT: Greenwood.

Sentencing Project. (2013). *The State of Sentencing 2013: Developments in Policy and Practice.* Washington, DC: Sentencing Project.

Shapiro, J. (2014). As Court Fees Rise, the Poor Are Paying the Price. *NPR,* May 23. Downloaded from: http://www.npr.org/2014/05/19/312158516/increasing-court-fees-punish-the-poor.

Shelden, R. (2007). *Controlling the Dangerous Classes: A Critical Introduction to the History of Criminal Justice* (2nd ed.). Boston, MA: Allyn and Bacon.

Thompson, H. (2012). The Prison Industrial Complex: A Growth Industry in a Shrinking Economy. *New Labor Forum, 21*(3), 38–47.

Walker, S. (2012). *Sense and Nonsense About Crime, Drugs, and Communities* (8th ed.). Belmont, CA: Wadsworth Pub.

Walker, S., Spohn, C., & DeLone, M. (2011). *The Color of Justice: Race, Ethnicity, and Crime in America.* Belmont, CA: Wadsworth Pub.

Western, B. (2006). *Punishment and Inequality in America.* New York: Russell Sage.

Zatz, N. (2008). Working at the Boundaries of Markets: Prison Labor and the Economic Dimension of Employment Relationships. *Vanderbilt Law Review, 61,* 857–958.

9

WOMEN AND SOCIAL JUSTICE

Women are not inherently passive or peaceful. We're not inherently anything but human.

Robin Morgan

Women may comprise the numerical majority of the general population, but they still exist and operate in a subordinate position in relation to men. While there are indeed biological differences between men and women, these biological differences must be separated from the gender differences and stereotypes that are the result of sexism and ignorance.

Sexism is the ideology that one sex is superior to the other. While the feminist movement in the 1960s has come to define the empowerment of women, pioneers were fighting for equal rights centuries prior. If one is in doubt as to whether women still exist as an oppressed majority, he or she need look no further than the relative socioeconomic positions that men and women occupy. This equality gap exists in employment, political power, and social standing. Table 9.1 illustrates that, generally speaking, women are underrepresented in positions of power—in this case among lawmakers—in the US today.

While women can and do occupy positions of power, those women are the exceptions and not the norm. This is not surprising, considering that women are often characterized as emotional, weak, and

TABLE 9.1 Gender and the Law

	Percent Women
State legislatures	23.7%
Congress	20%

Sources: Data is from the Washington Post, "The New Congress is 80 Percent white, 80 percent male and 92 percent Christian", by Philip Bump, January 5, 2015, http://www.washingtonpost.com/blogs/the-fix/wp/2015/01/05/the-new-congress-is-80-percent-white-80-percent-male-and-92-percent-christian/; and the National Conference of State Legislatures, "The Gender Gap Grows: Fewer Women in State Legislatures in 2015", by Katie Zielger, November 6, 2014, http://www.ncsl.org/blog/2014/11/06/gender-gap-grows-fewer-women-in-state-legislatures-in-2015.aspx.

irresponsible. Although the United States has made great strides to bridge the gap between men and women, there is still much work to be done. This chapter will first address gender roles before examining the legal battles that women engaged in to move towards equality in the United States. Our overriding goal is to identify the social justice implications of gender in America.

Gender Roles

Gender roles—the expected proper behavior, activities, and attitudes of males and females—are so pervasive and ingrained in our collective conscience that they are accepted as fact. As we discussed in Chapter 4, *socialization* (i.e., learning from social actors) related to gender occurs on virtually every level. From parents to teachers, the media to the government, women are encouraged to be feminine and men to be masculine. Deviating from these expectations often results in ridicule, bullying, as well as outright hostility.

There are two competing sociological perspectives on the utility of prescribed gender roles. First, the *functionalist perspective*—put forth by Talcott Parsons and Robert Bales (1955)—argues that gender roles help families function more efficiently. The need for division of labor within the household helped create particular roles and tasks that were better suited to one parent or the other. While this argument has some merit with regard to the needs of families, it does not sufficiently explain the gender associations in the workplace, such as the gender associations of teaching and nursing, business and science. The sexual labeling of entire professions does more harm than good by discouraging both sexes from pursuing a career that is outside of the social norms.

We are making strides towards the day when norms pertaining to sex and work no longer exist, but a quick visit into an elementary education class versus a business entrepreneurial class will show that we still have ways to go to achieve gender equality. Functionalists argue that breaking these gender norms would cause social disorder and confusion. Yet, a critique of the functionalist perspective is that it fails to acknowledge that both genders are fully capable of performing the entire range of duties present in family structure—from child-rearing to yard work—yet many men and women continue to parcel these roles out as if they were living on a pioneering homestead.

Second, the *conflict perspective* does not deny that there are indeed biological differences between the sexes. Instead, its proponents argue that these biological differences contributed to the growth of power for men during the preindustrial age. Their increased size, physical strength, and freedom from childbearing duties allowed men to dominate women, first physically, and later, socially and politically. While size and physical strength are no longer as functionally necessary in contemporary society, the established cultural beliefs and stereotypes still linger. Conflict theorists ultimately argue that gender norms are stifling societal growth by limiting the range of pursuits that men and women feel able and encouraged to pursue.

Gender roles have been the subject of many sociological studies. Prominent sociologist Patricia Adler and colleagues (1998) conducted a study of elementary school students, measuring how boys and girls achieved status in school. The status of boys was determined by their level of toughness, athletic ability, coolness, social skills, and success in relationships with girls. Girls gained social status based on their own physical appearance, their parents' social background, and through academic success. It is important to note that while girls generally are judged on more superficial characteristics, boys are also greatly impacted by gender roles. As Schaeffer writes, "Even when individuals are motivated to stretch the social boundaries of gender, social structure and institutions often impede them" (2011: 349).

Activity 9.1 Male/Female Characteristics

Make a list of characteristics or personality traits that you think of when you think of a female/woman and those when you think of a male/man.

What are the major differences between the two?

On what do you base the differences between the two groups?

It's interesting that, when discussing the oppression of women, the term *women's liberation* is often used. We argue that *gender liberation* would be more appropriate. After all, masculinity and femininity are two sides of the same coin. Progress is often stifled because gender theorists generally focus on women's roles without a reexamination of men's roles. In other words, men, too, need to be liberated from the constraints of the masculine value system. Thus, *gender liberation* entails freeing females *and* males from their prescribed societal roles.

Boys are socialized to think that they should be strong, fearless, dominant, and emotionless. These values manifest as *hypermasculinity*, where anything less than acting out these stereotypes would result in someone being less than a "real man." By encouraging boys and men to be dominant and aggressive, we are unintentionally promoting a culture where men may react physically, and sometimes violently, when their dominance is threatened. Additionally, we foster a system where men do not feel comfortable reporting their own victimization, particularly when it's sexual victimization. Lest you believe this is not a problem, consider that in 2012, the Pentagon stated that 53 percent of the sexual assaults reported in the military involved male victims (Department of Defense, 2012). Men often do not report sexual assault for fear that others will respond negatively to them. This cycle of aggression and shame can only be broken if we acknowledge that aggression does not make one strong and victimization does not make one weak. In short, we encourage a dialogue of male liberation as the counterpart to female liberation. We will not successfully free women of gender roles if we do not focus on doing the same for men.

Suffrage

From the founding of our country—in spite of the lofty social justice rhetoric related to liberty, equality, and even happiness—women were treated as less free, less human, and less worthy than men. This is just a reminder that the reality of America is often very different than our social justice ideals.

In the 1820s and 1830s, reform groups were proliferating across the United States. Religious movements, moral-reform societies, and anti-slavery groups were organizing and pushing for changes in legislation, including to gain for women the most basic of civil rights—the right to vote. In many of these organizations, women played a prominent role. At the same time, many women were beginning to feel frustration with the phenomenon called the *Cult of True Womanhood* that we discussed in Chapter 4. To say that a woman should be submissive, pious, and concerned mostly with home and family was stifling for many women. This critical attitude about how women are "supposed" to act combined with their lobbying efforts began to reshape what it meant to be a woman *and* a citizen in the United States of America.

First Feminist Movement

Feminist scholars generally recognize that feminism occurs in waves, the first of which started during the industrial age. In fact, the first formal feminist movement started in 1848. Before we examine this, it is first important to define what we mean by feminism. To the authors, *feminism* is simply the idea that women are people too, and thus deserve equal rights under the law.

Activity 9.2 Feminism

Do you think of yourself as a feminist?

Explain why or why not.

On July 19, 1848, the first women's rights convention convened in Seneca Falls, New York. Invited by Elizabeth Cady Stanton and Lucretia Mott, the group of mostly abolitionist-activists met to discuss how to move towards the direction of having their own political identities. They produced a document called the *Declaration of Sentiments* in which they wrote, "We hold these truths to be self-evident that all men *and women* are created equal, that they are endowed by their creator with certain inalienable rights, that among these are life, liberty and the pursuit of happiness." This is a simple reformation of the original text of the Declaration of Independence, shown in Chapter 1; the new language illustrates how the ideal of American equality had serious limitations. Their first action item for the group was *suffrage*, or gaining the right to vote, for it became clear that disenfranchisement severely hampered reformatory efforts.

The Civil War derailed the women's rights movement for a time; reform did follow at the conclusion of the war, but it did not include women. In Chapter 5, we discussed how the Fifteenth Amendment, passed in 1869, granted blacks the right to vote. The leaders of the women's rights movement thought that women would be granted the same rights shortly thereafter. They were wrong. Wyoming was the only state to grant women full voting rights in 1869.

Frustrated by the lack of progress in the wake of the Civil War, the suffragists broke into two factions. Elizabeth Stanton joined with Susan B. Anthony and together they created the *National Woman Suffrage Association (NWSA)*, which directed its efforts toward changing federal law; the NWSA went so far as to oppose the Fifteenth Amendment because it excluded women. The other faction was headed up by Lucy Stone, a well-known lobbyist for women's rights, and was called the *American Woman Suffrage Association (AWSA)*. This second faction disagreed with the NWSA's tactics of using racial division to gain the right to vote. While the AWSA was better funded, the NWSA had a national reach, thanks in part to the aggressive leadership of Stanton and Anthony. Figure 9.1 shows Susan B. Anthony.

FIGURE 9.1 Susan B. Anthony.

In 1872, Susan B. Anthony was arrested for attempting to vote in the presidential election. She was fined $100 for casting an illegal ballot. At her trial in 1873, Ms. Anthony brought the issue of suffrage to the forefront of the political debate with the following speech:

> Friends and fellow citizens: I stand before you tonight under indictment for the alleged crime of having voted at the last presidential election, without having a lawful right to vote. It shall be my work this evening to prove to you that in thus voting, I not only committed no crime, but, instead, simply exercised my citizen's rights, guaranteed to me and all United States citizens by the national Constitution, beyond the power of any State to deny.

The preamble of the Federal Constitution says:

> We, the people of the United States, in order to form a more perfect union, establish justice, insure domestic tranquility, provide for the common defense, promote the general welfare, and secure

the blessings of liberty to ourselves and our posterity, do ordain and establish this Constitution for the United States of America.

It was we, the people; not we, the white male citizens; nor yet we, the male citizens; but we, the whole people, who formed the Union. And we formed it, not to give the blessings of liberty, but to secure them; not to the half of ourselves and the half of our posterity, but to the whole people—women as well as men. And it is a downright mockery to talk to women of their enjoyment of the blessings of liberty while they are denied the use of the only means of securing them provided by this democratic–republican government—the ballot.

For any State to make sex a qualification that must ever result in the disfranchisement of one entire half of the people is to pass a bill of attainder, or an ex post facto law, and is therefore a violation of the supreme law of the land. By it the blessings of liberty are forever withheld from women and their female posterity. To them this government has no just powers derived from the consent of the governed. To them this government is not a democracy. It is not a republic. It is an odious aristocracy; a hateful oligarchy of sex; the most hateful aristocracy ever established on the face of the globe; an oligarchy of wealth, where the rich govern the poor. An oligarchy of learning, where the educated govern the ignorant, or even an oligarchy of race, where the Saxon rules the African, might be endured; but this oligarchy of sex, which makes father, brothers, husband, sons, the oligarchs over the mother and sisters, the wife and daughters of every household—which ordains all men sovereigns, all women subjects, carries dissension, discord and rebellion into every home of the nation.

Webster, Worcester and Bouvier all define a citizen to be a person in the United States, entitled to vote and hold office.

The only question left to be settled now is: Are women persons? And I hardly believe any of our opponents will have the hardihood to say they are not. Being persons, then, women are citizens; and no State has a right to make any law, or to enforce any old law, that shall abridge their privileges or immunities. Hence, every discrimination against women in the constitutions and laws of the several States is today null and void, precisely as is every one against Negroes.

Even in light of such a rational argument for why women deserved the right to vote, there were many groups opposing such a step. Alcohol distributors feared that, if given the chance, women would vote to pass laws regulating the sale and distribution of their products. The South was fearful of the possible impact of even more black voters. Black men had just won that right; now black women might be able to join them in the voting booth. Southerners had also not forgotten the role that women played in the abolitionist movement. They correctly realized that women could be a powerful force in shaping policy and, thus far, the laws were created to keep women powerless. One needed to look no further than the absolute control that husbands had over their wives to understand the way that men subjugated women in all aspects of life. Take, for example, *State v. Edens* (95 N.C. 693), the 1886 ruling by a North Carolina court that a criminal indictment cannot be brought against a husband unless the battery results in permanent injury, endangers life and limb, or is malicious beyond reasonable grounds. Yes, it was clear that women felt the need to gain social, legal, and political autonomy and so the battle for suffrage dragged on.

In 1890, the two factions merged to create the *National American Woman Suffrage Association (NAWSA).* This newly merged group was again led by Stanton and Anthony. Instead of arguing that women deserved the right to vote because they were equal to men, they decided to focus on how their votes might translate into creating a purer and more moral commonwealth. This angle served many political agendas, but the primary one being that middle-class whites realized that—since whites outnumbered blacks—white women would cancel out the black vote and would ensure that whites remained in the majority.

The activists gained traction in the Western states; Colorado granted full voting rights in 1893, followed by Utah and Idaho in 1896. Then, in 1913, a young Quaker named Alice Paul, who had experience with the English suffrage movement, formed the *Congressional Union* and adopted more militant tactics. She organized mass rallies, marches, and picketed to raise awareness and support for the cause. Paul also relentlessly attacked the Democratic administration of Woodrow Wilson for not supporting the right to vote for women.

Post-War Advances

While World War I initially slowed the suffragists' campaign, it ultimately helped them advance their efforts. With the men off to war, women worked tirelessly on behalf of the war effort, which helped them show that they were just as patriotic and deserving of citizenship rights as men. In total, over six million women filled positions in farms and factories, as nurses on the front line, and working for the Red Cross.

At the completion of the war, the men came home and the women were laid off from the positions that they had during the war. Not willing to be relegated only to the role of housewife, the combined efforts of civil disobedience and persistence eventually paid off. While the first Constitutional Amendment to grant women the right to vote was proposed in 1879, the Nineteenth Amendment was finally ratified in 1920. The text of the Nineteenth Amendment was short and to the point:

> The right of citizens of the United States to vote shall not be denied or abridged by the United States or by any state on account of sex. Congress shall have power to enforce this article by appropriate legislation.

As we've already established, achieving the right to vote does not automatically grant a group political power. Emily Blair, a suffragist and Vice President of the Democratic National Committee, said:

> Women were welcome to come in as workers but not as co-makers of the world. For all their numbers, they seldom rose to positions of responsibility or power. The few who did fitted into the system as they found it. All standards, all methods, all values, continued to be set by men.
>
> *(Woloch, 2010: 24)*

While women wanted to use their newly won right for promoting social change, they still did not have any representation in Congress. Also, suffrage had been the one issue that united women. Once that reform was achieved, their collective power was greatly diffused as they split along party lines. The reality was that changing the political culture, both in Washington DC and in the states, would take decades.

Second Feminist Wave

In fact, the second feminist wave didn't begin in earnest until four decades later. Feminism developed into two major branches: a *liberal feminist movement* that focused on women's equality in the workplace; and the *radical feminist movement*, which stressed that what goes on in the privacy of people's homes is deeply political. Women's liberation was spurred on by other social movements of the 1960s—student protests, anti-Vietnam movements, the Civil Rights movement, gay and lesbian movements, and so on. Collectively, these movements recognized that the current structure and function of society was one that was inherently oppressive to the working class, blacks, women, and homosexuals.

Second-wave feminism was theoretically neo-Marxist and heavily criticized capitalism. These feminists viewed capitalism as a means of perpetuating *patriarchy* and they fought to be free of the rigid gender roles that were so much a part of the previous decades. With a lack of social power and political influence, women felt like prisoners in their own homes and pushed back against constraints. As we discussed earlier in the chapter, women were historically under the complete control of their husbands; women who did not work outside of the home had no legal right to their husband's earnings or property. What's more, they also did not have control of their own earnings or property even if they did work outside of the home.

Sadly, not much progress had been made in protecting women from violence in the home. During this time, divorce was also difficult to obtain. A "no-fault" divorce was not an option; women had to prove wrongdoing to have the divorce granted. While a New York law was passed in 1966 citing beatings as grounds for divorce, women had to establish that a sufficient number of beatings had taken place (Bork, 2002).

Today, divorce is significantly easier to attain, although in some states, significant waiting periods exist. Practices limiting the ability of people to enter into as well as exit relationships (e.g., marriage, divorce) are inconsistent with American social justice ideals of libertarianism, egalitarianism, and utilitarianism. That is, they interfere with freedom, equality, and happiness. Because of the feminist movement—a movement of real people to expand rights for all people—significant progress has been made, however. This is yet another reminder that social justice does not occur on its own but instead is realized by the struggle of real people, assuring that it does.

Workplace Equality

Much like suffrage had been the focus of the first wave of feminism, workplace equality was initially the fuel that allowed the liberal feminist movement to grow. The state of affairs in the 1960s was that women were denied access to jobs in male-dominated fields, they received lower salaries than men across the board, and they were routinely let go from those jobs when they became pregnant. In 1961, John F. Kennedy established the *President's Commission on the Status of Women* to examine the different areas where inequality may exist. President Kennedy appointed Eleanor Roosevelt, former United States delegate to the United Nations as well as the widow of President Franklin D. Roosevelt, to chair the Commission. Eleanor Roosevelt had played a key role in the creation of the Universal Declaration of Human Rights (1948) and was recognized as a defender of both women's economic endeavors and women's traditional family role.

One point that was often lost on the detractors is that feminists did not want to create a society that mandated women to work. Instead, they wanted women to have the choice to stay home or go to work;

but, if they did enter the workplace, they demanded equal rights and equal pay. The Commission's report was published in October 1963, and found that substantial discrimination against women existed in the workplace. The Commission made specific recommendations for legislative changes including fair hiring practices, paid maternity leave, and affordable childcare. The *Equal Pay Act of 1963*, a direct result of the Commission's efforts, abolished wage disparity between sexes. Historically, men and women would get paid substantially different rates for doing the same work. The Equal Pay Act sought to correct that discrepancy.

Gender and Civil Rights

Women now had the floor on the national stage. They were determined to be included in the pending Civil Rights legislation. Women's rights had been overshadowed at the conclusion of the Civil War and the leaders of the women's rights movement were determined not to allow that to happen again. They were victorious when the Civil Rights Amendment was passed with the inclusion of "sex" as a category for prohibited discrimination. In addition to ending segregation as well as discrimination in voting and in education, the Civil Rights Amendment banned employment discrimination. Specifically, Title VII ordered that it is unlawful employment practice for an employer:

- to fail or refuse to hire or to discharge any individual, or otherwise to discriminate against any individual with respect to compensation, terms, conditions, or privileges of employment, because of race, color, religion, sex, or national origin; and
- to limit, segregate, or classify his employees or applicants for employment in any way which would deprive or tend to deprive any individual of employment opportunities or otherwise adversely affect his status as an employee, because of race, color, religion, sex, or national origin.
  (Civil Rights Act of 1964 § 7, 42 U.S.C. § 2000e et seq (1964))

The Civil Rights Act also established the *Equal Employment Opportunity Commission (EEOC)* to investigate complaints and impose penalties when discrimination was found. In situations where there was evidence of patterns of discriminatory practices, the EEOC would alert the Department of Justice for litigation. In 1965, Executive Order 11375 expanded *affirmative action* to cover discrimination based on gender. This order demanded that federal agencies take active measures to ensure that women enjoyed the same educational and employment opportunities as white males. Together, this legislation began the cultural shift towards fully incorporating women into both the public and private sectors. While this combined legislation afforded women the opportunity to seek out professional opportunities, it was difficult to pursue a career without the ability to control fertility and reproduction. As such, female control of contraception became a condition of the emancipation of women.

Before we move onto this issue, it's important to examine the state of the workplace in contemporary America. Table 9.2 illustrates some key facts regarding women and men in the workplace. As you can see, much progress has been made since the dawn of the feminist movement to gain equality in the workplace. Yet, for various reasons, women are still underrepresented among numerous professions, and still lag behind in terms of pay for men. This is clearly inconsistent with American social justice ideals.

Reproductive Rights

The argument over reproductive rights stems from the belief that, since women disproportionately bear the responsibilities associated with pregnancy and child-rearing, they should be allowed to determine if and when conception as well as birth should occur. There are two fundamental parts to the reproduction debate: contraception, and abortion. The first deals with whether and in what form women (and men) should have access to means to control whether they get pregnant in the first place. The second deals with whether and under what circumstances women (and couples) should be able to terminate pregnancies. The right to control reproduction soon joined workplace equality as an important issue that needed to be addressed.

Beginning with contraception, it's worth noting that the regulation of contraceptive measures has been in the public sphere since the 1800s. There are two distinct conversations that occur when policy issues arise and those are: the prevention and treatment of disease; and an aid in family planning. The prevention of disease was instrumental to the contraception debate because medical issues are far more concrete than issues of morality. By arguing that doctors should have the ability to provide contraception to prevent the spread of sexually transmitted diseases, lobbyists turned contraception into a public safety issue. Once the debate was successfully framed in a manner that focused on the rights of doctors to treat patients, contraception was made legal. This conversation, which was happening in the first quarter of the twentieth century, peaked the interest of individuals who were concerned about the decline of "native-born white Americans in face of massive immigration from southern and eastern Europe" (McBride & Parry, 2014: 81). Ironically, it came to pass that, in this manner, bigotry is what prompted policymakers to move forward with the family planning aspect of contraception, but it did so in a devastating way—the Eugenics Movement.

TABLE 9.2 Gender and the Workplace

Ratio of pay of women versus men, by occupation, 2010	
Food preparation/serving	112.1
Bill/account collector	109.5
Stock clerk/order filler	105.1
Postal service clerk	94.5
Social worker	91.1
Editor	88.3
Registered nurse	86.5
Pharmacist	83.2
Computer/information systems	81.8
Total, 16 years and older	*81.2*
Postsecondary teacher	77.3
Lawyer	77.1
Insurance sales agent	66.7
Property/real estate	65.3
Retail sales	64.7
Personal financial advisor	58.4

Source: Data is from the Bureau of Labor Statistics, "Women at Work", March 2011, http://www.bls.gov/spotlight/2011/women/.

Eugenics

The *Eugenics Movement* is among the darkest periods in American history. Eugenics, or the attempt to manipulate the human species through selective breeding, was popular in the first half of the twentieth century. It was built on the idea that science—specifically the recently founded Mendelian laws of heredity—could be used to solve social ills such as alcoholism, prostitution, and crime. While the quest for a "master race" is typically associated with Nazi Germany, the United States was in reality the forbearer of culling society of those they, the government, deemed unfit to live.

The policy implications of eugenics included the practice of compulsory sterilization of individuals. While Indiana was the first state to pass eugenics laws in 1907, 30 additional states would eventually follow suit over the next three decades. While eugenics was initially promoted as the sterilization of the disabled or mentally ill, it was also used extensively for socially disadvantaged groups. Cepko wrote, "In a culture with a creed of equality but a history of gender discrimination, the most obvious point of concern raised by sterilization statutes is that the application of sterilization laws [was] overwhelmingly directed at women" (2013: 123). As such, while compulsory sterilization did not begin as a women's rights issue, it evolved into one.

The story of the Eugenics Movement began in California, the epicenter of eugenics research and practice with roots in the 1800s. While the State of California was responsible for the greatest number of sterilizations, in this chapter, we will focus on the State of North Carolina, which arguably had the most aggressive eugenics laws in the country. Between 1929 and 1974, an estimated 7,600 individuals were sterilized in North Carolina against their will under the guise of public health and safety. The way for eugenics laws was paved by a 1927 Supreme Court decision in the case of *Buck v. Bell*, 274 U.S. 200 (1927). The State of Virginia involuntarily sterilized Carrie Buck and her infant daughter, Vivian, citing low IQ as the justification. In the opinion issued by the Supreme Court, Chief Justice Oliver Wendell Holmes wrote,

> It is better for all the world, if instead of waiting to execute degenerate offspring for crime, or to let them starve for their imbecility, society can prevent those who are manifestly unfit from continuing their kind . . . . Three generations of imbeciles are enough.

This decision opened the floodgates for thousands to be coercively sterilized or otherwise persecuted as subhuman. Years later, the Nazis at the Nuremberg trials quoted Holmes's words in their own defense.

Sterilization in North Carolina

Sterilization in North Carolina was overseen by the Eugenics Commission, which comprised five people appointed by the governor in North Carolina:

- the Director of Public Health Services;
- the Director of the Division of Social and Rehabilitative Services;
- a Chief Medical Officer of a state institution for the feeble-minded and insane;
- a Chief Medical Officer in the area of mental health services; and
- the State Attorney General.

In 1929, the North Carolina General Assembly approved a measure whereby any penal or charitable public institution could order the sterilization of any person that was deemed to be in the best interest of the public. North Carolina eugenics laws allowed social workers to make recommendations on who should be sterilized. Additionally, a next-of-kin or legal guardian could request sterilization at the public expense.

In the early years of the Eugenics Movement, there was a review and approval process that fell under the auspices of the Public Health Committee. Approximately 90 percent of the sterilization petitions brought before the board were approved. Then, in 1933, the General Assembly of North Carolina created the *Eugenics Board* to exclusively make these decisions (North Carolina Department of Cultural Resources, 1995).

Eugenics was widely discredited after it was adopted by Nazi Germany. As a result, many states ended their sterilization programs after the conclusion of World War II. North Carolina, on the other hand, was just getting started. Over 80 percent of North Carolina's sterilizations took place after the war. Part of the reason for the growth of the Eugenics Movement in the 1950s was due to concerns over mounting welfare expenditures. Decades before President Ronald Reagan created the myth of the "welfare queen," middle-class whites incorrectly believed that poor blacks were the primary recipients of general welfare and *Aid to Dependent Children* (later renamed *Aid to Families with Dependent Children*). This belief has roots in slavery and was based on the fact that slave owners would encourage their female slaves to have many children in order to increase their labor pool. The reality is that poor whites, particularly after the Great Depression, were receiving relief at a rate equal to poor blacks (Baldwin, 2010).

With little attention to the structural causes of poverty, and with increased racial tension and social unrest, the focus of the Eugenics Movement shifted to blacks. Unmarried women and children, particularly black women, were the most frequently targeted group. This trend is clearly seen in the racial composition of those sterilized. As Schoen (2011) points out: "Sterilization of the non-institutionalized rose from 23 percent between 1937 and 1951 to 76 percent between 1952 and 1966." Between 1960 and 1968, 98 percent of those sterilized were women, the majority of which were young black women.

Other than perhaps slavery and capital punishment, there is hardly an issue that so clearly violates our social justice ideals as eugenics/forced sterilization. Even with a valid social goal of bettering lives for the majority (i.e., utilitarianism), there can be no excuse for violating a person's right to autonomy and self-determination, a key part of liberty and freedom. Yet, up until the 1970s, state governments pursued the policy of forced sterilization, and many states today continue to use capital punishment.

Birth Control

While the Eugenics Movement and forced sterilizations were still in operation—and with the increasing stigma associated with large families—the Food and Drug Administration approved the birth control pill for use in 1960, but its availability remained a states-rights issue; this meant each state determined for itself whether citizens would have access to this method of birth control. By 1964, the pill was still illegal in eight states and, while five million American women were using the product, the controversy surrounding the pill was far from over.

Since the birth control pill did not prevent sexually transmitted diseases, it became the focus of the family planning debate. In 1965, the executive director of *Planned Parenthood*—an organization that distributed birth control pills—was arrested for providing contraception to married couples. The Supreme Court chose to hear the appeal on the case, *Griswold v. Connecticut*, 381 U.S. 479 (1965), and found that the state statute that criminalized the use of birth control violated a married couples' right to privacy. While the right to privacy is not explicitly granted by the Bill of Rights, and does not appear anywhere in the Constitution for that matter, the Supreme Court had long held that families are able to make certain decisions without governmental interference. Justice Douglas made this point clear in the *Griswold* decision by stating:

> We deal with a right of privacy older than the Bill of Rights—older than our political parties, older than our school system. Marriage is a coming together, for better or worse, hopefully enduring, and intimate to the degree of being sacred. It is an association that promotes a way of life, not causes; a harmony of living, not political faith; a bilateral loyalty, not commercial or social projects.
>
> *(Griswold Decision, 1965: 486)*

Of course, this ruling was related only to married persons and the same right to privacy was not extended to unmarried persons until 1972 when the Court heard a still controversial abortion rights case. The decades-long struggle for the right to contraception paved the way for what remains one of the most hotly debated legal issues: the right to a legal abortion.

Today, according to the US Department of Health and Human Service (2010), roughly 99 percent of women who have ever had intercourse have used some contraceptive method in their lives, including a male condom, oral contraceptive pill, and so on. Using the pill (82 percent) is the most common method used by women aged 15 to 44 years old. Further, according to the Guttmacher Institute (2012), since women only want to have an average of two children during their lives, they generally use contraception for about three decades!

The ability to regulate your own reproductive cycle is viewed by many women as well as men as a key facet of social justice; it is one thing that assures liberty and happiness for Americans. It also assures equality in terms of how the sexes are treated, for men already have complete freedom to regulate whether they have children (e.g., by being responsible in their sexual activity).

The controversy surrounding the right to a legal abortion goes back to the 1800s. In 1859, the *American Medical Association* passed a resolution that granted a fetus the title of "living being" and pledged to protect all life, regardless of the stage of development. By 1880, abortion was almost universally illegal except when the life of the mother was at stake. Abortion faded into obscurity in subsequent decades, but was brought back to the forefront of the public agenda in the mid-twentieth century by physicians who wanted fewer state regulations to govern their discretion of what was medically necessary. Feminists took up this charge and took it one step further by demanding a repeal of all abortion laws. To force the state's hand, abortion lobbyists began creating abortion clinics in direct defiance of state laws. Just when the public debate reached a fever pitch and state legislatures were struggling with an incredibly divisive issue, the Supreme Court emerged to establish a framework to help guide state policy making.

On January 22, 1973, the United States Supreme Court issued a decision in the case of *Roe v. Wade* (410 U.S. 113). *Roe v. Wade* was a legal challenge to a Texas law, which made it a crime to perform an abortion in situations where the woman's life was not at risk. At the time "Jane Roe," an unmarried Texas woman—whose real name was Norma McCorvy—wanted to terminate her pregnancy. When she filed the case, abortion was outlawed in nearly every state except for in select circumstances.

To understand the context in which this decision was made, one must recognize the reality of abortion when it was illegal. Statistically speaking, 17 percent of all deaths due to pregnancy and childbirth were the result of illegal abortion (Gold, 1990). With the Supreme Court ruling that the constitutional right to privacy "is broad enough to encompass a woman's decision whether or not to terminate her pregnancy," the Justices drew on decades of case law that set a standard for government non-intervention in personal decisions about procreation, marriage, and other aspects of family life. With this in mind, the Supreme Court highlighted four competing demands that needed to be reconciled:

1. the right of a woman to privately decide when and if to bear a child as outlined in the Griswold case;
2. the right of physicians to use their discretion in treating their patients and without government intervention;
3. the interest of state governments in protecting the life and health of the mother;
4. the interest of state governments in protecting the life and health of the unborn child.

The compromise that the Court outlined was a scenario that treated each of the three trimesters of a pregnancy as distinct periods. In the first trimester, the state may not regulate or interfere with the decision of the patient and the doctor to terminate a pregnancy. During the second trimester, the state may regulate medical conditions under which abortions are performed, but the practice itself cannot be restricted. Finally, abortions may be prohibited during the third trimester except to save the life of the mother. The justification for having policy that treated each trimester separately focused on both the changes in the fetus and the complexity of the procedure. For example, a first trimester abortion could be performed with outpatient surgery, while a second trimester abortion was considered a more serious procedure that has to be performed in a hospital setting. Further, a fetus in the first trimester is highly unlikely to survive outside the womb, whereas a fetus in the third trimester has a fighting chance.

The ruling in the *Roe* case was 7–2 that a woman's right to an abortion is essentially part of her right to privacy (recognized in the *Griswold* cases mentioned earlier), which is protected by the Fourteenth Amendment. Under the *Roe* decision, women were given complete autonomy to determine whether they allowed their pregnancies to continue during the first trimester of pregnancy, while recognizing that the state had a public interest in protecting fetuses during the second and third trimesters of pregnancy.

The passage of *Roe v. Wade* was not the end of the abortion debate. Opponents of legal abortion grew in strength and organization. Using terms such as *Pro-Life* and *Right to Life*, these groups worked diligently to strip government funding for any organizations that provided abortive services. Abortion-rights groups countered these efforts with lobbies of their own, but the general shift in the decades since *Roe v. Wade* has been towards increased restrictions.

Immediately after the Roe decision, Medicaid was permitted to cover the costs associated with abortions without restriction. That changed in 1976 with an amendment that was filed by Representative Henry Hyde. The *Hyde Amendment*, as it came to be known, specified what abortion services were to be covered under Medicaid. Congress wrestled over the exact circumstances that would be included in the Hyde Amendment, but, in 1993, they determined that coverage should be extended beyond life endangerment to include coverage for abortion services in cases of rape and incest. While there has been an incredible amount of debate over whether government funding can be used for non-emergency abortive services, it's important to understand that, at its core, while the *Roe* decision explicitly said that governments couldn't impose restrictions or barriers on a woman's right to choose, it remained up to state legislatures to decide whether to fund clinics that assist indigent women. This question of whether indigent women should have access to subsidized family planning cannot be isolated from the larger discussion about the feminization of poverty in Chapter 8.

Table 9.3 shows the number of abortions that have happened over the years since the *Roe* decision. As you can see, once abortions became legal, they quickly rose, eventually leveling off but still remaining quite high.

Activity 9.3 Abortion

Is abortion ever justifiable?

Should it be legal?

Explain.

Women as Victims

In patriarchal societies, there exists a long-standing cultural view that when someone is different from the status quo, they are seen as inferior. In this sense, violence against women was often seen as an expression of male superiority. When women "forgot their place," men reminded them. In fact, the common law doctrine of *coverture* that existed for centuries determined that a married couple became one person. Perhaps more precisely, the husband absorbed the wife so that the "one person" was really just he (Zaher, 2002). This subjugation of the wife to the husband's authority was present in the marriage contract. Women adopted their husband's surname, moved into the husband's home, became the husband's dependent, and swore to love, honor, and obey. Women were also required to have their husband's approval for all things including co-signing on contracts, managing her assets, and approving her will. In this sense, the wife became both legally and economically dependent on her husband.

It goes without saying that the wife did not have the same veto power over her husband's affairs. Since man's role was to rule his private household the same way that he ruled public affairs, it was considered the husband's duty to correct his wife, physically or verbally, should he have determined

TABLE 9.3 Abortion across the Decades

1973	615,831
1981	1,300,760
1991	1,556,500
2001	1,291,000
2011	1,059,500

Sources: Data is from Guttmacher Institute, "Abortion Incidence and Service Availability in the United States, 2011", http://www.guttmacher.org/pubs/journals/psrh.46e0414.pdf; and Christian Life Resources, "U.S. Abortion Statistics By Year (1973–Current)", http://www.christianliferesources.com/article/u-s-abortion-statistics-by-year-1973-current-1042.

it necessary. *Martial chastisement*, as it was called, did have some legal guidelines including that a husband could not beat his wife with an instrument of correction larger than the size of his thumb (hence the so-called "rule of thumb"). Additionally, the law of chastisement forbade the drawing of blood. The protection of the family was cited as the primary reason for the decriminalization of spousal abuse.

Domestic Violence

The National Coalition Against Domestic Violence (2014) defines *domestic violence* as "the willful intimidation, physical assault, battery, sexual assault, and/or other abusive behavior perpetrated by an intimate partner against another." Historically, domestic violence had been considered a states' rights issue. It was the Puritans who first sought to put an end to the physical infliction of harm of a wife by her husband. In 1641, the Massachusetts Puritans passed the first law against spousal abuse, calling it unnaturally severe and urging that males can assert themselves as superior through persuasion alone.

While the Puritans abstained from condoning domestic violence, their abstention was certainly not the norm for centuries to come. To illustrate this issue, we turn to the Mississippi State Supreme Court, who affirmed a husband's right to moderately discipline his wife (*Bradley v. State*, 1824). As part of the *Bradley* ruling, the court stated that domestic issues were best dealt with inside of the home instead of being brought to the legal system. This position was reaffirmed on numerous occasions and the general rule became that courts were only involved if excessive violence was used (*State v. Black*, 1864; *State v. Oliver*, 1979). The logic used by the courts was that, since a wife was a husband's property, he could do with her as he saw fit.

This was also believed to be true for sexual relations between spouses. An 1857 case in Massachusetts found that the "right" of a husband to sex with his wife also provided a husband with grounds for divorce if his wife did not comply with his request. This defense became part of rape laws in every state and created the *marital rape exception*, which stated that a man was not legally capable of raping his wife (such exceptions still exist in many other cultures and countries).

Remarkably, the criminal justice system propagated the idea until the 1970s that physical abuse and rape in spousal relationships did not constitute a crime. The *Women's Rights Movement* of the 1960s and 1970s, along with advocacy on behalf of victims, were instrumental in bringing these private struggles into the public consciousness. There was a call to redefine domestic violence as a criminal issue requiring criminal justice intervention instead of just a familial dispute that should remain between husband and wife. Advocates particularly fought to eradicate the legal distinction that existed between violent acts by a stranger and violent acts by an intimate.

Even so, the courts were slow to act. It wasn't until 1976 that Nebraska became the first state to eliminate the marital rape exception. Over the next decade, all of the other states followed suit and calls for reform of the criminal justice system followed.

Prior to the 1960s, the typical police response to domestic violence calls was non-intervention. That is to say that officers would leave without making an arrest. After domestic violence laws were passed, the police response shifted from non-intervention to mediation. Still viewing domestic violence as a family disturbance instead of a crime, officers were told to help mediate the situation. The problem with this tactic was that the officers often arrived on scene during what is known as the "reconciliation phase," which is the period of offender contrition immediately following the battering episode. Since both the offender and the responding officer often wanted the incident settled in a non-formal matter, the rights of the victim were still overlooked. It became clear that there was a need to change the way that the criminal justice system and criminal justice practitioners responded to domestic violence—from the initial processing of the case by law enforcement to intervention programs for batterers.

Beginning with the police response, research demonstrated that if the initial police response to a domestic violence incident was considered inadequate, the victim was less likely to contact the police in future domestic violence incidents (Erez & Belknap, 1998). In the 1980s, the call for stronger police response resulted in a more aggressive police response to domestic violence calls. This shift away from mediation was supported by research, which suggested that arrest had a deterrent effect on the offender (Sherman & Berk, 1984).

While law enforcement officers are considered the gatekeepers to the criminal justice system, and thus serve an important role, arrest is ultimately meant to result in prosecution. Considering the low probability of prosecution in domestic violence cases, victims often become skeptical of the criminal justice process if prosecution and or sentencing do not occur following arrest. The criminal justice paradigm of collecting evidence, gathering witnesses, and dealing with a single criminal event at a time makes it difficult for the proper processing of domestic violence cases. The nature of domestic violence is that it is often a series of escalating incidents that happen within the confines of the home, with very little concrete evidence and no witnesses. The victim and the offender often give vastly different accounts of what occurred and the result is that, even if prosecution does occur, the case is frequently prosecuted as a misdemeanor. Since many misdemeanors drop out off the prosecution process at various stages, reform of domestic violence legislation has targeted how these cases are handled post-arrest.

Beginning in the late 1980s, a push was made to issue more *protection orders*, produce more charging decisions, and shift the emphasis of the case towards evidence-based practices and away from victim testimony. Historically, and for a number of valid reasons, it has been difficult to gain the victim's cooperation during the criminal justice process. One of those reasons is fear of *secondary victimization*, or being exposed to the behaviors and attitudes of service-providers that are victim-blaming in nature and cause the victim to be doubly traumatized by events. To help limit this secondary victimization, many prosecutors' offices created victim advocacy programs to help streamline case processing and provide victims with information about court proceedings.

Another reform has been the recognition of *battered women syndrome* where a victim reacts to repeated violence by killing or injuring her abuser (Gillespie, 1989). This special defense for battery victims was necessary, since the victim frequently killed the batterer without provocation or while he was unable to defend himself (e.g., sleeping, intoxicated, etc.). The key to this defense was in showing that a victim perceived herself to be in imminent danger and to establish a pattern of aggression that supported this fear.

The first major federal effort to address domestic violence was the *Family Violence Prevention and Services Act* of 1984. The purpose of this legislation was twofold: to increase public awareness about family violence; and to fund shelters and other assistance for affected families. Additionally, it provided training and grant dollars to states and non-profit organizations to assist them with this cause.

One decade later, the *Violence Against Women Act (VAWA)* was passed, granting recognition to the fact that domestic violence remains a serious problem. The key provisions of VAWA were as follows:

- requiring that victim protection orders are recognized and enforced in all state, tribal, and territorial jurisdictions within the United States;
- full funding for rape kits and legal/court fees associated with protection orders;
- creating and funding of special domestic violence units at the local level; and
- allowing undocumented immigrants who are the victims of domestic violence to apply for a green card in exchange for helping law enforcement officials prosecute their abusers.

VAWA was a necessary complement to state legislation because it closed a number of loopholes that prevented the prosecution of certain abusers. For example, this Act addressed interstate travel for the purposes of violating a protection order or committing an act of domestic violence. This was an important provision because, historically, one jurisdiction did not necessarily recognize a protection order issued in a different jurisdiction.

While VAWA was a move in the right direction, not all victims were initially included in the provisions. To correct this, VAWA has been reauthorized three times since the original enactment. In the latest revision and reauthorization, which occurred in 2013, additional changes included extending services to LGBT victims, college students, Native American women with non-Native partners, and victims living in public housing. Much like the jurisdictional challenges that prompted the original VAWA, granting tribal courts the ability to try non-Indian spouses or intimate partners of Indian women in domestic violence cases closed the loophole for white offenders living on tribal lands.

Research on domestic violence illustrates the following realities about domestic violence in the US:

- One in every four women will experience domestic violence in her lifetime.
- An estimated 1.3 million women are victims of physical assault by an intimate partner each year.
- A large majority of domestic violence victims (85 percent) are women.
- Historically, females have been most often victimized by someone they know.
- Females who are 24 years of age are at the greatest risk of nonfatal intimate partner violence.
- Most cases of domestic violence are never reported to the police.

(National Coalition Against Domestic Violence, 2014)

Table 9.4 shows some key facts about domestic violence in the US.

Women as Offenders

Traditionally, the study of crime has been the study of young, male delinquency. The gender difference in crime is universal—women engage in criminal activity less frequently than men. As a result, the emphasis in criminology has been on the male offender to the almost utter exclusion of the female offender. Additionally, in both news and fiction, women have been portrayed primarily as victims of crime. This is partly due to the *hegemonic* discourse of gender, which has typecast males as aggressive and women as passive. Over time, criminologists became interested in female criminality but, even then, they began to examine women as offenders by applying male-derived theories to the behavior of women.

Before we begin to examine the participation of women in crime, let us examine the facts of how women are represented and processed in the criminal justice system. Women comprise less than 10 percent

TABLE 9.4 Domestic Violence in the US

- From 1994 to 2010, the overall rate of intimate partner violence in the United States declined by 64 percent, from 9.8 victimizations per 1,000 persons age 12 or older to 3.6 per 1,000.
- Intimate partner violence declined by more than 60 percent for both males and females from 1994 to 2010.
- From 1994 to 2010, about 4 in 5 victims of intimate partner violence were female.
- Females aged 18 to 24 and 25 to 34 generally experienced the highest rates of intimate partner violence.
- Compared to every other age group, a smaller percentage of female victims ages 12 to 17 were previously victimized by the same offender.
- The rate of intimate partner violence for Hispanic females declined 78 percent, from 18.8 victimizations per 1,000 in 1994 to 4.1 per 1,000 in 2010.
- Females living in households comprising one female adult with children experienced intimate partner violence at a rate more than 10 times higher than households with married adults with children and 6 times higher than households with one female only.

Source: Bureau of Justice Statistics, "Intimate Partner Violence (1993–2010)", http://www.bjs.gov/index.cfm?ty=pbdetail&iid=4536.

of incarcerated inmates but, today, they are the fastest growing prison population. Women are primarily arrested for property and drug crimes and women inmates are overwhelmingly minorities (65 percent), parents (75 percent) and single (66 percent) (Bureau of Justice Statistics, 2014).

It seems that the push to become tough on crime has coincided with a backlash against the quest for gender equality. These two movements have led to a hostile "equality with a vengeance" treatment of women who have found themselves in the criminal justice system (Steffensmeier & Schwartz, 2004: 113). While the FBI's *Uniform Crime Report* supports the assertion that the female-to-male gap in arrest rates is narrowing, the question remains as to whether that narrowing gap is a result of an increase in female offending or just an increasing in the willingness to arrest more females.

Scholars have been debating this question for decades, and both sides have valid points. Those who argue that the behavior of women is a changing point to a trend towards greater female freedom and assertiveness, which results in a "masculinized" female archetype who has a penchant for engaging in physical aggression and violence (Levin & Fox, 2000). Additionally, higher divorce rates result in single-parent households where women ultimately must take on the role of both the mother and father. The stressful economic circumstances in female-headed households may increase strain. *Strain*—a sense of frustration—combined with increased freedom, could result in increased criminal activity.

On the other side of the spectrum is the *policy change perspective*, which argues that the increase in female arrests is simply a result of the changes in how criminal justice officials enforce policy decisions. Law enforcement practices have moved towards allowing officers lower levels of discretion when deciding whether to arrest an individual. Definitions of the criminal law have been interpreted more expansively and law enforcement practices have become less tolerant.

One of these practices that may impact women is the policy of increasing the severity of the initial charges with the forethought that the individual is likely to accept a plea bargain for a lesser charge. Another relevant policy change is the criminalization of domestic violence and the associated mandatory arrest policies that often affect both parties involved.

Support exists for both hypotheses, but the true relationship is complicated by the fact that criminal justice actors do not treat all women equally. While being female tends to be a "protective" factor for white women, minority women do not experience the same advantage with regard to arrest, sentencing, and incarceration. The *chivalry hypothesis* asserts that actors in the criminal justice system treat women more leniently because they are perceived as weak and irrational. Theorists are quick to point out that this leniency only applies to "women who conform to a sex role which requires their obedience to men, their passivity, their acceptance of their status as the sexual property of only one man. Should they step outside of this boundary . . . chivalry is replaced by harsh exploitation and harassment" (Chesney-Lind, 1978: 204).

The feminists of the 1960s were predominantly white, middle-class, and heterosexual. They were women who did not want to be confined to the home but, with the exception of their biological sex, they shared many traits—and privileges—with their male counterparts. white women were disadvantaged by their gender, but privileged by their race. As Krolokke and Sorensen state,

In the context of the complex power relations of a postcolonial but still imperial and capitalist world, [non-traditional feminists] . . . raised the issue of differentiated-identity politics, based on the contingent and diversified but no less decisive intersections of gender, class, race/ethnicity, and sexuality.

(2005: 12–13)

Patricia Hill Collins (1998) discusses the theory of *intersectionality*, which analyzes how different systems of oppression interlock with one another. Traditionally, discussions of oppression used an additive approach for analysis. Holding the white, heterosexual male as the standard against which others are measured, the additive approach cumulates the areas in which an individual differs from the standard. This approach sees each area of oppression as distinct and different and considers racial differences separately from gender differences. When this additive approach is replaced by an interlocking approach, it results in a paradigm shift, or a shift in thought patterns. The new paradigm highlights how all groups possess varying degrees of penalty and privilege depending on their degree of "otherness" from the white middle-class heterosexual male. The *matrix of oppression* is one way to examine these differences. Figure 9.2 illustrates what the matrix of oppression looks like. As Collins writes:

The overarching matrix of domination houses multiple groups, each with varying experiences with penalty and privilege that produce corresponding partial perspectives, situated knowledges, and, for clearly identifiable subordinate groups, subjugated knowledges. No one group has a clear angle of vision . . . Given that groups are unequal in power in making themselves heard, dominant groups have a vested interest in suppressing the knowledge produced by subordinate groups.

(Collins, 1998)

	Race/Ethnicity	Class	Sex	Sexuality
Privileged	White	Upper/middle-class	Male	Heterosexual
Non-privileged	Non-white	Lower-class	Female	Non-heterosexual

FIGURE 9.2 Matrix of Oppression.

Returning to our example of white women, depending on the context, they can simultaneously be a member of an oppressed group—penalized for their gender—and an oppressor, depending on their attitudes about other individuals. Most individuals can readily recognize their own experiences within a system of oppression, yet this doesn't always translate to empathy for other groups who may be penalized for different characteristics. For example, women may be acutely aware of their own victimization in a system of oppression, yet still express a great deal of intolerance for people of other racial/ethnic backgrounds or different sexual orientations. Once we understand the complexity of how systems of oppression interlock to create these divisions between groups who should seemingly be sympathetic to one another, the division between different groups of feminists becomes clearer.

There is no universal female experience, just as there is no universal black experience. This point is of particular importance with regard to women because, historically, white, heterosexual, middle-class women had the ability to resist criminal labels in a way that other women could not. This largely remains true today, whereas women of color—especially poor women of color—are far less able to do so.

Conclusion

As this chapter shows, America still has serious problems with regard to sex and gender. That is, there is still evidence of significant disparities between men and women in important outcomes such as labor force participation and pay for work. Additionally, although we've made significant progress over the years, women are still vastly underrepresented among those in positions of power (e.g., lawmakers). This is a serious threat to social justice within society as well as within criminal justice practice, for the voices of women are largely not being heard or represented among state and federal lawmakers.

Further, women continue to be victimized by harmful acts such as domestic violence, generally committed within the context of intimate relationships. Progress has been made in American society with regard to bringing attention to acts of domestic violence, as well as taking them seriously and even preventing them; yet, the prevalence of domestic violence is still deeply troubling and obviously interferes with the realization of social justice.

Similarly, the crackdown on women offenders, especially poor women of color, for relatively minor crimes such as drug offenses, is troubling. Being deprived of one's liberty for non-serious crimes—the likelihood of which is highly impacted by one's color and class—is a threat to libertarianism as well egalitarianism. Further, lawmakers around the country seem to be aware of the threat to utilitarianism, for states have begun to reject overly punitive responses to crime.

Discussion Questions

1. What is sexism?
2. How does gender impact the criminal law?
3. Define gender roles.
4. Explain how socialization related to gender occurs in the US.
5. Differentiate the functionalist perspective of gender roles from the conflict perspective of gender roles.
6. Contrast sex liberation with gender liberation.
7. Outline and summarize the fight for suffrage and identify the main groups involved in the struggle to get women the right to vote.

8. Discuss the social justice implications of denying women the right to participate in the political process.
9. Provide a definition of feminism.
10. Contrast the liberal feminist movement and the radical feminist movement.
11. Identify and discuss disparities that exist within the workplace.
12. Discuss the social justice implications of disparities in the workplace based on gender.
13. How are gender movements an important part of the civil rights movement?
14. What are the social justice implications of birth control and abortion?
15. Describe the Eugenics movement and forced sterilization in North Carolina. What are the social justice implications of forcing people to be sterilized?
16. Discuss the terms coverture and marital chastisement and explain how they are related to social justice.
17. What is domestic violence? Discuss how prevalent it is in the US.
18. What is secondary victimization?
19. Define battered women syndrome.
20. How often, relative to men, are women involved in crime as offenders?
21. What is the chivalry hypothesis and how is it related to social justice?
22. Define the matrix of oppression.

References

Adler, P., & Adler, P. (1998). *Peer Power Preadolescent Culture and Identity*. New Brunswick, NJ: Rutgers University Press.

Baldwin, B. (2010). Stratification of the Welfare Poor: Intersections of Gender, Race, and "Worthiness" in Poverty Discourse and Policy. *The Modern American, 6*(1), 4–14.

Bork, R. (2002). Taking Fault with New York's Fault-Based Divorce: Is the Law Constitutional? *Journal of Civil Rights and Economic Development, 16*(1), 164–198.

Bureau of Justice Statistics. (2014). *Prisoners in 2013*. Retrieved from: http://www.bjs.gov/content/pub/pdf/p13.pdf.

Cepko, R. (2013). Involuntary Sterilization of Mentally Disabled Women. *Berkeley Journal of Gender, Law & Justice, 8*(1), 123–157.

Chesney-Lind, M. (1978). Chivalry Re-examined: Women and the Criminal Justice System. In Bowker, L. (Ed.), *Women, Crime and the Criminal Justice System*. Lexington, MA: Lexington Books.

Collins, P. (1998). It's All in the Family: Intersections of Gender, Race, and Nation. *Border Crossings: Multicultural and Postcolonial Feminist Challenges to Philosophy, 13*(3), 62–82.

Department of Defense. (2012). *Annual Report on Sexual Assault in the Military*. Retrieved from: http://www.sapr.mil/public/docs/reports/FY12_DoD_SAPRO_Annual_Report_on_Sexual_Assault-VOLUME_ONE.pdf.

Erez, E., & Belknap, J. (1998). In Their Own Words: Battered Women's Assessment of Systemic Responses. *Violence and Victims, 13*(3), 3–20.

Gold, R. B. (1990). *Abortion and Women's Health: A Turning Point for America?* New York: The Alan Guttmacher Institute.

Gillespie, C. (1989). *Justifiable Homicide*. Columbus, OH: Ohio State University Press.

Guttmacher Institute. (2012). *Facts on Contraceptive Use in the United States, Fact Sheet*. New York: Guttmacher Institute.

Krolokke, C., & Sorensen, A. (2005). *Gender Communication Theories and Analyses from Silence to Performance*. Thousand Oaks, CA: Sage Publications.

Levin, J., & Fox, J. (2000). *Dead Lines: Essays in Murder and Mayhem.* Needham Heights, MA: Allyn & Bacon.

McBride, J. & Parry, J. (2014). *Women's Rights in the USA: Policy Debates and Gender Roles.* New York: Routledge.

National Coalition Against Domestic Violence. (2014). Retrieved from: http://www.ncadv.org/need-help/what-is-domestic-violence.

North Carolina Department of Cultural Resources. (1995). *Eugenics in North Carolina.* Retrieved from: http://www.learnnc.org/lp/pdf/eugenics-in-north-carolina-p6164.pdf.

Parsons, T., & Bales, R. F. (1955). *Family, Socialization and Interaction Process.* Glencoe, IL: Free Press.

Schaeffer, R. (2011). *Racial and Ethnic Groups: Census 2010 Update* (13th ed.). Upper Saddle River, NJ: Prentice Hall.

Schoen, J. (2011). Reassessing Eugenic Sterilization: The Case of North Carolina. In Lombardo, P. (Ed.), *A Century of Eugenics in America: From the Indiana Experiment to the Human Genome Era.* Bloomington, IN: Indiana University Press.

Sherman, L., & Berk, R. (1984). The Specific Deterrent Effects of Arrest for Domestic Assault. *American Sociological Review, 49,* 261–272.

Steffensmeier, D., & Schwartz, J. (2004). Contemporary Explanations of Female Offending. In Price, B. R., & Sokoloff, N. J. (Eds.), *The Criminal Justice System and Women: Offenders, Victims, and Workers.* New York: Mc-Graw Hill.

US Department of Health and Human Services. (2010). *Use of Contraception in the United States: 1982–2008.* Retrieved from: http://www.cdc.gov/nchs/data/series/sr_23/sr23_029.pdf.

Woloch, N. (2010). *Women and the American Experience* (5th ed.). New York: Knopf.

Zaher, C. (2002). When a Woman's Marital Status Determined Her Legal Status: A Research Guide on the Common Law Doctrine of Coverture. *Law Library Journal, 94*(3), 459–486.

10

SEXUALITY AND SOCIAL JUSTICE

It may be an academically interesting puzzle as to why we are gay . . . but it is much more interesting and important to find out why people are homophobic.

Peter Nardi (US professor, 1947–)

When Americans think about twentieth-century social movements, they often think of the civil rights and women's rights gains of the 1960s. They are typically far less aware of the fact that the Gay Rights Movement has been simmering in the American underground for the better part of a century. LGBT (lesbian, gay, bisexual, transgendered) community members were not just historically ridiculed and scorned; they were systematically denied basic civil liberties such as their First Amendment freedoms of speech, press, and assembly. This shunning spanned all avenues of public and private life. While disapproval of homosexuality ebbed and flowed from decade to decade, anti-homosexual sentiments peaked during the Great Depression. Many Americans blamed the Depression on the excesses of the liberated Jazz Age that was punctuated with loose morality. There was this idea that once a man openly acknowledged and embraced his homosexuality, he threw off moral restraints of any kind.

The Great Depression also caused a massive crisis in gender and family dynamics as many men lost the ability to fill their role as the breadwinner. This backlash against gender liberation was visible in many avenues. For example, the Hayes Codes, which were in effect from the 1930s to the 1960s, prohibited Hollywood films from including homosexual themes. Homosexuals were also banned from working for the federal government, volunteering for the Boy Scouts of America, or even drinking at public establishments. The public intolerance of homosexuality was so high during the mid-century that LGBT community members had to use underground language to find one another. In an effort to find acceptance and welcome with like-minded individuals, people started using the word *gay*—originally meaning happy and carefree—to describe events or gatherings that were open to homosexuals. While the word gay eventually came to be used pejoratively, the original intent was one indicating acceptance.

Speaking of terminology, one word certainly does not even come close to describing the diverse group of individuals who are seeking equality as part of the sexual liberation movement. While individuals who identify as gay are certainly part of the LGBT community, they only comprise one part of a much larger group. As noted earlier, the phrase LGBT refers to the lesbian, gay, bisexual, and transgender community. This community is in reality a broad coalition of groups that are diverse with respect to their other defining characteristics, such as sex, race, ethnicity, and socioeconomic status. While we will be mostly referring to the LGBT community as a group with shared attributes, it's important to note that the members of this community have many divergent characteristics and concerns that may not be shared by all group members.

Concurrently, there is a shared experience—and stigmatization—common to all members of the group that will be the focus of this chapter, but first, there are important terms to be clarified. After we cover some basic terminology, we'll bring to light the historical events, grassroots efforts, and laws that have defined the Gay Rights Movement. We will also examine the treatment of LGBT community members in various institutions before discussing hate crimes as a new crime category.

Group Membership

Lesbians, gay men, and bisexual individuals are defined based on their sexual orientation. *Sexual orientation* is broadly defined based on the people to which one is sexually and emotionally attracted. When someone is attracted to an individual of the opposite sex, he or she is said to be *heterosexual*. *Homosexuals* are defined as individuals attracted to persons of the same sex and *bisexuals* are attracted to individuals of both sexes. In contrast, transgendered persons are instead defined by their gender identity and gender presentation. Members of this group identify with a gender that is different from the sex assigned to them at birth. Additionally, the *transgender* population is diverse with regard to sexual orientation and gender expression. While some transgendered individuals have undergone sexual reassignment surgery to alter their sexual anatomy to suit their gender, others have not and have no intention of doing so. While the differences between the groups are indeed many, all of the members have historically been marginalized once those differences became known. Society's cultural norms that emphasize traditional gender roles also emphasize exclusive heterosexuality. Any deviation from this norm has been categorized as deviant, immoral, sinful, and wrong, consistent with the idea that *straight* is normal (see Chapter 4).

Activity 10.1 Sexual Orientation

Is sexual orientation a choice?

Or is it something you are born with or that develops naturally?

Do some research online and explain your findings.

Discrimination and inequality faced by the LGBT community in the United States is widespread. While some Americans view the modern day social movement to end discrimination as a quest for special privileges, the truth is that LGBT community members simply want to enjoy equal rights—no more, no less. The agenda associated with the gay rights social movement is clear and transparent.

Advocates hope to eradicate the cultural norms that encourage practices that inflict harm on LGBT community members. This is not a new struggle, but, before we discuss the origins of the Gay Rights Movement, let us first examine how individuals who experienced same-sex sexual relationships were singled out and considered a minority group.

An examination of the history of mankind reveals that homosexual relations existed in all cultures and at all times (Adams, 1987). Greek and Roman literature provides many examples where same-sex sexual activity was considered normal and not stigmatizing. In Native American and Polynesian cultures, men partnering with men and women partnering with women also appeared to have been met with cultural acceptance. The same can be said of people in Africa, Egypt and South America. The point of all of this is that sexual relations between women and between men were virtually never separated out for the purpose of creating a distinct category of people known as homosexuals. It is only when a sexual preference puts an individual into a separate category of persons where the concept of a social movement for equal rights becomes possible.

This categorization of sexual preference began in nineteenth-century Germany where the term *homosexual* was coined by a Hungarian doctor named Benkert who argued that governments had no business dictating what consenting adults did in the privacy of their own homes. He pointed to dozens of productive and well-respected individuals—Charles IX, Pope Julius II, Napoleon I, Machiavelli, Michelangelo, Shakespeare, Moliere, Newton, to name a few—who would have been classified as deviant if Germany criminalized homosexual acts. He argued that not only did homosexuality not violate the rights of others, but also its presence in the sexual practices of all cultures was proof that it is a natural human phenomenon not worthy of persecution. Benkert did not succeed in his mission and Germany did end up criminalizing homosexual acts, but the roots of the Gay Rights Movement were formed. After the legislation was passed, homosexuals quickly became the target of psychiatric and medical intervention. The Nazis destroyed historic homosexual archives in Berlin and hundreds of thousands perished in concentration camps. While World War II was a major blow to the Gay Rights Movement in Germany, the beginning of a corresponding movement in the United States was well on its way.

Contrary to the freedom of speech espoused by the United States Constitution, state and city governments censored and banned LGBT art and politics. In fact, the only domain allowed to discuss sexuality was the medical field. While LGBT communities were quietly thriving in the underground of cities such as New York, Los Angeles, and San Francisco, doctors were classifying homosexuals as sexual perverts and recommending so-called "treatments" such as castration, hypnosis, surgery, electroshock, drugs, and hormones (Katz, 1976). Additionally, the American Psychiatric Association classified homosexuality as a disease, which further fueled the common societal belief that homosexuality was unnatural and undesirable. This type of feedback from the medical community further marginalized the LGBT population.

Though support for gay rights in the first half of the twentieth century was fleeting, there were attempts made to change the rhetoric. For example, in 1924, the Society for Human Rights was founded in Chicago. The Society's mission statement was:

> to promote and to protect the interests of people who by reasons of mental and physical abnormalities are abused and hindered in the legal pursuit of happiness which is guaranteed them by the Declaration of Independence, and to combat the public prejudices against them by dissemination of facts according to modern science among intellectuals of mature age.
>
> *(Gerber, 1962)*

While its existence was short-lived—the society was disbanded due to political pressure—it is recognized as the first gay rights organization in America. Following the disbanding of the Society, a 1926 *New York Times* article condemned homosexuality. This sparked a growing awareness of homosexuality in public consciousness.

The 1940s marked the founding of the first veterans group in America focused on LGBT community rights. An estimated 4,000 veterans of World War II were discharged under suspicion of homosexuality after the war ended. As a response to this, the Veterans Benevolent Association was formed to speak out against "blue" discharges. A blue discharge was less damning than an outright dishonorable discharge, but still a far cry from an honorable one. While the group was small in number, it marked the first time LGBT veterans gathered in an organized manner to advocate for veterans' rights; an issue that would follow us into the twenty-first century.

While the overwhelming majority of the research condemned homosexuality as an unnatural perversion, biologist Alfred Kinsey (1948) offered a different viewpoint in his research on male sexuality that was published in his book, *Sexual Behavior in the Human Male*. In his book, he argued that homosexual behavior is not limited to individuals who self-identified as gay and that one-third of the male population has engaged in homosexual activities at least once. With this research, Kinsey was instrumental in changing the national conversation about homosexuality. Shortly thereafter, the Mattachine Society was founded in Los Angeles in 1950. Named after the Medieval French secret societies of masked men who anonymously criticized monarchs, the organization, founded by Harry Hay, aimed to "eliminate discrimination, derision, prejudice and bigotry" (Adams, 1987). While the 1950s seemed to have a promising start, the rise of McCarthyism fueled a national panic over individuals seen as social deviants. As a result, the federal government dealt a major legislative blow to the quest for LGBT equal rights.

During the height of the *Red Scare*, or the fear of the potential rise of communism in the United States, a Senate report entitled, "Employment of Homosexuals and Other Sex Perverts in Government" was published. From the report:

> The primary objective of the subcommittee in this inquiry was to determine the extent of the employment of homosexuals and other sex perverts in Government; to consider reasons why their employment by the Government is undesirable; and to examine into the efficacy of the methods used in dealing with the problem . . . . In further considering the general suitability of perverts as Government employees, it is generally believed that those who engage in overt acts of perversion lack the emotional stability of normal persons [and are] not suitable for a position of responsibility.
>
> *(Davidson, Washington Post, 2012)*

As a result of this report, President Dwight D. Eisenhower issued Executive Order 10450, which banned gay men and lesbians from working for any agency of the federal government. The order made it legal to review and investigate government employees' private lives and even went so far as to mandate the firing of "security risks."

The President also ordered private contractors who engaged in business practices with the government to fire their gay employees as well. The logic used was that homosexuals were open to blackmail by foreign agents lest their behavior be exposed. In what became known as the *Lavender Scare*, thousands of individuals lost their jobs due to their real or perceived sexual orientation.

Emboldened by this victory, anti-gay rights legislation continued. In 1954, the FBI and the Postmaster General refused to deliver the magazine, *One: The Homosexual Agenda*, through the US mail system, citing that the material was obscene. The magazine sued and, while the courts initially ruled in favor of the Postmaster General, the case eventually found its way to the Supreme Court. In a landmark victory, the first of its kind for gay rights, the Supreme Court ruled in favor of the magazine (*One, Incorporated, v. Olesen*, 355 U.S. 371 (1958)). In a five-to-four decision, the justices ruled that a publication could not be considered obscene simply because it contained homosexual content. As such, homosexual publications could be distributed through the mail without further disruption.

Although many might even currently see efforts to restrict the rights of LGBT individuals as consistent with morality and especially traditional values, it should be noted that denying basic human rights as well as legal rights associated with institutions such as marriage is inconsistent with the American ideals of liberty and equality specified in the Declaration of Independence and US Constitution. This is true even if discriminating against LGBT individuals somehow contributes to the overall happiness of society and/or upholds even popular standards of moral decency.

As we have seen in the preceding chapters, the 1960s ushered in social change for many groups, and the LGBT community was no exception. Emboldened by increasingly critical discourse about gender roles, members of the LGBT community began to come out of hiding. As blacks were demanding service and women were emphatically demanding the right of choice (i.e., abortion rights), gay, lesbian, and transgendered individuals realized that sexual liberation required visibility in order to be normalized. This was aided greatly by changes in the heterosexual community. Divorce rates were rising, people were living together without getting married, and pre-marital sex became the standard. Entire communities were rejecting the mandate of assimilation and, instead, embracing their differences.

This, naturally, was met with serious resistance. Leading up to the 1960s, police officers in New York and San Francisco systematically rounded up and dispersed individuals who were considered socially undesirable. Blatant police profiling was routine thanks to Section 722, Subsection 8 of the United States Penal Law, which stated that it was lawful to arrest someone for their appearance or behavior patterns. In response, there were several small-scale riots protesting this treatment. LGBT community members experienced other types of discrimination as well. While it is commonly known that blacks were refused service at restaurants, many are not aware that members of the LGBT community were also routinely refused service. To bring attention to this disparity, a group of gay men staged a "sip-in" at Julius's bar in New York where places of business were not technically allowed to serve homosexuals. While Julius's was indeed a historically gay bar, they had recently been the target of a police raid and were under observation as a result. The ensuing arrests of the protesting opened the door for the courts to determine whether the New York State Liquor Authority can prevent establishments from serving homosexuals who are orderly. The courts, citing the First Amendment right to peaceably assemble, ruled in favor of the patrons, which granted LGBT community members the right to be served at the establishments of their choosing. Here it is important to note that societal progress does not just happen by chance; instead, it is won through great sacrifice and struggle by normal, everyday Americans motivated by their own sense of social justice.

Another victory was won on September 14, 1967, when the Senate passed a bill that prohibited the prying into the private lives of federal employees without a proven conflict of interest. The bill, intended to reverse the witch-hunt atmosphere created by McCarthy's reign of terror, was designed to protect government employees from having to submit to questions about religion, sex, and personal relationships.

Even with the ruling that prohibited the discrimination against serving LGBT community members alcohol, police raids continued. In June of 1969, New York police officers raided a Greenwich Village gay bar called the Stonewall. It had been the sixth bar raided in the preceding three weeks, but this time, the patrons fought back. Throwing both jeers and paving stones at the officers, three days of riots ensued. The Mattachine Society came in and organized a Gay Liberation Front meeting. The *Stonewall Rebellion*, as it was dubbed, was credited as the catalyst for the Gay Rights Movement.

Scholars have noted that police have been used in the past to uphold status quo arrangements in society, including during the civil rights movements of the 1960s but going even as far back as slavery when *Slave Codes* were enforced by local law enforcement officials. In this way, police have been a powerful force organized against social justice for a large majority of US history.

One year to the day later, thousands of members of the LGBT community marched through the streets of New York. This march launched gay pride parades all around the country. This first march was conducted in response to the extensive harassment that LGBT community members faced. Tired of being driven to the shadows, the marches and parades were done to show solidarity with each other. The goals of the Gay Rights Movement became clear:

- end police harassment of gay spaces (such as bars and clubs);
- end employment discrimination;
- end stigmatization by cultural authorities such as doctors, clergy, and government officials.

In other words, social justice was the goal here, in particular equal liberties such as those posited by scholars such as John Rawls and David Miller (see Chapter 1).

With grassroots efforts pushing for these goals across the nation, the 1970s ushered in a decade of repeals. In 1972, East Lansing, Michigan (the home of Michigan State University) became the first municipality to pass a gay rights ordinance. College towns across America followed suit. The importance of these ordinances, which amended anti-discrimination laws to add sexual orientation as a protected category, is that they effectively identified LGBT community members as a *minority group*.

Then in 1973, the board of the American Psychiatric Association voted to remove homosexuality from its list of mental illnesses. Additionally, the APA stated that it supported the repeal of legislation that criminalized sexual acts performed by consenting adults in private. This endorsement was critical because every state had anti-sodomy laws on the books; *sodomy laws* ban any sex between people of the same sex as well as anal or oral sex by members of the opposite sex. One by one, states—beginning with Illinois, Connecticut, Colorado, and Oregon—began repealing sodomy laws.

It is important to note that Southern states did not join in this trend in the early years of these repeals. In fact, another decade would pass before Southern courts dealt with the legality of private, consensual sex between adults.

Even religious organizations were coming out in favor of gay rights. Many churches issued statements in support of gay rights prior to 1980, including the Lutheran Church of America, the Unitarian Universalist Association, the United Methodist Church, the United Church of Christ, the Protestant

Episcopal Church, and the United Presbyterian Church. This is an important reminder that virtue is in the eye of the beholder—it varies by individual, religious affiliation, and even congregation.

This success was not without opposition. In 1977, Baptist singer Anita Bryant led a campaign to "Save Our Children" from a gay civil rights ordinance that was on the ballot in Dade County, Florida. Running a newspaper ad the day before the election, Bryant's organization claimed that, "the other side of the homosexual coin is a hair-raising pattern of recruitment and outright seduction and molestation" (Mello, 2004). The idea that seduction and molestation occurs at a higher rate among LGBT people is false and was motivated by unfounded fears. The idea that gay people seek to molest children, ironically, comes from particularly religious people, supposedly motivated by traditional moral and religious values; this is a reminder of the frequent conflict between social justice aimed at protecting virtue versus social justice aimed at achieving liberty and equality. The campaign worked and the ordinance failed.

Other cities quickly jumped on the bandwagon to try to either overturn existing ordinances or prevent them from passing. In 1978, San Francisco had one such ordinance come up for a vote before the Board of Supervisors. Harvey Milk, the first openly gay San Francisco City Supervisor, and Mayor George Moscone were among those in favor of passing the ordinance. The lone dissenter, board member Dan White, later went on to assassinate both Harvey Milk and Mayor Moscone. White's conviction for voluntary manslaughter instead of premeditated murder sparked the *White Night Riots*, which confirmed that tensions over homosexual rights were still quite high even in urban centers.

The 1980s brought with them a new president, Ronald Reagan, who ran on a platform of "traditional family values" and brought with him a conservative era characterized by vigorous crime control measures, regulatory rollbacks, and a reassertion of traditional American values (that are traditionally pro-heterosexual). Perhaps the most significant blow to the Gay Rights Movement came in 1986, when the case of *Bowers v. Hardwick* came before the Supreme Court. At that time, Georgia still had an anti-sodomy law on the books and the issue at hand was whether consensual homosexual sex is protected under the fundamental right to privacy.

The facts of the case were simple: a police officer, serving an arrest warrant after Hardwick failed to appear in court for a public intoxication citation, was let into the house by Hardwick's roommate. After being directed back to Hardwick's bedroom, the police officer observed Michael Hardwick having consensual sex with another male through the open door of the bedroom. Both Hardwick and his partner were arrested for sodomy. Hardwick then sued Michael Bowers, the state's Attorney General, in federal court seeking a declaration that the state's sodomy laws were invalid. The case made its way up to the United States Supreme Court and in a 5 to 4 decision, the court ruled that, while the Due Process Clause's right to privacy protects intimate marital and familial relations, the Court said that this does not extend to gay sodomy because "no connection between family, marriage, or procreation . . . has been demonstrated."

It's worth noting that at the time of this decision, the country was in a panic over AIDS, which the Centers for Disease Control originally named GRID, or Gay Related Immune Deficiency Disorder. The name was changed to *Acquired Immune Deficiency Syndrome (AIDS)* after individuals outside of the gay community were diagnosed, but the stigmatization of the initial name had already done considerable damage to an already marginalized population. While individuals with AIDS were excluded from all public life, the flawed belief that gay men were the primary hosts of the disease created an atmosphere of distrust and fear. Gay men were prohibited from donating blood and some doctors refused to operate on them.

> ## Activity 10.2 HIV/AIDS
>
> Do some research into the HIV virus and the AIDS illness.
>
> Start with the website of the Centers for Disease Control and Prevention: http://www.cdc.gov/hiv/default.html.
>
> Who is most at risk for HIV/AIDS and what can be done about it?

In the court of public opinion, anti-gay sentiment reached an all-time high in 1987 when 78 percent of individuals polled answered in the affirmative when asked if homosexual relations were always wrong. For comparison purposes, today about 55 percent of Americans believe homosexuality is acceptable (Gallup, 2014).

Thankfully, the tide began to turn in the 1990s, which brought new knowledge of the disease—as well as treatments—and some of the backlash against the LGBT community began to lessen. There was also a massive grassroots campaign occurring that focused on educated mainstream America about the reality of LGBT individuals. Organizations such as *Parents and Friends of Lesbians and Gays* (PFLAG) grew dramatically. What started out as a group of parents meeting in Greenwich Village in 1973 blossomed into a national organization of over 500 chapters with 80,000 members by the late 1990s. In the political sphere, politicians began showing up to Pride marches when they started seeing the LGBT community as a pool of motivated voters.

The 1990s also brought a major issue to the forefront of the national stage and that was LGBT community members serving in the military. Gays in the military shot into focus during the 1992 presidential election. Bill Clinton gave a speech at a gay fundraising event in Los Angeles where he stated that gay individuals were part of his national vision and that he would pursue ending military discrimination with "the stroke of a pen." Clinton won that election against incumbent George H. W. Bush in no small part thanks to Bush's decision to allow the religious right to push the traditional family values platform. The 1990s saw a prolific increase in the number of openly gay elected officials. President Clinton became the first president to appoint openly gay individuals to his administration and he issued executive orders banning discrimination on the basis of sexual orientation. He also no longer allowed sexual orientation to be a considered factor when determining security clearance, as it had been for decades before.

Perhaps the most telling signs of mainstream acceptance of the LGBT community were the increasing presence of homosexual themes in the media. From *Philadelphia* to *The Bird Cage* in the movies, to *Ellen* and *Will & Grace* on the small screen, positive gay themes were increasingly present with each passing year. Still, regardless of the fact that Americans had become increasingly accepting of the LGBT community, the debate over gays in the military was a caustic one with a long, divisive history.

Military Service

Historically, the United States military did not explicitly exclude LGBT community members from serving. While sodomy was classified as a criminal offense as early as the Revolutionary War, it was considered an unfortunate byproduct of having so many men bunked down together. This type of behavior is typically referred to as *situational homosexuality*, which is the term used when an individual engages in same-sex acts, but does not self-classify as being a homosexual. The issue of homosexuality and the military escalated in World War II when a psychiatric screening became part of the induction process for enlisting. Instead of maintaining the focus on eradicating homosexual *behavior*, the focus shifted to homosexual *persons*. The first appearance of distinguishing between homosexual and 'normal' persons occurred in the 1942 army mobilization regulations, and instructed officials on the proper procedures to reject gay draftees. Ironically, homosexuals were permitted to enlist when personnel shortages required the need for more bodies, but, with the end of the war, those individuals were involuntarily discharged.

There was very little conversation about the role of homosexuals in the military in the decades after World War II until the Gay Rights Movement brought the issue back to the forefront in the 1970s. The military pushed back against the quest for gay rights and, in 1981, the Department of Defense drafted a new policy, which explicitly stated that homosexuality is not compatible with military service (DOD Directive 1332.14). As a result of this report, nearly 17,000 individuals were discharged over the course of the 1980s. White women, though only representing 6 percent of personnel, comprised 20 percent of those discharged for homosexuality. At the end of the decade, current—and decorated—military members came out and openly advocated for a change in the policy banning homosexuals from military service. That change came in 1993 under the Clinton Administration in the form of *"Don't Ask, Don't Tell, Don't Pursue"* (DADT). Under the terms of DADT, military personnel could no longer ask explicitly about an individual's sexual orientation. Additionally, members of the military could not be discharged just for being gay. With that said, engaging in sexual conduct with a member of the same sex would still be considered grounds for discharge. DADT remained the official policy until 2011, but the way for the repeal was paved by increased pressure to allow homosexuals to serve openly following the September 11, 2001 terrorist attacks.

Gay Marriage

The right to marry whom you please has been a sought after right since the American Revolution. One of the tenets of slavery was that slaves could not enter into contracts, which marriage certainly is on the most basic level. Then, once slavery was abolished and former slaves had the right to marry, there were limitations as to *whom* they could marry—interracial marriage was not universally allowed until the Civil Rights Movement. In Germany, the Nazi party was adamant that Jews could not marry non-Jews and, in fact, marriage equality became such a divisive issue that the General Assembly of the United Nations included the "right to marry" as a fundamental human right in the 1948 Universal Declaration of Human Rights. Major rights of the Universal Declaration of Human Rights are shown in Table 10.1.

TABLE 10.1 Universal Declaration of Human Rights

PREAMBLE

Whereas recognition of the inherent dignity and of the equal and inalienable rights of all members of the human family is the foundation of freedom, justice and peace in the world,

Whereas disregard and contempt for human rights have resulted in barbarous acts which have outraged the conscience of mankind, and the advent of a world in which human beings shall enjoy freedom of speech and belief and freedom from fear and want has been proclaimed as the highest aspiration of the common people,

Whereas it is essential, if man is not to be compelled to have recourse, as a last resort, to rebellion against tyranny and oppression, that human rights should be protected by the rule of law,

Whereas it is essential to promote the development of friendly relations between nations,

Whereas the peoples of the United Nations have in the Charter reaffirmed their faith in fundamental human rights, in the dignity and worth of the human person and in the equal rights of men and women and have determined to promote social progress and better standards of life in larger freedom,

Whereas Member States have pledged themselves to achieve, in co-operation with the United Nations, the promotion of universal respect for and observance of human rights and fundamental freedoms,

Whereas a common understanding of these rights and freedoms is of the greatest importance for the full realization of this pledge,

Now, Therefore THE GENERAL ASSEMBLY proclaims THIS UNIVERSAL DECLARATION OF HUMAN RIGHTS as a common standard of achievement for all peoples and all nations, to the end that every individual and every organ of society, keeping this Declaration constantly in mind, shall strive by teaching and education to promote respect for these rights and freedoms and by progressive measures, national and international, to secure their universal and effective recognition and observance, both among the peoples of Member States themselves and among the peoples of territories under their jurisdiction.

Article 1.

- All human beings are born free and equal in dignity and rights. They are endowed with reason and conscience and should act towards one another in a spirit of brotherhood.

Article 2.

- Everyone is entitled to all the rights and freedoms set forth in this Declaration, without distinction of any kind, such as race, colour, sex, language, religion, political or other opinion, national or social origin, property, birth or other status. Furthermore, no distinction shall be made on the basis of the political, jurisdictional or international status of the country or territory to which a person belongs, whether it be independent, trust, non-self-governing or under any other limitation of sovereignty.

Article 3.

- Everyone has the right to life, liberty and security of person.

Article 4.

- No one shall be held in slavery or servitude; slavery and the slave trade shall be prohibited in all their forms.

Article 5.

- No one shall be subjected to torture or to cruel, inhuman or degrading treatment or punishment.

Article 6.

- Everyone has the right to recognition everywhere as a person before the law.

(continued)

TABLE 10.1 *(continued)*

Article 7.

- All are equal before the law and are entitled without any discrimination to equal protection of the law. All are entitled to equal protection against any discrimination in violation of this Declaration and against any incitement to such discrimination.

Article 8.

- Everyone has the right to an effective remedy by the competent national tribunals for acts violating the fundamental rights granted him by the constitution or by law.

Article 9.

- No one shall be subjected to arbitrary arrest, detention or exile.

Article 10.

- Everyone is entitled in full equality to a fair and public hearing by an independent and impartial tribunal, in the determination of his rights and obligations and of any criminal charge against him.

Article 11.

- (1) Everyone charged with a penal offence has the right to be presumed innocent until proved guilty according to law in a public trial at which he has had all the guarantees necessary for his defence.
- (2) No one shall be held guilty of any penal offence on account of any act or omission which did not constitute a penal offence, under national or international law, at the time when it was committed. Nor shall a heavier penalty be imposed than the one that was applicable at the time the penal offence was committed.

Article 12.

- No one shall be subjected to arbitrary interference with his privacy, family, home or correspondence, nor to attacks upon his honour and reputation. Everyone has the right to the protection of the law against such interference or attacks.

Article 13.

- (1) Everyone has the right to freedom of movement and residence within the borders of each state.
- (2) Everyone has the right to leave any country, including his own, and to return to his country.

Article 14.

- (1) Everyone has the right to seek and to enjoy in other countries asylum from persecution.
- (2) This right may not be invoked in the case of prosecutions genuinely arising from non-political crimes or from acts contrary to the purposes and principles of the United Nations.

Article 15.

- (1) Everyone has the right to a nationality.
- (2) No one shall be arbitrarily deprived of his nationality nor denied the right to change his nationality.

Article 16.

- (1) Men and women of full age, without any limitation due to race, nationality or religion, have the right to marry and to found a family. They are entitled to equal rights as to marriage, during marriage and at its dissolution.
- (2) Marriage shall be entered into only with the free and full consent of the intending spouses.

- (3) The family is the natural and fundamental group unit of society and is entitled to protection by society and the State.

Article 17.

- (1) Everyone has the right to own property alone as well as in association with others.
- (2) No one shall be arbitrarily deprived of his property.

Article 18.

- Everyone has the right to freedom of thought, conscience and religion; this right includes freedom to change his religion or belief, and freedom, either alone or in community with others and in public or private, to manifest his religion or belief in teaching, practice, worship and observance.

Article 19.

- Everyone has the right to freedom of opinion and expression; this right includes freedom to hold opinions without interference and to seek, receive and impart information and ideas through any media and regardless of frontiers.

Article 20.

- (1) Everyone has the right to freedom of peaceful assembly and association.
- (2) No one may be compelled to belong to an association.

Article 21.

- (1) Everyone has the right to take part in the government of his country, directly or through freely chosen representatives.
- (2) Everyone has the right of equal access to public service in his country.
- (3) The will of the people shall be the basis of the authority of government; this will shall be expressed in periodic and genuine elections which shall be by universal and equal suffrage and shall be held by secret vote or by equivalent free voting procedures.

Article 22.

- Everyone, as a member of society, has the right to social security and is entitled to realization, through national effort and international co-operation and in accordance with the organization and resources of each State, of the economic, social and cultural rights indispensable for his dignity and the free development of his personality.

Article 23.

- (1) Everyone has the right to work, to free choice of employment, to just and favourable conditions of work and to protection against unemployment.
- (2) Everyone, without any discrimination, has the right to equal pay for equal work.
- (3) Everyone who works has the right to just and favourable remuneration ensuring for himself and his family an existence worthy of human dignity, and supplemented, if necessary, by other means of social protection.
- (4) Everyone has the right to form and to join trade unions for the protection of his interests.

Article 24.

- Everyone has the right to rest and leisure, including reasonable limitation of working hours and periodic holidays with pay.

(continued)

TABLE 10.1 *(continued)*

Article 25.

- (1) Everyone has the right to a standard of living adequate for the health and well-being of himself and of his family, including food, clothing, housing and medical care and necessary social services, and the right to security in the event of unemployment, sickness, disability, widowhood, old age or other lack of livelihood in circumstances beyond his control.
- (2) Motherhood and childhood are entitled to special care and assistance. All children, whether born in or out of wedlock, shall enjoy the same social protection.

Article 26.

- (1) Everyone has the right to education. Education shall be free, at least in the elementary and fundamental stages. Elementary education shall be compulsory. Technical and professional education shall be made generally available and higher education shall be equally accessible to all on the basis of merit.
- (2) Education shall be directed to the full development of the human personality and to the strengthening of respect for human rights and fundamental freedoms. It shall promote understanding, tolerance and friendship among all nations, racial or religious groups, and shall further the activities of the United Nations for the maintenance of peace.
- (3) Parents have a prior right to choose the kind of education that shall be given to their children.

Article 27.

- (1) Everyone has the right freely to participate in the cultural life of the community, to enjoy the arts and to share in scientific advancement and its benefits.
- (2) Everyone has the right to the protection of the moral and material interests resulting from any scientific, literary or artistic production of which he is the author.

Article 28.

- Everyone is entitled to a social and international order in which the rights and freedoms set forth in this Declaration can be fully realized.

Article 29.

- (1) Everyone has duties to the community in which alone the free and full development of his personality is possible.
- (2) In the exercise of his rights and freedoms, everyone shall be subject only to such limitations as are determined by law solely for the purpose of securing due recognition and respect for the rights and freedoms of others and of meeting the just requirements of morality, public order and the general welfare in a democratic society.
- (3) These rights and freedoms may in no case be exercised contrary to the purposes and principles of the United Nations.

Article 30.

- Nothing in this Declaration may be interpreted as implying for any State, group or person any right to engage in any activity or to perform any act aimed at the destruction of any of the rights and freedoms set forth herein.

Source: http://www.un.org/en/documents/udhr/index.shtml.

People may wonder why all the fuss about marriage, but it was more than just wanting a public declaration of love. Marriage affords couples both private and public rights and benefits and, in that sense, it's a deservingly big deal. Some of these rights are shown in Table 10.2.

TABLE 10.2 Rights Granted by Marriage

According to the Human Rights Campaign and NOLO, there are 1,138 benefits, rights, and protections granted from the federal government to married couples. They include:

Consumer benefits

Employee benefits

Estate planning benefits

Family and medical leave benefits

Health care benefits

Housing benefits

Immigration benefits

Medical benefits

Social security benefits

Tax benefits

Sources: Human Rights Campaign, "Overview of Federal Benefits Granted to Married Couples", http://www.hrc.org/resources/entry/an-overview-of-federal-rights-and-protections-granted-to-married-couples; NOLO, Law for All, "Marriage Rights and Benefits", http://www.nolo.com/legal-encyclopedia/marriage-rights-benefits-30190.html.

Going back to the earlier fights about marriage equality, the United States Supreme Court said their piece about interracial marriage in the 1967 case of *Loving v. Virginia*. The case dealt with a black man married to a white woman, illegal in the state of Virginia! The Court stated: "The freedom to marry has long been recognized as one of the vital personal rights essential to the orderly pursuit of happiness by free men." With that statement falling so in line with the language put forth in the Declaration of Independence, an important precedent was formed.

There were other factors that would eventually pave the way for same-sex marriage equality. For example, marriage has always been a civil matter. The religious ceremony aspect of marriages was not only separate from the legal contract of marriage, but they were also non-binding in the eyes of the government. In fact, the rules established by many churches on which two individuals could marry were not legally enforceable. In short, marriage is a state matter that is not subject to religious restrictions. The idea of codifying the institution of marriage as a union between one man and one woman gives supremacy to a single religious view, which is antithesis to the religious freedoms purported to matter in our founding documents.

The Women's Rights Movement also helped move the evolution of marriage along, because it created more gender neutrality. Gone were the days when women were mandated to stay in the home and became the ward of their husband upon marriage. That's not to say that gender roles didn't still exist; they did, but things were changing. The roles in families—who works, who stays home, who makes more money—were no longer solely determined by biological sex and assigned gender roles. These changes made the idea that marriage can only consist of a union between a man and a woman no longer appear so obvious or necessary. Ironically, LGBT members did not universally agree upon the idea that same-sex couples should want to even seek state-sanctioned marriages. Some wanted nothing to do with gender roles and the patriarchal institutions that supported them; others wanted access to everything that heterosexual couples have access to—benefits such as tax breaks, benefits of spouses (Social Security, Medicare, disability, public assistance, veterans' and military benefits). Eventually, what the LGBT community agreed upon was the belief that they, at a minimum, wanted the choice available to them. The need for this choice reached an urgent pitch during the AIDS crisis of the 1980s and 1990s. Ultimately, it was the realization that same-sex partners had no legal standing with regard to hospital visitation, property, child custody, end-of-life decisions, and so many other benefits that married couples took for granted. The time had come to fight for marriage equality.

Legal analysts and advisors knew that the words "gay marriage" would yield a battle much like that fight for gay rights in the military. With this in mind, step one became advocating for domestic partnerships to provide some legal protections. These began being passed in the early 1990s, but the limitations were clear. While they did help with insurance benefits, the presence of a domestic partnership did not help with social security benefits, pension protections, and hospital visitation rights. Hawaii became the battleground state for the first quest to make the leap from partnership to marriage. In 1993, the Hawaiian Supreme Court ruled that the marriage ban for same-sex couples violated the state's Equal Rights Amendment. They sent the court case back to the trial courts to determine whether there is a "compelling state interest" in denying same-sex couples the right to marry.

The trial court sat on the issue for years, but that one small victory became enough to spur the United States Congress into action. In 1996, the Senate voted 85–14 for the *Defense of Marriage Act (DOMA)*. The House followed suit with a 342–67 vote. DOMA altered the federal definition of marriage to be the union of one man and one woman. Taking it a step further, DOMA declared that no state needed to recognize a same-sex marriage performed in another state. Finally, it denied federal benefits to such married couples. The passage of DOMA violated the spirit of our Constitution in a number of ways, but, primarily, the codification of marriage as a union between one man and one woman gave supremacy to a single religious view.

This is not only the antithesis of the ideals put forth in separation of church and state, but it clearly is also inconsistent with equal liberties as posited by social justice scholars such as John Rawls and David Miller (see Chapter 1). It is another reminder of how efforts to uphold morality and virtue often conflict with American principles of liberty and equality.

Knowing that DOMA could not stand for long, same-sex marriage advocates forged on. Vermont became the next battleground state. With a long history of tolerance, it seemed as though same-sex marriage had a good chance for success. The case of *Baker v. Vermont* was filed in the courts seeking the ability to marry for three same-sex couples. In 1999, the case made its way to the Vermont Supreme Court, who agreed that same-sex couples should not be denied the benefits of marriage. The Supreme Court sent the issue to the state legislature and instructed them to find a remedy. The legislature's solution came in the form of *civil unions*, which granted same-sex couples the legal benefits of marriage under a different name. While this seems like a victory, civil unions provided none of the federal benefits, such as tax considerations and social security. Plus, it should be obvious by now that separate does not and cannot yield equality. This was separate drinking fountains all over again.

The fight continued in Massachusetts. Here, Gay and Lesbian Advocates and Defenders attorneys focused their arguments on one of the primary arguments against same-sex marriage—the ability to procreate. Many supporters of the "one man and one woman" brand of marriage highlighted procreation as a key condition of marriage. This argument was antiquated in a number of ways. First and foremost, people who cannot or choose not to procreate are never denied marriage contracts. Moreover, marriage was not a necessary condition of procreation. An increasing number of people gave birth to children out of wedlock, to say nothing of those who used fertility methods or who chose adoption. The court case made its way to the Massachusetts Supreme Court and, in her majority opinion, Chief Justice Marshall wrote the following:

> The Massachusetts Constitution affirms the dignity and equality of all individuals. It forbids the creation of second-class citizens. In reaching our conclusion we have given full deference to the arguments made by the Commonwealth. But it has failed to identify any constitutionally adequate reason for denying civil marriage to same-sex couples.

The most important point made above is that marriage has always been, first and foremost, a civil matter that is entirely separate from a religious matrimonial ceremony. In fact, the religious ceremony is non-binding in the eyes of the government until which time a legal contract is signed and submitted to an officer of the court. Additionally, the rules established by many churches about who could marry whom have never been legally enforceable. In short, marriage is a state matter not subject to religious restrictions. Over the last ten years, more and more states agreed with Justice Marshall. It seemed that Massachusetts was the tipping point. Today, all states have legalized marriage because of a Supreme Court Decision.

In 2013, The United States Supreme Court issued their first ruling on same-sex marriages. This historic ruling came in the form of striking down Section 3 of the Defense of Marriage Act. Based on this ruling in the case of *US v. Widsorm 570 US*, couples who are legally married in states that recognize same-sex marriage must receive the same federal benefits that heterosexual couples receive. In his decision, Justice Kennedy wrote, "DOMA writes inequality into the entire United States Code." He went on to say that withholding federal recognition of marriage when the states have sanctioned it relegated same-sex couples to the "unstable position of being in second-tier marriage[s]."

Hate Crimes

Over the course of this book, we've established that prejudice and bias have been root causes of oppressive policy. Similarly, hatred born of this same prejudice has been the motivator for many crimes committed against any group categorized as different. In this sense, hate crimes are most definitely not a new phenomenon; however, the recognition of a *hate crime* as a separate crime category and the codification of it into law is quite novel indeed. Since specific statutes vary from state to state, for the purposes of this text, we will use the definition put forth by the Federal Bureau of Investigation:

> A *hate crime*, also known as a bias crime, is a criminal offense committed against a person, property, or society which is motivated, in whole or in part, by an offender's bias against a race, religion, disability, sexual orientation, or ethnicity/national origin.

Historically, bias-related crimes were prosecuted—if they were prosecuted—under a number of different laws including the Civil Rights Act of 1866, the Enforcement Act of 1870 and the Civil Rights Act of 1875. These federal laws were directed towards trying to curb the violence against African Americans during reconstruction; however, these laws did not protect other minority groups who may also be victims solely because of certain extrinsic characteristics. Not much was done with regard to bias-motivated offenses during the first half of the twentieth century, but the issue quickly came to the forefront during the Civil Rights movement. This concept of a *hate crime* was first formulated in the 1970s, as law makers scrambled to explain what they perceived was an increase in crime that occurred simply because of the victim's race or religion. While the 1960s ushered in significant policy changes aimed towards equality, the cultural shift in viewing all people as equal was slower to follow suit. By criminalizing hate-motivated intimidation and violence, the hope was to send a message that hate would not be tolerated.

Before we move on, it should be noted that there is not universal agreement that hate crimes should even be a category unto their own. Some of the questions raised include:

1. *Is it possible to fully know a perpetrator's motive for committing a crime?* More precisely, the question that we have to ask ourselves is whether criminal justice professionals have the capabilities to measure motive in a legal sense. Sure, there are instances where a defendant provides a full confession; but in many cases, criminal justice professionals are left to piece together what they can, based on the evidence.

2. *Should we consider motive at all?* Some people steal for fun and some steal to feed their families; if they are caught and prosecuted, the statutes are not written separately based on these motivations. While motive can sometimes be considered a mitigating factor in the presentation of a defense, some scholars argue that bias or hate statutes are setting a precedent that could be loosely interpreted as considering motive; in essence, this is a strong statement of our social justice principles.

3. *Do hate crime statutes take the focus away from the core offense?* As a society, we've been moving away from assigning different punishments based on extra-legal variables for the same crime. Hate crime critiques see these statutes as opening the door for these extra-legal factors to again be considered.

Now, let's cover a few of the reasons why supporters of hate crime statutes think that they're a necessary inclusion.

1. *Hate crimes typically result in more harm.* Research has shown that hate-motivated crimes are often more violent, have multiple perpetrators, result in greater physical injury, and have increased consequences for the victims—both emotional and physical (Iganski, 2001).

2. *Enhanced hate crime penalties send the message that society considers these types of crimes intolerable.* When examining the history of punishment, we typically can make inferences about any given society's values on the basis of what crimes are punished most severely. By increasing the sanctions associated with hate-motivated offenses, the criminal justice system and society are collectively saying that these crimes are more serious than their non-bias motivated counterparts.

3. *The protected populations have historically been underserved by the criminal justice system.* While the police motto is "to protect and serve," there is a great deal of mistrust in communities with non-white, upper class, and hetero-normative populations. As an institution, the criminal justice system protected individuals who were represented by those in power. Others did not receive the same service. To correct for this, hate crime statutes include provisions for training law enforcement officers to be more effective in serving all individuals living within their communities.

The 1980s saw the first hate crime laws passed, with Washington and Oregon leading the charge, and, over the next two decades, virtually every state had some form of a hate crime statute on the books. Most of these laws were modeled after hate crime legislation drafted in 1981 by the Anti-Defamation League, a prominent Jewish Civil Rights organization, who saw the need for a comprehensive response to violence targeting minority groups. While each state has a slightly different definition of what constitutes a hate crime, the major provisions of most state statutes include: (1) a listing of protected groups; (2) identification of predicate crimes, or crimes eligible for hate crime provisions; (3) penalty enhancements for hate crimes; (4) stipulations for collecting hate crime data.

Initially, there were numerous legal challenges to hate crime statutes. The primary argument made against hate crime statutes is that they were a violation of the First Amendment's Freedom of Speech provisions. There were several important cases that made their way up to the United State Supreme Court. The first of these was a case where a group of white youths who burned a cross in a black family's yard. Seventeen-year-old Robert Viktora was convicted of violating St. Paul, Minnesota's bias-motivated crime ordinance that specifically banned displaying swastikas and burning crosses. Viktora appealed the conviction and the district court ruled in his favor, stating that the ordinance was too broad, a violation of the First Amendment, and as such, unconstitutional. The city of St. Paul filed a counterappeal that was brought before the United States Supreme Court in 1992 in the case of *R.A.V. v. City of St. Paul*. The Court agreed that the St. Paul ordinance was a violation of the First Amendment because the verbiage of the ordinance focused on bigoted ideas—in the form of white supremacy—and not on the actions. Additionally, no one was physically harmed in the cross-burning case, which the Court determined made the actions symbolic of hateful thoughts.

In a second Wisconsin case, the United State Supreme Court did establish that, when physical harm is present, hate crime legislation is legal. In the case of *Wisconsin v. Mitchell*, a group of young African Americans gathered in an apartment complex. The group, having recently finished discussing a scene from the movie *Mississippi Burning* where a white individual beat a black individual, the group spotted a white boy on the street and one of the group members shouted, "There goes a white boy, go get him." The boy was severely beaten and comatose for four days.

During the trial, the perpetrator was convicted of aggravated battery and also received a sentencing enhancement based on the fact that the victim was selected solely on the basis of race. The defense once again used the First Amendment's protection of offensive thought as an argument against the sentencing enhancement and, once again, the Wisconsin court agreed with the defense. The United States Supreme Court agreed to hear the appeal and this time, they reversed the ruling of the Wisconsin lower court. In a unanimous decision, the Supreme Court determined that the hate penalty enhancement is not a violation of the First Amendment due to the "greater individual and societal harm." The Justices went on to say that the statute does not stifle free speech because it punishes bias-motivated acts, not their thoughts. This became the precedent of the Court: while expressions of hate are protected by the Bill of Rights, actions of hate are not.

The 1990s were an active decade for hate crime legislation. The federal government first passed the *Hate Crimes Statistic Act*, which was meant to serve as a means of both documenting and understanding these types of crimes. This Act required the US Department of Justice to collect data on crimes that "manifest prejudice based on race, religion, sexual orientation, or ethnicity" (US Public Law, 101–275). Furthermore, the Act determined that the Federal Bureau of Investigation should issue a summary of these findings annually. The following year, a bias crime data collection program was included in both the *Uniform Crime Reporting* system as well as the *National Incident Based Reporting program*.

The *Violent Crime Control and Law Enforcement Act of 1994* expanded on the previous law to include disability as a reported victim category and also included a provision for sentencing enhancements "for offenses that the finders of fact at trial determine, beyond a reasonable doubt, are hate crimes." Unfortunately, gender and gender-identity were omitted from the list of protected groups until two highly publicized cases provided the attention needed to create more progressive hate crime legislation. Table 10.3 shows the number of hate crimes known to the police in 2012 according to the FBI.

TABLE 10.3 Hate Crimes in the US

According to the FBI, there were 5,796 hate crimes involving 6,718 different offenses in 2012. These consisted of:

5,790 single-bias incidents that involved 6,705 offenses, 7,151 victims, and 5,322 offenders.

6 multiple-bias incidents reported in 2012 involved 13 offenses, 13 victims, and 9 offenders.

Of the offenses:

- 59.1 percent were crimes against persons
- 37.9 percent were crimes against property
- the remainder were crimes against society
- 39.6 percent were simple assault
- 37.5 percent were intimidation
- 21.5 percent were aggravated assault
- 0.6 percent consisted of 10 murders and 15 forcible rapes
- 0.8 percent involved the offense category *other*, which is collected only in the National Incident-Based Reporting System
- the majority of the 2,547 hate crime offenses that were crimes against property (74.8 percent) were acts of destruction/damage/vandalism
- the remaining 25.2 percent of crimes against property consisted of robbery, burglary, larceny-theft, motor vehicle theft, arson, and other crimes.

Further:

- 28.4 percent were destruction/damage/vandalism
- 23.4 percent were simple assault
- 22.2 percent were intimidation
- 12.7 percent were aggravated assault.

Additionally:

- 79.6 percent were directed at individuals
- 4.6 percent were against businesses or financial institutions
- 3.0 percent were against society
- 2.9 percent were against government
- 2.7 percent were against religious organizations
- the remaining 7.2 percent were directed at other, multiple, or unknown victim types.

Of these incidents:

- 48.3 percent were racially motivated
- 19.6 percent resulted from sexual-orientation bias

- 19.0 percent were motivated by religious bias
- 11.5 percent stemmed from ethnicity/national origin bias
- 1.6 percent were prompted by disability bias.

Of the offenses:

- 49.2 percent stemmed from racial bias
- 19.7 percent were motivated by sexual-orientation bias
- 17.4 percent resulted from religious bias
- 12.3 percent were prompted by ethnicity/national origin bias
- 1.5 percent resulted from biases against disabilities.

Of those racially motivated offenses:

- 66.1 percent were motivated by anti-African American bias
- 22.4 percent stemmed from anti-Caucasian bias
- 4.1 percent resulted from anti-Asian/Pacific Islander bias
- 4.1 percent were a result of bias against groups of individuals consisting of more than one race (anti-multiple races, group)
- 3.3 percent were motivated by anti-American Indian/Alaskan Native bias.

Of those ethnically motivated offenses:

- 59.4 percent were anti-Hispanic bias
- 40.6 percent were anti-other ethnicity/national origin bias.

Of those based on religion:

- 59.7 percent were anti-Jewish
- 12.8 percent were anti-Islamic
- 7.6 percent were anti-multiple religions, group
- 6.8 percent were anti-Catholic
- 2.9 percent were anti-Protestant
- 1.0 percent were anti-Atheism/Agnosticism/etc
- 9.2 percent were anti-other (unspecified) religion.

Of those based on sexual orientation:

- 54.6 percent were classified as anti-male homosexual bias
- 28.0 percent were reported as anti-homosexual bias
- 12.3 percent were prompted by an anti-female homosexual bias
- 3.1 percent were classified as anti-bisexual bias
- 2.0 percent were the result of an anti-heterosexual bias.

Source: The Federal Bureau of Investigation, 2012 Hate Crime Statistics, "Incidents and Offenses", http://www.fbi.gov/about-us/cjis/ucr/hate-crime/2012/topic-pages/incidents-and-offenses/incidentsandoffenses_final.

On June 7, 1998, James Byrd, Jr. was murdered in Jasper, Texas. Targeted because of his race, three men drove him out to the countryside, beat him, and then dragged him behind their pick-up truck for three miles. This brutal murder left James's three children without a father. Then on October 7 of that same year, Matthew Shepard, a 21-year-old student at the University of Wyoming, was severely beaten and then left to die tied to a fence post in Laramie, Wyoming. Matthew was targeted due to his sexual orientation. These two cases culminated in an important piece of legislation, which was called the

Matthew Shepard and James Byrd, Jr. Hate Crime Prevention Act (HCPA) in their honor. Below is a description of the law from the Department of Justice (emphasis included in the original):

> The Matthew Shepard and James Byrd, Jr., Hate Crimes Prevention Act of 2009, 18 U.S.C. § 249, was enacted as Division E of the National Defense Authorization Act for fiscal year 2010. Section 249 of Title 18 provides funding and technical assistance to state, local, and tribal jurisdictions to help them to more effectively *investigate and prosecute hate crimes.*
>
> It also creates a new federal criminal law which criminalizes willfully causing bodily injury (or attempting to do so with fire, firearm, or other dangerous weapon) when:
>
> (1) the crime was committed because of the actual or perceived race, color, religion, national origin of any person or (2) the crime was committed because of the actual or perceived religion, national origin, gender, sexual orientation, gender identity, or disability of any person and the crime affected interstate or foreign commerce or occurred within federal special maritime and territorial jurisdiction.
>
> The newly enacted § 249 has three significant subsections. Subsection (a)(1) criminalizes violent acts (and attempts to commit violent acts undertaken with a dangerous weapon) when those acts occur because of the actual or perceived race, color, religion, or national origin of any person. This section of the statute has a broader reach than existing hate crime statutes. (18 U.S.C. § 245, for example, requires that government prove not only that the crime was motivated by animus but also because of the victim's participation in one of six enumerated federally protected activities). Section 249(a)(1) was passed pursuant to Congress's Thirteenth Amendment authority to eradicate badges and incidents of slavery. *The government need prove no other "jurisdictional" element to obtain a conviction.*
>
> Subsection (a)(2) of § 249 protects a wider class of victims. Subsection (a)(2) criminalizes acts of violence (and attempts to commit violent acts undertaken with a dangerous weapon) when motivated by the actual or perceived gender, disability, sexual orientation, or gender identity of any person. It will also apply to violent acts motivated by animus against those religions and national origins that were not considered to be "races" at the time the Thirteenth Amendment was passed. This portion of the statute was passed pursuant to Congress's Commerce Clause authority. *Thus, to obtain a conviction, the government must prove that the crime was in or affected interstate or foreign commerce.* Subsection (a)(2)(B) of the statute contains a detailed description of the ways the commerce clause element may be fulfilled.
>
> Subsection (a)(3) of § 249 provides for prosecution of crimes committed because of any of the characteristics defined in (a)(1) or (a)(2), whenever such crimes occur within the Special Maritime and Territorial Jurisdiction (SMTJ) of the United States.
>
> The statute criminalizes only violent acts resulting in bodily injury or attempts to inflict bodily injury, through the use of fire, firearms, explosive and incendiary devices, or other dangerous weapons. The statute does not criminalize threats of violence. Threats to inflict physical injury may be prosecutable under other hate crimes statutes, such as 42 U.S.C. § 3631 or 18 U.S.C. § 245. *Such threats may also be prosecutable under generally applicable federal laws preventing interstate communication of threats.*

The *Anti-Defamation League* highlighted how the HCPA is different than previous iterations of hate crime legislation.

1. It closed a critical loophole that previously only allowed federal involvement in hate crimes when the victim was attacked while engaged in federally protected activities (such as attending public school or serving on a jury). Outside of those scenarios, federal agents could not intervene.
2. This legislation finally expanded protections to include the victim's real or perceived sexual orientation, gender identity, gender to the already protected categories of race, religion, national origin, and disability.
3. It increased protections to all individuals regardless of their state of residence. At the time of signing, only 30 states included sexual orientation, 26 states included gender, and 12 states included gender identity as a protected category.

The HCPA effectively put pressure on the local jurisdictions to act. This was especially important given the previously dismissive nature of how the courts treated hate crimes against LGBT community members. For example, Jenness and Broad (1997) discussed a 1988 case that involved the beating to death of a homosexual man. A Broward County judge asked the prosecuting attorney, "That's a crime now, to beat up a homosexual?" To which the prosecutor replied, "Yes, sir. And it's also a crime to kill them." The judge replied, "Times have really changed" (1997: 50). While this demonstrates the perception of LGBT community members as being somehow less than human, it also illuminates the fact that violent hate crimes committed against gay, lesbian, and transgender people are especially brutal. A New York hospital official was quoted as saying, "Attacks against gay men were the most heinous and brutal I encountered . . . They frequently involved torture, cutting, mutilation . . . showing the absolute intent to run out the human being because of his (sexual) preference" (Winer, 1994).

The first national self-report study examining antigay violence was conducted in 1984 by the National Gay and Lesbian Task Force. In the early years of data collection for LGBT violence, self-report was the only means to gather any information, but it remained useful as a comparative measure even after official statistics began to be compiled. Not surprisingly, the self-reported victimization statistics varied greatly from government collected official statistics. For example, in 2001, the FBI reported 1,555 incidents of attacks on LGBT community members while the National Coalition of Anti-Violence Programs (NCAVP) had 2,210 attacks on record for the same period. In reality, the discrepancy was much greater than even those numbers show, since the FBI was reporting national statistics and the NCAVP only included a dozen reporting regions that covered 51 million people.

Activity 10.3 Hate Groups

Read about active hate groups from the Southern Poverty Law Center: http://www.splcenter.org/hate-map.

What kind of hate groups exist today?

Where do they exist?

How do they differ?

Do you notice any patterns about where such groups are located?

Typically, crime victims are more likely to report their attacker if they are strangers to the victims. This was not the case with LGBT community members. Many LGBT individuals did not want their status as such to be widely known, so being involved in a criminal case where they were targeted for a trait that they had perhaps not yet disclosed added additional complications. Adding to this, LGBT community members are often still distrustful of law enforcement as a result of both the harassment that was mentioned earlier in the chapter as well as an unwillingness on the part of the police to get involved.

Perhaps one of the best-known examples of this involved the serial killer, Jeffrey Dahmer. One of Dahmer's 14-year-old victims had escaped from his apartment, naked and in a drugged stupor. Two teenagers spotted him and called the police. The officers arrived to the scene at around the same time as Dahmer did. Dahmer told the officers that he and the victim were having a "lovers' quarrel" and the officers let the victim leave with Dahmer indicating that they didn't want to get involved in a homosexual dispute. It's hard to believe that if the victim had been a naked 14-year-old, drugged female that the outcome would have been the same. Sadly, that was the last time anyone saw Dahmer's victim alive.

Recently, there has been a push for law enforcement officers to receive increased training, often called cultural awareness training, on how to handle cases of a sensitive nature. A number of departments have passed *zero tolerance* ordinances, regardless of the nature or severity of the hate crime, and some, such as the Metropolitan Police in Washington DC have created LGBT liaison units to help improve community relations. These departments realize that, when fear of reporting decreases, they can create safer neighborhoods, improve reporting statistics, and help normalize the transition of LGBT members from being part of a marginalized group to mainstream society.

Summary

Issues related to the LGBT community remain somewhat controversial in America. Opposition to homosexual behavior is one thing, as many are opposed to it for religious reasons and for reasons related to their own sense of virtue. Yet, opposition to gay marriage has lessened over time and courts have consistently begun to explain that the legal benefits of marriage cannot be denied to human beings based on with whom they choose to sleep and live. Today the battle is mostly about whether people can deny service to members of the LGBT community based on their own religious beliefs.

Other rights such as being able to serve in the military are also being upheld, based on the principles of liberty and equality. This is suggestive that, with regard to issues of sexuality, America is becoming a more socially just nation. Gone are the days of seeing, framing, and declaring homosexuality as a mental disorder; but efforts to discriminate remain. Yet, Americans continue to struggle and work hard for change in this area, even standing up to efforts to give people the right to discriminate against LGBT individuals based on their own religious beliefs.

Discussion Questions

1. What does the acronym LGBT stand for? Does this acronym make sense as a category? Explain.
2. What is sexual orientation? Do you think people choose this or is it inborn? Explain.
3. On what basis do you think the American Psychological Association declared that homosexuality was a mental disorder?
4. Describe the Lavender Scare in the context of the Red Scare.

5. How have US courts helped assure equality when it comes to sexual relations? Explain, using examples from the chapter.
6. Summarize the history of "gays in the military" and explain how the issue has changed over time.
7. Summarize the major legal rights associated with marriage.
8. If marriage is a legal institution rather than a religious institution, can governments legally deny associated rights of marriage to people based on their sexual orientation?
9. What are hate crimes? Based on the discussion in the chapter, do you think hate crime statutes are necessary? Explain.

References

Adams, B. (1987). *The Rise of a Gay and Lesbian Movement*. Boston, MA: Twayne Publishers.

Davidson, J. (2012, March 2). Uncle Sam Didn't Welcome Gay Employees. *Washington Post*. Retrieved from http://www.washingtonpost.com/politics/uncle-sam-didnt-welcome-gay-employees/2012/03/01/gIQAny0PmR_story.html.

Gallup Poll. (2014). *Same-Sex Marriage Support Reaches New High*. Retrieved April 27, 2015, from http://www.gallup.com/poll/169640/sex-marriage-support-reaches-new-high.aspx.

Gerber, H. (1962, September 1). *One: The Homosexual Agenda*. Chicago, IL: The Society for Human Rights.

Iganski, P. (2001). Hate Crimes Hurt More. *American Behavioral Scientist, 45*(4), 626–638.

Jenness, V., & Broad, K. (1997). *Hate Crimes: New Social Movements and the Politics of Violence*. Hawthorne, NY: Aldine De Gruyter.

Katz, J. (1976). *Gay American History: Lesbians and Gay Men in the U.S.A.: A Documentary*. New York: Crowell.

Kinsey, A. (1948). *Sexual Behavior in the Human Male*. Philadelphia: W. B. Saunders.

Mello, M. (2004). *Legalizing Gay Marriage*. Philadelphia: Temple University Press.

Winer, A. (1994). Hate Crimes, Homosexuals, and the Constitution. *Harvard Civil Rights–Civil Liberties Law Review, 29*, 387–438.

11

SUMMARY AND PROSPECTS FOR THE FUTURE

... the arc of the moral universe is long, but it bends towards justice.

Martin Luther King, Jr., 1967

We've seen throughout this book that Americans are a just people. We put our principles of justice on paper when we declared our independence from Great Britain with the Declaration of Independence and again when we founded our country with the US Constitution. Their principles include *liberty*, *equality*, *happiness*, *virtue*, and *justice*.

Yet, throughout our nation's history, we've struggled to assure that our actions match our ideals. Whether it be slavery and Jim Crow, the oppression of Latinos, the subjugation of women, the suppression of labor, the delayed nature of accepting full rights for LGBT (lesbian, gay, bisexual, transgender) individuals, or some other large issue dealing with race, class, gender, sexuality, or other categories of exclusion, our practice often falls short of our ideals. And change is often slow.

Yet, like the Reverend Martin Luther King, Jr. said in his speech against the Vietnam War referenced above, change does eventually happen, and that is because there is morality in people and thus in the universe. This does not mean that change is inevitable, and assuming it is might actually slow down the speed of our progress. In fact, societal change toward greater liberty, equality, and happiness, and thus social justice—all American virtues—requires a lot of struggle by a lot of people over a long period of time. Then, eventually, change occurs, often when you least expect it. The recognition of *marriage equality*—or the legalization of gay marriage, if you prefer—is a great example of how change can occur suddenly across the country.

In this chapter, we summarize the main arguments of the book and then turn to the prospects for future change. The goal of the chapter is to provide a summary of what we know and to make some predictions of where we will likely go in the near and distant future.

Summary of the Book

In this book, we've outlined different theories of and approaches to justice. Below we offer a summary of the main points from each chapter. Our goal here is not only to summarize what we've already covered throughout the chapters but also to meaningfully demonstrate connections between them.

Chapter 1

We showed in Chapter 1 that the meaning of justice is in the eye of the beholder. For example, to a victim of crime, justice often simply means punishing the offender (*retributive justice*), but to a person arrested and charged with a crime, justice is likely to refer to assuring fairness in the criminal justice process (*procedural justice*). As noted in the book, Americans expect criminal justice agencies to achieve both conceptions of justice, as the goals of the criminal justice system are to achieve *crime control* and *due process*. This reality is reflected in our most common conception of justice—Lady Justice or Justitia—regularly depicted carrying a sword (as a sign of punishment) and wearing a blindfold and holding scales (one a sign of fairness and the other of balance).

Throughout the book, we've shown that Americans also logically expect more from their criminal justice system, since they strongly hold values related to social justice. As shown in Chapter 1, *social justice* refers to a broader sense of justice that exists when all people enjoy equal liberties and are treated equally. Yet, there are different theories of and approaches to social justice, each of which emphasizes one of three major concepts: *welfare* (providing a good life for people); *freedom* (protecting people's liberty); and *virtue* (protecting morality).

Utilitarianism emphasizes welfare, well-being, or happiness. According to this school of thought, something is just if it maximizes welfare, well-being, or happiness in society. A major limitation of this theory of justice is it does not protect the rights of individuals. *Libertarianism* emphasizes liberty or freedom. According to this school of thought, something is just if it respects and protects liberty or freedom. Free market libertarians focus their attention mostly on property rights. A major limitation of this theory of justice is it does not help assure equality in society. *Egalitarianism* emphasizes equality in society. According to this school of thought, something is just if it assures equality of opportunity, and if it helps take care of the least advantaged members of society. A major limitation of this theory of justice is it does not necessarily achieve morality in society. Finally, *virtue-based theories* emphasize morality or doing the right thing. According to this school of thought, something is just if it helps protect morality and our common values. A major limitation of this theory of justice is that someone has to decide whose values dominate in society, and it is not clear how that is determined in cases where morality varies.

Chapter 2

As we showed in Chapter 2, Americans generally support each major approach to justice, meaning they have values consistent with utilitarianism, libertarianism, egalitarianism, and virtue-based theories. Our founding documents—the Declaration of Independence and the US Constitution—show that America was founded mostly on the principles of libertarianism and egalitarianism. Yet, they also reflect our utilitarian values, most notably our desire to achieve happiness, and are suggestive of the virtues on which our country was founded.

As we showed in Chapter 2, key terms related to justice found in the Declaration of Independence include *equality*, *rights*, *life*, *liberty*, and the *pursuit of happiness*. And key terms related to justice found in the US Constitution include *justice*, *domestic tranquility*, *common defence*, *general welfare*, and *liberty*. These documents illustrate that America's founders valued crime control as well as due process. Further, the documents suggest they held conceptions of social justice rooted in utilitarianism, libertarianism, egalitarianism, and virtue, at least on paper.

Yet, Americans are a conflicted people, as our principles often conflict with one another because we emphasize one set of values in one context or set of circumstances and another set of values in another context or set of circumstances, as shown by David Miller in his theory of justice. Opinion polls show, for example, that we continue to value liberty and hold free market principles, yet we also value equality and recognize that large inequalities in society are not justified because they are not based on differential claims of desert and because they are harmful to people, especially the most needy. We thus generally support government programs that help assure equality even as we simultaneously want to shrink the size of government.

Public opinion polls also demonstrate that our values are indeed changing over time, and Americans are generally becoming a more tolerant people. While some see specific trends as evidence of weakening of our morals—at least with regard to traditional moral values—our increased acceptance of diversity is consistent with the argument that our commitment to equality is growing over time. Americans also clearly value happiness and helping the less fortunate, for polls illustrate that we want to spend more on attacking social and economic problems rather than on law enforcement and prison, and that we would prefer to spend more on education.

Two contemporary theories of justice that emphasize libertarianism and egalitarianism are John Rawls's *justice as fairness* and David Miller's *pluralistic theory of social justice*. Rawls's theory presents three major principles of justice, including the *equal liberties principle* (all people should have the same basic liberties or freedoms), the *equal opportunity principle* (all people should have the same opportunities for success), and the *difference principle* (economic inequalities should be arranged to most benefit the least advantaged). These principles are ordered, meaning equal liberty is the most important thing to Rawls, and the last two principles only pertain to the inevitable inequalities that result in society.

Miller's theory also presents here major principles of justice, including *need* (providing for people their basic necessities), *desert* (giving people what they deserve), and *equality* (treating people equally). He emphasizes need over desert, and desert over equality, but whether one principle is prioritized over another depends on the *mode of human relationship* one is in at the time, meaning whether one is in a *solidaristic community* such as a family (where need is most relevant), an *instrumental association* such as work (where desert is emphasized), or in matters of *citizenship* (when equality is seen as most important).

Both Rawls and Miller agree that inequalities will inevitably arise in competitive societies but that those seen in contemporary capitalist societies such as the US are not justifiable; further, public opinion polls illustrate that citizens generally agree with this sentiment. This means that Americans support reasonable limits on free markets in order to assure greater equality in society. Further, Rawls and Miller also see that protecting human rights are important for achieving social justice, and Americans hold many values consistent with protecting *human rights*.

To Rawls, social justice is present when liberty and equality are protected and when the most needy are cared for. To Miller, social justice is prevalent when people's needs are met, when people are given what they deserve, and when all people are treated equally. Any condition or occurrence that interferes with these goals is a threat to social justice. Throughout the book, we examined criminal justice practice, from the law all the way though police, courts, and corrections, and showed ways in which each is consistent with the social justice principles laid out in Rawls's and Miller's theories (as well as in other approaches to justice).

It should not be surprising that criminal justice practice is both consistent and inconsistent with social justice—that it helps achieve and often interferes with realizing a socially just society—because America's whole historical experience is characterized by conflicts between the principles on which our country was founded and our actual practice. Our centuries' long history of wiping out Native people, enslaving Africans, and oppressing women shows that American practice has always been in conflict with our own ideals. In fact, critical interpretations of the US Constitution suggest the document may have been primarily meant as a means to maintain status quo arrangements in society aimed at assuring continued control over government and power by wealthy, white men.

Whatever the truth, rights have been extended over time to more and more groups in more and more situations, making American practice more consistent with our ideals of liberty and equality found in the US Constitution. Public opinion polls today show that Americans continue to embrace these values, as well as happiness and morality, meaning that the theories of utilitarianism, libertarianism, egalitarianism, and virtue-based approaches are still embraced by us.

Chapter 3

In Chapter 3, we showed that all activities of the police, courts, and corrections stem from the criminal law, as each agency of criminal justice is an enforcement mechanism. The *substantive criminal law* defines harmful acts as crimes and specifies punishments, and the *procedural criminal law* specifies the rules of due process that must be followed as a person is processed through the system. The law is thus the primary mechanism we use to try to achieve our crime control and due process goals, and to thus assure that we achieve social justice goals such as happiness, liberty, and equality.

The whole criminal justice process begins when an act is defined as a *crime*, which is an act that violates the criminal law. From this point, since many harmful acts are not defined as crimes or serious crimes—including some forms of killing and some forms of property-taking—criminal justice is characterized by a serious problem. That problem is that the most serious and harmful behaviors are *not* vigorously pursued by criminal justice agencies.

It is lawmakers who determine which acts are crime and *serious crime*. In America, there is differential access to law-making in the form of voting and lobbying activities. The poor and people of color are underrepresented among voters and legislators themselves and are also least likely to donate money to political campaigns. This raises the significant possibility of bias in the criminal law, the outcome being that certain groups have their voices and interests represented more than others and that certain acts are more and less likely to be criminalized, not based on degree of harm caused but instead on other political and ideological grounds.

In fact, an analysis of available data shows that *white-collar crimes* and *corporate crimes* are more common and produce more harm than *street crime*, yet the latter are generally defined as serious whereas the former tend not to be. Incredibly, culpable acts of corporations even injure and kill more people than street crime. This is a serious threat to justice in the United States; it is inconsistent with libertarianism, egalitarianism, and even utilitarianism (because it does not contribute to our overall happiness).

After laws are made, *police* investigate cases where it is suspected that a person has violated them. Yet, police serve four additional roles beyond this *law enforcement* role, including *peace preserver*, *crime preventer*, *service provider*, and *rights upholder*. Thus, policing is ideally aimed at goals consistent with social justice, including protecting people's liberty and life, assuring happiness in society, and assuring equality.

Yet, the reality of policing is also in some ways inconsistent with social justice. For example, police are focused almost exclusively on street crime, ignoring the culpable behaviors that produce the most harm in society. Further, they tend to be located in poor areas inhabited by people of color, assuring higher rates of stops, searches, and arrests of some different groups of people. Evidence from studies shows that police in some jurisdictions use race and ethnicity to profile people (i.e., *racial profiling*), and that African Americans and Hispanics are more likely to be stopped, questioned, searched, and arrested; this is consistent with *contextual discrimination*.

After policing, *courts* take over, and the many duties of courts are consistent with social justice in the ideal as well. For example, courts convict and sentence the guilty, consistent with our crime control goals. They also guarantee by law that people will not be deprived of life, liberty, or property without *due process of law*, consistent with our due process goals.

Yet, the reality of courts is also at times inconsistent with social justice. For example, due process in the form of trials is rarely followed. This is because, with an enormous number of cases and limited resources, courts are forced to resort to *plea bargaining*, especially for those who cannot afford a competent criminal defense. Evidence from studies shows that, in some places, race and ethnicity impact pre-trial decisions and jury selection at trials, and harsher sentences for some of the poor and people of color for some types of crimes in some jurisdictions; this is also consistent with *contextual discrimination*.

After courts, *corrections* take over. The great bulk of offenders are handled in *community corrections*, yet *institutional corrections* (e.g., jails and prisons) are more severe and costly. In the ideal world, correctional punishment is necessary to assure social justice, for without the incapacitation and deterrence offered by corrections, the life, liberty, and happiness of citizens would be at greater risk. Yet, with the move away from rehabilitation toward mass incapacitation, most forms of punishment are highly ineffective at achieving these goals. The shift from rehabilitation toward punishment was organized and brought about by conservative politicians at the state and federal level beginning in the 1960s—both Republicans and Democrats—who hold a political ideology that sees criminals as completely responsible for their behaviors and criminal justice as the only means to protect society from crime.

A summary of Chapter 3 shows that criminal justice is ideally aimed at goals consistent with social justice—things such as protecting our life and liberties (as valued by libertarianism), public safety and happiness (as valued by utilitarianism), equality (as valued by egalitarianism), and even our values or morality (as valued by virtue-based theories). Further, the criminal law (e.g., the Bill of Rights in the US Constitution) was set up to protect civil liberties and to provide for equality, at least on paper. American criminal justice agencies that enforce the law are thus ideally dedicated to outcomes consistent with social justice from an egalitarian perspective (e.g., due process and equal protection). And all of criminal justice can be viewed as a means to enforce the people's values or morality—or at least those that are reflected in the criminal law—making it consistent with virtue-based theories of justice.

Yet, the reality of actual criminal justice practice puts criminal justice at conflict with social justice in many ways. Criminal justice practice often fails to assure happiness, protect life and liberty of citizens, and is at times dramatically unequal. For example, the poor and people of color—and especially young, poor, men of color—are disproportionately likely to be exposed to probation, jail, and prison. There are also significant racial disparities, class disparities, and gender disparities in capital punishment practice. Scholars nearly universally agree that these problems stem from systemic biases (i.e., *systematic discrimination*) pertaining to characteristics of both defendants and victims. To the degree that this is not due to disparate criminality of these groups, it is not consistent with social justice, especially libertarianism and egalitarianism—because it interferes with their liberty and exemplifies unequal treatment at the hands of the criminal justice system. This means future struggle, dedication, and hard work are still needed to bring the reality of criminal justice practice more in line with American ideals.

Chapter 4

In Chapter 4, we showed that it is not just the law but all of American society that is characterized by *social stratification*, where categories of people are arranged in a hierarchy characterized by power differentials that most benefit those at the top. This system of stratification is based on the belief in *essentialism* and is maintained by *hegemonic* cultural beliefs and practices pertaining to categories of difference in society.

Different societal contexts inform the creation of *categories of difference*. Relevant institutions that impact categories of difference include the family, educational system, peer groups, religion, the media, the economy, and the government. The *family* is the first institution to impart information about society to children, which helps define their sense of identity, including to which groups they belong (and don't). We learn through words and actions what is right and wrong, what is moral and immoral, what is normal and abnormal, and so forth. Many of these lessons revolve around different groups in society, including racial and ethnic groups, genders, social classes, people with different sexual orientations, and so forth. Parents are children's first teachers.

The *educational system* takes over where parents leave off; teachers become secondary parents, and schools help shape what children believe to be true as well as shape social interactions between students. There is no question that children learn what behaviors are acceptable in schools, and lessons learned at home are either reinforced or challenged in the school context. Many of these lessons also revolve around different groups in society, including racial and ethnic groups, genders, social classes, etc.

Peer groups become very important to children especially during the teenage years; young people begin to look to friends for reinforcement on how to dress, what to think, and how to behave, as well as how to treat people who are different than they. Thus, peer influence impacts how people view different groups in society.

As for *religion*, the United States of America features people who profess a wide variety of faiths and non-faiths—from atheist to fundamentalist. Most religions have a particular *ideology*, which is a set of beliefs and values about the way the world ought to be and the way that individuals ought to act. Inherent in this ideology is the idea of what is right versus what is wrong. Our sense of morality is directly impacted by the religion we follow, as different religions offer their own "truths" about what is right and tolerable and what is not; many of these so-called truths pertain to categories of difference (e.g., sexual orientation). For many people, religion takes precedence over other institutions, which has incredible importance for matters of virtue.

The *media* is a term that refers to a method of communicating entertainment or information. The news media serve as a gatekeeper to decide which stories and issues receive attention and which do not. While the media generally cannot tell the general public what to think, they can focus their attention on what to think about, and decisions about what is newsworthy and what is not is directly impacted by profit-seeking by the corporations who own the news media. Since Americans spend so much time interacting with the media, it is clear that the media can influence beliefs about different groups of people, creating or reinforcing certain stereotypes.

The US *government* is ideally "of the people, by the people, for the people," meaning it has the responsibility of creating and supporting our rights as individuals, as well as creating new laws and managing the welfare of all that live within our country's borders. Our government also determines which behaviors are legal and illegal. Unfortunately, the behaviors that we criminalize disproportionately affect a particular group of people more than another. An example is US drug control policy; it has taken literally decades of evidence to finally convince various state and our federal governments to make changes to policies and laws to reduce inequalities in criminal enforcement and sentencing to benefit poor people and people of color. Several states and municipalities have even gone as far as decriminalizing and even legalizing marijuana!

The *economy* regulates the use and expenditure of material resources. America's mixed economy makes the government the primary driver of a number of industries, including the criminal justice system, education, national defense, and infrastructure. The strength of the economy heavily influences other institutions in society, as in the case when a strong economy generates more taxes for education and when a weak economy generates strain for families and individuals. In periods of economic turmoil, people are less likely to identify with people who are different than they, making categories of difference more relevant.

As we showed in Chapter 4, the effects of any one institution on a person will vary across the course of a person's life. For example, some will impact a person earlier in life beginning in infancy (such as families). Others will impact them a bit later in late childhood and adolescence (such as friends and the education system). Still others will impact people across the entire span on a person's life (such as the media, the economy, and the government). And others may or may not directly impact people, depending on how they are raised (such as religion). But the point is that we are impacted by all of these institutions at some point in our lives.

Interpersonal and internal contexts are also relevant for categories of difference. The *interpersonal context* is defined by an individual's interactions with others. We get feedback, both verbal and non-verbal, on what is desirable and "normal" or undesirable, from others. We take this feedback and fuse it with the lessons and norms put forth in institutional contexts to internalize values and beliefs (i.e., internal context), and these values and beliefs alter future behavior and become the lens through which we all see the world. *Social construction theory* asserts that what we know as real is the combined result of all of these interactions. These cultural products, or lessons, are then taken for granted and, ultimately, taken for fact. This is how common stereotypes focusing on different groups in society come into existence; our views of what is just and unjust are highly impacted by these institutions.

The main categories of difference examined in the book deal with race, ethnicity, social class, gender, sexual orientation, and so forth. *Race* is a descriptive term using to refer to a group of people that share, or are perceived to share, common hereditary traits such as skin color, hair texture or eye shape. *Ethnicity* is more broadly defined as shared cultural traits like language, food, religion, customs and traditions. There are distinct traits for eye shape, skin color and hair texture, but these traits are entirely independent of each other, meaning there is no genetic basis for race. Furthermore, there is more genetic differentiation within a local community than there is between different communities.

Racial stereotypes thus arise from sources other than genetic differences between groups and the behaviors that may result from those differences. And they began to arise during the initial colonization of North America; early settlers used physical and cultural differences between themselves and indigenous populations to support their belief that the Native Americans were a primitive and less evolved group; racial and ethnic differences were codified into law and used as the reasoning for taking lands away from Native Americans and relocating them to the least desirable parts of the country; all of this is inconsistent with America's ideals.

The settlers also relied heavily on slave labor and indentured servants to support the local economy. After various rebellions, states enacted formal *slave codes* to limit the rights, associations and mobility of slaves. Between these laws and the use of Africans as slave labor, race emerged as a visible and tangible difference between landowners and those who were owned. The distinct physical appearance of the Africans, combined with their lack of command over European languages and non-Christian origins, began being used as a justification for their continued enslavement; all of this violates our beliefs in social justice.

Social class describes access to economic, social and/or lifestyle resources. Thus, establishing the social class of any given individual is more complicated than simply adding up his or her income and wealth and comparing it to the poverty threshold, which is considered to be the official divide between the middle and lower classes. *Economic resources* include income and wealth, where *income* is defined as money earned on a regular basis through work and investments and *wealth* refers to the ownership of all property that has a monetary value minus one's debt.

Social resources refer to the degree to which groups can exercise cultural authority or political influence, and is measured by the ability to shape popular consciousness through access to mass media, education, or other platforms of public communication found in the institutional context. An important form of social resources is *social capital*, which refers to the connections within and between social networks. *Lifestyle resources* refer to the degree to which group-based patterns of behavior and belief are valued or devalued within our society, and they include styles of dress, modes of speech, and even expressed attitudes and beliefs. According to many scholars, middle-class and at times upper-class lifestyles are most revered in society, which makes realizing social justice more difficult.

Gender refers to the social roles expected of males and females and falls along a continuum with masculinity on one end and femininity on the other. The process of "doing gender" begins from birth; starting in the earliest stages of childhood, we learn how to be a woman or how to be a man based on lessons we are taught by our parents, teachers, friends, the media, and so forth. Current gender stereotypes are traced back to the beliefs about how women should act in the nineteenth century—the Victorian Era. The virtues of *piety*, *purity*, *submissiveness*, and *domesticity* became associated with what it meant to be a woman. In a patriarchal society such as the United States, the masculine archetype is still dominant over the feminine. That is to say masculine traits are valued over feminine ones.

When gender differences result in structural inequalities, women have less power, status and economic rewards than men (often for the same jobs). This inequality in power is clear when you examine how men dominate positions of authority and leadership in government, the criminal justice system, the military and religion. The combined message sent from all of these different examples of the gender power differential is that women are not seen as being as capable as men of being leaders; this is another threat to social justice.

As a society, we have historically recognized two *sexual orientations*: straight and gay. The term *straight* is indicative of society's general view of the rightness or wrongness of someone's sexual preference; if something is not straight, it is crooked, broken, bent. This imagery indicates not being straight is a condition that warrants fixing. Our rigid guidelines for our thoughts and feelings about sexual orientation often lead to alienation for non-straight people, or a sense of not fitting in with the greater community. Youth often go through a period of identity crisis where they are trying to figure out why they are having bad thoughts. This can also lead to self-alienation.

In fact, there are not just two sexual orientations. Yet, heterosexuality is valued above all other options. Particularly within certain branches of the religious community, homosexuality is looked upon as an abomination and a sin. While there is evidence that sexual preference is as much a part of the individual as eye color or hair color, in a large number of communities, it is still unacceptable to be openly gay; this violates American social justice ideals.

The purpose of creating stereotypes about some groups and power differentials that benefit some at the expense of others is to help create a *negative ideology*, or false consciousness. Negative ideology helps hide the essence of what the power structure in society really is, which is beneficial to the ruling class at the time. The crux of a successful negative ideology is getting the citizenry to buy into the ideology being presented as reality, a reality socially constructed by the powerful who control the law and media.

There is inequality in American society, and evidence of specific kinds of discrimination within criminal justice, as well. Yet, Americans often do not see these realities. This is in part due to the negative ideology of the *American Dream* and our "colorblind" society. As shown in Chapter 4, this negative ideology helps us account for continued disparities we see in American society organized around race, ethnicity, social class, gender, and sexual orientation.

Chapter 5

In Chapter 5, we showed that whites make up a large majority of all Americans (about 78 percent of the population). Yet, African Americans make up 13 percent of the population, and Latinos make up about 17 percent of the population. These *minority groups* are distinct racial or ethnic groups that have significantly less power or privilege than the members of the dominant or majority group.

The primary problem between having a dominant group in dialectic with minority groups is that the process of socially constructing race and ethnicity clearly benefits the dominant group; they are most able to have their norms reflected in the criminal law, consistent with the theory of *culture conflict* and the *conflict school of criminology*. Further, they are most capable of constructing and reinforcing *stereotypes* or generalizations about all members of any given group without allowing for individual differences. Stereotypes about racial and ethnic groups can lead to *prejudice*, *racism*, and ultimately *discrimination*.

From the very founding of our country, African Americans have been treated unequally, first as *chattel* or property (i.e., slaves), then as second-class citizens in *Jim Crow*. *Slave codes* and later *Black codes* specified acceptable and unacceptable behaviors for African Americans that did not even apply to whites. Our history is thus inconsistent with egalitarianism and violates the major principles of John Rawls's theory of justice as fairness as well as David Miller's pluralistic theory of justice. That is, the practice of slavery and "separate but equal" laws stand in direct opposition to equal liberties, equal opportunities, the difference principle, as well as equality in matters of citizenship.

Ultimately, after much struggle that included a Civil War, a period of reconstruction, and then a massive *Civil Rights Movement*, measures were enacted to outlaw slavery and mandate that discrimination against people of color be eliminated in education, transportation, voting, and so forth. Civil rights acts were passed beginning in the 1860s and the US Constitution was amended, as well. As groups such as the KKK used violence to maintain white power structures and other "legitimate" groups such as *White Citizens' Councils* used legal means to intimidate and oppress minorities, people of color engaged in acts of *civil disobedience* and used the courts to insist on equal treatment under the law. New civil rights laws (e.g., the *Civil Rights Act of 1964* and the *Voting Rights Act of 1965*) codified the American virtue of equality. While it was the law that permitted differential treatment of people of color throughout US history, it is also the law that has been used to change this.

Yet, white supremacists and political actors continued to use whatever means necessary to assure continued white dominance in US society, including the infamous *Southern Strategy*, a coordinated plan by Republican party leaders to win back the South for the purposes of gaining power and eroding social welfare programs. The South has largely voted Republican ever since.

Sadly, there is evidence that racism still exists in the US. For example, after the US Supreme Court struck down Section 4 of the 1965 *Voting Rights Act*, several states passed laws (e.g., voter ID laws) that are predicted to "have a discriminatory impact on minority voters" according to the US Department of Justice. This is one of the reasons that the 2014 mid-term elections featured the lowest voter turnout in several decades.

Finally, there is strong evidence, consistent with the conflict school, that discrimination still exists in criminal justice to this day. Specifically, there is evidence that *racial profiling* exists in some police agencies and that race continues to impact criminal sentences, consistent with *contextual discrimination*.

Blalock's *power threat hypothesis* aims to explain such findings, asserting that the presence and growth of minority groups is associated with increased social control mechanisms. Reformulations of his theory account for concepts such as *criminal threat*, describing the perceived danger posed by minorities. *Fatal controls as a mechanism of social control* include the vigilantism, lynching, police use of deadly force, and the death penalty, all found to be historically biased against people of color. *Coercive controls as a mechanism of social control* include arrest and imprisonment, also historically found to be disproportionately applied to people of color. Finally, *beneficent controls as a mechanism of social control*—which appear to aid the threatening population, but in reality serve as a behavioral constraint (e.g., welfare and asylums)—tend to have most impacted people of color.

At the individual level, discrimination also can occur in matters of criminal justice, as in cases where stereotypes related to race lead to perceptions of *blameworthiness*, which are also impacted by legal factors such as *offense seriousness* and *prior record*. Interestingly, discrimination in sentencing seems to occur only when it is possible for it to occur; as crime seriousness increases, judicial discretion in sentencing decisions decreases, making discrimination less possible; in this way, progress has been made, because legal factors primarily determine sentencing outcomes.

One of the most alarming assertions about discrimination in criminal justice comes from Michelle Alexander who claims America's policy of mass imprisonment is an intentional *racial caste system* that evolved from slavery and Jim Crow. Alexander's argument is that this started during the birth of the Civil Rights Movement as part of the "law and order" approach to crime control. The long-term result is a conflation of criminality with blackness, so that being black is now essentially equated with being a criminal.

In Chapter 5, we reviewed issues of citizenship, and paid particular attention to the role that ethnicity plays in American society. While many immigrants come to the US in pursuit of the *American Dream*, others come here merely to be with and/or provide for their families. Even though most Americans also strive for these goals of prosperity, security, and success, not all Americans support even legal immigration. Many more reject the idea of illegal immigrants staying here, especially if granted full citizenship rights.

Incredibly, the total foreign-born population in the US in 2011 was 40.4 million, comprising 13 percent of the US population; only about one-quarter of these are *unauthorized immigrants*, including people who snuck into the country illegally. The largest minority group in the US is now Latinos, who, according to the 2012 census, made up 16.9 percent of individuals living in America. In 2012, there were almost 34 million Latinos of Mexican origin living in the US, including 11.4 million immigrants born in Mexico and 22.3 million Mexicans born in the US. About half of Mexican immigrants are illegal immigrants and three-quarters of illegal immigrants are Latino.

Chapter 6

Citizenship is a status of a person as a citizen of a country that guarantees him or her certain rights and privileges, as well as duties. Although this is a nation of immigrants, the issue of immigration is currently one that is controversial, and that has great importance for issues of social justice.

Although about 40 million Americans are foreign-born, only about one-quarter are *unauthorized immigrants*; Mexicans make up the largest portion of illegal immigrants in the US. This is largely because legal immigration is so greatly restricted, suggesting one way to solve the problem of illegal immigration is to raise per country limits for Latin American countries.

Hispanics now make up the largest *minority group* in the United States, ahead of African Americans. Almost two-thirds of the total Latino population identify as Mexican. Other notable populations in the US include Cuban Americans and Puerto Rican Americans, each with their own issues and history related to social justice. The dominant issue of social justice in America today that deals with social justice is the effort to deny equal rights to Latinos, which is inconsistent with principles of *libertarianism* and *egalitarianism* reflected in the theories of Rawls and Miller introduced in Chapter 1, as well as our nation's founding documents.

In Chapter 6, we showed similarities and differences between Mexicans (who make up 63 percent of the Latino population in the US), Puerto Ricans (who comprise 9.2 percent of the Latino population in the US), and Cubans (who make up only 3.5 percent of the Latino population in the US). Each has faced its own challenges, including Mexicans, who lost land to the US and who are currently viewed by politicians from major political parties in the US as a threat to national security due to illegal immigration; Puerto Ricans, who are counted as citizens of the US but who cannot vote; and Cubans, whose country has faced an economic boycott from the US for decades and whose country was invaded by forces working on behalf of the US government.

A large majority of Americans favors providing a way for illegal immigrants to stay in this country, and almost half think those who are here illegally should be allowed to apply for citizenship. Americans are evenly divided about whether the recent increase in deportations is a "good thing" or a "bad thing," and Republicans and whites are much more supportive of deportations than Democrats and Latinos; only liberal Democrats generally favor allowing illegal immigrants to become citizens, which is a good reminder of the contextual nature of social justice—responses often depend on the issue and who is being asked.

One barrier to effective immigration reform is that corporations in the United States have invested in and exploited Mexican labor. As long as this remains true, it is unlikely that any meaningful changes will occur with US immigration policy. Thus, it might be expected that especially border states will continue to make efforts—such as, most recently, Arizona—to pass their own laws in an effort to try to deal with illegal immigration. This is problematic for two reasons: it is the federal government that is authorized by the US Constitution to deal with this issue; and state laws tend to be motivated by free market concerns rather than realizing social justice.

We also reviewed numerous pieces of legislation in US history—some of which have aimed to restrict illegal immigration (such as the 1986 *Immigrant Reform and Control Act* and the 1996 *Illegal Immigration Reform and Immigrant Responsibility Act*) and other legislation that has tried to make it easier for people to immigrate and contribute to American economic success (such as the *Immigration Act of 1990* and the *Illegal Immigration Reform and Immigrant Responsibility Act*)—showing our conflicting principles and values related to social justice. Stated simply, our own experience shows that lawmakers seek to stop illegal immigration to reduce crime and protect public lands and health (consistent with our *crime control* principles) while often also passing measures to ease immigration restrictions to benefit corporations and the economy (consistent with our *libertarian* principles). Meanwhile, some state laws reportedly passed to restrict immigration will actually serve to benefit corporations who, for example, house illegal immigrants in private prisons. The social justice principles at work here are related to free market libertarianism—profit above all else.

Some measures also seek to ease the burden on immigrant families, consistent with our virtues of compassion. An example is the *Deferred Actions for Childhood Arrivals (DACA)* program, begun in 2012. Another example, yet to be passed, is the *Development, Relief, and Education for Alien Minors Act* (also known as the Dream Act), which is motivated by compassion and a concern for equality of opportunity for children of immigrants, consistent with our egalitarian ideals.

Yet, there is also evidence that at least some of our anti-immigration legislation was put into place to control Latino immigrants due to a *moral panic* that is based on false notions about immigration and crime. Here, immigrants and refugees are often characterized as "enemies at the gate" so they can be dehumanized and more easily controlled. Part of our concern over illegal immigration likely stems from issues of racism and ethnocentrism; the term immigrant has become nearly synonymous with the term criminal, particularly with regard to the Latino population, similar to Michelle Alexander's claims about blackness being conflated with crime. This convergence of terms has brought about a moral panic over illegal immigration in the US, where Latino populations have been dehumanized, making it easier to deny them even basic human rights.

Finally, there is evidence of *contextual discrimination* against Latinos when it comes to policing and court activity (e.g., sentencing). To a degree, this helps explain why Latinos make up a disproportionate amount of clients in the courts and correctional facilities. The irony here is that, the longer Latino immigrants stay in the country, the more likely they are to commit crime! One concern of the public is that immigration increases crime, yet the scholarly consensus is that it does not. There is, however, evidence that Latinos are consistently sentenced more harshly than whites. This stems in part from racial profiling by the police, as well as contextual discrimination in the courts, leading to overrepresentation of Latinos in corrections populations as well as overburdened correctional agencies and further racial stratification and subsequent racial and ethnic exclusion in society. None of these outcomes are consistent with the American social justice principles of liberty and equality.

Chapter 7

Since just about the time when white European settlers arrived in what would become the United States of America, *Native Americans* have been subjugated and oppressed—in fact, the majority of tribes were ultimately wiped out. For those that survive, nearly one-third live on more than 550 reservations in 33 states, where rates of crime and drug abuse are exceptionally high.

The primary ideologies used to justify the treatment and mistreatment of Native Americans were *Social Darwinism* (which holds that the fittest will survive; since Europeans were seen as superior to native populations, the fact that whites survived and thrived was proof that Native Americans were inferior) and *Manifest Destiny* (the idea that Europeans had the God-given right and, indeed, the duty to expand their territory and cultural influence throughout North America).

The eradication of the Native Americans was accomplished by *genocide* as well as *ethnocide*, not to mention through an abuse of the law; even treaties and US Supreme Court cases were ultimately ignored to the detriment of native populations. Actions by white settlers (and later by white "Americans")—motivated by their own desire to own and control as much land as they could—violated the American ideals of liberty and self-determination, and our actions were clearly unequal in their outcomes and thus inconsistent with the American principle of equality.

In spite of the numerous efforts to improve the lives of Native Americans—many through the law—as well as to merely respect their right to self-determination, a large number of the Native Americans living in urban areas live in poverty and experience increased involvement with the criminal justice system. Plagued by poverty, social isolation, drug and alcohol abuse, and high rates of unemployment, crime rates are very high among native populations, and Native Americans are overrepresented in the criminal justice system. Further, Native Americans also generally receive longer sentences and serve a higher percentage of those sentences than similarly situated whites, due to both legal factors (e.g., offense seriousness and prior record) and extra-legal factors (e.g., ethnic discrimination). So, today, Native Americans must continue to work to achieve social justice outcomes promised to all people in our nation's founding documents.

Chapter 8

In Chapter 8, we showed that we remain a nation obsessed with crime—especially *serious street crimes*. This has been true through nearly all of our nation's history, so it should not be surprising that, for most of our nation's history, we've used criminal justice agencies to control those people perceived to be most engaged in these acts—the poor. Simultaneously, we largely ignore acts of white-collar crime and corporate crime, so that the powerful people who commit these very harmful acts rarely are arrested, convicted, and sentenced to prison.

Some scholars point out that the criminal justice system is biased against the poor at all stages of the process, starting with the criminal law and continuing into policing, courts, and corrections. It is in the interests of the powerful to focus so heavily on street crimes rather than other types of harmful behaviors, including white-collar crimes, corporate crimes, and even governmental deviance. To the degree that this is true, American criminal justice is not consistent with our own ideals.

American governments have for decades rounded up young, poor, minority males and subjected them to government-controlled institutions like jail or prison or community alternatives such as halfway houses and boot camps, amounting to a form of population control used to keep the poor in their place. This not only harms the poor but also people of color, who generally have lower incomes than whites, less overall wealth, and are more likely to suffer from unemployment, poverty, and child poverty. It is these groups, according to scholars, who are viewed as the *dangerous classes*—those people who need most attention from criminal justice agencies in order to protect society from crime.

The main reason that criminal justice tends to focus its attention on street crime rather than other, more harmful, behaviors is because of who makes the law, votes for it, and funds it. In a nutshell, these people are *not* demographically representative of the US population, but instead are made up largely of older, wealthy, white males. None of these outcomes are consistent with any conception of social justice; they do not promote or respect liberty, equality, happiness, or virtue.

Other biases against the poor occur in criminal justice, as well. For example, whereas the right to counsel in criminal cases has been extended to the *indigent*, the right to quality representation has generally not been. Thus, due process remains an illusion for many Americans, inconsistent with the concept of equality and thus the realization of social justice. Problems with legal defense are found even in capital cases, where the outcome is literally life or death.

Finally, the *collateral consequences* of convictions tend to be suffered mostly by the nation's poor, assuring that, even after serving time in prison or jail, many Americans have nearly no chance of making it on the outside. Many felons even lose their right to vote and thus participate in democracy, referred to as felony disenfranchisement. These practices cause harm to the least advantaged citizens in the US and are thus not consistent with the idea of the difference principle.

Chapter 9

Women make up the majority of the general population, yet they still face sexism and subjugation in US society. In spite of the enormous progress that has been made in America over time, the *gender roles* that specify the proper behavior, activities, and attitudes of males and females are so pervasive and ingrained in our collective conscience that they remain accepted as fact. Males remain the dominant gender in US society, even as more and more rights have been extended to females over time.

Incredibly, even as the nation was founded on principles such as liberty and equality, women were not even allowed to vote—not until women forced the issue through the suffrage movement. Today, women are more likely than men to vote. Yet, workplace equality has still not been achieved. Even after federal action, women continue to make less on average than men, often for the same jobs and careers.

Further, there remain even contemporary efforts to reduce and restrict the reproductive rights of women. Efforts to restrict access to contraception as well as abortions have been more common in the past five years than in the past several decades, and many view this as a denial of liberty and self-determination.

In these issues, we see how law was used to first oppress and subjugate women but has most recently been used to liberate women in order to realize our social justice ideals of liberty, equality, and happiness across society. In fact, it has become virtuous in and of itself to pursue these social justice ideals.

When it comes to issues of gender and criminal justice, women are overrepresented among victims of some forms of crimes, especially domestic violence—a crime of power and control. Women, however are underrepresented among "clients" in criminal justice, including arrestees, defendants, and probationers/inmates. The *chivalry hypothesis* asserts that actors in the criminal justice system treat women more leniently because they are perceived as weak and irrational.

Chapter 10

In Chapter 10, our focus was on the LGBT community. The term *sexual orientation* refers to the sex or gender of people to whom you are attracted. We showed that, throughout US history, *straight* has been considered normal, whereas *gay* has been equated with different and thus abnormal. In part because of this, as well as because of a long history of laws identifying and punishing LGBT individuals and their sexual behaviors, widespread discrimination against the LGBT community has existed in the United States.

From specific laws that have banned *sodomy* to *gay marriage* to even military service, the LGBT community has faced legal discrimination in the US. Events like the *Lavender Scare* caused fear in American society, to the detriment of the LGBT community, which interfered with the realization of our social justice ideals. The American Psychological Association once even considered homosexuality to be a mental disorder!

Yes, as our nation and its people have progressed, the law has come to protect the rights of all humans—gay, straight, or other. An excellent example, discussed in Chapter 10, is the institution of *marriage*—now available to not only heterosexuals but also LGBT individuals. Marriage is a *legal institution* that grants many privileges from the government, and thus cannot be denied to any human being based on *extra-legal* factors (i.e., things outside of the law); this argument has been recognized by the courts as they have extended marriage rights to all.

Thankfully, *hate crimes* are relatively rare in the United States, and their recognition in the law is evidence of our strong social justice ideals. The fact that they still occur—and that active hate groups operate in the US—is evidence that we still have progress to make when it comes to realizing social justice.

The Future

After reading this book, there can be little doubt about where we as a people are heading in the future. Whether it be with regard to any aspect of criminal justice (i.e., the criminal law, policing, courts, or correctional practice) or to the law more generally as it pertains to race, ethnicity, social class, sex, gender, sexual orientation (or any other similar factor), the US has become and is still becoming a more socially just country. That is, America is become freer and thus more assuring of liberty, as well as more equal, which we argue has more utility because it assures greater happiness for more and more people in society.

We are thus confident that Martin Luther King's claim that "the arc of the moral universe is long, but it bends towards justice" is correct. America is becoming a more just place, and its people are increasingly becoming a more just people who actually strive to live up to the ideals of equality, Rights, Life, Liberty, the pursuit of Happiness, Justice, domestic Tranquility, common defence, and general Welfare stated in our nation's founding documents—the Declaration of Independence and the US Constitution.

Yet, as shown in this book, progress works this way: two steps forward, one step back; two steps forward, one step back. That is to say simply that, with each effort to achieve social justice, there are also efforts to stop progress. Often, these latter efforts are justified in terms of morality of virtue, reminding us of the inherent conflict between those things that assure liberty and equality and those that are claimed to protect one's religious or moral values. In this way, virtue-based approaches to justice often interfere with efforts to achieve greater social justice. If we value liberty, equality, and happiness, we must not be silenced by those who stand in the way of change based on religious or moral principles. After all, on what principle(s) can preventing freedom (i.e., liberty), welfare (i.e., well-being or happiness) be justified if liberty and happiness as well as equality are actually the values on which this country was founded?

Helpful Reforms

In order to assure that America continues to march toward a more socially just place, we offer the following reforms. Our belief is that working toward these reforms will bring about more just and equitable criminal justice practice, as well as a more just society:

1. Seek procedural justice over retributive justice. Procedural justice is aimed at assuring fairness in criminal justice practice and, as such, it is related directly to realizing *equality* in society and thus social justice. Retributive justice is also an acceptable goal of criminal justice, for achieving justice for crime victims is necessary to a peaceful society. Yet, we argue that states and the federal government should seek above all else to assure fair procedures of criminal justice. That is, we argue that American criminal justice practice should be more concerned with due process than crime control. Even though the latter is still important, most crime that is prevented in the US is prevented *not* by criminal justice but instead by other social institutions such as those identified in the book.
2. Increase the representative nature of law making—today the lawmaking process is biased in favor of some people and interests and against others. This must change if we hope to achieve socially just criminal justice agencies. Since criminal justice practice (i.e., policing, judicial processes, and correctional activity) amounts to an enforcement of the criminal law, any bias in the law will be found in all of criminal justice. It is mostly wealthy whites who have their voices heard and interests served in the law-making process. To change this, we must make people from all racial, ethnic, social classes, and other groups involved in the legislative process, from law-making, to voting, and even funding the law.
3. Define crime and serious crime based on the degree of harm it causes, not who commits it. Currently our focus in criminal justice is nearly exclusively on street crime even though white-collar crimes and corporate crimes cause far more damage than street crimes. This can be changed easily by legislating on offenses based on the degree of harm they actually cause, as demonstrated through empirical data. Ironically, pursuing white-collar and corporate offenders will go a long way toward assuring social justice outcomes, for it will greatly reduce the racial, ethnic, and social classes disparities we see in contemporary criminal justice agencies.
4. Protect human rights. Human rights are expansive and are espoused in documents such as the United Nation's Universal Declaration of Human Rights. As we showed in Chapter 1, they include rights pertaining to general freedom; dignity; life; liberty; security; equality before the law; fair and

public hearings by independent and impartial tribunals; presumption of innocence until proven guilty; freedom of movement and residence; right to seek and gain asylum from persecution; right to a nationality; the right to marry and have a family; right to own property; freedom of thought, conscience and religion; freedom of opinion and expression; freedom of peaceful assembly and association; the right to participate in government; the right to social security; the right to work by free choice and to have protection against unemployment; the right to equal pay for equal work; the right to rest and leisure; the right to an adequate standard of living, including "food, clothing, housing and medical care and necessary social services, and the right to security in the event of unemployment, sickness, disability, widowhood, old age . . . "; the right to education; the right to participate in the community and "to enjoy the arts and to share in scientific advancement and its benefits"; and the right to the "protection of the moral and material interests resulting from any scientific, literary or artistic production of which [one] is the author." Additionally, people enjoy freedom from slavery or servitude; torture or cruel, inhuman or degrading treatment or punishment; discrimination; arbitrary arrest, detention, or exile; and arbitrary interference with privacy, among many others. These rights ought to be codified into US law so that all Americans—regardless of race, ethnicity, social class, gender, sexual orientation, and so forth—will be treated the same in the eyes of the law.

5. Fight against the forces of essentialism and hegemony that posit that differences between people are inborn and natural and that assure stereotypes and discrimination against some groups in certain contexts or situations. This requires first recognizing the social institutions (i.e., family, education, peers, religion, media, economy, government) that impact the development of the negative ideology positing some people are superior to others by nature, and, second, ultimately using each of these institutions to enshrine our dedication to social justice ideals. In essence, this means using families, educational institutions, peer groups, religious organizations, the media, governments, and, to the degree possible, economic institutions, to state, work toward, and then protect liberty, equality, happiness, virtue, and justice in society.

6. Recognize the role that federalism can play in hindering social justice. States have historically resisted efforts by the federal government to bring about social justice in America. The US Department of Justice fights with states even today to assure equal liberties on matters related to voting rights and marriage.

7. Continue to confront unjust laws and change them in order to achieve our social justice ideals. As we showed in this book, the law has been changed in much of society—in many areas of American life—and can be further changed to being about more liberty, equality, happiness, virtue, and justice in society. Yet, it takes the dedication, hard work, sacrifice of real people to make this happen.

INDEX

Made in United States
North Haven, CT
24 July 2023

39423436R10161